In his forewo... Dr. Bennett tells us that "Brother Anthony has been in a position to ponder long, and to search a great deal." And he goes on to say about the Hermit Brother ". . . true discoverers are modest . . . . In this book the author seldom obtrudes himself. He does not lecture, nor is he sermonizing. He wants to make the black and white letters sing, and so they do."

The monk (Brother Alberic) is a Trappist of an Abbey in the Eastern part of the United States. The author lives as a hermit in an Abbey in Eastern Canada.

THE
BREAD
OF GOD

THE

BREAD

OF GOD

By

A TRAPPIST MONK WHO PRAYED
FOR A CARMELITE HERMIT WHO WROTE

VANTAGE PRESS

New York   Washington   Atlanta   Hollywood

Nihil obstat

James T. O'Connor, S.T.D.

Censor Librorum

Imprimatur

James P. Mahoney, D.D.

*Vicar General, Archdiocese
of New York*

FIRST EDITION

Copyright © 1975 by Brother Anthony

Published by Vantage Press, Inc.
516 West 34th Street, New York, New York 10001

Manufactured in the United States of America

Standard Book No. 533-00605-8

To

the

Virgin of the Poor

Mother

of

Perfect Understanding

I confess to almighty God,
and to you, my brothers and sisters,
that I have sinned through my own fault
in my thoughts and in my words,
in what I have done,
and in what I have failed to do.

I was selfish, arrogant and unkind.
I was jealous and coveted what was not my own.
I was angry and wanted to kill.

I lied and let others be blamed for what I had done.
I robbed the glory of another and turned honor into shame.

I took what did not belong to me and kept what was not mine.
I was miserly towards others yet a spendthrift to myself.

I was a glutton and drank to excess.
I sought forbidden pleasures and consorted with every kind.
I was unfaithful to the one I loved.

I left unheeded the cries of the needy and gave no comfort
to those who craved a kind word.
I was unforgiving and cruel in my revenge.

I was proud and ungrateful.
I was shallow and cynical to those who sought my trust.

And I was indolent when I should have worked.

I ask blessed Mary ever virgin,
all the angels and saints,
and you, my brothers and sisters,
to pray for me to the Lord our God.

CONTENTS

Background of the Parable
On the Terms "Good Seed" and "Darnel"
On "Sleeping Men"
On the Appearance of the "Fruit" and Exposure of the "Darnel"
Some "Darnel" of Today
On Fidelity to His Words
Keep the "Good Seed" of His Word for It is Truly Good Inside and Out
The Glory of the "Good Seed" is in the Fruit of the Golden Ear
On "Collecting" the "Darnel" and "Gathering" the "Wheat"
His "Bondservants" Must Wait Until They Have Brought Forth "Fruit" and Become Thereby Free "Harvestmen"
Truth Is the Wages Free "Harvestmen" Receive from Him
Truth Begets Truth
Those Who Hold Fast and Do the Truth Become True Themselves and Bring Forth Truths to His Glory
On the "Work" of the Seed of Truth in the Heart of the Ground
On the Unfolding of His Words in the Hearts of Those Who Hold Them Fast
The Word of God Gives Light to Those Who Do What It Commands
The Light of His Word Shall Expose All Errors and Lies
The Word as "Wheat" (Scriptural and Rabbinic Sources)
The "Ground" of "His Field" is Perfected by Holding Fast to the "Good Seed" the Son Sowed
The "Fruit" Brought Forth by the Good Ground Bears Witness to the Truth of His Word and Gives Glory to Him
The Lord Will Cause the Truth to Spring Forth from the Heart of the Good Ground When the Time Comes for All Lies to Be Silenced
The "Darnel" in His Field are the Lies Brought Forth by the Ground Which Held Fast and Acted upon the Evil Seeds Sown by the "Devil"
Lies Bring Forth Lies
The Mystery of "Lawlessness" is at Work in the Heart of the Evil Ground
The Meaning of the Term: "The Field Is the World"
Of the Two Types of Seed Found in His Field and How to Distinguish Them
The Seed Determines the Man
The Sword of Truth is Given to the "Harvestmen" Before They Are Sent to Reap
The "Harvestmen" Shall Understand and Know How to Silence the Lies by "Binding" Them
Those Who Have Brought Forth Lies Shall Also Be Punished
The Punishment of Liars is to Be Silenced and Bound Up with Their Own Lies
On "Binding" the "Bundles"
On "Collecting" Darnel
On the End of "Stumbling Blocks"
When the "Darnel" is Collected Out of His Field We Shall See the Glory of His Wheat
On "Gathering" the "Wheat" into His "Barn"
On Cleaving Fast to His Word that We May Be Gathered Along with It
Those Who Have Kept His Word Shall Have Light in Themselves: "The Fruit of Light"

On the "Barn" of the Lord
The Coming Purification by "Fire"
Why the "Righteous" Shall "Shine"
The Righteous Shall Shine Forth Like the Sun in the Kingdom of Their Father
Why the Parable of the Good Seed and the Darnel Is Found Only in the Gospel According to St. Matthew

FOREWORD

Brother Anthony paid me a great compliment in asking me to furnish a foreword for his remarkable book. There are many works of critical scholarship on the market, and many works of piety, many commentaries, and many meditations. This work has something of all of these, and yet cannot be described faithfully as any one of them. It is a highly individual work, and I have met nothing like it before.

It deals with the teaching of Jesus with special reference to certain parables, and, in a special combination of philological, cultural, and spiritual research, draws from the bare words of the texts their fullest meaning. There are moments when the careful investigation of the words brings to light treasures not dreamt of by the all-too-rapid reader that most of us are. There are moments, too, when Brother Anthony's practised eye sees there more than some scholars will be ready to see. But they may think again, and be better informed. An example is the commentary on Mt. 13:31, Lk. 13:19. 'Took and sowed' amounts to much the same as 'sowed'. Few will think that semitic idiom (did Jesus utter his parables in Aramaic, or in Mishnaic Hebrew?) will make more out of 'took and sowed' than a simple 'sowed.' Yet it is a fact that the compilers (and their anonymous and unknown specialist advisers and their churches) deliberately preferred to read 'took and sowed' instead of St. Mark's simple 'sowed', and that proves that they saw something special in the 'took'. If Brother Anthony does not say the last word on their reasons he draws our attention to the fact that a reason has to be found.

Again and again he traces out the true implications of the choice of word which we, with our all-too-familiar eyes and ears, take for granted. And he insists on wishing us, whether we know any Greek or not, not to slide over passages without asking why the writer put it in that way and not in another. At Mk. 4:29 the usual translation runs 'as soon as the crop is ripe'. Bauer-Arndt-Gingrich in their indispensable *Greek-English Lexicon to the New Testament* would translate 'when the (condition of the) crop permits', much more nearly literal. Brother Anthony shows us that the original text, curiously, insinuates that the fully grown plant (the ex-seed, as it were) presents itself for harvesting. The Gospel is full of half-and quarter-expressed ideas and allusions, similar to this, and, taking a fairly small scope as his text, Brother Anthony has compiled, with delicate care, a marvellous commentary, enriching the story with apposite quotations, and filling out the Jewish background from the Old Testament and other suitable material, including the Dead Sea Scrolls, where relevant.

He is not interested in polemic. He will not be concerned at the objections many will raise to his manner of proceeding. Some, I do not doubt, will say that he has assumed too much: (1) That the texts carry these allusions and nuances, unimaginable to a literal Anglo-Saxon; (2) that the linguistic apparatus at his command is always faithful and adequate; (3) that the text of the gospels he uses is critically sound and reliable; (4) that the parables are correctly, and only, to be taken and studied in the very order and in the very contexts in which they appear in the gospels; (5) finally, that these are the words of Jesus and the implications are to be traced to him. At one place he (rightly to my mind) rebukes the less imaginative (and very much more common) student of the New Testament who insists on translating Mt. 13:28 rejecting the word 'man' as a mere literal Aramaism. And they, in return, will accuse him of being fanciful and over-imaginative.

The answer to the doubts must lie in two parts. Of the hundreds of connections which Brother Anthony has seen, many have been seen before, but have not always been used in quite this way. Many others are original and show what can be done when the vocabulary and the basic ideas of the New Testament are taken seriously by someone who understands the oriental mind. For the authors of the New Testament were either orientals or were faithful pupils of orientals. There we see the operation of biblical themes, unseen, through gospel passages, weaving, as it were, the New Testament on the threads of the Old. To many this will seem authentic, and the examples will appear convincing. The message will be impressive. Others perhaps will not meet their target immediately. It is the exercise that is impressive, even if all the rays from this huge light do not penetrate equally far.

Of one thing I am sure, namely that others will be stimulated to make similar adventures into other areas in the New Testament by similar methods, and will be similarly rewarded, namely by a number of convincing discoveries, and by a number of curious finds, not actually amounting to discoveries, which nevertheless may fertilise a budding idea at some later stage.

Since we do not possess a signed testimonial from Jesus or any of his students to the effect that this, and nothing more or less, was intended by a particular piece of teaching, or a particular action, we must rely on inspired research, tireless ingenuity, and literary and spiritual insight to make the bare words sing. And this is what Brother Anthony is doing. I have a notion of how successful he will be from a small experience of my own, which serves as a partial answer to sceptics. It is true that we cannot *prove* that Jesus spoke those very words, still less in that order, or in that context; and (as Matt. 19:16-17; Mk. 10:17-18; Lk. 18:18-19 show only too plainly) we are to approach, in faith, documents adjusted and even transmuted by those who transmitted the information to us. It is true that there is no *proof* that the exact vocabulary, and style, was the chosen vehicle for so much hidden meaning and arcane promptings. There is no *proof* that a bald, superficial, and rapid understanding is not a sufficient and faithful interpretation. But this little anecdote will serve for me, and many minded as I am. Before I tell it, I must announce my conviction that, all in all, after massive research and prolonged meditation Brother Anthony has furnished a hundred stimulating and important ideas for each one that figures below.

Metaphors, which usually figure commonplace things, are not chosen hastily, and must normally fit, or they will not work at all. The Hebrews, when they wanted to speak of a principal authorising his agent to do a job for him, did not use a highly technical, still less an abstract term. They called an agent 'he who is sent', and the principal 'he who sends'. Agency was 'being sent', an abstract, probably not an ancient term in itself. The Greek for 'agent', in the biblical setting, was *apostolos*, a word everyone recognises, for it is our Apostle. The Apostles were Jesus's agents. And who was Jesus? This is an important question, for according to Jewish law 'an agent is even as the principal', he has the qualities and attributes of his principal, whom he represents. Now I did not want to go into that, but mentioned these facts about Jewish law in connection with the Unjust Steward, who could represent his master and so get away with transactions which might not have been authorised specifically.

Brother Anthony has been in a position to ponder long, and to search a great deal of apposite sources, and he has put together much more than two and two: yet who can say which of his discoveries is more valuable than the location of a good sound biblical authority for God's agent (and a son can be an agent, indeed none better) being as God himself?

The value of a discovery, of a notion, depends not on the intention, or the motive, behind the discovery, but on its fertilising capacity for others. That is why true discoverers are modest—and why modest, hidden-away people, can be discoverers. In this book the author seldom obtrudes himself. He does not lecture, nor is he sermonising. He wants to make the black-and-white letters sing, and so they do.

Do not read it rapidly. Take your time over each section. Have an old version of the Old Testament handy. It will be more like the Hebrew text (with all its corruptions and mistakes) with which Jesus's generation were equipped. For the New Testament use a version with several translations in parallel, if you cannot use the original. If Brother Anthony's parallels and arrangement do not strike a spark at once, it does not mean they never will. And maybe you will find something, and there is no place too remote for something startling to be discovered in it. Fertilisation is not confined to big cities, nor luxurious faculty rooms.

This book does not purport to answer all the questions you could ask. It raises a vast number. It provides a means of study, and fruitful meditation. To me, if not to all, it tells an authentic tale, movingly recreating the baroque thought-patterns of the ancient world, so unlike our own. Was Jesus's teaching meant to come into our world too? How were we supposed to understand this strange language, so simple on the surface, about seeds, birds, stones, money, and such like, and yet so involved and loaded with overtones, about reward and punishment, about sin and forgiveness, about personal righteousness, and what makes it tick? It is uncongenial to us, as many unsympathetic minds, even learned minds, had said in almost as many words. Is anyone sent to us with the message? Will he use words from the Bible, or out of his own head? Brother Anthony keeps to the Bible, and warns us that to sophisticate the teaching of Jesus is a sin.

How do we know whether the message is truly conveyed, after all? Not, I suggest, by *a priori* ideas about what kind of message we like to hear. The message is conveyed if it is understood. If the person to be communicated understands, the messenger is indeed 'sent' by the Master. Otherwise he is deluding himself. How do we know whether the hearer understands? By having a degree in theology? I wonder. Another possible answer is that he does what the Master bids him do. From the fruit one may know the nature of the tree, not from its appearance. The quality of a book lies in the effect it has on the lives of the readers, and of the hearers of those who are stimulated by it to pass on the message faithfully. 'If ye love me, keep my commandments' says Jesus, as St. John understands him (Jn. 14:15), which is no more than common sense. It is fine to be a messenger, but finer to hear the message and perform what it commands (Lk. 11:28). The test of a man's spiritual adventures in the text of the New Testament is not critical scholarship (which has another arena) but their capacity to cause the will of God to be done. Happy the messenger who communicates the message undefiled!

J. Duncan M. Derrett, Ph.D., LL.D.,
D.C.L.

London,

ABBREVIATIONS

I The books of the Bible in alphabetical order of abbreviations

Ac	Acts	2 K	2 Kings
Am	Amos	Lk	Luke
Ba	Baruch	Lm	Lamentations
1 Ch	1 Chronicles	Lv	Leviticus
2 Ch	2 Chronicles	1 M	1 Maccabees
1 Co	1 Corinthians	2 M	2 Maccabees
2 Co	2 Corinthians	Mi	Micah
Col	Colossians	Mk	Mark
Dn	Daniel	Ml	Malachias
Dt	Deuteronomy	Mt	Matthew
Eph	Ephesians	Na	Nahum
Est	Esther	Nb	Numbers
Ex	Exodus	Ne	Nehemiah
Ezk	Ezekiel	Ob	Obadiah
Ezr	Ezra	1 P	1 Peter
Gal	Galatians	2 P	2 Peter
Gn	Genesis	Ph	Philippians
Hab	Habakkuk	Phm	Philemon
Heb	Hebrews	Pr	Proverbs
Hg	Haggai	Ps	Psalms
Ho	Hosea·	Qo	Ecclesiastes (Qoheleth)
Is	Isaiah	Rev	Revelation
Jb	Job	Rm	Romans
Jdt	Judith	1 S	1 Samuel
Jg	Judges	2 S	2 Samuel
Jl	Joel	Sg	Song of Songs
Jm	James	Si	Ecclesiasticus (Sirach)
Jn	John	Tb	Tobit
1 Jn	1 John	1 Th	1 Thessalonians
2 Jn	2 John	2 Th	2 Thessalonians
3 Jn	3 John	1 Tm	1 Timothy
Jon	Jonah	2 Tm	2 Timothy
Jos	Joshua	Tt	Titus
Jr	Jeremiah	Ws	Wisdom
Jude	Jude	Zc	Zechariah
1 K	1 Kings	Zp	Zephaniah

II Other Abbreviations

AV	Authorized Version (King James)
B.T.	Babylonian Talmud
En	Enoch (Book of)
Er	Erubin (Mishnah)
2 Esd	Second Book of Esdras (Fourth Ezra — 4 Ezr)
Gk	Greek Text
Gn R.	Genesis Rabbah (Midrash)
Kidd.	Kiddushin (Mishnah)
J.T.	Jerusalem Talmud
Kal. R	Kallah Rabbah (Midrash)
L.B.	Epistle (Letter) of Barnabas
L.T.	Literal Translation
L.V.	Latin Vulgate
M.T.	Masoretic or Hebrew Text of the Bible
Meg.	Megillah or "Scroll of Esther" (Mishnah)
Men.	Menahoth or "Meal Offerings" (Mishnah)
Midr. R.	Midrash Rabba
O of Sol.	Odes of Solomon
P.A.	Pirke Aboth or "Sayings of the Fathers"
P.A.—R.N.	Pirke Aboth of Rabbi Nathan
Pes.	Pesachim or "Feast of Passover" (Mishnah)
Ps of Sol.	Psalms of Solomon

Q II D.S.S., Fig.	Qumran Cave II Dead Sea Scroll Fragment
RSV	Revised Standard Version
S of En	The Book of the Secrets of Enoch (Slavonic)
Sanh.	Sanhedrin (Mishnah)
Sept.	Septuagint or Greek Text of the Bible
Si O	Sibylline Oracles
Siph. Dt	Siphre on Deuteronomy (Tannaitic Mishnah)
Stob. Herm. Exc.	Stobaeus, Hermetica Excursus
Sy	Syriac Text of the Bible
T.A.	Testament (XII Patriarchs) of Asher
T.B.	Testament of Benjamin
T.D.	Testament of Dan
T.G.	Testament of Gad
T. Iss.	Testament of Issachar
T. Jos.	Testament of Joseph
T.J.	Testament of Judah
T.L.	Testament of Levi
T.N.	Testament of Naphtali
T.R.	Testament of Reuben
T.S.	Testament of Simeon
T.Z.	Testament of Zebulon

IMPORTANT

Please read the right hand pages first from top to bottom, then read the notes on the left hand pages at your leisure.

The right hand pages are for the "hungry" and the notes on the left hand pages—for the "bakers."

THE
BREAD
OF GOD

PROLOGUE

He waits whom my soul loves and my heart yearns for
He stands and waits by the door.

Peering through the windows, seeing through the lattices
that I did not hear the sound of His gentle knocking
because I was sitting completely enthralled reading one of His letters.

He smiles for He knows from my joy that I now understand
what He long tried to tell me.

He has seen me get up and gather His words then rush to make
out of them bread of understanding for Him.

The loaf is done, the fruit of a first baking, somewhat awkward
and a little lumpy here and there. . .
But there it is!

I must go now for I hear Him coming,
He has opened the door.

My Beloved has come for the Bread of His Word.

INTRODUCTION

*"**POOR IN SPIRIT**": The era of the New Testament was characterized even as today by great intellectual pride. Scoffers were rampant as the Dead Sea Scrolls reveal and excoriate:

"They do not hearken to Thy voice nor do they give ear to Thy Word, of the vision of knowledge they say, 'It is unsure', and of the Way of Thy heart, 'It is not the Way' " (Thanksgiving Hymn 4:17, 18).

"Furthermore they defile their holy spirit and open their mouth with a blaspheming tongue against the Laws of the Covenant of God saying, 'They are not sure', they speak abominations concerning them" (Zadokite Fragment VII. 11-12, edit. C. Rabin).

The "poor in spirit" were the "humble", devoid of pride who faithfully accepted the "yoke of the heavens" with spiritual docility. The term betokened obedience to the Laws of the Covenant. In this light we find "the poor in spirit" in the Scrolls of Qumram:

"He has opened the mouth of the dumb that they might praise His mighty works.

He has taught war (against the sons of darkness) to the hand of the feeble and steadied the trembling knee; He has strengthened the back of the weak.

By the *poor in spirit*. . .(missing portion) the hardened of heart and by the perfect of way all nations of wickedness have come to an end: not one of their mighty men stands" (War Rule 14:7, Dead Sea Scrolls IQM).

Again in the Scroll (War Rule 11:9-10), the "stricken in spirit" are equated with the "righteous":

"Thou wilt kindle the *stricken in spirit* and they shall be a flaming torch in the straw to consume ungodliness and never to desist until iniquity is destroyed" (IQM 11:9-10).

"The *righteous*—in the time of their Visitation shall shine forth, and as sparks among the stubble they shall run to and fro" (Wisdom 3:17).

Also in another Dead Sea Scroll fragment (Commentary on Psalm 37) the "humble" and the "congregation of the poor" are equated:

"But the *humble* shall possess the land and delight in abundant peace" (Ps. 37:11).

"Interpreted (idem.) this concerns the *congregation of the poor* who shall accept the season of penance and shall be delivered from all the snares of Satan. . .the *congregation of the poor* shall possess the portion of all. . .they shall possess the high mountain of Israel" (Commentary on Ps. 37 Fragment A: col. I.11):

In another work called the Psalms of Solomon, which was written in the same era, the "God-fearers," are variously called "the pious," "the righteous," and "the poor" (Psalms of Solomon 2:37, 39; 3:4, 5, 7, 8, 10, 14; 4:1, 9; 5:14; 8:28, 40; 9:6; 10:3, 7; 12:6, etc.).

The "poor in spirit" shall be exalted in the end for "humiliation follows the proud and glory shall uphold the humble of spirit" (Prov. 29:23).

"Humble thyself and thou wilt find mercy in the sight of God for many are the mercies of God and to the humble He reveals His secret" (Sirach 3:18, 20).

"The Mysteries of God He reveals to the lowly" (Sirach 3:18 Sinaiticus and Syriac Text).

"Whosoever therefore shall humble himself as this little child, he is the greater in the Kingdom of Heaven" (St. Matt. 18:4), in the realm of those who shall understand the "Mysteries of God" (IQM 14 Dead Sea Scrolls). Because "with the humble is Wisdom" (Prov. 11:2) and "the counsel of the Lord is with them who fear Him" (Psalm 25:14).

"His secret is with the righteous" (Prov. 3:32).

Thus by the "poor in spirit" He shall make to understand "the hardened of heart" who "understood not. . .because their hearts were hardened" (St. Mark 6:52; Isaiah 6:10; St. Matt. 13:15).

For the "poor in spirit" are taught by God and it is to them that He reveals His secrets.

So, if you want to "be taught by the Lord" (Isaiah 54:13) be "poor in spirit" and remember that the Lord "teaches the humble" (Ps. 25:9) not the proud.

"Not because you were more excellent than all other people hath the Lord had pleasure in you, but because you were poor in spirit and more humble than all the nations" (Palestinian Targum on Deut. 7:7).

He teaches "the poor in spirit" for "they that give heed unto Him are the poor of the flock" (Zadokite Fragment 10:1 B. Text).

*Bethlehem: Beth="House" and Lehem="Bread"

*"**CARING**": Because when we care for someone our hearts are soft towards that one. "The Word of the Kingdom" (St. Matt. 13:19), is sown as a Seed in the ground of our hearts, and the best time to sow is when the ground is soft and moist.

There are two great poverties in the world
That of goods and that of spirit,

Am 8:11   Two great hungers for the Bread of God
Pr 9:5   That of body and that of soul,
Is 55:2

Dt 8:3   For it is written: "Not by bread alone does man live
Mt 4:4   but by every Word that proceeds from the mouth of God."
Jr 15:16

Thus it is that there are two Blessed —

Lk 6:20   The poor
               and
Mt 5:3   The poor* in spirit.

For to be poor and empty of self
Is to be rich in the possession of God

Lk 17:21   Whose kingdom is in our hearts;

1K 3:7   And to be poor in spirit and little before Him
Jr 1:6   Is to be able to enter, to see and to share
Mt 18:4

The infinite treasures of His domain
Which is: the Kingdom of Heaven.

This is known to the little ones here on earth
Mt 11:19   As the Wisdom of God.
Lk 7:35

Dt. 29:29   "The secret things belong to the Lord"
Is 28:9   But the things that are revealed
Mt 11:25   Belong to the children.
P.A.—R.N.34

1 Co 2:7   The greatest Mystery of all
Lk 2:10   Was born to us
            In the little town of the House of Bread called Bethlehem.*

Lk 2:12   A Mystery "wrapped in swaddling clothes and lying in a manger"
Is 1:3   Because a manger has but one use
Jn 6:33   To hold food — "the Bread of God,"

Jn 6:51   A "living Bread" that is "the Word of God."
Jn 1:1

Lk 17:20   The Kingdom of God always comes unawares
            Yet every time it comes upon us

It does when we are caring* for someone else
For something other than ourselves.

*"**SHEPHERDS**": There were two flocks in the field that night: the Lord's own flock (Ezek. 34:31; 36:38; Isaiah 40:11; Micah 7:14; Ps. 23:1-2; 78:52; 80:1; 95:7; 100:3; St. Luke 12:32; St. John 10:11 etc.) and their sheep beside them. St. Luke 2:8 as written in Greek states: "and there were shepherds in that country lodging in the fields" *(agrauleo)*. The word *agrauleo* is derived from *agros*="field" and *aule*="fold." The shepherds in that particular spot were lodging as a fold in the field and God watched over them for they in turn were watching "over their flocks." In Hebrew the word for "shepherds" is *roim*, a word derived from the verb *raah*="to see." *Roim* also means "seers."

Notwithstanding the fact that Abraham and David were of the same occupation, strict Jews despised shepherds because their type of work made them neglectful of religious observances (Baba Kamma 7:7; 80a; Shekalim 7:4 B. Talmud).

Rabbi Jose bar Hanina (3rd century) taught that in the whole world there is no occupation more despised than that of a shepherd (Midrash Rabbah on Ps. 23 sect. 2).

In Egypt shepherds were regarded as "an abomination" (Gen. 46:34; Exod. 8:6).

"Egyptians reject all shepherds" (Palestinian Targum on Gen. 46).

"Egyptians keep at a distance all shepherds of flocks" (Targum of Onkelos on Gen. 46).

"Let not a man bring up his son to be a shepherd for their occupation is that of thieves" (Abba Gurja, Jer. Talmud).

Thus the Sanhedrin ruled that no shepherd was capable of bearing witness owing to their habit of encroaching upon the pastures belonging to others (Sanhedrin 25a B. Talmud).

In the region near Bethlehem where the shepherds were keeping watch there stood the "tower of the flock" the *Migdal*-*Eder* ("flock") of Genesis 35:21 and Micah 4:8: "and thou Migdal-Eder ("tower of the flock") stronghold of the daughter of Sion, unto thee shall it come; yea, the former dominion shall come, the kingdom of the daughter of Jerusalem" (In this passage: Micah 4:6-8, the Lord promises the exaltation of the lame and rejected ones for whom He will restore His Kingdom. *See also* Isaiah 40:9-11; Ezek. 34:11-16; 37:24-28; Zeph. 3:19; St. John 10:7-16).

Among the Jews there was an ancient tradition as found in the Palestinian Targum on Genesis 35:21 that states on that passage: "and Jacob proceeded and spread his tent beyond Migdal-Eder, the place from whence it is to be that the King Messiah will be revealed at the end of days" (*See also* Targum Jonathan and Targum Onkelos in Lightfoot's *Decas Choregr.* IV. 4-5).

That particular "tower of the flock" was still standing in the time of Christ. The Oral Law (Mishnah) mentions it as a boundary point for acceptable Temple offerings. "Any cattle or sheep found within a radius of Jerusalem as far as Migdal-Eder can be offered as whole offering or peace offering unto the Lord" (Shekalim 7:4. See also *La Geographie du Talmud* p. 152 by A.N. Neubauer, Paris 1868). The "tower of the flock" Migdal-Eder was still extant in the time of St. Jerome (c.350-400 A.D.) and was mentioned by him: "about a thousand paces (approximately 1 mile in 'Roman paces') from Bethlehem is the Tower of Ader which means, "Tower of the Flock," a name which seems to be a prophetic allusion to the shepherds' future witness to the Nativity of the Lord" (St. Jerome O.S. 43 also *Onomastikon* of Eusebius 62, 68 and St. Jerome's Epistle to Paulae CVIII). A few decades before the year 385 A.D. there was already in that spot a famous monastery called the Poimenion ("of the flock") and this was visited by Palladius (c380-420 A.D.) when he lived with the holy monk Possidonius not far from Bethelem (*See* Syriac text of the *Paradise of the Fathers*, translated by E.W. Budge, London 1907, Chatto and Windus Vol. I, p. 173, and *Historia Lausiaca* Migne P.G. XXXIV. 1179 and others*).

Ancient Christian tradition mentions that the shepherds of the gospel were natives of the village of Beth-Zur in Judea which was located in the area belonging to the Calebites of the tribe of Judah for Beth-Zur was in their portion (Josh. 15:38; Neh. 3:16; 2 Macc. 11:5; Josephus *Antiq.* 12:7, ⁵). Although the Calebites were a branch of the tribe of Judah, they were of mixed blood having derived origin from the Gentile Kenizzites (Numbers 32:12; Genesis 15:19) and as such were considered racially inferior, the very name of their eponymous ancestor: *Caleb* means "dog" in Hebrew. The Kenites as well were identified with the admirable Rechabites (1 Chr. 2:55; 4:23) to whom it was promised by the Lord that there would not lack a man before them to stand before Him forever (Jer. 35:5-10, 16-19). In Psalm 71 (Sept.) they were promised the gift of praise to the Lord and Jewish tradition said of them that the rich reward of the revelation of the Messiah would be theirs (Aboth de Rabbi Nathan, chapter 35).

Yet to the people of His time these poor shepherds were an insignificant lot, but not to God, for it was to these despised shepherds of mixed parentage who bore the opprobrious name of "dogs" *(calebites)* that the Good News was first given. In turn it was they who first spread the Good News of His birth (St. Luke 2:17) and the glad news of salvation: "Glorifying and praising God" (St. Luke 2:20). They, who were not allowed by the Oral Law to bear witness to the Truth, "made known abroad the Word which was told them concerning this Child" (St. Luke 2:17).

For when God reveals Himself it is to the foolish, the weak, the base and despised (1 Cor. 1:27-28), and it is to them that He makes manifest His glory (St. Luke 2:9).

"So that no human being might boast in the Presence of God" (1 Cor. 1:29).

*Others who mention the monastery at the site of Migdal Eder and the "church of the shepherds" are Cyril de Scyth, *Vita S. Euthymii* LXXXVI idem. *Vita S. Sabae* LXXXIV; Metaphrastes, *Vita S. Theodosii*; Armenian Lectionary (450-500 A.D.) and Georgian Calendarium; Procopius, *De Aedificaciones* V. 9; Arculf (650 A.D.) mentions: "I visited the tombs of the three shepherds who are buried in a church beside the Tower of Ader, they are a thousand yards east of Bethlehem" (*Itinera Hierosolymitana*, CSEL, Vienna, 1898, Trans. by P.G. Geyer); Pilgrim of Piacenza (570 A.D.) mentions that "opposite to Bethlehem there is a monastery surrounded by a wall, where a great number of monks are gathered together" (Edit. Tobler et Molinier, p. 107, 171 also Vol. II p. 514a); Monk Bernard (870 A.D.) mentions a visit to the "monastery of the shepherds a mile out of Bethlehem" Daniel (1160 A.D.) mentions "the holy meadow" and Moslem Idrisi (1154 A.D.) tells about the "church of the angels" there.

That is why the first good news was to a few shepherds*
Watching over their flock

Because it was a special kind of watching
A "keeping watch": a caring for in the night.

The night that brought Light to the darkness
And joy into the world.

Alleluia!
Alleluia!

*"**MYSTERY**": "The Mystery (Singular) of the Kingdom of God". Both St. Mark 4:11 and St. Luke 8:10 are in the singular in the Latin Vulgate, Syriac Peshitta, Harkleian, Old Latin and Georgian texts based on the ancient Greek texts.

*"**FOUR**" or five times if St. Matthew 19:24 is included. However, the Latin Vulgate and the Syriac texts retain "Kingdom of Heaven" instead of "Kingdom of God". The early Church fathers, viz., St. Clement of Alexandria (c.210 A.D.), Eusebius (c.340 A.D.) and St. Chrysostom quote it as the "Kingdom of Heaven" also.

There are two hidden things in the Gospel
Which we must search for:

Mt 13:11   The "Mysteries of the Kingdom of Heaven"
            And
Lk 8:10   The "Mystery* of the Kingdom of God."
Mk 4:11

            St. Matthew alone tells about the Kingdom of Heaven
Mt 6:33   And on the Kingdom of God he writes four* times.
12:28
21:31, 43
            The other Gospels proclaim the Kingdom of God.

            St. Matthew wrote for the Jews: His people
Rm 3:2   Who "are entrusted with the Words of God."

            The Jews have great reverence for His name
            and they are careful not to profane It.

            Thus they call Him the Blessed One,
            The Almighty, the High and Lofty and Holy One
            And many other names meaning: God.

            Every Jew is in a way a son of Solomon
            For they love Wisdom as their fathers did.

            Solomon was the wisest man the world ever knew
            Until Emmanuel came to us.

            St. Matthew's Gospel is the good news of the Wisdom of the Lord
            And of His Understanding
            Which He gave to us in the form of Keys.

            Two Keys:

            One for the righteous
            and
            One for the merciful

            Because only the pure can see the Wisdom of God
            and only the compassionate can understand it.

Pr 25:2   "It is the glory of God to conceal a thing"

            And wait. . .

            For the merciful to become faithful
            And the righteous to be kind.

7

*"WORD": "The source of Wisdom is the Word of God" (Sirach 1:5; Syriac, Sahidic, Latin Vulgate and Greek ms. 248).

*"BE GOOD": "Blessed are ye righteous ones for unto ye are revealed the deepest secrets of the Law" (Zohar. Sect. Idra Rabba 2:26). "God...will give the upright insight into the Knowledge of the Most High and into the Wisdom of the sons of heaven, and (He will give) to the perfect of Way Understanding" (Community Rule IV. 20, 22, Dead Sea Scrolls).

*"KNOWLEDGE": No one finds the treasures of Wisdom unless he understands where to search and where to find the "Parables of Knowledge" that are kept in them. For the Lord gives Widsom to the wise but knowledge He gives only to those who understand (Daniel 2:21). "A man of understanding has Wisdom" (Prov. 10:23) and true knowledge from God.

*"BE VERY GOOD": "For I say unto you, unless your righteousness exceeds that of the Scribes and Pharisees, you will never enter the Kingdom of Heaven" (St. Matt. 5:20). "For the bewitching of naughtiness obscureth good things and the wandering of concupiscence doth undermine the understanding of the innocent" (Wisdom 4:12; Sept.).
So be good!—"lest wickedness should alter 'your' understanding" (Wisdom 4:11; Septuagint).
"I, in righteousness, I see Thy face" (Ps. 17:15; Literal translation).
"Blessed are the pure in heart for they shall discern (orao) God" (St. Matt. 5:8).
"With the pure (barar) thou dost show Thyself clearly" (barar)-Ps. 18:26; 2 Sam. 22:27.
"Unhappy" are the wicked for they shall "not discern Thee in all Thy Words" (Liturgical Fragment Q I Dead Sea Scrolls).
"Happy the soul which has not been sullied by evil deeds for it has discerned its Creator and understood its origin" (Sepher Ha Tapuach).
God is Truth and He "reveals what is hidden to the pure" (2 Baruch 54:5).
"I found Wisdom in purity and through her guidance I obtained Understanding" (Sirach 51:20; Hebrew Text).
"From my youth Thou hast appeared to me in the Wisdom of Thy Law and by Thy fixed Truth Thou hast supported me" (Hymn 9:31, Dead Sea Scrolls).
"Put away the imagination of evil from your hearts and there will speedily be revealed to you the glory of the Lord" (Palestinian Targum on Leviticus 9:6).

*"UNDERSTAND": "If thou desire to hear, thou shalt receive Understanding, and if thou incline thine ear, thou shalt be wise" (Sirach 6:33 Syriac Text).
Listen closely for "there is no understanding to him that hears" (Isaiah 33:19; Sept.) without paying attention.

Come, let us go into the field of the Lord and search for hidden
treasure among the Parables.
For they are full of hidden Wisdom.

Pr 2:4   "Search for Wisdom as for hidden treasure."
Mt 7:7   "Seek and you shall find."

Si 6:27 Sept. "Search, and seek, and Wisdom shall be made known to you"
Jn 5:39   If you "search the Scriptures."

For it is in holy scripture that true Wisdom is found.

Ba 3:15   "Who has come into the treasures of Wisdom?"
2 Ba 44:14   "They who have acquired for themselves the treasures of Wisdom,"
              are they who have sought Wisdom in the field of the Lord.

Jb 28:12   "Where is Wisdom to be found?
              and where is the place of Understanding?"

              Wisdom is found in the Truth of His Word*
Jb 38:36   And the place to understand it is in our hearts.

Pr 14:33   "Wisdom rests in the heart of him that has Understanding"
Jb 28:28   Because he has departed from evil.

Si 18:28   "Every man of Understanding knows Wisdom"
              And he understands that Wisdom rests in his heart because:
Si 33:3 L.V. "A man of Understanding is faithful to the Law of God."

Ws 1:4   "Wisdom will not enter a deceitful soul nor dwell in a body enslaved
              to sin."
              So that if you want to find rich treasure: be* *good*

Ws 8:5   For after all "what is richer than Wisdom?"
Ws 7:14   "Wisdom is an infinite treasure to all mankind"
Si 1:24 *Sept.* And "the Parables of Knowledge* are in the treasures of Wisdom."

Si 38:33 Sy   But if you hope to "understand the parables of the wise": be *very**
              good.
Si 39:1,2,3. Because it is "he that applies himself to the fear of the Lord and sets
Gk and Sy   his mind upon the Law of the Most High," who shall "enter into the
              deep things of parables" and understand "the dark sayings of
              parables."

Si 11:4 L.V. "For the works of the Most High are wonderful, secret and hidden."
Si 6:35   "Be ready to listen to every divine discourse and do not let the
L.T. Sept.   *Parables of Understanding* escape you."
              Hold fast to each and every Word and listen carefully.
              Remember that the "Parables of Understanding" came to us from
              the mouth of God.

Mt 13:19   "He who has ears to hear let him hear"!! and understand.*

"Come to Wisdom as one that plows and wait for her good fruits."

Sirach 6:19; Septuagint.

CHAPTER 1

THE PARABLE OF THE SOWER

According to St. Matthew 13:3-9, 18-23

[3] And He spoke to them many things in parables, saying, "Behold, the sower went forth to sow. [4] And as he sowed some seeds fell by the wayside and the birds came and devoured them. [5] And other seeds fell upon rocky places, where they had not much soil and they sprang up at once, because they had no depth of soil. [6] But when the sun rose they were scorched and because they had no root they withered away. [7] And other seeds fell among the thorns. And the thorns sprang up and choked them. [8] And other seeds fell upon good ground and yielded fruit, some a hundredfold, some sixtyfold, and some thirtyfold.
[9] He who has ears to hear, let him hear."

[10] And the disciples came up and said to Him, "why do you speak to them in parables?"
And He answered and said, "To you it is given to know the Mysteries of the Kingdom of Heaven but to them it is not given."

[18] "Hear therefore the parable of the sower. [19] When anyone hears the Word of the Kingdom but does not understand it, the evil one comes and snatches away what has been sown in his heart. This is he who was sown by the wayside. [20] And the one sown upon rocky places, that is he who hears the Word and receives it immediately with joy; [21] yet he has no root in himself but continues only for a time, and when trouble and persecution come because of the Word, he at once falls away. [22] And the one sown among the thorns that is he who hears the Word; and the cares of this world and the deceitfulness of riches choke the Word and it is made fruitless. [23] And the one sown upon good ground that is he who hears the Word and understands it; he indeed bears fruit and makes in one case a hundredfold, in another sixtyfold and in another thirtyfold."

*"**Wisdom of God**": This Truth is beautifully manifested in St. Matthew 21:8; St. Mark 11:8 and St. John 12:13. In narrating Christ's triumphal entry into Jerusalem, each one of the evangelists uses a different word for "branches": *Klados*, *Stoibas* and *Baion* respectively. *Baion* denotes a palm branch, *Klados* and *Stoibas* are the two other types of branches needed to fulfill the directions found in Lev. 23:40 as regards making the *Lulab* or "festive branch" which is composed of three different types of branches, a palm branch and myrtle and willow branches tied up together. St. Luke makes no mention of branches.

There was an ancient Jewish tradition that decreed that at whatever time of the year the Messiah was to appear, the Jews were expected to greet and hail Him by taking up *Lulab* clusters and singing Hosannas to Him as the Holy One of Israel (Pesikta de Rab Kahana 27:3).

Our Lord said there were two secret things in the Gospel:
The Mysteries of the Kingdom of Heaven
and
The Mystery of the Kingdom of God.

Come, let us speak to the Sower in St. Matthew
And ask Him there, about the Mysteries of the Kingdom of Heaven.

He will tell us to look for impersonal things —
The broad and non-specific pluralities,
The grand design — the holy reasons
For which we must listen very closely
In order to hear and understand.

In the light of the Kingdom of Heaven —
Notice that the Parable of the Sower as found in St. Matthew is full
of pluralities:

"some seeds fell"—	13:4
"the birds devoured them"—	13:4
"other seeds fell"—	13:5
"they had not much soil"—	13:5
"they sprang up"—	13:5
"they had no depth of soil"—	13:5
"they were scorched"—	13:6
"they had no roots"—	13:6
"they withered away"—	13:6
"other seeds"--	13:7
"choked them"—	13:7
"other seeds"—	13:8

And when they yielded they gave:

"some a hundredfold"	13:8
"some sixtyfold"	13:8
"some thirtyfold"	13:8
"He who has ears to hear let him hear"	13:9

And let him listen very closely.

Because: "When anyone hears the Word of the Kingdom and does
not understand it, the evil one comes and snatches away what has
been sown in his heart."

Parables are intended to provoke thought and make us ponder over
the words to seek their meaning for us.
And to draw us to seek the answer from Him—when we do not fully
understand them.

We shall learn a very important thing:
That just as we help one another so do the Gospels depend on one
another
To reveal the Wisdom* of God

For they are truly Christian Gospels.

*"HEAVEN": "The eternal secrets which are in heaven and which men strive to learn" (Book of Enoch 9:6, Greek Text, Syncellus Fragment and Akhmim fragment).

There are two kinds of seed in the parable of the Sower —
The many seeds for the heart to ponder
And the one Seed for the heart to hold.

From the many seeds we learn about the Kingdom of Heaven*:
About the things in store for us in this world and the next.

From the one Seed we learn how to be like Him
For this is the work of the Kingdom of God.

Those who enter the Kingdom of Heaven
Are those who understand the Word.

Those who force themselves into the Kingdom of God
Are those who do what the Word says.

Mt 13:3-9   The Sower went forth to sow His Truths
And this St. Matthew tells us.

Mk 4:3-9   The Sower also went forth to sow Himself
Lk 8:5-8   And this we learn from St. Mark and St. Luke.

Mt 13:18-23   When you understand the general things
You become particular in your explanation.

Mk 4:13-20   When you know who the particular One is
Lk 8:9-15   You shall explain all things.

Those who hold fast to His Truths keep Him in their hearts
And those who keep Him there hold on to the Truth.

Mt 13:19   Let us now go to St. Matthew and ponder. . .
"What has been sown in his heart?"

Mt 7:7   St. Matthew does not tell you
But He says: "Seek and you shall find."

Lk 11:19   Go to St. Luke for He said there the same thing
Lk 8:5   And find that the "Sower went to sow his seed."

Lk 8:11   What kind of a seed is "his seed"?
"The seed is the Word of God."

Jn 1:1   The Word of God is God.

Mk 4:15   "The Word has been sown in their hearts". . .
For it is there that the Word desires to be understood.

*"**SNATCHES AWAY**" *(harpazo):* The Greek word *harpazo* means "to snatch away" to "take by force" (See notes opposite page 25). St. Matthew in this parable speaks of the Kingdom of *Heaven:* the understanding of the Wisdom of God. In St. Matt. 21:43 a different word is used because our Lord refers to the Kingdom of *God:* "Therefore I say to you that the Kingdom of God shall be taken (*airo*="lifted up") from you, and given to a nation yielding the fruits thereof."

*"**RECEIVES**" *(lambano):* The word *lambano* corresponds to the Hebrew word *laquach* which means either to "receive" or "take," ex. "receive *(laquach)* instructions from His mouth" (Job 22:21; Hebrew Text), "receive *(lambano)* a declaration" (Job 22:21; Septuagint).

*"**ROOT IN HIMSELF**": In the time of our Lord, contemporary Jewish thought expressed Wisdom as a root implanted in the heart of man: "The glory of those. . .who have planted in their heart the root of Wisdom" (2 Baruch 51:3). "The root of Wisdom and the riches of understanding and the fount of Knowledge" (2 Baruch 59:7). Naturally, this root of Wisdom sprung forth from the seed of the observance of the Law: "Prepare your hearts to sow in them the fruits (seeds) of the Law" (2 Baruch 32:1a). This was of vital importance because the advent of the Messianic Age was to be preceded by the period of the Messianic "woes," a time of great tribulation for all the inhabitants of the world. The root of Wisdom and the seeds of the Law then "shall protect you in that time in which the Mighty One is to shake the whole creation" (2 Bar. 32:1b). "To whom has the root of Wisdom been revealed?" (Sirach 1:6); "the root of Wisdom that never fails?" (Wisdom 3:15). "Wisdom's root that cannot fail" (*Idem.* Holmes Translation) and "the root of the just that shall prosper—and never be moved" (Prov. 12:12,3), are identical, for they are both grounded in the fear of the Lord. Because "to fear the Lord is the root of Wisdom" (Sirach 1:12; Job 28:28).
If "the prolific brood of the ungodly will be of no use and none of their illegitimate seedlings will strike root or take a firm hold" (Wisdom 4:3 RSV), it is because the ungodly do not have the fear of the Lord: "All who forget God wither before they bear fruit for such are the paths of all who forget God" (Job 8:11-13). The foolish may appear to flourish for a while: "He thrives before the sun and his shoots spread over his garden, his roots twine about the stone heap, he lives among the rocks" (Job 8:16-17). But how long do you think he will last when the "sun of Justice" (Mal. 4:2) comes forth? "The children of the ungodly shall not bring forth many branches, they are unhealthy roots upon sheer rock" (Sirach 40:15 *RSV*). "If he is destroyed from his [rocky] places then it will deny him, saying, 'I have never seen you.' Behold this is the joy of his way" (Job 8:18-19 RSV).
"We strike root downward and bear fruit upward" (Isaiah in 2 Kings 19:30). If Wisdom is a root it searches for the waters of Understanding. The good ground is well watered and so it is, that the root of Wisdom from the seed of His Word bears fruit in those who understand.
The seeds that fell among the thorns sprung roots and grew as well because the ground was receptive and not hardened. But how could the young and tender plant of His Word thrive amidst the evil company of the thorns? It bore no fruit because: "To depart from evil is Understanding" (Job 28:28) for among the wicked "the best of them is as a brier and the most upright is as a thorn hedge" (Micah 7:4). So be good even if you have to go to the desert to avoid your own weakness for the wrong company. Seek God first and do not be afraid. Remember that the date palm of the desert thrives in the most inhospitable places and it thrives unafraid of the burning sun. Even with its head in a furnace the date palm bears the sweetest of fruits because the roots of its feet are dipped in the waters of Paradise. And that is Understanding. Solomon had a long root but in the end he ran out of water.

Because St. Matthew understood what had been sown in the heart,
He explains the meaning of the parable more intimately,
The general becomes particular;
The non-specific becomes specific;
The impersonal becomes personal.

Mt 13:19-23   Thus he writes:
"When *anyone* hears the *Word of the Kingdom* but does not understand *it*
the evil one comes and snatches* away what has been sown in *his* heart.
This is *he* who was sown by the wayside
And the *one* sowed upon rocky places,
This is *he* who hears the Word and receives* it
Yet *he* has no root* in *himself*
he at once falls away.
The *one* sown among the thorns:
This is *he* who hears the Word—
riches choke the Word;
it becomes unfruitful.
And the *one* sown on good ground:
This is *he* who hears the Word and understands *it. he* indeed bears *fruit* and makes in *one* case a hundredfold in *another* sixtyfold and in *another* thirtyfold."

Mt 13:19   Notice that St. Matthew writes: "the word of the Kingdom" but does not say which
Because it is not the words of the Kingdom of Heaven but the Word of the Kingdom of God hidden and unspoken until the time of the Reign of Understanding: today.

There are two things that prevent hearing and understanding.
The first one is the sin of pride
And the second is hardness of heart.

Pride is the sin of the "wise" of this world
Who "know" so much that they no longer listen
With awe and delight as a child does to the Word of God.

And so they breed among themselves the sin of indifference—
A sin
Because it is indifference to the Words of God.

They reap their own punishment
For indeed they hear but do not understand and they see but never perceive:

The hidden Wisdom of God.

*"**GOOD AND KIND**": "The wicked err when they devise evil but **compassionate** and **righteous** men do all kinds of good. The workers of iniquity do not understand Truth and Mercy; Kindness and Truth are with the workers of good things" (Prov. 14:22; Syriac Text). Those who are both merciful and righteous understand the Truth and with their knowledge of it they are able to devise true things full of good words for "there is Wisdom in the *good* heart of a man" (Prov. 14:33; Septuagint).

*"**ASKED**": "Ask and learn" (I Macc. 10:72), according to Hebrew usage the two imperatives "ask and learn" are not coordinated but subordinate the one to the other thus "ask and you will then know for you will learn the answer."

*"**EAGERLY**": Children hear well and they listen attentively: "A good ear will hear Wisdom with all desire" (Sirach 3:31 Latin Vulgate). If "an attentive ear is the desire of a wise man" (Sirach 3:29; Septuagint) it is because the desire of a "wise man" is someone who understands him. "He who has ears to hear let him hear" (St. Matt. 11:15; 13:9, 43; St. Mark 4:9, 23; 7:16; St. Luke 8:8; 14:35). "Listen therefore. . .understand. . .and learn" (Wisdom 6:1 RSV).

*"*MATHETEUO*" means "instructed" in Greek. St. Matthew was "instructed (*matheteuo*) in the Kingdom of Heaven" (St. Matt. 13:52).

*"**SAGES** are found where parables are spoken" (Sirach 38:33), because they know that "a parable is found on the lips of the wise" (Sirach 21:16; Sinaiticus Text).

*"**HAPPY**": "Hear my son and be wise and make your heart happy in the way" (Prov. 23:19). And be good for "Wisdom. . .is not discerned in the heart of fools" (Prov. 14:33; Septuagint).

1P 1:23	Remember that the Word of God is a living Word
Heb 4:12	And living things are not really understood by the mind but by the heart that is good* and kind.

1 Jn 4:8   Because true understanding is born of God who is Love in our hearts
And only He can teach us all things.

Pr 18:15, Sept. "The ear of the wise seeks understanding"
Pr 28:5   And "those who seek the Lord understand all things."

Mk 4:33   When they did not know the meaning of a parable,
Mk 7:17   They went to Him.

Mk 4:34   "And He explained all things to them"
Mk 4:10   Because—"they asked* Him."
Lk 8:9

For Wisdom loves to make wise
The little ones who listen eagerly*

And who give Wisdom delight
When they understand.

Before He explained the parable of the Sower to them
Our Lord said something very important.

Mk 4:13   He said: "Do you not understand this parable?
How then will you understand all the parables?"

Pay close attention then to the parable of the Sower.

If the "Kingdom of Heaven" means the Reign of Understanding then
St. "Matthew"—which is a play on the Greek word *mathe-teuo**—should not have found it necessary to ask the Lord for explanations concerning this parable.

And so it was that although the disciples in St. Luke and St. Mark asked Him for the meaning of the parable
They did not in the Gospel according to St. Matthew.

Mt 13:10   Instead they asked Him why He spoke to the "crowds" in parables.
Mt 13:10   And the Lord replied, "To you it is given to know the Mysteries of the Kingdom of Heaven but to them it is not given"

Mt 7:7   Until they ask Him.
Lk 11:10

To St. Matthew were assigned the treasures of His Wisdom because St. Matthew was a tax collector called Levi who was trained to account.

And so he accounted for each and every Word that proceeded from the mouth of God.

He kept a ledger on the things that were spoken
And remembered when he wrote for the Jews that:
Si 3:31   "The heart of a sage* will ponder a parable and an attentive ear is the wise man's joy."

Be happy* now.

*"**BIRDS**": Both St. Matthew and St. Mark were Jews and the early Fathers[1] of the Church tell us that their ministry was primarily directed towards their own countrymen in Judea and abroad. Tradition[2] holds that St. Mark wrote the gospel based on the preaching of St. Peter. Needless to say, St. Matthew wrote down what he saw and heard himself.
As Jews these two evangelists were cognizant of the Jewish Apocryphal and Apocalyptic writings prevalent in their day. This premise is supported by the fact that both of them retain the word "birds" by itself unqualified by the usual designation; "of heaven" (ouranos). Thus it is written:[3] "and the birds came and devoured them" (St. Matthew 13:4), "and the birds came and devoured it" (St. Mark 4:4). The omission of the phrase "of heaven" is deliberate in these verses because elsewhere St. Matthew (6:26; 8:20; 13:32) and St. Mark (4:32) keep the usual[4] scriptural qualification. It is omitted in the parable of the Sower because in that parable the "birds" represent "the evil one" (St. Matt. 13:19) or "Satan" (St. Mark 4:15) and the Jews were taught that Satan was cast down from "heaven" (Ouranos) and given the "air" (aer) for his habitation. Thus we find Satan referred to as: "the spirit of the air (aer) Beliar" — Test. of Benjamin 3:4 (C. 125 B.C.). "I threw him (Satan) out of the height with his angels and he was flying in the air (aer) continually" — Secrets of Enoch 29:5 (C.25 B.C.). "Solomon—controlled and mastered all spirits of the Air" (aer)—Test of Solomon 1:1. "Beliar ascended in the air (aer) where he lives"—Ascension of Isaiah 10:29 (C. 70 B.C.). St. Paul, a Jew, also knew that "the prince of the power of the air" (aer)-Eph. 2:2, was none other than "Beliar the great, evil, angel, king of the air (aer) of the world" (Ascension of Isaiah 4:2). However, St. Paul demoted him to "chief" (archon) or "prince" (archon), because with the "understanding of Christ" (1 Cor. 2:16; St. John 12:31), St. Paul knew that to be a "king" one must have a "kingdom" and the air (aer) is no realm.
When our Lord told the parable of the Sower in the Hebrew-Aramaic of His day He simply said "birds" as He did on another occasion recorded in St. Luke 12:24 and in so doing His listeners would understand that "birds" not "of heaven" (ouranos or shamayim) were "birds of the air" (aer) up there where the "evil one", "Satan-Beliar" lives. He did not say "air" i.e. "birds of the air" because there is no word for "air" in either Aramaic or Hebrew.
Thus we should not make the common mistake of altering "birds of heaven" (ouranos) into "birds of the air" because "heaven" (ouranos) is "heaven" (ouranos) and "air" (aer) is "air" (aer) and never should the twain be confused for we do not beat "heaven" "as one that beats the air" (aer)-1 Cor. 9:26. If "ye shall speak into the air" (aer)-1 Cor. 14:9, and think ye are being heard in "heaven" (ouranos)—ve are mistaken.
Who "threw dust in the air" (aer)—Acts 22:23, so that "the sun and the air (aer) were darkened" (Rev. 9:2) but not heaven (ouranos) above?
"Ask now. . .the birds of heaven (ouranos) and they shall tell thee" (Job 12:7 Septuagint and Hebrew Text), that you cannot darken "heaven" because "heaven" (ouranos) is always full of light.
Read now the Babylonian Talmud Sanhedrin 107a and find out that the devil can assume any form such as that of a "bird" of the "air."

[1] "Fathers": St. Ireneaus, St. Clement of Alexandria, Eusebius, Papias, St. Jerome, Origen, Tertullian and St. Justin Martyr.
[2] "Tradition": See Eusebius "Hist. Eccl". Vol. II, 15; Vol. III, 29; Vol. VI, 14, 25 Patrol. Grec. Vol. VII, 878; Vol. VIII, 45 also Vol. VI, 724; Vol. VII, 878; Vol. XX 172, 300, 552, 581. Patrol. Lat. Vol. II, 367: Vol. XXIII, 621, Muratorian Fragment1.: Tertullian Contra Marc." IV, 5, St. Justin Martyr Dial. 106, St. Jerome's De. Vir. Ill. 8; Ad Hedib. ep. 120 (Patrol. Lat. Vol. XXII, 1002).
[3] "written": All the best and earliest Greek codices viz; Vaticanus, Sinaiticus, Alexandrinus, Ephraemi, Regius, Sangallensis, Rosanensis etc. and the old Latin texts prior to the Sixtine and Clementine Vulgate have simply "birds" in St. Matthew 13:4 and St. Mark 4:4.
[4] "usual": The phrase "birds of heaven" (ouranos) is found widely used throughout the Greek Septuagint which was the Bible quoted by our Lord and His disciples in the gospels. The term is the Greek translation of "birds of heaven" (shamayim) of the Hebrew Text. St. Luke was a Greek physician native of Antioch and very well versed in the Septuagint. He was a Gentile convert and he probably did not share the familiarity St. Matthew, St. Mark and St. Paul had with the Jewish Apocryphal and Apocalyptic works. "The air produces oblivion. . .the air makes one forget" (Sanhedrin fol. 109 Col. I. B. Talmud).

22

CHAPTER 2

THE PARABLE OF THE SOWER

According to St. Mark 4:2-20

[2] And He taught them many things in parables and He said to them in His instruction, [3] "Hear ye! Behold! the sower went forth to sow: [4] and it came to pass that as he sowed some seed fell by the wayside and the birds* came and devoured it. [5] And other seed fell upon rocky places where it had not much soil and it sprang up at once, because it had no depth of soil; [6] but when the sun arose it was scorched and because it had no root it withered away. [7] And other seed fell among thorns, and the thorns grew up and choked it, and it yielded no fruit. [8] And other seed fell into good ground and yielded fruit that grew up and increased and bore, one thirtyfold, one sixtyfold and one a hundredfold."

[9] And He said to them, "He that has ears to hear let him hear."

[10] And when He was alone, those who were around Him with the twelve asked Him about the parable. [11] And He said to them, "To you it is given to know the Mystery of the Kingdom of God; but to those outside everything is in parables; [12] that seeing they may see and not perceive; and hearing they may hear, and not understand; lest they might be converted and their sins should be forgiven them."

[13] And He said to them, "Do you not understand this parable? How then will you understand all the parables? [14] The Sower sows the Word. [15] And those by the wayside are they who are where the Word is sown; as soon as they have heard Satan at once comes and takes away the Word that has been sown in their hearts. [16] And those likewise who are sown in the rocky places are they who when they have heard the Word, receive it immediately with joy; [17] and they have no root in themselves but continue only for a time then when trouble or persecution arises because of the Word, they at once fall away. [18] And those who are sown among the thorns are they who hear the Word, [19] but the cares of the world and the deceitfulness of riches and the lusts about other things entering in choke the Word, and it becomes unfruitful. [20] And those who are sown upon good ground are they who hear the Word and accept it and bring forth fruit, one thirtyfold, one sixtyfold and one a hundredfold."

*PERSONAL: In St. Mark 4:16, the word is "received *(lambano)* with joy" but it bears fruit only in those who "hear and accept *(paradechomai)* it" (v. 20). The Greek Word *paradechomai* is made up of two words: *para* ("beside") and *dechomai* which means "to receive gladly," "to welcome" or "to give a ready and willing reception to." Thus to *paradechomai* the Word is to welcome it gladly alongside as one would welcome a friend beside him. For we are to cleave to the Word and "hold it fast" *(katecho)* St. Luke 8:15, just as we should cleave to God (Deut. 11:22; 13:4; Joshua 22:5; 23:8; 2 Kings 18:6) and "cleave to that which is good" (Romans 12:9).

There is no mention of *paradechomai* or *katecho* in the parable of the Sower as recorded in St. Matthew, because the emphasis there is on understanding the Word. In St. Mark and St. Luke the emphasis is on loving it faithfully.

Furthermore the impersonal "evil one" of St. Matthew 13:19 is personally identified as being "Satan" in St. Mark 4:15 or "the Devil" in St. Luke 8:12. Even the temptations in St. Mark 4:19 and St. Luke 8:14 are of a more personal nature: "the lusts *(epithumia)* of other things" and *sensual* "pleasures" *(hedone)* actively "enter in" *(eisporeumai)* to displace love for the Word. The displacement of the Word in St. Matthew 13:22 is on a less intimate and more intellectual plane, *viz.,* "The cares of the world and the deceitfulness of riches" act as distractions keeping one from listening attentively to the Word and pondering over it so as to be able to understand it and bear fruit.

Again, the personal respect due the Word of God is brought forth in St. Mark 4:15 and St. Luke 8:12 through the use of the word *airo* ("to lift up," "to take up"): "Satan" or "the Devil" takes away *(airo)* the Word from their hearts" (See notes on page 18 *re* the same use of the word *airo* in St. Matthew 21:43 because there our Lord referred to the "Kingdom of God" not the "Kingdom of Heaven").

The parable of the Sower as recorded by St. Matthew was told in a certain way by our Lord to illustrate "the Mysteries of the Kingdom of Heaven" thus in St. Matthew: "the evil one comes and snatches *(harpazo)* away what has been sown in his heart." The evil one does not "lift up" what has been sown, he "snatches away" what the "ground" should have grappled with: the hidden Wisdom of God found in the Truth of His Word. For in St. Matthew the stress is on *understanding* the Word, and we must with "all 'our' getting get understanding" (Proverbs 4:7). We must grasp His Words with the same violent effort that the evil one uses to "snatch away" what had been sown in the heart. For thus is the Kingdom of Heaven "taken" by our understanding: "My soul wrestled with Wisdom" (Sirach 51:19 Septuagint). "Take hold of Wisdom and do not let her go" (Sirach 6:27). "They that watch for Wisdom shall embrace her" (Sirach 4:13 Latin Vulgate). "Draw near to Wisdom. . .and when you draw close to her do it as a hero and as a mighty one" (Sirach 1:22 Sinaiticus Greek Text). So grab a hold on Wisdom and hold her fast or the evil one will snatch her away from you.

*INDIVIDUALLY: In the original Greek it reads *eis—en—en i.e.,* "one thirty, another (one) sixty, another (one) a hundredfold." "One" corresponds to the aramaic *dah*="one." It would have been natural for St. Matthew to do as St. Mark did and use "it" and "one" as there was no specified word for "some" in Hebrew-Aramaic. Yet St. Matthew deliberately used the indefinite Greek ending *'o—' o—' o, i.e.* "Some a hundredfold, some sixtyfold, some thirtyfold."

24

Lk 17:21   "The Kingdom of God is within you."
Do not look for it anywhere else
For it is the Lord in you

To rule, love and transform you
To be a child of God again

Which is what we were created for
And why we were redeemed.

In the parables of the Kingdom of God
Everything is more personal* and deals
Between God and you
And between Him and me.

The Kingdom of Heaven may be a delight to the understanding
But the Kingdom of God is joy to the heart.

You will be reading the same parable in St. Mark and St. Luke
But the Sower will be sowing in a different way.

The heart can only hold one thing at a time.
In the parable of the Kingdom of God the Sower sows one seed at a time.

Read "it":

Singular "some *(allos)* seed fell"	St. Mark 4:4
"birds devoured it"	St. Mark 4:4
"another seed fell"	St. Mark 4:5
"it had not much soil"	St. Mark 4:5
"it sprang up"	St. Mark 4:5
"it had no depth"	St. Mark 4:5
"it was scorched"	St. Mark 4:6
"it had no root"	St. Mark 4:6
"it withered away"	St. Mark 4:6
"another seed fell"	St. Mark 4:7
"thorns grew up and choked it"	St. Mark 4:7
"it yielded no fruit"	St. Mark 4:8

Even the ones that brought forth fruit yielded individually*:
"one thirtyfold" v. 8
"one sixtyfold" v. 8
"one a hundredfold" v. 8

Mk 4:9   "He who has ears to hear let him hear."

            If there are hidden differences in the same parable
Pr 25:2   It is because His glory is to conceal a thing
And wait. . .
For the little ones to ask Him where.

25

*"**JOY**": "The ear that listens to Wisdom rejoices" (Sirach 3:29 Hebrew Text).

Mk 4:10 Lk 8:9	In the Gospel according to St. Mark and St. Luke those who asked Him for the meaning of the parable are the disciples themselves.
	And so He explained it to them.
Mk 4:11 Si 39:3, 2 Sy	But to the rest and to us: "everything is in parables" that are full of "dark sayings" and "deep things" to make us ponder. And to make us also seek Him when we do not understand.
Mt 7:7 Si 39:2 Sy	"Ask, and it will be given you. . . Knock, and it will be opened to you" And you shall"*enter* into the deep things of parables."
Jm 1:5-6	You shall understand Because you asked Him with Faith, for the answer.
	He hides Truth in His parables so that we may seek the meaning from the author of the parable Himself.
Mt 13:23 Mt 13:23	In the Kingdom of Heaven the Seed bears fruit in you If you *hear* and *understand* the Word.
Mk 4:20 Lk 8:15	In the Kingdom of God the Seed bears fruit in you If you hear and *accept* the Word and *hold it fast*.
	But in both instances the bearing of fruit also depends on the kind of soil we provide for the Seed.
2 Esd 9:17	For "as is the soil, so is the seed."
Mk 4:16 Mt 13:20 Lk 8:13	If we knew that the seed is the Word of God We would receive it now as they did then: "immediately" and with "joy"*
	Rejoicing in the Wisdom of the Lord.

*"MOISTURE": "Does the rush flourish without water or shall the reeds grow up without moisture? When it is yet on the root, and though it has not been cut down, does not any herb wither if it does not receive moisture? Thus then shall be the end of all that forget the Lord" (Job 8:11-14 Sept.).

CHAPTER 3

THE PARABLE OF THE SOWER

According to St. Luke 8:4-15

[4] And when a great crowd came together and people from town after town came to Him, He said by a parable: [5] "A sower went forth to sow his seed: and as he sowed some fell by the wayside; and it was trodden down and the birds of heaven devoured it. [6] And some fell on the rock and as soon as it had sprung up it withered away, because it had no moisture.* And some fell among thorns and the thorns sprang up with it and choked it. [8] And some fell upon good ground and sprang up and it made fruit a hundredfold." As He said these things He cried out, "He who has ears to hear let him hear."

[9] And when His disciples asked Him what this parable meant, He said, "To you it has been given to know the Mystery of the Kingdom of God; but for others this is in parables, so that seeing they may not see, and hearing they may not understand. [11] Now the parable is this: The seed is the Word of God [12] and those by the wayside are they who have heard; then the devil comes and takes away the Word from their hearts that they may not believe and be saved. [13] And the ones on the rock are those who, when they hear the Word, receive it with joy; but these have no root, they believe for a while and in the time of temptation fall away.

[14] And as for what fell among the thorns, they are those who hear, but as they go on their way they are choked by the cares and riches and pleasures of life and their fruit does not mature. [15] And as for that in the good ground they are those who, hearing the Word, hold it fast in an honest and good heart, and bear fruit with patience."

*"**PATIENCE**": We must have "patience" (*hupomeno*) and "endurance" (*hupomeno*) to the very end for "through much pressure *(thlipsis)* we must enter the Kingdom of God" (Acts 14:22). Being "born again" (St. John 3:3; I Peter 1:23) is not easy either for the mother or child—it takes time and "labor." Both St. Mark 4:8, 26-28 and St. Luke 8:15 stress the gradual growth of the Kingdom of God and the necessity of not only "receiving" and "accepting" gladly the Word of God but also holding it fast with endurance to the bearing of the "hundredfold" for Him (St. John 15:8). Moreover in St. Mark the sequence of yield is progressive: "one thirtyfold, one sixtyfold and one a hundredfold" (St. Mark 4:20) but not in St. Matthew 13:23.

Lk 8:11 Lk 8:5	St. Luke knew that "the seed is the Word of God," "His seed": the Sower's own;
Mt 13:37 Jn 10:36	The Sower who is the Son of Man And also the Son of God
Lk 8:12	From this understanding came belief "Believe and be saved."
Pr 4:1 RSV Lk 1:3	By hearing instruction and being attentive we gain insight As a good evangelist St. Luke: "considered all things carefully from the first" And so he gained insight.
	He understood it is a child of God we are making In the good soil of our hearts.
Col 4:14	Because St. Luke was a physician.
Lk 8:15 Lk 8:15, 5	When we understand the Kingdom of God as he did We shall also "hold it fast in an honest and good heart" With "patience" and love for this: "his seed".
Lk 8:8	There are no "thirty" or "sixtyfolds" in St. Luke Because when we love we give nothing but the "hundredfold." Which is the maximum yield to that one Seed.
	For only by yielding all self to it Will the Seed give all itself to us.
	Because the Kingdom of God is an exchange Between the Lord and you Between your will and His Between His Heart and yours
Lk 8:15 Mt 10:22 Mk 13:13	All this takes "patience"* (*hupomeno*) Which is the Greek Word for endurance and perseverance "He who perseveres *(hupomeno)* to the end shall be saved"
Eph 1:14	And the end of the Seed is to bear fruit in you To possess your soul So that you may acquire possession of the fruit.
	The fruit that you shall have brought forth To the glory of His Word.

*"IN ST. LUKE": The Parable of the Sower was told by our Lord on three different occasions with minor variations in each instance designed to bring out a different facet of His teaching. St. Luke preserves the version of this Parable told by our Lord at the time "He went throughout every city and village preaching and bringing the good news of the Kingdom of God. . .and when a great crowd came together and people from town after town came to Him He spoke" (St. Luke 8:1, 4) to them, the version of the Parable retained by St. Luke. He was inside a house on this occasion for we are told that "His mother and His brothers came to Him then but they could not reach Him because of the crowd. And He was told: 'Your mother and Your brothers are standing outside (exo-outside of doors) desiring to see You'." (St. Luke 8:19-20). This is verified by St. Matthew who tells us that on that "same day Jesus went out of the house and sat by the seaside" (St. Matt. 13:1) and there told the same Parable again with the variations recorded by St. Matthew (13:1-23). On another day when "He began again (palin) to teach by the seaside" (St. Mark 4:1), He told the multitude the third version of the Parable of the Sower which is preserved for us in the Gospel according to St. Mark (4:1-20).

*POIEO—"to make in Greek and denotes active effort.

*"BECAME": "You who conceive Christ through your Faith; bring Him to birth through your good works" — St. Ambrose, Sermon 192.2 (C. 340 A.D.). "And he (Abraham) blessed the Creator who had created him in his generation according to His good pleasure for he knew and perceived that from him would arise the plant of righteousness, and from him a holy seed so that it should become like Him who made all things" (Book of Jubilees 16:26 written C. 153-105 B.C.). Become a new Adam who was from the "ground" (adamah) raised to be "Adam who was the son of God" (St. Luke 3:38 RSV). Because He "was of God" (St. Luke 3:38 Douay Version).

*"LISTEN": "My son — if thou desire to hear, thou shalt learn and thou shalt receive understanding, if thou love to hear thou shalt be wise" (Sirach 6:32, 33 collated from the Greek, Latin Vulgate and Syriac Hexaplar Texts). "Hear me and I will instruct thee" (4 Ezra 7:49), "Be meek to hear the Word of God that you may understand and return a true answer with Wisdom" (Sirach 5:13 Latin Vulgate). "Hear now, my sons and I will uncover your eyes that you may see and understand the works of God—that you may choose that which pleases Him and reject that which He hates" (Damascus, Rule 2:14-15, Dead Sea Scrolls). "These things I know by the Wisdom which comes from Thee for Thou hast unstopped my ears to marvelous mysteries" (Hymn 1:21 Dead Sea Scrolls). "The people of the holy ones of the Covenant" are those "instructed in Thy Laws and learned in Wisdom, whose ear has been unstopped and who have heard profound things" (War Rule 10:10-11 Dead Sea Scrolls). "Hear, o you wise men, and meditate on knowledge" (Hymn 1:35 Dead Sea Scrolls) "Hear ye and understand" (St. Matt. 15:10) that He "groaned" (St. Mark 7:34) because He knew what comes after we are given Understanding and do not turn to Him (Heb. 6:4-6). "But they did not understand this and were afraid to ask Him" (St. Mark 9:31) lest they should be given understanding and not repent. "But they did not understand this saying and it was hidden from them, that they might not perceive it" (St. Luke 9:45) and understand. Pray to the Lord that His "Mercy and Truth" be always together when we understand Him.

One child is born from one seed
So that in* St. Luke "his seed" is sown as one seed

Lk 8:5-7   For "it was trodden"
"it was devoured"
"it sprang up"
"it withered away"
"it had no moisture"
"thorns sprang up with it"
"and choked it"

Lk 8:8   But when "it" found good soil in a good heart
"It" literally "made *(poieo*)* fruit a hundredfold."

"It" became* in you
What you have always been meant to be:

Jn 1:12   Truly — a son of God.
Rm 8:16

Lk 8:17   "Nothing is hidden that shall not be made manifest nor anything secret that shall not be known and come to light."

Mk 4:24   "Take heed then how you hear" — the Parable of the Sower
Lk 8:18   Because God Himself told it to us.

Lk 8:8   "He who has ears to hear let him hear"
And listen* very closely

Rm 10:17   Remember that "Faith comes from hearing and hearing by the Word of God."

Mk 7:34   *"Ephphatha"!!*

*"VERSION": The Greek of St. Matthew clearly states as regards the seeds, that "the birds came and devoured **them**" *(auta*-plural) and "the thorns sprang up and choked **them**" *(auta)*. But in St. Mark and St. Luke it states that "the birds devoured **it**" *(auto*-singular) and "the thorns sprang up and choked **it**" *(auto)*.

CHAPTER 4

ON FIDELITY IN RENDERING THE TEXT OF
THE PARABLES INTO THE VERNACULAR

Take heed what Bible you read: the Parable of the Sower
For there is another sower sowing seeds
That bear fruit in misunderstanding

And this sower "plants" in the same field
Where the Word was sown

He scatters here and there his weeds
With absolute impunity

Mt 13:25 Because "men are sleeping" who should have been awake
Guarding and holding fast to His Word

Beware!!
Because when we do not understand "it" the evil one comes
Mt 13:19 and snatches away what has been sown in the heart.
Mk 4:15 "Satan immediately comes and takes away the Word"

And this he can easily do had you been reading this parable in some
of the modern translations of the Bible.

Take the Knox version* for instance
If you had read the parable of the Sower there
You would have never really understood "it."

Because instead of "it" you would find "some," "these," "they,"
"them"
and all kinds of seeds in St. Mark and St. Luke
In place of "it": the Word of God.

You might even find the "Kingdom of Heaven" in St. Mark 4:26 and
the Kingdom of God in St. Matthew 13:11
Which have no business there.

Have we grown bored?
Have we lost enthusiasm for His Words that we now play the literary
game of altering them?

Who are we to dare change the Word of God?
Who are we to seek to "improve" it
To make it more literate more up to date by substituting our jargon
To replace His spoken Words?

Who gave us permission to do so?

35

*"PISHON": One of the rivers of Paradise (Gen. 2:11) and allegorically the river of Wisdom (Sirach 24:23).

For we insult God when we attempt to improve Him
And we push Him aside when we supplant His Word with the weeds
of our arrogant presumption.

An orthodox Jew would never dream of doing to the words of a
harlot in Joshua the things we do to the spoken Word of God in our
own New Testament.

And we wonder today why God is dead—to us
When it is we who are famished and dying

Jn 6:63   For His Words are spirit and life
And they are Words we have cast aside.

Woe to you! Who do this to the Words of God
For the Lord can use asses like us
To spring forth Pishon* you

May you swim in it and remember from now on
Jn 10:35   That "the scripture cannot be broken"
If you hope to understand what was spoken.

*GREEK MANUSCRIPTS

Codex Vaticanus	4th Century A.D.	Vatican Library
Codex Sinaiticus	4th Century	British Museum
Codex Alexandrinus	4th Century	British Museum (quot. of St. John 12:40 only)
Codex Ephraemi	4th Century	Natl. Lib. Paris
Codex Washingtonianus I	4th-5th Century	Freer Lib. Wash. D.C.
Codex Bezae	5th Century	Cambridge Library
Codex Dublinensis	6th Century	Trinity College (only St. Matthew)
Codex Rossanensis	6th Century	Rossano, Italy (only St. Matthew)
Codex Laudianus	7th Century	Bodleian Library, Oxford
Codex Regius	8th Century	Natl. Libr. Paris
Codex Sangallensis	9th Century	St. Gall Switzerland
Codex Tischendorfianus	9th Century	Bodleian Library, Oxford (only St. John)

*Old Syriac MSS.	Peshitta Ms. 14459	5th Century	British Museum
	Harkleian Ms. 936	10th Century	British Museum
*Coptic	Sahidic Ms.	4th Century	British Foreign Bible Society (St. John's Gospel)
	Bohairic Ms.	11th Century	Bodleian Library, Oxford
*Georgian	Opiza and Tbet' Mss.	11th Century	Publ. British and Foreign Bible Society
*Old Latin	Codex Vercellensis	3rd-4th Century	Vercelli, Italy
	Codex Veronensis	4th Century	Verona, Italy
	Codex Brixianus	6th Century	Brescia, Italy
(Early Copies) *Latin Vulgate	Codex Fuldensis	5th-6th Century	Fulda, Italy
	Harleian Gospels	6th-7th Century	British Museum
	Stonyhurst Gospels	7th Century	Stonyhurst College
	Codex Amiatinus	8th Century	Laurentian Libr. Florence
	Codex Dunelmensis	8th Century	Durham, England
(Later Copies) *Latin Vulgate	Sixtine Vulgate		
	Clementine Vulgate		

Among the English Versions that have kept understanding in the "heart" are the King James Version; Douay and Challoner Rheims; Revised Version 1881; Revised Standard Version 1946; Jerusalem Bible 1966, and Common Bible 1973.

And understanding is with the heart
As it is written in the oldest Greek* Texts of St. Matthew 13:15:
"For the people's heart *(kardia)* has grown dull
and their ears are heavy of hearing
and their eyes they have closed
lest they should perceive with their eyes
and hear with their ears
and understand with their heart *(kardia)*
and turn for me to heal them" (from Isaiah 6:10 Septuagint).

The Greek word *kardia* and its equivalent for "heart" in the Syriac,*
Coptic, Latin and Georgian are found in all the best and earliest
codices and manuscripts of the New Testament.

In all these understanding is kept in the heart
Where it belongs.

*Kardia
158 x in
the N.T.

Whenever the word *kardia** is used in the New Testament
It means heart and nothing else

The Greeks had a word for everything and they were the first great
thinkers of the world so that they had many words for mind and the
mental processes of thinking.

For the things of the mind the following words are found in the New
Testament:

dianoia *ennoia* *gnome* *noema* *phronema*	"mind"	*phroneo*—"to think" *homophron*—"of one mind" *homothumadon*—"with one mind" *hupotithemi*—"put in mind" *boulomai*—"to be minded" *mimneskomai*—"to be mindful" *mnemoneuo*—"to bring to mind" *sophroneo*—"to be of right mind".

Yet they still kept understanding in the "heart" *(kardia)*

Because it is in the heart where love abides
That His Word is understood

For His Word is a living Word
And living things are not really understood by the mind
But by the heart.

Jn 14:23
Mk 4:15

"If anyone love Me, he will keep My Word": in his *heart.*
"The Word that was sown in their hearts."

39

*"**HEART**": The people of the Bible thought with their hearts as regard to the Words of God because His Words are meant to be acted upon and so the Jews kept them in the seat of all action. It is *in* the heart that His Words persuade our innermost being and turn us towards Him. It is written: "The Word is very near unto thee, it is in thy mouth and in thy heart that thou mayest *do* it" (Deuteronomy 30:14). Commenting on this verse the Rabbis said conversely that the Word comes near you into your heart when you "mean to do" what the Word says. (Tract Erubim Ch. 5 B. Talmud).

Even the Greeks who kept things in their minds feared anything kept in the heart for it inevitably meant action. Thus in Homer's *Iliad* 9.434 Phoenix is greatly alarmed because Achilles had "set the homeward journey to his heart" *(kardia)* and Phoenix knew that such a course resulted in action. Again in the *Iliad* 1.297, 4.104, 13.55: "to place it in the heart" *(kardia)* was to turn the heart towards a positive action. When the gods set an idea in the heart *(Iliad* 1.55; 4.104) it meant that the person had to execute it.

The Jews did all their meditating, pondering, remembering and thinking in their hearts and so they were moved in their hearts towards God. Minds never yearn, it is the heart that "longs for" and "clings to" His Word.

"Blessed is the man who meditates on these things, and he that lays them up in his heart shall become wise" (Sirach 50:28) because it is *in* the heart that he shall understand them. For when God created man "He gave them a heart to understand" (Book of Enoch 14:3). That is why "he that considers the ways of Wisdom in his heart shall also have understanding in her secrets" (Sir. 14:21 Septuagint).

"Blessed is the man that meditates good things in Wisdom and that reasons holy things by his understanding"—heart (Sirach 14:20 Septuagint). When the Alexandrian Jewish Scribes in the year 250 B.C. translated the Hebrew Bible into Greek they rendered "Wisdom will enter your heart" (Prov. 2:10 Hebrew Text), into "Wisdom will enter your understanding" (Prov. 2:10 Septuagint) because in those days it meant the same thing.

"The heart is deep beyond all things and it *is* the man" (Jeremiah 17:9 Septuagint). That is why God seeks your heart not your "mind" because only your heart can understand Him with love. The Lord made the heart "deep beyond all things" because He made it the place to understand His Wisdom: "For the thoughts of Wisdom are wider than the sea and her counsels profounder than the great deep" (Sirach 24:29 Septuagint).

The day is near when "the earth shall be full of the Knowledge *(deah)*[1] of the Lord as the waters cover the sea" (Isaiah 11:9).

And the heart that is "deep beyond all things" shall hold this sacred knowledge then, and it shall also understand it, for it shall see and hear clearly the wonders of God with its own eyes and ears. "My heart has seen *(raah*=to see, to behold) abundantly Wisdom and Knowledge" (Eccle. 1:16 Literal Translation). "Give Thy servant therefore a heart that hears" *(shamea*-to hear, to hearken)—1 Kings 3:9 Literal Trans., and the Lord did.

[1] Knowledge: The usual word for "knowledge" is *daath* which is the knowledge of man. The Knowledge which pertains to God is a different word: *deah*. Thus it is written: "for the Lord is a God of Knowledge" *(deah)*—I Samuel 2:3. He is not like "man who is brutish in his knowledge" *(daath)*—Jer. 10:14; 51:17. "Whom shall He teach Knowledge?" *(deah)*—Isaiah 28:9. "I will give you shepherds after My own *heart* who will feed you with Knowledge *(deah)* and understanding" (Jeremiah 3:15). "He that is perfect in Knowledge *(deah)* is with you" (Job 36:4) if you keep His Words in your heart (St. John 14:23).

The Hebrew of the Old Testament had no word for mind
But it had three words for heart: *leb, lebab* and *libah*

Because the heart* was esteemed.
They believed that in the heart was the innermost spring
The ultimate source of all the physical, emotional, intellectual and
volitional activity of man.

The heart was the seat of action and the unifying force of a man's
life
It was the one thing sought by the wise father:

Pr 23:26   "My son give me your heart" *(leb)*.

When men really believed in God
The heart was a wonderful thing

And things were done in the heart that we can only do in the mind
today.

1 Ch 29:18   Long ago men thought with their hearts and prayed:
    "O Lord. . .keep forever such purposes and thoughts in the hearts
(lebab) of Thy people."

They meditated with their hearts:

Ps 4:4   "Meditate with your own hearts *(lebab)* on your beds and be
silent"

And considered with their hearts:

Dt 4:39   "Know therefore and consider in your heart *(lebab)* that the Lord
is God"
So they knew in their hearts:

Qo 8:5   "The heart *(leb)* of the wise knows"

And could plan in their hearts:

Pr 16:9   "The heart *(leb)* of man deviseth his way"

Because there, in the heart, men retained His Words:

Pr 4:4   Let your heart *(leb)* hold fast to My Words"

Applying their hearts to what He revealed:

Pr 22:17   "Apply your heart *(leb)* to My knowledge"

For to the heart it was given to understand:

Dn 10:12   "Do not fear Daniel for from the first day you gave your heart
(leb) to understand and to humble yourself before your God."

And to keep His things:

Dn 7:28   "I kept the matter in my heart" *(leb)*

So that Daniel:

Dn 1:18   "determined in his heart" *(leb)*

And Jeroboam:

1 K 12:33   "devised of his own heart" *(leb)*

And even the Queen of Sheba spoke to Solomon:

1 K 10:2   "all that she had in her heart" *(lebab)*

The Gospels make sure that thinking upon the Words of God be
done in the heart.

For it is written that the mother of the Saviour:

Lk 2:51   "Kept all these sayings in her heart"

Lk 2:19   "Pondering them in her heart"

And having her own soul pierced by a sword:

Lk 2:35   "that the thoughts of many hearts may be revealed"

41

1 Jn 3:20	If today "our heart blames us" It does because we no longer keep His Words in our hearts.
	We have become "word"ly wise and keep His Words instead in our minds Where they are easily forgotten.
Pr 3:3; 7:3	When God wants man to remember He writes on the tablets of the heart (Jer. 31:33; Heb. 8:10).
Jb 22:22	For He knows that if we "lay up His Words in our hearts" We shall never forget them
Is 32:4 L.T. Mt 24:35	Let us hope that "the heart *(lebab)* of the rash shall understand" That when Our Lord said: "Heaven and earth will pass away but My Words will not pass away"— He meant what He said.
Is 40:8	For "the Word of our God endures forever"
2 Tm 3:16	And if "all Scripture is inspired by God" Then every Word of it becomes a sacred thing And we dare not cast aside a single word said to be uttered by Him.
	Yet we did
	In the Confraternity Version of St. Matthew 13:15 and St. John 12:40 Someone changed "understand with the heart" to "understand with the mind."
	Because someone rejected the word "heart" as being archaic and too old-fashioned for the sophisticated ear of this rational age.
Jn 14:24	Someone who forgot in his "mind" what the Lord said: "He who does not love Me does not keep My Words. And the Word that you have heard is not Mine but the Father's who sent Me."
Jn 12:48	We should remember that He also said: "He who rejects Me and does not accept My Words has one to condemn him. The Word that I have spoken will condemn him."
	The word "heart" that someone cast aside.
Jn 12:49-50	For the Lord said: "I have not spoken on My own authority but He who sent Me, the Father has commanded Me what I should say and what I should declare. . .the things therefore that I speak, I speak as the Father has bidden Me."
Jm 1:17	And He was bidden to say "heart" and not "mind" because the Father does not contradict Himself.
	And the Son was quoting from the Father who spoke through Isaiah 6:10 and said there: "Understand with the heart"
1 Jn 5:10	So that someone who changed "heart" to "mind" "Made Him a liar because he did not believe the witness that God has borne concerning His Son."
Mt 13:11, 15	And the witness was St. Matthew who quoted our Lord as having said: "Understand with the heart."
Jn 8:17 Mt. 18:16	If St. John 12:40 quoted the same phrase of our Lord Who are we to dare contradict the statement of two witnesses?

43

For the Lord knew all about:
  "troubled hearts" (2 Kings 6:11)
  "sad hearts" (Nehemiah 2:2)
  "discouraged hearts" (Numbers 32:7)
  "fearful hearts" (Isaiah 35:4)
  "sick hearts" (Proverbs 13:12)
  "hardened hearts" (Psalm 95:8)
  "divided hearts" (Hosea 10:2)
  "rebellious hearts" (Jeremiah 5:23)
  "envious hearts" (Proverbs 23:17)
  "vexed hearts" (Ezekiel 32:9)

And "grieved hearts" (Ezekiel 13:22)
because "proud hearts" (Proverbs 16:5)
and "evil hearts" (I Sam. 17:28)

No longer hold fast to His Words.

"God knows 'our' hearts" (St. Luke 16:15)
For He saw us:
  "doubting" in our hearts (St. Mark 11:23)
  "arguing" in our hearts (St. Luke 5:22)
  "imagining evil" in our hearts (Genesis 6:5)
  "erring" in our hearts (Psalm 95:10)
  "thinking evil" in our hearts (St. Matt. 9:4)

And "committing adultery" in our hearts (St. Matt. 5:28).

Mk 7:21-23   "For out of the heart of man come evil thoughts, adulteries, immorality, murders, thefts, covetousness, wickedness, deceit, shamelessness, jealousy, blasphemy, pride, foolishness. All these evil things come from within. . .the heart of man."

And those of you who discard His Words with full approval
Better believe this in your hearts

Because it is with the heart that a man believes (Romans 10:10).

1K 10:24   God gives Wisdom to the heart
2 Ch 9:23   For it is the heart that understands: Wisdom.
Qo 1:17; 2:3; And it is the heart that knows, searches out and seeks wisdom with
7:25   reason

Because we do "reason" in the heart (St. Mark 2:6)
And "wonder" in the heart (St. Luke 3:15)
And "say" in the heart (St. Luke 12:45)

That we hope you "resolve therefore in your hearts" (St. Luke 21:14)
From now on—
To be more faithful to the Word of God.

Jn 15:7   For His Words are meant to abide in us
Jn 15:3   And it is by His Word that we are made clean.

So keep "understanding with the heart"
As a more faithful scribe did in the same Confraternity Version (Acts 28:27)

And you will then understand
That when you are touched in the heart by the Words of God
You repent and turn for Him to make you clean and whole again

But when you are touched in the head,
Brother,
You've had it.

God is Truth
And He sows His Word as a seed

So we should watch that seed sown in the ground of our hearts
We should take good care of it and hold it fast

Cherishing and warming it with our love.

We must till the ground of our hearts and keep it clear of weeds
Because His seed flourishes only in the ground that is good.

We must act upon the seed of His Word
For unless we do the seed remains intact.

But if we act upon it a wonderful thing will happen:
The seed shall break open for us

And we shall begin to understand the Truth of His Word

When that seed is understood it grows rapidly
It increases and springs forth from the heart

To be seen by all

Then, if the ground of our hearts remains good
The grown plant will bear fruit

Fruit so beautiful that all the other plants shall lower their branches
in awe
And drop their fruits in homage

Then the world shall hear the fruit of light sing forth the praises of
His glory
Because that fruit is full of the seeds that come from His sown Word.

Hold fast to the Truth.

CHAPTER 5

THE PARABLE OF THE GOOD SEED AND THE DARNEL

St. Matthew 13:24-30, 36-43

[24] Another parable He set before them saying, "The Kingdom of Heaven has become like a man sowing good seed in his field, [25] but while men are sleeping, his enemy came and sowed darnel in the midst of the wheat and went away. [26] And when the blade sprang up and bore fruit then the darnel appeared also. [27] And the servants of the householder came and said to him, 'Sir, didst thou not sow good seed in thy field? how then does it have darnel?' [28] And he says to them, 'A man, an enemy has done this'; and the servants said to him, 'Wilt thou have us go forth and collect them?' [29] And he said, 'No, lest in collecting the darnel you should uproot with them the wheat. [30] Suffer both to increase together until the harvest, and in the time of the harvest I will say to the harvest men, Collect first the darnel and bind them into bundles to be burned but gather the wheat into my barn'."

[36] Then He sent away the crowds, and went into the house*: and His disciples came to Him saying, "Explain to us the parable of the darnel of the field." [37] And He answering them said, "He who is sowing the good seed is the Son of Man. [38] The field is the world, and the good seed, these are the sons of the Kingdom, and the darnel are the sons of the evil one, [39] and the enemy who sowed them is the devil, and the harvest is the completion of the age, and the harvest men are messengers. [40] As therefore the darnel is collected and burned in the fire, so will it be at the completion of the age. [41] The Son of Man will send forth his angels and they shall collect out of his Kingdom all the stumbling blocks and those doing the lawlessness, [42] and cast them into the furnace of fire; there shall be weeping and gnashing of the teeth. [43] Then shall the righteous shine forth as the sun in the Kingdom of their Father. He who has ears to hear let him hear."

BACKGROUND OF
THE PARABLE OF THE GOOD SEED AND THE DARNEL

Unless we try to understand His parables as having been uttered by a Jew for the Jews, we shall not be able to understand them fully.

Mt 15:24
"I am not sent except to the lost sheep of the House of Israel."

Jn 4:22
"Salvation is from the Jews."

The infinite Wisdom behind His word reveals itself in the light of the Sacred Scriptures.

Mt 3:15;5:17
These are perfectly fulfilled by Him and in Him. If ignorance of the Scriptures is ignorance of Christ the saying may well include the Jewish Apocalyptic writings of His era and the two centuries preceding it.

There were some things already growing in the field of Sacred Scripture before His coming.

The Messiah was clothed in the imagery of a plant:

Is 53:2
"He grew up before Him like a young plant and like a root out of dry ground."

Is 11:1, 10
"There shall come forth a shoot from the stump of Jesse and a branch shall grow out of his roots. . .the root of Jesse shall stand as an ensign to the peoples; him shall the nations seek and his dwelling shall be glorious."

Jr 23:5, 6
"I will raise up for David a righteous branch and he shall reign as king and deal wisely and shall execute justice and righteousness".

Ezk 34:29
"I will raise up for them a plant for renown."

En 93:10;
84:6
He was to be "the eternal plant of righteousness" from "the eternal seed."

Jn 15:5, 1
He said when He came; "I am the Vine. . .the true Vine."

The righteous and humble were also compared to plants of the Lord:

Ps of Sol.
14:2,3
"The Paradise of the Lord, the trees of life are His pious ones. Their planting is rooted for ever; they shall not be plucked out."

Ex 15:17
"Thou wilt bring them in and plant them on Thy own mountain."

O of Sol.
11:15
"Blessed O Lord, are they who are planted in Thy land."

Is 61:3
"The planting of the Lord that He might be glorified."

En 62:8
"The congregation of the elect and holy shall be sown."

En 84:6
"The flesh of righteousness and uprightness establish as a plant of the eternal seed."

En 93:10
"The elect righteous of the eternal plant of righteousness"

En 93:5
"A man shall be elected as the plant of righteous judgement and his posterity shall become the plant of righteousness for ever more."

Jb 5:26
"You shall come to your grave in ripe old age, as a shock of grain comes up to the threshing floor in its season."

Si 10:18
"God has made the roots of the proud nations to wither and has planted the humble of these nations."

Ml 2:15
"What does one seek but the seed of God?"

L.T.
Do not receive "the evil seed" (4 Ezra 4:30) of the "father of lies" (St. John 8:44) and do not forget that the wicked "shall not be planted, yea, they shall not be sown" (Isaiah 40:24).

Is 40:24
If someone else sows them "their stock shall not take root in the earth and He shall blow upon them and they shall wither and the whirlwind shall take them away as stubble."

51

Mt 15:13	For "every plant which My Heavenly Father has not planted will be rooted out."
	Therefore:
Ho 10:12	"Sow for yourselves righteousness and reap the fruit of your steadfast love,"
Pr 22:8; Jb 4:8	For "he who sows injustice will reap calamity"
T.L. 13:6	"If you sow evil things you will reap every trouble and affliction."
T.L. 13:6	"Sow then for yourselves good things in your soul that you may find them in your life."
	Remember that:
Is 55:10	His word cast upon the earth shall "bring forth and sprout"
Ps 85:11	And "Truth shall spring out of the earth" like a blade to cut off:
En 93:4	"The deceit that shall have sprung up" for "there shall arise great wickedness"
Si 3:28; M.T.	Because "the scorner. . .an evil plant *(nata)* is his plant" *(nata)*, full of evil seeds.
	And thus:
Mt 24:12	"Iniquity shall abound"
S of En 34:1	"For I know the wickedness of men that they will not carry the yoke which I have laid upon them, nor sow the seeds which I have given them, but having cast off My yoke they will take another yoke and will sow empty seeds" of "untruths."
En 10:16	But "the plant of righteousness and truth shall appear and prove a blessing"
En 38:1	For "when the congregation of the righteous shall appear. . .sinners shall be judged for their sins and shall be driven from the face of the earth."
En 10:20,22	"All oppression. . .all unrighteousness, all sin and all godlessness and all uncleanness that is wrought upon the earth" shall be destroyed and "all the earth shall be cleansed from all defilement and from all sin and from all punishment and from all torment."
Mt 13:41	"His angels shall collect out of His Kingdom all the stumbling blocks and those who do the lawlessness."

*"LOOK ALIKE": The "weeds" of the New American Bible and The Good News For Modern Man, and the "thistles" of The Living Bible miss the point for at no time in their development do "weeds" and "thistles" resemble "wheat."

*"DEVIOUSNESS": The Rabbis of the 3rd and 4th Centuries also commented on the deviousness of rendering unclean things clean by plausible argumentation with particular emphasis on the decisions of the members of the Sanhedrin on this (Midrash Rabbah on Ruth 2:2 re "Cozeba"). Again, in St. Matt. 15:4-6, the Law of Moses explicitly stated: "He that curseth his father or his mother, let him die the death" (Exodus 21:17; Lev. 20:9) but the Rabbis decreed "he that curseth his father or his mother is not guilty, unless he curses them with the express mention of the name of Yahweh" (Sanhedrin 7:8). Also: "It is more punishable to act against the words of the scribes than against those of Scripture" (Sanhedrin 11:3). To this type of thinking our Lord applied St. Matt. 15:9 and St. Mark 7:7, 8.
Many examples of the greater emphasis placed on the Oral Law over and above the Law of Moses are found in Rabbinic thought to give a few examples:
"The study of Scripture is a doubtful habit; that of the Mishnah (Oral Law) is one for which a reward is received; but nothing is more commendable than the study of the Gemmara" (Commentaries on the Oral Law)—Baba Metzia fol. 33 Col. 1. Rabbi Yochanan 3rd Century A.D.
"Give heed, my son to the words of the scribes, rather than to the words of the Law, for the words of the Law consist of positive and negative precepts (not all capital offenses) but whosoever transgresses any of the words of the scribes is guilty of death" (Erubin Fol. 21 Col. 2 Raba 3rd Century A.D.).
Rabbi Yochanan said: "The Holy One blessed be He has made the covenant with Israel for the sake of the words delivered by mouth" (Oral Law) only (Gittin fol. 60 Col. 2. See Titus 1:14).
"The Oral Law (Mishnah) is more precious than the Torah" (Peah 2:6 Jer. Talmund. See also Ber. 8a; 13; Chagigah 10a. J.T.).

The Parable of the Good Seed and Darnel

On the terms "good seed" and "darnel"

The ladder of Understanding is ascended step by step and we have to start from the bottom rung and ask ourselves why the Lord chose to contrast *"good seed"* to *"darnel."*

Obviously because both seeds look* alike and cannot be distinguished in growth from one another until the grain is in the ear. One is a good seed and the other a "bad" one, for from one is made good bread but if bread be made from the other it would be hazardous to partake of it because eating darnel results in dizziness, vomiting, circulatory disturbances and hallucinations.

But there are other reasons for the choice; the Mosaic Law (Lev. 19:19; Deut. 22:9) forbade the Jews to sow a field with different kinds of seeds; needless to say no farmer would sow a field with both "darnel" and "wheat" no matter if both seeds appeared to belong to the same family.

However, although the Oral Law elaborating on Leviticus 19:19, forbade the Jews from planting barley and wheat alongside in the same field (Kilayim 1:9), it allowed wheat and *darnel* to grow legally together. The Rabbinic Oral Law ruled that "wheat and darnel are not two kinds," *i.e.;* they are both considered the same kind of seed and not being accounted "diverse kinds," provision was made in the Oral Law (Kilayim I:I) for darnel and wheat to be planted legally in the same field or if found mutually growing in the same field to be left together untouched. Darnel was just held to be "degenerate wheat" (Jerusalem Kilayim I:26) and as such not a different kind of seed altogether. It was again a way of circumventing the written Law of Moses by oral rulings. Our Lord accused the deviousness* of these oral rulings. (St. Mark 7:1-13) For they eventually led to overemphasis being placed on the oral tradition above the greater commandments (St. Luke 11:38-39; St. Matt. 23:25-27).

Mt 13:25, 28
2Tm 1:14

Thus in the parable of the Good Seed and Darnel our Lord brings our attention to the fact that "darnel" is not just "degenerate wheat" but "darnel," a harmful weed that has no business being in "his field." Whatever has not been sown by Him can only have been sown by *"his enemy"* who often needs *"a man, an enemy"* to do this thing for him *"while men are asleep"* and no longer "guard the Truth that has been entrusted to" them.

The field of Holy Scriptures is sacred and the Words that have been sown in that beautiful field are His Words. We dare not plant some of our words here and there between His Words or substitute any of them by some of our own because in so doing we shall be casting His Words aside and rejecting them as being too archaic for this modern age. We shall have dared to improve or correct Him and bring Him up to these times forgetting that the Word of our God endures forever and is not easily cast aside but shall return to judge the presumption of some of our modern scribes.

Jr 23:28

Jr 8:8, 9

Jeremiah in his day had already contrasted the "wheat" of His Word to the false "chaff" and even then he had excoriated the "lying pen of the scribes" who "have rejected the Word of the Lord."

55

*"LEVEL": "I will not level God with man" (Job 32:21 L.V.).

*"WATCH": An attentive conscientious disciple that was diligent in his studies was known as a "wakeful one." In the section Sotah 9:15 of the Babylonian Talmud it was said of "Rabbi" Ben Asai (c., *110 A.D.*) that: "since the death of Ben Asai there are no longer any wide awake ones" (*i.e.*, untiringly studious ones). Although considered as such for his erudition and insight, Ben Asai was never made formally a rabbi, he remained a student all his life. Thus he was the model *par excellence* of a good student and disciple: a wakeful one, "watchful and diligent in the Law" (Palestinian Targum on Numbers 21) for "when dreams increase many empty words abound" (Eccle. 5:7 Literal Translation).

2 Esd 14:25
2 P 1:19

Yesterday's faults are today's offenses because we have forgotten that we do not bring God down to our level* of understanding but we must climb up to His, and we must hold on to what was given us to hold fast until the glorious day when He shall come to "light up in 'our' hearts the lamp of understanding."

Mt 13:24-30,
37-41

Those who supplant His Word sow the "darnel" of *"stumbling blocks"* which never bear true fruit because they are not His *"good seed"* and they do not bear within them the *"wheat"* of His Word. The darnel carry inside of them *"stumbling blocks"*—nothing else. Thus He said in this parable that *"darnel"* was *"sowed," "darnel"* appeared and *"darnel"* was *"collected"* to be burned. *"Darnel"* is *"darnel"* from the beginning to the end. And the *"darnel-stumbling blocks"* are said to be sown *"in the midst of the wheat"* for what is inside the *"good seed"* is known to be *"wheat"* once it is in the ground of *"his field"* but the "darnel" is "darnel."

On "Sleeping men"

Mt 13:25

The parable commences in the aorist (present-indefinite) tense relating a sad occurrence: *"the Kingdom of heaven has become like a man sowing good seed in his field but while men are sleeping his enemy comes and sows darnel in the midst of the wheat."* Because of this, the Realm of Understanding has become a tract of misunderstanding—there is "darnel" in the once well ordered field of His Word. The "darnel" is there because men slept instead of guarding the Truth. The Lord knew that they would continue sleeping because St. Matt. 13:25 literally reads: *"while men are sleeping his enemy comes and sows."*

Is 56:10-11

For "His watchmen are blind they are all without knowledge; they are all dumb dogs, they cannot bark; dreaming, lying down loving to slumber. The dogs have a mighty appetite they never have enough. The shepherds have *no understanding."*

Jr 3:15
Ezk 34:2-3

Perhaps they have forgotten that they are called to be shepherds after His own heart who will feed us with "knowledge and understanding" but sometimes they are too busy feeding themselves and unaware that sheep without shepherds are still sheep—but shepherds without sheep are not shepherds; they who neglect to watch* and care for what is His are not servants of the Lord, they are sleeping *"men."*

Mt 13:25

Lk 2:8

Do not forget that the shepherds who saw the glory of God were shepherds "keeping watch over their flock at night"—the time for watching. And even at noon when the porter of the house who is supposed to be "cleaning the wheat" falls asleep, the unguarded king is stabbed (2 Sam. 4:5 Sept. and Latin Vulgate). And darnel is sown over the honor of his field.

57

*AMOS 8:11: "A famine on the land, not a famine of bread, nor a thirst for water, but of hearing the Words of the Lord." For the "Word of the Lord was rare in those days" (I Samuel 3:1). "Save me, O Lord, for there is now no saint: truths are become rare from among the children of men" (Psalm 12:1 Sept.).

*"ALONE": Another word for "gourd" is found in the book of Jonah the prophet: "the gourd (kikayon) that the Lord God prepared" (Jonah 4:6) to try Jonah. This "gourd" (kikayon) can be said to have truly come from a "light" (orah) plant for it has long been identified to have been the gourd of the castor-oil "tree" (L. Ricinus Communis) known to the early Egyptians as kik or kiki from which the Hebrew word kikayon is derived (See Herodotus II.94; Pliny's Hist. Nat. XV. 7; Dioscorides Mat. Med. IV. 161). Oil from the castor plant was used by the Hebrews to light up the Sabbath lamps (Shabbath 21 a B. Talmud) and was known as shemen kik it was said by Rabbi Simeon Ben Lakish (3rd Century A.D.) that this oil originally came from the "gourd" (kikayim) that the Lord prepared for Jonah (Mishnah II. 1 on Shabbath 21a). Jeremiah (2:21) knew about the "wild gourds" (paqquoth) found in the field and where they came from: "I planted you as a choice vine (soreq) wholly a true (emeth) seed. How then have you turned degenerate and become a strange (nokri) vine (gephen)?" bearing strange fruit. Thus St. Ignatius of Antioch (c. 110 A.D.) in his epistle to the Trallians 11:2 wherein he warns them against false doctrines says: "shun these wild plants which bear nothing but deadly fruit for when one tastes it, he is doomed to die outright." If we want the light of truth we must go to the "True Vine" (St. John 15:1).

Mt 13:26 The parable continues: *"And when the blade sprang up and bore fruit then the darnel appeared also."*

The Greek word used for "appeared" is *phainomai* which also means "to shine." *Phainomai* is derived from *phao* which means "to give light." When the good seed springs up to give light the darnel is exposed. The Hebrew word for "light" is *or* and from it is derived another word for light: *orah*. We shall now see why plants shine.

Let us look for "light plants" in the field of the Lord and ask the "son of the prophet" (2 Kings 4:38-44) where to find some as they are difficult to see with all the darnel about and we sometimes must translate literally if we are to come upon these beautiful plantings of the Lord.

In the days of 2 Kings 4:38-44 there was a famine in the land, the type of famine Amos* 8:11 spoke about:— "And the sons of the prophets are sitting before him (Elisha) and he (Elisha) says to his young man: 'Set on the great pot and boil pottage for the sons of the prophets.' And one (of the sons of the prophets) goes out into the field to gather herbs *(orah)* and finds a grapevine *(gephen)* of the field and gathers of it gourds *(paqquoth)* of the field—the fulness of his garment—and comes in and splits them into the pot of pottage, for they knew them not; and they pour out for the men to eat and it comes to pass at their eating of the pottage, that they have cried out and say, 'Death is in the pot, O man of God!' and they have not been able to eat.

2K 4:38-41
L.T. And he (Elisha) says, 'Then bring ye meal'; and he casts into the pot and says, 'Pour out for the people' and they eat; and there was no evil thing in the pot."

Shortly after they had eaten there appeared a man from Baal-Shalisha bringing along "bread of first fruits," "twenty loaves of barley" and "full ears of corn in its husk" (2 Kings 4:42) just in case we might be thinking about a different type of famine in the land with lean ears and no first fruits of the harvest to give away.

The episode of the "gourds" is a gem of Wisdom with a hidden lesson in the narrative. Instead of finding "light" *(orah)* or an "herb of light" *(orah)*, the disciple of the prophet found a "grapevine" *(gephen)* of the field. The word *gephen* is used 50 times in Holy Scripture and in all instances it means "grapevine." Thus we would expect the son of the prophets to have found the *gephen* to be bearing "grapes" *(enab)* or a "cluster" *(staphule)*, perhaps "immature grapes" *(semadar)* or "grape gleanings" *(oleloth)* but sad to say not a "single grape" *(peret)* was there, not even "wild grapes" *(beushim)* or the "sour grapes" *(boser)* that prophets rage about. That "grapevine" *(gephen)* had nothing growing on it but a lapful of "gourds" *(paqquoth)*. They were strange "gourds" indeed because *paqquoth* is a word used only once in the Bible, in that particular passage alone*.

The *paqquoth* were split and put in the great pot for the sons of the prophets to *know* and determine whether they were good or bad for "they knew them not." Adam and Eve will tell you that the knowledge of good and evil was acquired by eating the fruit (Gen 3:6) but unfortunately Eve picked the wrong tree. When the sons of the prophets had tasted what was in the pot they all said there is "death in the pot!" just as there was "death" in the fruit our first parents ate. The pottage was redeemed by the addition of meal. The meal that comes from the "wheat" of His Word (Jer. 15:16; 23:28; Deut 8:3; Prov. 9:5; Wisdom 16:26; Sirach 15:3; Isaiah 55:2). The lesson in the passage is that if we want "light" it comes only from one source: His Word.

Is 26:19 "Light plants" may take a long time to grow but in the end they always give their light: "Thy dead shall live, their bodies shall rise. O dwellers in the dust awake and sing for joy for thy dew is as the dew of herbs" *(orah)* the kind of "herbs" that spring up in the

Ps 97:11
Ml 4:2
Is 18:4 end because "Light *(or)* is sown for the righteous." When "the sun of justice" shall rise "like clear heat on an herb" *(or)*, men shall see the "light" *(or)* else!

*"CRAVE FOR": When the people hungered for the flesh pots of Egypt, they also craved for "*chatsir*" which is kindly rendered "leeks" in Numbers 11:5.

*"MANGER": "The ox knows its buyer (*qanah*) and the ass its master's manger (*ebus*) but Israel does not know. My people does not understand" (*bin*)—Isaiah 1:3. The word *ebus* in Isaiah 1:3 is usually rendered "manger" but it actually means a closed grain crib or granary as in Jeremiah 50:26: "Open up her granaries" (*ebusek*).
In the first chapter of Isaiah the Lord reprimands His people by upbraiding them that the ox knows its "owner" (*qanah*) or "buyer" (*qanah*) i.e., the one who "redeemed" (*qanah* as in Neh. 5:8) it, but Israel does not know nor acknowledge the Redeemer. They were redeemed from the bondage of slavery (Exod. 6:6; 15:13; Deut. 7:8; Ps. 77:15; 106:10 *etc.*) by the Lord through His wonderful saving acts yet they remained recalcitrant and not heeding His call: "Return unto Me for I have redeemed thee" (Isaiah 44:22). The ass knows where the good grain is found and craves for it "but My people does not understand" the Word of the Lord nor do they hunger for it as bread for their souls.
"My people are foolish they *know* me *not*, foolish sons are they, yea they have *no understanding*" (Jer. 4:22).

Mt 13:27

"And the servants of the householder came and said to him, 'Sir, didst thou not sow good seed in thy field? how then does it have darnel?' "

Notice that they are called "servants" not sleeping "men." And the servants are very respectful towards their Master the "householder," they address him as "Lord" (*kurios*) or "Sir" (*kurios*) and use the polite "thou" (*soi*) towards him even though the "servants" know that the "householder" himself is the "man" who performed the seemingly menial task of "sowing good seed in his field" (v. 24).

We know these "servants" kept watch because the moment the fruit "appeared" and revealed the darnel, they reported the matter to their Lord. They were zealous as well for his field because they asked permission to clean it up and said to him:

Mt 13:28

"Wilt thou then that having gone forth we should collect them?"

Mt 13:29-30

"And he said, 'No, lest in collecting the darnel you should uproot with them the wheat. Suffer both to increase together until the harvest—' "

While waiting the servants read and searched the Scriptures to see if anything like this case of double appearance had been written up before their time. Sure enough, with the aid of the Lady of the house they found it in Proverbs 27:25 where they literally read:

"When the hay (*chatsir*) is revealed (*galah*)
And the tender grass (*deshe*) appears (*raah*)
the herbs (*eseb*) of the mountains are gathered (*asaph*) in."

There are some asses who will explain this verse to the horses and mules.
The Hebrew word for "common grass" or "hay" is *chatsir*. When the wicked and foolishness are compared to "grass" such as in 2 Kings 19:26; Job 8:12; Ps. 37:2; 90:5; 129:6, etc., they are always compared to *chatsir*. *Chatsir* was the common grass fed to "horses" and "mules" (I Kings 18:5) but never offered to the asses because they know better than to eat that kind of "hay" which foolish people crave* for

What asses really like is "tender grass" (*deshe*) and "provender" (*belil*) and so it is given to them because they *understand* (Numbers 22:23-33).

Ps 32:9

They are "not like a horse or a mule without understanding"; good donkeys like Balaam's ass fear the Lord and obey and depart from evil and so they teach their Masters for that is Wisdom and Understanding (Job 28:28).

Jb 6:5

"Does the wild ass bray when he has tender grass (*deshe*)?
Or does the ox low when he has provender (*belil*)?"

No, Sir! Asses and oxen know that the Master provides in his manger* for them nothing but the best food. Ask the Judges, Job or Isaiah what asses like to eat:

Jg 19:21
Jb 24:5, 6

"he brought him into his house and gave the asses provender" even "wild asses. . .gather their provender (*belil*) in the field and provide bread (*lechem*) for their children" because they want nothing but the best for their own.

Is 1:3
Pr 20:17
Pr 4:17
Is 32:6

"But My people have no understanding", they love to eat other things instead, they crave for the "bread of deceit" and the "bread of wickedness."

Well did Isaiah say: "the fool speaks folly and his heart plots iniquity: to practice ungodliness and to utter error concerning the Lord, to leave the craving of the hungry unsatisfied and to deprive the thirsty of drink" and "corrupt the poor with lying words" instead of the true Bread of His Word.

Is 32:7
Jn 6:32

*"**TEACHERS**": Isaiah 30:20 is in the plural.

*"**GOOD**": The just and their seed "shall flourish like the herb *(eseb)* of the earth" (Ps. 72:16), and "their bones shall flourish like the tender grass" *(deshe)*—Isaiah 66:14.

*"**EXPOSED ETC.**": "Evil deeds shall be uncovered to all Israel at the end of time" (Dead Sea Scrolls, Q4 Commentary on Nahum 3:6-7a). "Thy righteousness shall be revealed before the eyes of all Thy creatures" (Hymn 14:16, Dead Sea Scrolls). Because "the plant of Truth which was hidden and was not esteemed being unperceived," (Hymn 8:10, D.S.S.) shall suddenly spring forth from the ground (Ps. 85:11; Isaiah 43:19, 21). Then "all the nations shall acknowledge Thy Truth and all the peoples Thy glory" (Hymn 6:12, D.S.S.). In that day scoffers "shall stumble, and they shall not prevail, they shall be greatly ashamed; for they shall not **understand** *(sakal)*, their everlasting confusion shall never be forgotten" (Jer. 20:11). Because they did not comprehend that it is *in* the righteous that: "**Truth** *(emeth)* will spring up from the ground" (Ps. 85:11) of their hearts. "As the earth brings forth her bud. . .so shall the Lord make justice and praise to spring forth before all the nations" (Isaiah 61:11) from the heart of the good "ground." "O Lord. . .let Thy work appear *(raah)* unto Thy servants, and Thy glorious honor unto their children" (Ps. 90:13, 16). "Dark deceits vanish when exposed to the clear light" (St. Augustine, *Ep ad Donatists*). "Where shall the ungodly and the sinner appear?" (2 Peter 4:18; Prov. 11:31 Sept.), when "their folly shall be made plain to all" (2 Tim. 3:9). "Meditate upon these things. . .attend to the public reading of Scripture, to exhortation and doctrine. . .devote yourself to them that your good progress may appear to all" (I Tim. 4:15, 13, 15b). "Let your light so shine before men that they may see your good works and give glory to your Father who is in heaven" (St. Matt. 5:16).

Is 30:24   But Isaiah (30:20-25) promised that when the Teachers* arrived: "the oxen and young asses that till the ground will eat salted provender that has been winnowed with shovel and fan" because the asses dislike "chaff" and they will kick the "towers"

Is 30:25   down who have allowed darnel to be sowed in the field of the Lord.

The Lord created *deshe* ("tender grass") and *eseb* ("herb") and so they are good grasses and their seed is good*:

Gn 1:11-12   "God said, 'Let the earth yield tender grass (*deshe*) and herb (*eseb*) sowing seed'. . .and so it was"—that "God saw that it was good."

The Lord did not create "*chatsir*" and so the wicked are compared to it and this common "*grass*" is "exposed" *(galah)*.

But when the good tender grass shows itself it always "appears" *(raah)* to remind you that when the Lord "appears" in Holy Scripture the word *raah* is used (ex. Gen. 12:7; 17:1; 18:1; 26:2; 35:9; 48:3; Exod. 3:2, 16; 4:5; 6:3 etc.) and so *raah* is used when the "tender grass" from the "good" seed "appears."

Eph 5:13   "When anything is exposed by the light it becomes visible."

When "*chatsir*" is exposed it is "revealed" *(galah)*. The word "*galah*" is used in the Bible in the sense of being "uncovered," "revealed," "discovered," "disclosed" and "exposed"* frequently in the derogatory sense as in Jeremias 13:22: "it is for the greatness of your iniquity that your skirts are lifted up" *(galah)*. Lewd things do not "appear," they are "exposed" *(galah)* (See Lam. 4:22; Ezek. 16:37; 23:10, 18; Hosea 2:10; Nahum 3:5, etc.)

"Hay" and "darnel" may "appear" to be "revealed" but they are really literally "exposed" *(galah)* by the bright "light plants."

The Lord *gathers* the mountain "herb" *(eseb)* as He *gathers* His good seed the "wheat" into His barn to feed His faithful ones.

Gn 1:29   Do not forget that *eseb* was the food of Paradise: "and God said: 'Behold I have given you every plant *(eseb)* yielding seed which is upon the face of all the earth. . .for food'." God gathers in the good things before the deluge (Gen. 6:21; 2 Peter 2:9; 3:7). When He comes you may be sure the grass of the wicked shall have been mowed down:

Ps 72:6-7,L.T.   "He comes down like rain on mown grass
As showers. . .sprinkling the earth
The just shall flourish in His days
and peace shall abound until the moon is no more."

This generation shall pass away, there is no escape from the great Sickle that shall come to reap all that is in His field but

Am 7:1   another one shall rise like "the latter growth that comes *after* the mowings of the King"—the reign of the just with their Lord. To

Lk 14:14   them belongs the first resurrection: "the resurrection of the just" (See also Rom. 11:15; Isaiah 60:1-2; Eph. 5:13-14; Rev. 20:1-6). For many have been called (St. Matt. 24:14) and the few are still

Mk 10:31   His chosen (Rom. 11:1-11, 25, 28).

"Many that are first will be last and the last first."

*"**REJECT**": "They speak evil of the things they understand not" (2 Peter 2:12) thinking that they know everything yet forgetting that "he who thinks he knows anything knows nothing yet as he ought to know" (I Cor. 8:2). But "let no man deceive you through philosophy and vain deceit" (Col. 2:8). "Take heed to yourself and unto the Teaching, hold to that, for by so doing you will save both yourself and your hearers" (I Tim. 4:16). For "what shall be the end of those who believe not the Gospel of God?" (I Peter 4:17). Theirs is an end of shame before all (2 Tim. 3:9). "When His Truth becomes known the teaching of falsehood are silenced" (St. Gregory *Morals on Job* Book XXXIII. 18).

*"**SOW**": "The scoffer. . .an evil plant (*nata*) is his plant" (Sirach 3:28 Hebrew Text).

Jn 12:48   "He who rejects Me and does not accept My Words has a judge: the Word that I have spoken will be his judge."

Those who cast His Words aside to plant in their stead the "darnel" of their own "stumbling blocks" shall find that:

Ho 10:4   "judgement also springs like the poisonous weeds in the furrows of the field" they have sowed.

Many today dare set themselves up above the inspired words of the sacred writers. These men "have conceived chaff and brought forth stubble."

Is 33:11

What they do not understand they reject*. Here are some rejections of Our Lord's explanation of the parable (St. Matt. 13:36-43):

"We shall do well to forget this interpretation as completely as possible" (C.H. Dodd, *The Parables of the Kingdom*).

"It is impossible to avoid the conclusion that the interpretation of the parable of the tares is the work of Matthew himself" (J. Jeremias, *The Parables of Jesus*). These modern scribes "shut up the Kingdom of Heaven against men."

Mt 23:14

They sow* the "darnel" of doubt for "it is impossible" from their statements to avoid the conclusion that their "Matthew" *lied* when he said specifically that "He (the Lord) answering them said" (St. Matt. 13:37), and if "Matthew" said some lies here how can we be sure he did not make up some extra ones throughout the gospel? The "wise men" of today seem to have the last word on what He said and what He did not say more than nineteen hundred years ago. Well did Our Lord say, *"an enemy, a man did this" (v. 28)* and what they do is make "stumbling blocks." These "men" better believe this "Whoever causes one of these little ones who believe in Me to *stumble* it would be better for him if a great millstone were hung around his neck and he were thrown into the sea."

Mk 9:42
Mt 18:6

Pr 14:15   Notice that our Lord said "little ones" for it is the "innocent," "simple" "little ones" who "believe every Word" the big ones no longer do and so they have no understanding (St. Matt. 11:25).

Let the big ones remember that the "millstone" is written in St. Matt. 18:6 as the *mulos onikos* which means in the Greek "the millstone of an ass" and it is these asses here who are going to hang it around their necks for making void His Word. Let them weigh these words and think over their heavy pieces while they are still growing in the field of the world.

Pr 26:27   "He who rolls stumbling stones gets rolled over by them"
Pr 28:10   "He who misleads the upright into an evil way will fall into his own pit of error"
Si 6:21, 22   "He that lacks understanding cannot abide in Wisdom. Wisdom
Mt 18:6   shall be to him as a mighty stone of trial,"
Hung around his neck.

*"**BROKEN**": Even in the 14th Century it was considered a grievous offense to "loosen" the Scriptural Text by substitution of a word or in any way tampering with it: "The Scriptures cannot be loosed for the precious things (i.e., the Words) are joined together by Wisdom"—Ibn Adonijah (c. 1524 A.D.) in his *Introduction to the Rabbinic Bible.*

*"**SPEAK**": "I shall not go beyond the Word of the Lord" (2 Sam 22:31 Septuagint). For "these are the Words which the Lord spoke...and He added no more" (Deut. 5:22; 12:32). "Keep the teachings which you have received adding nothing and subtracting nothing"—Letter of Barnabas 19:11 (c. 79 A.D.). "These are the precepts which the Lord commanded unto Moses and which not one must be trifled with or modified" (Palestinian Targum on Leviticus 27). The wise Egyptian scribes also taught respect for Truth: "Grasp hold of Truth and do not add to it"—Instruction of Ptah-Hotep (c. 2450 B.C.) Prisse Papyrus (National Bibliotheque of Paris, France). As St. Paul said: "do not go beyond what is written" (in Scripture)—I Cor. 4:6.

En 104:10;
1 Tm 4:1

En 104:11

Mt 5:18
2 Tm 3:16
Jn 10:34

Rev 22:18-19

More than two thousand years ago and at least a hundred years before His time the Book of Enoch prophesied that "sinners will alter and pervert the words of righteousness in many ways and will speak wicked words and lie and practice great deceits and write books concerning *their* words."

Instead of "writing. . .down truthfully all my words in their languages and not change or take anything away from my words but write them all down truthfully" to the last "jot or one tittle" because "all Scripture is inspired by God" and "the Scripture cannot be broken"*. St. John again emphasized this respect due when he said at the end of the Apocalypse:

"I warn everyone who hears the words of the prophecy of this scroll, and if anyone takes away from the words of this scroll of this prophecy, God will take away his share in the tree of life, and in the holy city, and the things written in this scroll."

Qo 3:14

"Whatever God does endures forever, nothing can be added to it, nor taken away from it; God has made it so, in order that men should fear Him."

Dt 4:2
Ps 18:30

"You shall not add to the Word which I command you, neither shall you take away from it." For "the Word of the Lord is tried."

Pr 30:5,6

"Every Word of God is fire-tried. . .do not add to His Words lest He reprove thee and thou be found a liar."

Is 40:8
2 S 22:31 Sept.
Nb 24:13 Sept.
Jr 26:2

"The Word of our God endures forever."
"The Word of the Lord is mighty and tried in the fire."
"Whatsoever things God shall say, them will I speak."*
"All the Words I command you to speak to them; do not hold back a word."

Jr 23:28

"For what has straw to do with wheat? Let him who has My Word speak My Word truthfully."

And let him who writes render it faithfully holding fast to His Words

Is 55:8

For His thougths are not our thoughts nor are our ways His ways.

Is 55:9

"For as the heavens are higher than the earth so are My ways higher than your ways
And My thoughts than your thoughts."

Si 15:18
Si 1:23

"For great is the Wisdom of the Lord."
"He will *hide* His Words for a time and the lips of many shall declare His Wisdom"
When they discover them in His light.

Pr 25:2

"It is the glory of God to hide a thing and the glory of kings to search out a matter."

Jr 15:16

"Thy Words were *found* and I ate them and Thy Word became to me a joy and the delight of my heart."

Mt. 13:15
Is 6:9-10

Because it is the *heart* who *understands* the Word of God.

*"FRUIT": The "fruit" in this parable is the grain in the ear. The Rabbis knew that when the grain is in the "ear" (az) it is time to "ponder" (az) and understand (see Yebamoth 21a and Erubin 21b B. Talmud).

Si 9:17	"The leader of a people is proved wise by his words."
Pr 12:8	"A man is praised according to his wisdom."
Ws 3:20 Sept. & L.V.	"There shall be respect rendered Him by His Words."
Mk 4:22	"For nothing is hid except to be made manifest; nor is anything secret except to come to light."
Mt 13:11	"To you it has been given to know the secrets of the Kingdom of Heaven but to them it has not been given."
Mt 13:13	"I speak to them in parables because seeing they do not see and hearing they do not hear, nor do they understand."
Rm 11:8	Because "God gave them a spirit of stupor, eyes not to see and ears not to hear" Until the Reign of Understanding.
Jn 16:12,14	Then shall the Son of Man be exalted by "The Spirit of Truth. . .He will glorify Me for He will take what is mine and declare it to you." And what is His and can be declared are His Words and His Wisdom.
Is 52:13,15	"Behold My Servant shall prosper, he shall be exalted and lifted up and shall be very high. . .for that which has not been told them they shall see and that which they have not heard they shall understand."
Mt 13:26 Mt 7:16	The time for Understanding is when the fruit* appears. The "servants" understood: "*when the blade sprang up and brought forth fruit*" because people and things are known "by their fruits."
Mt 7:15 Mt 7:16	"Beware of false prophets who come to you in sheep's clothing but inwardly are ravenous wolves." "You will know them by their fruits."
Mt 7:17-18	"Every good *(agathos)* tree brings forth good *(kalos)* fruit but a rotten *(sapros)* tree brings forth evil *(poneros)* fruit. A good *(agathos)* tree cannot bring forth evil *(poneros)* fruit neither can a rotten *(sapros)* tree bring forth good *(kalos)* fruit."
Lk 6:43	Ordinary good *(kalos)* trees bear good *(kalos)* fruits "For no good *(kalos)* tree bears rotten *(sapros)* fruit"
Lk 6:43	"Nor does a rotten *(sapros)* tree bear good *(kalos)* fruit." A rotten *(sapros)* tree either bears no fruit at all or if it has any on the branches it has "rotten" *(sapros)* fruit or "worthless" *(kakos)* fruit but not "evil" *(poneros)* fruit.

*"INSIDE": "Their hearts are eaten out as when creeping things devour" (Epistle of Jeremias v. 20, Septuagint). "Their heart is ashes and they err" (Isaiah 44:20 Sept.) because there is no understanding in them to comprehend the Truth. "Every work that is corrupt shall fail in the end and the worker along with it" (Sirach 15:20 L.V.). "The name of the wicked will rot" (Prov. 10:7).

*"KALOS": The Greek word *kalos* denotes external goodness or beauty and the word *agathos* signifies internal goodness or wholesomeness.

Mk 7:23	Unless that tree is rotten and corrupt because it is a tree full of evil *inside.* *
Mt 15:19	"For all these evil *(poneros)* things come from within"
Eph 2:1,5; Col 2:13	From inside those who are "dead in their trespasses and sins."
	A corrupt *(sapros)* tree and a good *(agathos)* tree may look *alike* on the *outside.* They may both be "good" *(kalos* *)* to behold with "beautiful" *(kalos)* fruit in their branches. But the beautiful fruit you may see in the branches of a corrupt tree is not really a true fruit it is a *false fruit.*
Lk 6:43 Ho 10:13 Pr 11:30	Because "a corrupt *(sapros)* tree cannot bear good *(kalos)* fruit" it can only make the evil "fruit of lies" The "fruit of lies" is always dressed up to look like the Truth which is the beautiful fruit of righteous trees.
	Corrupt trees making evil fruit are most hazardous when they are found in a field assumed to have nothing but good fruit trees.
Mt 12:33	"Either make the tree good *(kalos)* and its fruit good *(kalos)* or make the tree rotten *(sapros)* and its fruit rotten *(sapros)*." Let the fruit be wholly good or wholly rotten inside out.
Mt 12:33 Jude 12	"For the tree is known by its fruit" and no one will go near a tree that is "twice dead" rotten inside out or eat putrid fruit from its branches.
	If many eat evil fruit it is because it looks attractive and wears a "good" beautiful skin to make people think it is also good *(agathos)* inside. Good enough to eat and take it where all poisons do their deadly work.
Lk 6:45	"The good *(agathos)* man out of the good *(agathos)* treasure of his heart produces good *(agathos)*. . .his mouth speaks": *Truth.*
Lk 6:45	"The evil *(poneros)* man out of his evil *(poneros)* treasure produces evil *(poneros)*. . .his mouth speaks": *lies* Because the evil man has the evil one *(poneros)* dwelling inside of him.
Jn 8:44	"The devil"—is the "father of lies" and he "has nothing to do with the truth because there is no truth in him."
Pr 10:16 Ho 10:13	"The fruit of the wicked" is a "fruit of lies" and all "lies" come from their "father" within that evil and corrupt tree.
	Notice that St. Luke 6:45 speaks of the evil treasure of the evil man but where is "his heart"? He has lost it to the evil one.
Lk 8:5,8 Lk 8:11	It is the "good *(agathos)* ground" that "bears fruit a hundredfold" because it "believes" "accepts" "holds fast" with "perseverance" "His Seed": "the Word of God" inside its
Lk 8:15	"beautiful *(kalos)* and good *(agathos)* heart."
Mt 13:24	The "*good (kalos) seed*" sown in "*his field*" is "good" *(kalos)* on the outside.
Mt 13:25,29,30	Inside that "*good seed*" is the "*wheat*" of His Word and because "wheat" is food needless to say it is "good" *(agathos)* to eat. The "*good seed*" is thus good *(kalos)* on the outside and good *(agathos)* on the inside where the "wheat" is.
Mt 13:24	Although the "*field*" is "*his*" Our Lord does not say that the "*good seed*" is his Because the "*good seed*" belongs to the "Father."
Mt 13:37 Mt 13:37 Pr 11:18; Sept.	The "*good seed*" was given to "*He who sows the good seed*" who "*is the Son of Man*" as a reward from His Father. For "the seed *(sperma)* of the righteous is a reward of Truth."

71

The *"Son of Man"* is a good Son and He is first to acknowledge that what He has, He *received* from His Father for He knew that "a man's glory comes from honoring his father."

Si 3:11 RSV

The Son of God said:

Jn 7:16 "My teaching is not Mine but His who sent Me."

Jn 8:26 "He who sent Me is true and I declare to the world what I have heard from Him."

Jn 8:28 "When you have lifted up the Son of Man you will know that I am He and that I do nothing on My own authority but speak thus as the Father taught Me."

Jn 12:49 "I have not spoken on My own authority but He who sent Me; the Father has commanded Me what I should say and what I should declare."

Jn 12:50 "The things therefore I speak, I speak as the Father has bidden Me."

Jn 7:16;14:24 "The Word that you have heard is not Mine but the Father's who sent Me."

Jn 17:7-8; 8:38,40 "They know that everything that Thou hast given Me is from Thee; for I have given them the Words which Thou gavest Me."

The "field" is "his" but the "good seed" belongs to the Father. Because the "good seed" contains the "wheat" of His Word by which the Father shall glorify the Son through the Holy Spirit:

Jn 14:26 "The Counselor; the Holy Spirit whom the Father will send in My name,
He will teach you all things and bring to your mind all that I have said to you."

Jn 16:14 "He will glorify Me for He will take what is Mine and declare it to you."

When the good seed shall have accomplished the task of glorifying the Son; then shall we remember that He also said: "I am glorified in them."

Jn 7:10

73

*"**SET**": "Another parable He set *(paratithemi)* before them" (St. Matt. 13:24,31). "Eat such things as are set *(paratithemi)* before you" (St. Luke 10:8). The same word *paratithemi* ("set") is used in describing the feeding of the multitudes (St. Mark 6:41; 8:6, 7; St. Luke 9:16; 11:6). We are meant to partake the Word of God as food (Deut. 8:3; Jer. 15:16) thus Moses "came and called the elders of the people and set *(paratithemi)* before them all these words which the Lord had commanded him" (Exod. 19:7 Sept.).

*"**HIM**": "Everything that is made by God is beautiful *(kalos)* and good" *(agathos)*-St. Maximus (*c.* 600 A.D.) on the Ascetic Life, Paragraph 7.

*"**GOOD INSIDE OUT**": His fruit is therefore "good *(tob)* and beautiful *(yapheh)* to eat" (Eccle. 5:18 Hebrew text). "For if He has anything good *(agathon)* and if He has anything beautiful *(kalon)*" you may be sure that His good thing is also beautiful and His beautiful thing good (Zech. 9:17 Septuagint). "If you are able to understand God then you will understand the beautiful *(kalon)* and the good *(agathon)*"— *Corpus Hermeticum Lib. VI,*5. edit. W. Scott.

Heb 6:5	"Have you tasted the good *(kalos)* Word of God?"
	Eat! and be filled that you may know that the outwardly good *(kalos)* Word of God is also inwardly good *(agathos)*.
Lk 1:53	"He has filled the hungry with good *(agathos)* things." Because those who are filled have eaten and having eaten they *know* His things are really good *(agathos)*.
	Never forget that He set* His parables before us (St. Matt.13:24, 31) As food in a banquet for us to partake Because His Words are meant to nourish our souls.
	Beautiful *(kalos)* things are to be looked at But they also have to be good *(agathos)* before they can be taken inside of us.
Mt 7:11	We do not crave beautiful food but we do hunger for good food Even those "who are evil *(poneros)* know how to give good *(agathos)* gifts to their children" who are *hungry*.
Mt 7:11	"How much more will your Father in heaven give good *(agathos)* things to those who ask Him" for the Bread of God.
Lk 11:13	"How much more will your Father in heaven give the Holy Spirit to those who ask Him" for the Bread of His Word.
Lk 6:45	"The good *(agathos)* man out of the good *(agathos)* treasure of his heart brings forth that which is good" *(agathos)*. Because what makes a man good *(agathos)* is God inside of him.
Mk 10:18 Lk 18:19	"No one is good *(agathos)* but God alone."
	A thing may be outwardly beautiful but rotten inside (St. Matt. 23:27-28) or clean on the outside but evil within (St. Matt. 23:25). But when you see anything that is beautiful *(kalos)* on the outside and good *(agathos)* inside: you may be sure it belongs to Him*
	For all the beautiful things of God are good* inside out.
Col 1:5,6	Rejoice! Rejoice! For "the Word of Truth. . .which has come to you. . .is bearing fruit. . .*in* you." So that you may understand and turn to Him with all your heart and give Him praise.
	Repent! Repent! For when the fruit is ripe the reapers are sent (Amos 8:1; St. Matt. 13:30) And the time of the Harvest has come for all.

*"FRUIT": The Father is glorified by the fruit of our praise full of the seeds of the Word of Truth: truthful praise. "The lips of the wise sow (*zarah*=to sow) knowledge" (Prov. 15:7). "The mouth of the wise brings forth *(nub*=to sprout forth) Wisdom" (Prov. 10:31 Hebrew Text). "Draw near to Wisdom as one that sows and reaps and wait for the abundance of her fruits" (Sirach 6:19 collated from the Hebrew, Syriac, Greek and Latin Vulgate Texts). "Even from the time of the flowering until the fruit was ripe my heart delighted in Wisdom" (Sirach 51:15 Sept.).

A father, glorifies his child when he reveals him proudly to the rest;
A child glorifies his father when he becomes the fruit of his expectations.

Jn 15:8   "By this My Father is glorified in that you bear much fruit."*

We are all derived from the seed of our fathers.
The seed by bearing fruit gives glory to the sower.

Jn 16:21   There is great joy at the birth of a child into the world and all sorrow is forgotten.
Who remembers then that the child was once a seed?

A seed silent and hidden away for many months in the womb that suddenly brought it forth for all to hear.
The seed is no longer silent then, but cries out in the child that is born.

A child is born only to those who have held fast the seed.
All things have their season, and all seeds bear fruit in the fulness of time, provided they find good ground.
When the ground holds the seed fast—the seed bears fruit in its season.

Jn 17:6-7   "They kept Thy Word, *now* they know"—
As everyone shall when the seed of His Word brings forth: the fruit of Understanding.

1 Th 5:21   Hold fast in your good *(agathos)* heart: "that which is good" *(kalos)*

Jm 3:17   That the One in your heart who is the only good One may bring forth in you: "good *(agathos)* fruits."

1 Co 3:7   "Only God gives the growth."
We are the ground that holds fast His good seed.
"Ground" is all *we* are in His field.

1 Tm 2:4   "To come to the full knowledge of the Truth," we must hold fast to it until the time comes for it to be seen by all.

Ps 85:11
Ps 85:12   For He promised that *"Truth* shall spring out of the earth"
"and our land shall yield her fruit,"

Her fruit of Understanding.

Ws 3:9   And "they that trust in Him shall understand the Truth"
Because Trust is Faith in Him and believing is holding fast to His Word.

77

*"HUNDREDFOLD GRAINS": As the wise man Bildad said to Job: "Though thy beginning was small (as one seed) yet thy latter end shall greatly increase" (Job 8:7).

*"GARBAGE": For it is written: "Thou hast made light of all them that err from Thy statutes; for their deceit is falsehood. Thou puttest away all the wicked of the earth like refuse" (sig)—Ps. 119:118-119 Hebrew Text. "For they are all refuse" (Ps. 14:3) they and their works, and refuse is "collected." Even the Egyptians knew that "a man remains over after death and his deeds are placed beside him in heaps" (Instruction for King Meri Kare Leningrad Papyrus 1116 a fol. L.55). When weeds are "collected" they are plucked out. The Hebrew word for "to pluck out" is arah which also means "to expose," "to discover out," "to uncover," and to reveal in a shameful light, i.e., "to make naked." Similarly the Hebrew word for "sin": chataah comes from a root meaning "to err" viz, chata and again the Hebrew for "to heap up": chathah is the same word for "to take away." When sinners and their sins are taken to the furnace, those who have erred shall be "dismayed" (chatath).

*"WAIT" until the time comes when "He shall not suffer unrighteousness to dwell anymore in their midst nor any man that knows wickedness" (Ps. of Solomon 17:29).

The Truth that springs out of the ground is the same Truth that was hidden under the surface.
The wheat found in the full ear of grain is the same "wheat" within the "good seed" that was sown.
For the wheat of His Word endures forever.

From the one grain sown sprung forth the full ear of a hundredfold* grains of wheat.
So that the fruit of Understanding may praise the good seed of His Word.
For it takes one hundred words to give perfect praise to the One Word of God.

In the burst of the rich harvest the husk reveals the wheat it once held fast and discloses it.
That is all it does because the wheat vouches for itself.
The husk without the wheat is chaff.

We are the husk that voices the Words that are His.
We are the ground in His field and the fruit of the full ear
Because all these hold within them the wheat of His Word.

But never forget that the wheat grains of His Words are His.
And what is His shall be gathered when it has accomplished the purpose for which it was sent

Is 55:11

"My Word. . .that goes forth from My mouth shall not *return* to Me empty"
But it shall return.

On "collecting" the "darnel" and "gathering" the "wheat"

Mt 13:30

"*In the time of the harvest I will say to the harvest men collect first the darnel and bind them into bundles to be burned but gather the wheat into my barn.*"

Notice that the darnel is "*collected*" but the wheat is "*gathered.*" Our Lord differentiated between the wheat and the darnel also in the manner they were to be harvested. The darnel is always "*collected*" like garbage*. Only the wheat is "*gathered.*"

The Greek word for "collected" is *sullego* which means "to lay together" or "to pile up together." It is a word derived from *lego* which means "to pick out."

On the other hand the word for "gather" is *sunago* which actually means "to gather" or "to bring together." Good things are gathered. The servants understood this when the fruit "appeared" for when they asked His permission to pull out the

Mt 13:28,29

darnel they said to Him: "*wilt Thou then, that we go forth and collect* (sullego) *them?*" "*But He said: 'No' lest in collecting* (sullego) *the darnel ye should uproot with them the wheat.*" He

Mt 13:30

asked them to wait* until the time of the harvest when: "*I will say to the harvest men collect* (sullego) *first the darnel.*"

Mt 13:40,41

Even in the explanation of the parable which some of the "wise men" deny Him He said: "*as therefore the darnel is collected* (sullego) *and burned in the fire. . .the Son of Man will send forth His angels and they will collect* (sullego) *out of His Kingdom all the stumbling blocks and those who do the lawlessness.*"

79

*"**FAITHFULLY**": The *Diatessaron*, a harmony of the four gospels written by Tatian (c. 170 A.D.), preserves the same distinction. The darnel is picked out and "collected" and the wheat is "gathered" (*Diatessaron* 17:6,7,23,24). Unfortunately the *New English Bible* "gathers" the darnel and "collects" the wheat.

*"**TODAY**": Modern translations of the Bible no longer differentiate. It is these "little things" that give glory to God. Take for instance St. John 15:1-7 where Our Lord says: "I am the True Vine and My Father is the Vinedresser. . .you are the branches." "Every branch in Me that bears no fruit. He takes away (*airo*="**to lift up**" or "to take away" as in St. John 1:29) and every branch that bears fruit He cleanses (*kathairo*="to cleanse," "to make pure" it is derived from *katharos* which means "pure" as in St. Matt. 5:8) that it may bear more fruit—he who abides in Me and I in him, he it is that bears much fruit: for without Me you can do nothing." Those who are not joined to Him "are cast out as an unprofitable branch" (Isaiah 14:19). Thus we see that the unproductive branches are taken away because they never really "took" to the Vine. The withered branches are not "cut away" or "cut off" as the *Jerusalem Bible* says it, because in doing so you would be cutting the Vine as well and no one cuts God in any form whatsoever! The branches bearing fruit are "cleansed" not "pruned." The Greek words for pruning are *apotemuo, apokopto* and *klademo* not *kathairo* because even "the black poppy" is not cleansed (*kathairo*) with harsh treatment" (Isaiah 28:27 Sept.) such as the "pruning" found in modern bibles. The branches that did not take are *not* "collected and thrown on the fire" (v. 6 *Jerusalem Bible*) or "picked up" (v. 6 *Knox Bible*) they are "gathered (*sunago*) and thrown into the fire" sadly but with *respect* because they once formed part of the True Vine. While you are gathering ask the Confraternity Version people how they can expect you to see "the day dawn and the morning star rise in your hearts" (2 Peter 1:19) when they have taken away "the eyes of the heart" (*kardia*) in Ephesians 1:18 and put them in "the mind"? (Ephesians 1:18 *Confraternity Version*).

*"**COLLECTED**": In the Old Testament there are 24 different words for "gather together" in Hebrew, but there was a special word used for "collect" or "pile up," and the word corresponding to *sullego* is *tsabar* which means to "pile up" or "heap up." Everytime the word *tsabar* is used in the Old Testament it is used in a derogatory sense as "collect" in the New Testament. Here are some examples: dead frogs were never gathered they were "collected": they "collected (*tsabar*) them together in heaps and the land stank" (Exodus 8:14). Foolish words were also "collected" as Job said to the "wise" who spoke foolishly: "I could speak as you do. . .windy words I could collect (*chabar*) or heap up against you" (Job 16:4-5) but he did not because it is up to the Lord "to collect (*tsabar*) their mischiefs upon them" (Deut. 32:23), as He did in His parable: "They will collect (*sullego*) out of His Kingdom all stumbling blocks and those who do the lawlessness" (St. Matt. 13:41). "The wickedness of the wicked shall be upon him" (Ezek. 18:20). The word *tsabar* is seemingly used in a good sense in Genesis 41:35 but do not forget that what Joseph was "gathering was *Egyptian* corn not Israelite. The Scribes never used *tsabar* for gathering the corn of Israel. In the New Testament the sense of collecting and heaping up error is found in 2 Tim. 4:3. St. Stephen who was full of "grace," "power," "Wisdom" and "the Spirit" (Acts 6:8, 10) and who had "the *understanding* of Christ" (I Cor. 2:16) knew all those fine points of the Word of God. That is why he used a very special word to describe the "grain" or "corn" of Egypt for he said in Acts 7:12: "when Jacob heard that there was grain (*sitia*) in Egypt, he sent forth our fathers the first time." The word for "grain" in the New Testament is *sitos* or *siton. Sitia* is a very rare word used only one time in the New Testament and one time in the Old Testament Greek Version: "If a fool be filled with meat (*sitia*)"—Prov. 30:22. St. Stephen knew that only good "wheat" (*sitos* or *siton*) belongs to Israel.

80

Mt 13:30	*"But gather* (sunago) *the wheat into My barn."*

The Latin Vulgate faithfully* rendered the difference using the word *colligo* for "collecting" the darnel, and *congrego* for "gathering" the wheat.
But today* we "gather" everything in "his field" without distinction and thereby lose a great deal of His precious Wisdom. We have become "learned" like the arrogant son who returns from school to criticize the diction of his father at table. Now we have arbiters who glibly reject whole segments of Holy Scripture because these portions do not quite fit their preconceived notions. These learned ones had better remember that those who do the lawlessness of rejecting His Word are also going to be "collected" from "His field."

Mt 13:41	
En 98:15	"Woe to you who write down lying and godless words."
Lk 11:52	"Woe to you. . .for you have taken away the key of knowledge; you did not enter yourselves, and you hindered those who were entering."

The "wheat" is gathered *(sunago)* because holy things and persons are gathered *never* "collected*".

Jn 6:12,13	"He told His disciples, 'Gather up the fragments left over that nothing may be lost', so they gathered *(sunago)* them up."
Jn 11:52	"Gather *(sunago)* together into one the children of God."
Is 57:1 Sept.	"The righteous are gathered" *(sunago)*.
Mt 25:32	"Before Him shall be gathered *(sunago)* all the nations."
Lk 11:23	"He that does not gather *(sunago)* with Me scatters".

Thus "wheat" is always "gathered" *sunago* (St. Matt. 3:12; 13:30; St. Luke 3:17) and fruits are "gathered" *sunago* (St. Luke 12:17, 18; St. John 4:36) but not darnel or strange fruits, these are "collected."

Mt 7:16	Whenever the word collect *(sullego)* is used in the New Testament it is employed in a derogatory manner: "Do men collect *(sullego)* grapes out of thorns?"

No, Sir! because out of thorns men collect nothing but thorns as grapes are gathered from a grapevine and nowhere else.
However, if you see some grapes growing from a thornbush be sure to collect them because they are just as weird as the darnel in His field of wheat.

Lk 6:44	What about figs, do men collect figs out of thorns?

No, Sir! "out of thorns men do not collect *(sullego)* figs" because out of thorns men collect nothing but thorns and they can use these thorns to teach the men of Succoth some lessons (Judges 8:16).

Is 28:26,29	"He is instructed aright whom God teaches. . .for *He* is wonderful in counsel and excellent in Wisdom."

The Wisdom of God is revealed in His Words but these are understood only by those who hold fast to them.
As the "good seed" holds fast to the "wheat" and the "good ground" holds fast to the "wheat" and as the full ear in each grain of the "fruit" holds fast to the "wheat" of His Word.

Qo 3:1	For "all things have their season."

*"WAIT": His Word is sown and we must wait until it bears fruit. "He who sows a plant unless it grows till the time suitable to it does he who planted it expect to receive fruit from it?" (2 Baruch 22:6). Have patience for the harvest shall surely come.

*"MELILAH": "Ripe ear of grain" as in Deut. 23:25. Millah- "say or speak" as in Job 36:2 also "to extol" (See Psalm Scroll of Cave 11, Ps. 151:3 Dead Sea Scrolls). Closely related to these words is mille which means "to fulfill" or "to accomplish" cf. Jer. 44:25; I Kings 2:27; 8:15,24; Ps. 20:5-6; 2 Chron. 36:21. "Who can withold himself from words (millah)" when the time is ripe for understanding? (Job 4:2). Hold fast to His Words and keep them as precious seeds in the ground of your heart and some day you shall bring Truth forth and become "father of the right answer" (AdG i. See Akkadische Gotterepitheta, K. Tallquist, Helsinki 1938 also the Textes Religieux Sumeriens de Louvre II Paris, 1950; Journal of Cuneiform Studies III, F. Kraus). Then you shall be able to "gather thy understanding" (idem). "If thou art a man of understanding one sitting in the counsels of the Lord, gather thy understanding" (Instruction of Ptah-Hotep 365. Papyrus Prisse National Library, Paris).

*"BOUND FAST TO HIS WORD": "Put your feet into the fetters of Wisdom and thy neck into her chain. Bow down thy shoulder and bear her and be not grieved with her bonds. Keep her ways with all thy power. . .for at the last you shall find her rest and that shall be turned to thy joy. Then shall her fetters be a strong defence for thee and her chains a robe of glory. For there is a golden ornament upon her and her bonds are purple lace" (Sirach 6:24-26, 28-31 Sept.). Those bound to the obedience of doing His Word shall be given liberty of the sons when they are sanctified by the Truth that shall set them free. In the meantime they must remain bound to Him and His Word. They must bear His Yoke: the yoke of His Commandments. "But if I suffer I shall then become the freedman of Jesus Christ and in Him I shall arise free" (St. Ignatius of Antioch c. 102 A.D. in his Epistle to the Romans 6:22).

We have to wait,* hold fast and be patient until the day the full ear becomes fully ripe.
For then the grain shall suddenly break forth releasing some of the wheat of His Word
For all to hear.

Pr 23:9

The *melilah** ("ripe ear") shall *millah* ("speak") and everyone shall wonder at "the Wisdom of *His* Words" (*millah*).

Mt 13:30
Mt 13:30

In the meantime *"suffer to increase together* (sunauxano) *both"*: the wheat and the darnel, *"until the harvest."*

Now is the time to tell the difference between the "good seed" and the "darnel."
Between Truth and the lie of the "stumbling blocks."
Because the fruit has appeared to make us understand and turn to Him before the reapers come.

Mt 13:27

Those who understand must be prompt to serve the Lord and zealous for the honor of His Word. The *"servants"* appear the moment the fruit appears. The action is continuous in the original Greek which literally reads: *"When the blade (or herb) sprang up* (or sprouted) *and brought forth* (or made) *fruit then appeared also the darnel. Now the servants of the householder approaching, said to him, 'Sir* (or Lord) *do you not sow good seed in thy field, whence then has it the darnel?'"*

Mt 13:28-29

When Our Lord explained why the darnel is there, the servants immediately want to do something for Him, they ask Him if He will allow them to go forth and collect the darnel. Again we have the present tense being used and the verses literally read: *"now the servants are saying to Him: 'wilt Thou then that having gone forth we should be collecting them?' But He is saying: 'No'"*

Ac 6:7
Jn 15:8

because the Word of God must increase in His field so that it may be multiplied in the number of those who believe and hold fast to His Word. "My Father is glorified in that you bear *much* fruit."

Mt 13:27
Mt 13:30

Although the "servants" *(doulos)* understand the difference, they must wait until *"the time of the harvest."* They have to remain bound* fast to His Word until they have also achieved full maturity. Then they may go forth from their bonds for these "servants" belong to the lowest class of workers who are known as "bondmen" *(doulos)* or "slaves" *(doulos)* which is what the word *doulos* really means.

Until they have given satisfaction to their Lord and paid by their labor some of the great debt they owe, they must remain bound to Him hoping for His Mercy at *"the time of the harvest,"* because at that particular time kind Masters occasionally freed their "bondmen" or "slaves."

The very word meaning "to set free" in the Greek, viz., *eleutheros* is derived from *eleos* which means "to have mercy" or "pity" on someone and *therizo* which means "to harvest" or "to reap" *(theros*="summer"), because "bondmen" were usually freed at the time of the "harvest" *(therismos).* The word "liberty" is in turn derived from the identical Roman custom of freeing "bondmen" or "slaves" in honor of *Liber,* god of grape-gathering and harvesting, better known these days as Bacchus.

*"FREED": The same transition from *doulos* (bondservant) to *diakonos* (attendant) is evident in the Parable of the Marriage Feast (St. Matthew 22:3,4,8,9, v. 13 and in the Parable of the Ten Pounds, St. Luke 19:13 v. 24). The "spirit of bondage" leads to the "spirit of adoption" and the freedom of the sons (Romans 8:15).

*"OWNED": Slaves and bondservants were regarded and treated as the master's purchased chattel. Thus in Genesis 17:23, 13 the word for "slave" is *miknah* which means "purchase": "He that is bought" (*miknah*) and "all they that were bought" (*miknah*) are "slaves." See also Leviticus 25:45 wherein "slaves" are referred to as "possessions" or *achuzzah* which also means "what is held fast" (*achuzzah*).

*"HOUSEHOLDER": He is Householder because "we are His house *(oikos)*" and He is the "builder" of this "house" *but* "we are His House *if* we hold fast our confidence and pride": in the Truth and Wisdom of His Word (Hebrews 3:6,3).

*"SHARE": "The thresher threshes in hope of a share in the crop" (I Cor. 9:10). "Happy the righteous! for well shall they fare. For the fruit of their deeds they shall eat, woe to the wicked for the work of their hands shall be paid back to them" (Isaiah 3:10, *see also* Jer. 16:19). Even the pagan Babylonians knew that the reward of the wicked is their own lies: "With lies and not truth they (the gods) endowed them (the wicked) forever"—Babylonian Tablet 34773 (British Museum).

*"WAGES" or "REWARD": "The ordinances of the Lord are true and righteous altogether. . .in keeping them there is a great reward": Truth (Psalm 19:9, 11). "Errors! who does understand?" (Psalm 19:12 Literal Translation of the verse directly following v. 11) Answer: Those who have been rewarded by the gift of Truth in the fruit of Understanding. "Who sows righteousness—a reward of Truth" *(emeth)*—Prov. 11:18 Literal Translation. "For Thou wilt reward the righteous with loving kindness and Truth" (Targum of the Amidah or 18 Benedictions). "My Word shall be thy reward" (Palestinian Targum on Genesis 15).

*"GO FORTH": "For the mystery of lawlessness is already at work and will continue until He who restrains will no longer restrain those who shall spring out of the midst. And then the lawless one will be revealed whom the Lord Jesus will slay with the breath of His mouth and destroy him by His appearing and coming" (Free rendering of 2 Thess. 2:7-8 in sense of context. *See also* Psalms of Solomon 15:6-7 and Odes of Solomon 31:1,2). The "ground" remains in the ground while the seed is still growing. It is not yet ready to arise and "go forth" because until the Word has fully "increased" in the heart of the ground the maturation must still complete its course. Only when the fruit has become fully mature and the work is finished does all growth stop. Having done the job it was given to do, the "ground" may now arise; "sanctified" and "made free" by the "Truth" of His Word (St. John 17:19; 8:31,36). The "ground-bound" "servants" are now free "harvestmen." They may be said to have become "sons of the field" (Job 5:23 Lit. Trans.) having been brought forth from it. The "field" in the end becomes "His Kingdom" (St. Matt. 13:41) and so the "sons of the field" may also be called "sons of the Kingdom" (St. Matt. 13:38).
It is by keeping and "doing" all His Words that are sown in the field of Holy Scripture that the "ground" of His field becomes transformed.
"Gods *(elohim)* have I seen coming out of the earth" (I Sam. 28:13).

84

Needless to say "bondservants" *(doulos)* and "slaves" *(doulos)* receive no pay from their Masters because they are "owned" by them however when they are freed* and become "freedmen" *(apeleutheros)* they are entitled to receive payment for their labors.

Mt 10:22
1 Co 7:22

"Freedom" *(eleutheria)* for a slave is always a reward of long and faithful service to his Lord and Master and that takes "endurance," "perseverance" and "patience" which you know is the same word *hupomeno* in the Greek. "He that perseveres to the end shall be saved." "He who was called in the Lord as a slave *(doulos)* is a freedman *(apeleutheros)* of the Lord" at "the time of the harvest" when even the fruits set their own seeds free.

Truth is the Wages Free "Harvestmen" Receive From Him

Rm 8:21

The work of the Word of God is to make us sons of God. Our work is to hold fast to His Word that it may work in us to set us free from the bondage of sin and obtain for us all: "the glorious liberty of the children of God."

Jn 4:36

Only "freedmen" can be "harvestmen" *(theristes)*
Because "he who reaps receives *wages*"
And "slaves" *(doulos)* may not apply because they are "owned."*

Mt 13:30

Thus it is written: "*in the time of the harvest I will say to the harvestmen,*" not to the "servants" because they are still "bondmen" *(doulos)*.

Mt 13:30

There is no doubt as to who will send the harvestmen because He said: "*I will*" and He had already identified Himself with the "householder"* *(oikodespotes)* in St. Matt. 10:24-25.

We know that "bondmen" *(doulos)* received no wages and were bound to their Masters' service until their debt was paid in full but the freedmen in turn or the "harvestmen" had the right to expect recompense for their labors.

"Harvestmen" were customarily paid with a share* of the harvest crop instead of "money."

In this parable the good crop of "*his field*" is the "*wheat*"
Thus the "*harvestmen*" receive a share of the "*wheat*".
If the "*wheat*" is the "*Word of God*" then the "wheat" is *Truth* (1 John 1:8, 10).

Is 61:8

"I will give *(nathan)* them their wages* *(peullah)* in Truth" *(emeth)*.

Jn 8:31-32

"If you continue in My Word, you are truly My disciples and you will know the Truth and the Truth will make you free."

Mt 13:28

Because the bond "servants" *(doulos)* continued increasing with the "wheat" they are free to "*go* forth" in the time of the harvest because it is the season then for the wheat of His Word to break forth from its bonds. When the husk at full maturity releases the "*wheat*" the "*servants*" in turn are "freed" and they are now ready to work as harvestmen in "*his field.*"

Mt 13:24

*"**HELP**": "He who makes himself a slave in this world on account of the Words of the Torah will be free in the world to come" (B.T. Baba Metzia 85b). He who holds fast and works to exalt Truth shall become free and no longer bound to error (St. John 8:31-32; St. James 3:2), for having become true he shall speak the Truth brought forth from the good ground of his heart.

*"**WORK**": "Everyone born of God. . .God's Seed (*sperma*) abides in him" (I John 3:9). God's Seed is His Word (St. Luke 8:11). "The Word of God which is at work in you believers" (I Thess. 2:13) is "the Word of Truth" (Eph. 1:13) for His "Word is Truth" (St. John 17:17; 14:6). This "Truth. . .which abides in us" (2 John 1:1,2) is "the implanted. . .Word of Truth" (St. James 1:21,18) which thus works as a "Seed." The work of a seed is directed into propagating itself into many children seeds, this it does with the cooperation of the ground. We are the "ground" of His field or Territory within which the Seed of His word of Truth reigns. If we obey the directives of the Seed, His Truth shall beget Truths through us. These new ("children") Truths may be said to be the offspring products or "children of the Reign" (St. Matt. 13:38) of the Word of Truth in the heart of the obedient ground. The "good seed" are not "the subjects of the Kingdom" (*Jerusalem Bible*) or "people who belong to the Kingdom" (*The Good News for Modern Man*) or the "citizens of the Kingdom" (*The New American Bible*). "The Good seed these are the children (*uioi*="sons", "children" *i.e.*, direct offspring) of the Reign" (St. Matt. 13:38). They are the result of the rule of "the Word of the Kingdom" (St. Matt. 13:19) in the heart of the good ground.

86

Those who persevere and continue holding fast to His Word are freed in the time of the harvest because they have become His children then, and must come forth from their voluntary bondage.

Shall He bring the fruit to maturity and not cause it to bring forth? (Isaiah 66:9); sons of God are free indeed! (St. Matt. 17:26).

If the Son of Man makes you free you will be free indeed because He is both Son of Man and Son of God (St. John 8:28, 36). What He sows as Son of Man (St. Matt. 13:37) He reaps as Son of God and "Lord of the Harvest."

Mt 9:38
Lk 10:2

Jm 1:18

Those who are "brought forth by the Word of Truth" are the children of the Father of Truth and as such they speak and write the Truth which is according to their own nature for they are "of God."

Jn 8:47

1Jn 3:9

"Everyone born of God does not sin because God's seed *(sperma)* abides in him."
"The good *(kalos)* Word of God" is "the Word of Truth."

Heb 6:5;
2 Co 6:7;
Eph 1:13
2 Jn 1:2

It is "the Truth which abides in us."

Mt 13:24
Jm 1:21,18

The "good *(kalos)* seed" is "the *implanted*. . .Word of Truth"
Which is sown in our hearts by the Son of Man.
For *we* are the *ground* in *"his field."*

A seed is sown into the ground so that it may bring forth fruit full of seeds.
Each of the seeds inside the fruit is alike and true to the seed that was sown.
Because the seeds inside the fruit are its "children."

It is the "work" of a seed to bring forth fruit full of seeds.
With the help* of the ground.

Mt 13:19
Mk 4:14
Lk 8:4,11.

"The Word of the Kingdom" is sown as a seed for "the Sower sows the Word" and we know that "his seed. . .is the Word of God."

The "work"* of "the Word of the Kingdom" is to bring forth fruit full of the Words of the Kingdom.

1 Th 2:13

"When you received the Word of God which you heard from us you accepted it not as the word of men but as what it really is, the Word of God which is at work in you believers."

Heb 4:12

"The Word of God is living and active."
If it is sown as a seed it "works" as a seed to bring forth fruit full of children seeds.

Col 1:5,6

"The Word of the Truth of the gospel. . .has come to you as indeed in the whole world and it is bearing fruit and increasing so among yourselves"—
Acting in you as a seed does in the heart of the ground.

| Jm 1:18 | "Of His own will He brought us forth by the Word of Truth that we should be a kind of first fruits of His creation." Full of the good seeds of His Word of Truth. |

Mt 13:38   *"The good seed: these are the sons of the Kingdom."*
They are the children of the "Word of the Kingdom" brought forth from the heart of the ground.

From the heart of the *good* ground that held fast to the seed of the Word.

1 Jn 3:9   "Everyone born of God" has "God's seed" abiding in him,
2 Jn 1:2   God's seed which abides in him is "the Truth which abides in us."

Jm 1:21,18   It is called "the implanted. . .Word of Truth" because we are the ground and the Seed of His Word is sown in our hearts.
1 Th 2:13   "The Word of God which is at work in you believers" has but one
Jn 1:1, 12-13   job to do and that is to make us children of God.
Gn 1:26-27   The Seed is sown to transform the "ground" to His own image
1P 1:23   and likeness again.

When the job is done the finished work receives the seal of approval
The worker is the Word of God.
The seal* is Truth.

The ground transformed by the Seed of His Word brings forth fruit that is full of words to the glory of the Seed
So that the fruit may bear witness to the Truth of the implanted Word (1 John 5:7; St. John 15:26-27).

The Son of Man is the perfect example of complete submission to the Rule of God (St. John 8:29).
He is also the living embodiment of the Kingdom of God: the unimpeded Reign of God in the heart of man.

To the Son of Man belong all the Words of the Father (St. John 16:15; 17:7-8) and through them he bears witness to the Truth (St. John 18:37).
In turn He sows the good seed of His Words in us so that we may bear witness to the Son (St. John 15:26-27) and the Truth of the Father found in Him (Eph 4:21; St. John 5:23).

Mt 13:37   *"He who sows the good seed is the Son of Man."*
Mt 13:24,38   Because the *"field"* of the *"world"* is *"his"* and in order to
Si 37:23   bear "the fruits of. . .Understanding" the good seeds must be
Mt 13:23   sown in the ground.

Jm 1:21   The Son of Man sows Truth so that the ground "may be sanctified through the Truth" "implanted" in it.
The holy ground sanctified by the Word of Truth (St. John 17:17)
Jm 3:18   is the ground that shall bear "the fruit of righteousness" full of His Words of Truth.

2 Th 2:13   But to "be sanctified through the Truth" we the ground must
2 Th 2:10   "believe in the Truth" and we must "love the Truth" so that
Rm 1:18   we may really "hold the Truth" fast in our hearts (St. Luke 8:15).

2 Tm 3:7   Only then shall we "come to the Knowledge of the Truth" and
Ws 3:9   truly "understand the Truth"
Because the good seed of His Word will unfold in our hearts.

*"THE GENES": The early Fathers had none of the genetic knowledge we have today but they had insight: "Let us behold the fruits of the earth. Everyone sees how the seed is sown. The sower goes forth, and casts it upon the earth...the seed...in time dissolves and from the dissolution, the great power of the providence of God raises it again; and of one seed many arise, and bring forth fruit" (First Epistle of St. Clement I to the Corinthians 11:19-20, 1st. Century A.D.).

*"IN": "For the works of the Lord are wonderful, and His works among men are hidden" (Sirach 11:4 L.V.). "The power at work within us is able to do far more abundantly than all we can ask or think of" (Eph. 3:20). So let us be "wise by means of the Spirit of Understanding," (Ps. of Solomon 17:42; Isaiah 11:2) at work within us. Never forget that "understanding grows with us" (4 Ezra 7:71) if we keep and treasure His Words within us. And remember that the Word of God is an *active* Word working within us (I Thess. 2:13; Hebrews 4:12; Romans 1:16; St. James 1:18; 1 Peter 1:23; Ps. 33:9; 107:20; Isaiah 55:10-11; Wisdom 9:1-3; Sirach 42:15), unto our salvation.

*"OF ITSELF": Conversely if the ground is bad it produces nothing. Evil ground is the ground that holds fast to the evil seed of deceit bringing forth the "fruit of lies" (Hosea 10:13) which is "the fruit of the wicked" (Prov. 10:16). As the Egyptians said "he is a mean person...void of the bringing forth of good speech" (Instruction of Ptah-Hotep 320 Papyrus Prisse, National Library, Paris).

*"HOSEA 2:22": The Hebrew word used in Hosea 2:22 for "answer," "hear" and "shout" is the same word *anah, viz.,* "Then the Lord answered *(anah)* Job" (Job 38:1. See also Gen. 18:27; 31:31; Num. 11:28; Josh. 1:16; Judges 5:29 *etc.*). "I the Lord will hear *(anah)* them" (Isaiah 41:17; see also 1 Sam. 8:18; Ps. 3:4; 4:1; 86:1, 120:1; Jonah 2:2; Hosea 2:21 etc.) "He will roar mightily against His fold, and shout *(anah)* like those who tread grapes" (Jer. 25:30. *See also* Deut. 27:14; Exod. 32:18). The grain, the wine and the oil shall testify *(anah)*[1] that it is God who sows His Words.

[1] *Anah* also means to testify as in "*one* witness shall not testify *(anah)* against any person" (Num. 35:30) "but in the mouth of *two* or *three* witnesses every word shall stand" (Deut. 19:15). Not just the grain (Truth) but the wine (Understanding) and the oil (Wisdom) shall testify to His Word.

Before it can unfold, the seed must "die."
It must break open and disintegrate as a seed
So that it may spring forth and reappear in the glorious garments
of the golden ear.

Unless the seed "dies" the genes* cannot commence the "work"
of the seed; the task of raising up from the body of the seed a
plant that shall bear the fruit full of "children" seeds.

The "children" seeds are really the offspring of the "work" of the
seed because the parent seed "died" to give them life.

Mt 13:38   *"The good seed these are the sons of the Kingdom"* because they
really are the "sons" of the Reign.

Mt 13:19   They are the "children" of the "work" of the "Word of the
Kingdom" in the "heart" of the ground.
A "work" that commenced when the parent Seed "departed" (St.
John 16:7).

The genes are the "Spirit" of the Word and the "work" takes
place in* the heart of the ground.

While the "Spirit" works towards raising up children to the Seed,
the ground is being transformed and sanctified.
The "Spirit" continues working producing first a sprout from the
body of the seed, then a blade, an ear, and the mature full grain
in the ear (St. Mark 4:28).
All the while the "ground" is becoming more perfect and holy.

The "ground" knows nothing about how the "Spirit" of the
Word or the genes do their work, neither does a "man" know (St.
Mark 4:26,27).

The only thing the "ground" knows is that the work continues
and progresses if the ground is good
But if the ground turns bad, all the work stops.

For the ground produces of* itself, if it is good: production is
good, and the growth of the plant continues until the fruit is fully
mature and all the seeds are ripe.
When that day arrives all the work ceases because the job is done.
The "ground" is sanctified.
And the "children" seeds bursting forth from the golden ear fall
upon the "ground" sealing the holy with Truth.

Rev 19:9   Then shall the lips of the "ground" joyfully cry out: the "Words
Jn 3:33   of God are True" because "God is True."

Ho 2:22*   "In that day, says the Lord, I will answer the heavens and they
L.T.   shall answer the earth; and the ground shall hear the grain, the
wine and the oil and they shall shout: God sows!!"

And God reaps.
Repent! Repent!
For on the day of the Harvest the Reapers are sent.

*"**LITTLE ONES**": The Jewish scribes who translated the Hebrew bible into the Greek of the Septuagint rendered "simple" (Heb. *pethi*) into *nepios* (Gk. "little ones" or "babes," see Ps. 19:7; 119:130; St. Matt. 11:25) and sometimes into *akakos* (Gk. "without evil," "innocent," see Prov. 14:15). It is the "little ones who believe in Him" (St. Matt. 18:6; St. Mark 9:42) and it is in their hearts that the Word unfolds to give them "light and understanding" (Ps. 119:130). For "the light of the glorious gospel of Christ who is the Image of God" shines in the hearts of them who "believe" (2 Cor. 4:4,6; Coloss. 1:12; Prov. 14:15 M.T.).

*"**ECCLE. 12:10**": The upright do not lie (Jer. 23:31) thus when St. Matthew says that "He said"—— you better believe He did. For "it may not be said that Truth is a lie, nor right wrong" (Test. of Asher 5:4). "Follow the Truth with singleness of face" (*idem.* 6:1). Take His word for it and remember that Dodd is not God.

2 Co 6:2	"Behold, now is the acceptable time." Now is the time for Understanding (Job 28:28), that we may bear much fruit (St. Matt. 13:23).
Jn 12:24 1 Co 15:36	"Unless a grain of wheat falls into the ground and dies, it remains alone; but if it dies it bears much fruit."
	But for a seed to break open and "die," it must be acted upon by the ground. If the ground is indifferent to it: the seed remains intact.
	However if the heart of the ground holds it fast, responds to it and gives it warmth: A wonderful thing happens to the seed: it opens up and begins to unfold.
Ps 119:130	"The unfolding of His Words gives light and understanding to the simple"
Pr 14:15	Because "the simple believe every word."
Ps 19:7	They hold fast to His Words for they know "the testimony of the Lord is sure, making wise the simple."
	These "little* ones" who believe in Him (St. Matt. 18:6) are made wise because it is in their hearts that the seed of His Word unfolds.
Ws 3:9	It is to them that He reveals Himself for He promised that "they that trust in Him shall understand the Truth."
Pr 3:32 M.T. & L.V.	"His secret (sodh) is with the simple" (simplicibus).
Mt 11:25;	"I thank Thee, Father, Lord of heaven and earth, that Thou hast hidden these things from the wise and prudent and revealed them to babes."
Lk 10:21	For after all there is no one simpler than a baby.
	Hold fast (as babies do): to the seed of His Word. Because "God's seed" encloses "Truth," "light and under-standing"
Pr 19:8 Sept. & L.V.	And "he that keeps understanding shall find good things" with His Light.
Rev 21:5	He shall find that the "Words" of God "are trustworthy and true"
Pr 8:8,9.	They "are righteous Words, there is nothing twisted or crooked in them, they are all straight to him who understands."
	Hold fast to His Word
Pr 22:21 Jr 8:8 Is 33:11 Qo 12:10.*	And you shall "know the certainty of the Words of Truth that you may answer with words of Truth" to "the lying pen of the scribes" who "conceive chaff" and "bring forth stubble." Because they have no understanding of "the upright who wrote the Words of Truth."

*"FRUIT OF RIGHTEOUSNESS": By sowing His Words of good counsel in the ground of our hearts, the Sower "sows righteousness" (Prov. 11:18). The ground that holds fast these seeds of righteousness brings forth "the fruit of righteousness" (St. James 3:18) which is the Truth. Thus in the end "he who sows righteousness (has) a reward of Truth" *(emeth)*-Prov. 11:18. The Truth (Fruit) brought forth from the Word (Seed). This fruit is the "fruit of righteousness. . .to the glory and praise of God" (Philip. 1:11). The Truth brings justice and justice brings peace. Thus "the fruit of righteousness" is also called "the peaceable fruit of righteousness" (Heb. 12:11) which "yields" itself "to those exercised by it." Those who possess the fruit (Truth) in the end, are those who have kept and obeyed the seed (Word). The task of the Seed is our perfection and perfection brings forth the Fruit of praise and peace. "Blessed are the peacemakers for they shall be called children of God" (St. Matt. 5:9).

*"DOES": "If a man. . .hath walked in My Commandments and kept My judgments to do *(asaph)* truth; he is just, (and) he shall truly live, saith the Lord" (Ezekiel 18:5, 9. Hebrew Text). "Hezekiah did that which is good, and that which is right and that which is true before the Lord his God" (2 Chr. 31:20). . .and "prospered" (v. 21). "Go and do thou likewise" (St. Luke 10:37). "For whosoever is watchful and diligent in the Law is builded up and perfected" (Palestinian Targum on Num. 21). "That they may hold fast to all good so that they may practice Truth, righteousness and justice upon earth" (Community Rule 1:5, Dead Sea Scrolls).

*"GREAT": The common word applied to a "teacher" in Israel is *lamad* or *yarah*. When a teacher is great he is called simply "Rabbi" or "great one" derived from *rab* and *rabah:* "abundant." "Everyone therefore who hears these Words of Mine and *does* them shall be likened to a *wise* man. . .And everyone that hears these Words of Mine and does *not* do them shall be likened to a *foolish* man". . .(St. Matt. 7:24,26). "Keep the statutes and ordinances and do them for that [the doing] will be your Wisdom and Understanding in the sight of the peoples" (Deut. 4:5).

*"LIGHT": Just as the seed that is in the dark *inside* of the ground comes to light *outside* the ground in the fruit, so is man raised from the ground that he is formed from, to walk in the presence of His Light. Man dies and goes back into the ground. He is formed again and raised on the Last Day if he has done what is true. If we do the things that are true and hold fast to His Truth we shall come to the light of understanding it. In its time and season "Truth will return to them that *practice* her" (Sirach 27:9) just as the seed returns into view clear and multiplied in the fruit wearing the glorious golden garment of the full ear of grain. Truth returns to those who are true to God. "All that the Lord has spoken" we will hear and understand *after* we have done it (Deut. 4:5). The people in the book of Exodus said: "All that the Lord has spoken he will do and hear" *(shamea)*-Exodus 24:7. For "a good understanding have all who do His Commandments" (Ps. 111:10). "Hear and understand" now (St. Matt. 15:10). Never forget we are just the "ground" in "His field": the "world," for "from the ground" (Gen. 2:7) we were "formed. . ."As "Solomon" said; we are "ground born" *(gegenes)*—Wisdom 7:1. Where else can Wisdom plough and sow? Where else shall He sow Himself to transform us? To sanctify us with His Truth? In the ground of our hearts, of course.

It is not enough to hear the Word of God and accept it. The Word of God must be obeyed when it commands and it must be pondered and acted upon by the heart of the "ground." For only then shall it open to give us Light and Understanding.

Jm 3:18
Heb 12:11
Ph 1:11

And only then shall it increase to bear in us: the "fruit* of righteousness" full of the Words of Truth.

Mt 13:23

"He who hears the Word and understands it; he indeed bears fruit."

Jn 3:21

The Word of Truth must be obeyed inside the ground before it can bring forth the glory of Truth for all to see and hear.
"He who *does** what is True comes to the Light"
And lights up the darkness.

Gal 4:19

It is those who hear His Words and *"do them"* who are His "mother" and His "brothers" (St. Luke 8:21).
Because it is they who shall have brought Him forth from their hearts and it is they who shall have become like Him.

Rm 10:5

Those who hear His Words and *"do them"* are the ones who build upon the rock that will always stand (St. Luke 6:47).
It is "the man who *practices* the righteousness which is based on the Law who shall live."

Jm 1:22,25

"Be doers of the Word and not hearers only."

Lv 18:5

"You shall therefore keep My statutes and ordinances by doing which a man shall live."

Gal 3:12

"The Law does not rest on faith," for "He who *does* them shall live". . .

Mt 5:19

"He who does the least of these commandments and teaches men so, shall be called great"*. . .
In the Reign of Understanding.

Jn 3:21
1 Jn 1:15
Jn 1:9
Jn 8:12

Because "he who does what is true comes to the light*" and shall understand that: "God is Light," "the true Light that enlightens every man": "The Light of the world" and "the Light of Life."

Jn 1:1, 7-9
Jn 1:14

"The Word" of God is "Light" and "the Word became flesh."

Jn 12:36

"Believe in the Light that you may become children of Light."

Ph 2:16,13
Ph 2:15

"Hold fast the Word of God" for "God is at work in you" and "you shall shine as lights in the world"
If you hold fast.

Ph 2:14-15

Obey the Word of God
"*Do* all things without grumbling or questioning that you may become blameless and innocent children of God without fault in the midst of a crooked generation that has been perverted" by the *"darnel"* that was sowed in *"His field."*

95

*"**DO NOT ACCEPT**": "Accept not the seeming good as the genuine good" (Testament of Asher 4:3).

*"**EXPOSE**": The Greek Text of the New Testament differentiates between the way evil is exposed and the way Truth is made manifest: "Have no communion with the works of darkness but instead expose, (elegcho) them" (Eph. 5:11). "All things that are exposed" (elegcho) are evil things. "Everyone who does evil hates the light and does not come to the light that his deeds may not be exposed (elegcho) as evil. But he who does the Truth comes to the light that it may be manifested (phaneroo) that his works are done in God" (St. John 3:20-21). "For whatsoever doth make manifest (phaneroo) is light" (Eph. 5:13).

*"**WORD OF TRUTH**": Held fast by those who are good (agathos) and righteous (dikaios). Only they can bring forth the fruit of the Word of Truth: the fruit of Light and Understanding full of the seeds of Truth. "If you continue in My Word you are truly My disciples, and you will know the Truth, and the Truth will make you free" (St. John 8:31-32). So "be firm, I pray you, for if you persevere then your fruit shall be good" (agathos)-Job 22:21, Sept., and "you will go down into the grave like ripened corn to be harvested at the right time or like a stack on the threshing floor that is garnered at the appointed time" (Job 5:26; St. Clement, 1st Epistle to the Corinthians 1:56). Then you and your good (agathos) fruits shall be gathered to the glory of God.

*"**KINGDOM**": The word "Kingdom" rendered basileia in the Greek of the New Testament is the Hebrew-Aramaic word malkuth which means "rule," "dominion" or "sovereignty." Malkuth is derived from malak: "to reign" (malik="king"). The good seed are the "sons of the Reign" or "Rule," not the territory. The term "sons of the Kingdom" derives its origin from that portion of the book of Jeremiah known as Baruch (c. 580 B.C.) therein the disciple of the prophet Jeremiah speaks of the final return of the Jews from all the places of exile to a glorified Jerusalem: "Arise, O Jerusalem; stand on high and look about towards the east, and behold thy children gathered together from the rising to the setting sun, by the Word of the Holy One rejoicing in the remembrance of God. For they went out from thee on foot, led by the enemies: but the Lord will bring them to thee exalted with honor as sons (filios) of the Kingdom" (regni)—See Baruch 5:5-6 Latin Vulgate, Armenian, and Greek Alexandrinus Text.
The term "sons of the Kingdom" in the popular usage of the time meant the righteous ones who were to inherit the blessings of the new world in the "days of King Messiah." These were also known as the "sons of the coming world" (Taanith 22a B.T.) Only the righteous were to partake of the joys to come in the reign of King Messiah (Cant. R. to II. 13. Also Aboth de Rabbi Nathan 28).
The righteous became righteous through accepting and obediently ("doing") the "Law of Righteousness" (Rom. 9:31) which was embodied in His Commandments: "all Thy Commandments are righteousness" (Ps. 119:172). These holy precepts stemmed from "the Word of Thy righteousness" (Ps. 119:123, 144).
God is Truth (Isaiah 65:16; Deut. 32:4; Jer. 4:2; St. John 14:6; 10:30; Exod. R. to 29:1; Ber. 46b. B.T.) And He is True (St. John 3:33) and so are all His Words (Ps. 119:160). Thus the Psalms declare: "perfect Truth are Thy testimonies"; "Thy Law is Truth," "all Thy Commandments are Truth" (Ps. 119:138 Sept.; Ps. 119:142,151 Hebrew Text). The Truth and righteousness of His Commandments are directed to make righteous and true all those who observe them. Those who subjected themselves to the dominion of His Law in their hearts (Ps. 37:31; 119:11,34,36,69,80), become gradually transformed into righteous ones through submission and conformation to His Laws of Truth and Righteousness. As products of the faithful observance of His Commandments the righteous ones in His time came to be known as "sons of righteousness" (Community Rule III., Dead Sea Scrolls) and "sons of Truth" (Community Rule IV, D.S.S.) and they remained so as long as they accepted and did His Counsels. Conversely the wicked and the faithless were called "sons of error," "children of falsehood" and "sons of perdition" (idem.). Needless to say the seed of lies came from the lips of the "children of falsehood" just as the seeds of Truth shall come forth from the lips of the "sons of Truth": "the children (fruits) of the Reign" of God in the heart of man (St. Luke 17:21; Jer. 24:7; 31-34). Both the Greek and Latin Texts of St. Matt. 13:38 preserve the emphatic: "these are the sons of the Kingdom" viz.,
"These (outoi) are (eisin) the sons of the Kingdom" (Greek).
"These (hi) are (sunt) the sons of the Kingdom" (Latin).
In Holy Scripture whenever God points with pride at anything, He uses the emphatic "these things" or "these are" or "they are," thereby drawing attention to them and to their qualities (See Isaiah 66:2; Malachias 3:17; Gen. 2:4, etc.). The Rabbis had commented on this in the Midrash Rabbah Bereshith 12:1 (See also St. Matt. 18:4; St. Luke 8:47; St. Mark 3:34-35). Thus while actually telling the parable our Lord could point at His own mouth while speaking and draw attention to the words proceeding from there and say "these are the sons of the Kingdom": the "children" of the Truth abiding in Him and brought forth as the fruit of His obedience to the Truth of the Father in Him (St. John 5:17, 20; 8:29; 10:30,38; 14:10,11,20; 15:10; 16:32). He emphasized by saying "these are" because the people were being taught that the "sons of the Kingdom" or "sons of the world to come" (B. Shabbath 153a; Pesahim 8a), were they themselves purely by virtue of belonging to the "seed of Abraham." Our Lord taught that the real "sons of the Kingdom" are the righteous themselves who bring forth words of Truth: fruits ("offspring") of their own righteousness.

Eph 5:8	"Once you were darkness, but now you are light in the Lord; walk as children of light," As children of the light of His Word.
	Take no part in the sowing of darnel and do* not accept it in the ground of your heart.
Eph 5:11	"Have no communion *(koinonia)* with the unfruitful works of darkness."
Eph 5:11,13.	"But instead expose* them—for when anything is exposed by the light it becomes visible."
Mt 13:26	Thus *"when the blade sprang up and made* (epoiesen) *fruit then the darnel appeared as well."*
Eph 5:9 L.T.	Because it was exposed by "the *fruit* of *light.*"
Eph 5:9	And "the fruit of light is found in all that is goodness *(agathosune)*, and righteousness *(dikaiosune)*, and *Truth*" *(aletheia).* Because it is fruit from the "good seed" of His Word* of Truth.
Eph 5:9,10	"The fruit of light" is for "proving what is acceptable to the Lord" Because the Lord accepts nothing but the Truth.
Ho 10:13 Pr 20:17	And there is nothing like the Truth to expose the "darnel" of lies and the "fruit of lies" from which is made "the bread of deceit."
Mt 13:38 L.T. Gk and L.V.	*"The good seed these are the sons of the Kingdom*"* They are the sons of the "reign" or "work" of the "Word of the Kingdom" in the "heart" of the "ground" in "his field."
	A "work" that produces fruit full of Words of Truth and thereby sanctifies the ground that holds fast to the Seed. In the end the fruit is there because the "genes" were obeyed and because the "ground" worked along with the Spirit of the Word.
Meg. J.T. 1.7	The "good seed" "died" when it opened up, just as a word of prophecy "dies" when it is fulfilled.
Ps 117:2 Is 40:8	But the Truth of His Word lives and endures forever.
Mt 13:38	Our Lord said: *"The good seed these are the Sons of the Kingdom"* because in His time the people were taught other things about being the "good seed" and "sons of the Kingdom" or "sons of the world to come."
Jn 8:44	Things that did not come from the Father of Truth but from the "father of lies."
Mt 15:13	In His time there were some strange plants growing in His field of Truth: "plants which My heavenly Father has not planted" and which had to "be rooted out."
Mt 15:14	These strange "plants" arose from the "stumbling blocks" the "blind guides" sowed.

*"**BIBLICAL PERSONAGES**": The patriarchs and the great personages descended from Abraham were considered to have been perfectly righteous (Gen. R. 63,90; Sanhedrin 107a; Shab. 56a; Sifre 72b; Yalkut 1:94; Meg. 13b etc.). However in Abraham's case it was purely due to the grace of God (Gen. Rabbah 60). "The world was created only for Israel; none are called the children of God but Israel, none are beloved before God but Israel" (Gerim 1 J.T.).

*"**ETC.**": "The seed of an alien is like that of a brute. . .aliens have no father" (Yebamoth fol. 97, col. 2; fol. 98, col I). "The all-merciful has thoroughly eliminated all holiness from the seed of gentiles" *(idem. See also* Baba Kamma fol. 49, col. 1).

*WHY is Israel compared to wheat? No doubt because the Lord said: "I will sow *(zara)* them among peoples" (Zech. 10:9).

*"**ALONE**": "The Jews are entrusted with the Words of God" (Rom. 3:2). Because His Word was first given to them, they are the elect, the chosen among all peoples, and they remain so (Rom. 11:1-2,5) as long as they hold fast to His Word and His precepts. In the time of our Lord they lost sight of the relationship between election and fidelity to His Law and began to claim election on the basis of blood relationship and on the merits of their forefathers: "Even among those of Israel who transgress the Law the fire of Gehinnom will have no power" (Chagigah fol. 27,A). Only they alone were entitled to do good, not the gentiles: "Almsgiving exalteth a nation that is to say the nation of Israel; but benevolence is a sin to nations—that is to say for the gentiles to exercise charity and benevolence is a sin" (Baba Bathrah fol. 11 col. 2).

Mt 15:9	The people were being taught as "doctrines the precepts of men"
Mt 15:14	and the teaching was being done by the "blind guides" who were sowing these errors.

The "blind guides" taught that all blessings fell on those who were of the "seed" of Abraham regardless of personal merit. Salvation was guaranteed to those fortunate enough to have had Abraham for "their father" (St. Matt. 3:9; St. Luke 3:8; St. John 8:33-58).

The people were taught by them that:

Sanh 10:1 "All Israel has part in the world to come."

Siph. on "Everything comes to Israel on the merits of the Fathers."

Dt p. 108 (b) Abraham's merit would avail even to the morally dead (Midrash Rabbah Bereshith Gen. p. 80 b).

The sins of biblical* personages descending from Abraham were not really sins at all (Shabbat 55b; Baba Bathra 10a; Jerusalem Chagigah 76a; Vayikra Rabbah on Lev. 36).

Blood relationship to Abraham exempted sinfulness on their part (Baba Metzia 7:1; Baba Kama 91a).

It was also taught that Abraham sat by the gates of *Gehenna* saving all Israelites from punishment (Bereshith Rabbah on Gen. 48; Shemoth Rabbah on Exod 19; Yalkut Shimeoni 1 p. 236; Pirke de Rabbi Eliezer c.29 and Midrash Rabbah on Ps. 6:1).

They were taught that the "good seed" or the "wheat" was Israel alone for all the rest of the nations were "chaff" etc.* "The world was made for the sake of Israel" (2 Esd. 7:11):

"Israel is the grain of the world" (Pesikta Rabbah 10 p. 36). "As the world cannot exist without wheat it also cannot do so without Israel" (Midrash Tillim 2:12).

At the time of the harvest only the "grain" or "Israel" shall remain as all the rest of the growth will be cut down and thrown into the fire (Shoher Tob 2:12).

"When the people of Israel are numbered they are numbered as kors of wheat" (Midrash Rabbah on Numbers 1:2).

"Why* is Israel compared to wheat?" (Rabbi Simeoni B. Lakish 3rd Cent. A.D.).

"Israelites are righteous, *all* of them are as wheat for storage" (Midrash Rabbah on Canticles 7:3).

"Just as the farmer pays no attention to the baskets of dung or of straw or of stubble or of chaff because they are not worth anything, so the Holy One blessed be He pays no attention to the other nations"—to whom then does He pay attention?

"To Israel as it is written," etc. (Midrash Rabbah on Canticles 7:3).

"The straw, the stubble and chaff were arguing with one another each claiming that for its sake the ground had been sown. Said the wheat (Israel) to them: 'wait till the threshing time comes and we shall see for whose sake the *field* has been sown' " (Midrash Rabbah on Canticles 7:3).

"Just as wheat seed is carefully measured before sowing and when it is brought in from the threshing floor it is again measured, so it is with Israel" etc. (Midrash Rabbah on Canticles 7:3).

"Israel is the heave offering (wheat sheaves) of the Lord" (Midrash Rabbah on Exod. 31:9).

Our Lord told the parable to gently remind His people that what made them and makes them the chosen seed is the Word of God given to Israel alone* among all the nations and through them "to fill the face of the world with seed" (Isaiah 27:6). They are His good seed as long as they cleave to the "wheat" of His Word.

Because the good seed of God are those who hold the "wheat" of His Word of Truth *tight* inside of them as all grains of wheat do and Christians should.

For without the "wheat" of His Word all of us including Israel are nothing but "chaff," "stubble," "straw" and "dung."

*"EARLY" AND LATER SIMILITUDES: As seen in the writings of Bar-Hebraeus (c. 1246 A.D.) in his poem *Carmina:* "My disciple caused me great anguish for he desired chaff and despised my flour, he should have occupied himself with knowledge but is instead attached to idle thoughts."

*"SEEDS OF TRUTH": The early church fathers frequently mention the "seeds of Truth"—*viz.*, "and these men, preserving the *true* tradition of the blessed teaching directly from Peter and James, John and Paul, the holy Apostles, son receiving it from father, came by God's providence even unto us, to deposit among us those seeds (of Truth) which were derived from their ancestors and the Apostles" (Clement of Alexandria, c.150 A.D., Stroma I, 1, 11; *cf.* Eusebius, *Hist. Eccle.,* V, 11). Conversely evil men sow seeds of deceit: "I have heard of certain persons from elsewhere passing through, whose *doctrine* was *bad*. These you did not permit to sow their seed among you; you stopped your ears, so as not to receive the seed sown by them" (St. Ignatius of Antioch, C. 110 A.D., in his Epistle to the Ephesians 9:1).

Jeremiah 23:28 and Isaiah 55:10-11 had already compared the Word of God to "wheat" and "seed" for the "Sower." Error was compared to "chaff" and "stubble" (Isaiah 33:11).

The same allegory was followed by the Rabbis who compared the Torah frequently to wheat and to bread and the words of the Talmud to grain: "they shall keep themselves alive with grain" (Midrash Rabbah on Numbers 8:1).

The ear was compared to a "grain receiver" when it was attentive to the Torah (Midrash Rabbah on Numbers 14:4).

Wheat was also compared to Knowledge (Yalkut Gen. 21).

"The fruit of the Tree of Knowledge was wheat" (Midrash Rabbah on Gen. 15:7; Berakoth 40a).

A scholar was compared to an "ear" of "wheat" (Sotah 5a).

Rabbi Ismael (c. 130 A.D.) compared proud scholars to the tops of the ears of corn that shall be cut off (Sotah 5a) and mediocre and poor Jewish scholars were compared to "husk" (Ben Azzai 2nd Cent. A.D.; Bechoroth 58a).

"A man devoid of knowledge is as one who has never eaten wheaten bread" (Rabbi Meir 2nd Cent. A.D.).

The "Master of the wheat" was the erudite scholar well versed in all the Law (Horayoth 14a and Baba Batha 145b Mishnah). Early* similitudes dating from the 1st Century A.D. refer to the words of the Torah as "wheat" (Canticles Rabbah to 4:11; Mechilta to Exod. 16:13; Yalkut Shimeoni quoting Rabbi Simeon ben Johai 2nd Cent. A.D.; Jerusalem Shekalim 5 p. 486) and for comparison to words of oral law see Erubin 1:1 (B. Talmud) and Targum Song of Songs 5:11.

Sin was referred to as a degenerate or perverse wheat: "the evil inclination is like a kind of wheat that crouched at the entrance of the heart" (Yalkut Gen. 37; Berakoth 61a).

The Midrash was compared to a thousand measures of grain (Exodus Rabbah 30:14; Shabbath 31a).

By saying 'the good seed these are the sons of the Dominion or Reign' our Lord ruled out any sonship derived from racial links or patriarchal relationship.

Furthermore by saying 'the good seed' were the 'sons of the Reign' He emphasized that the sonship was acquired through *obedience* to the *rule*. The good seed are not *ipso facto* sons of the "Word" or of the "Son of Man," they are sons of the *Rule* of the Word in the "heart" of the ground.

Mt 13:37	*"He who sows the good seed is the Son of Man"* Because the "Son of Man" embodies the perfect reign of the Father in the heart. And so He sows what He brought forth: the seeds* of Truth.
Jn 17:19	We "follow Him" because He set the example for us: "Santify them in the Truth; Thy Word is Truth. As Thou didst send Me into the world, so I have sent them into the world. And for their sake I sanctify Myself, that they *also* may be sanctified *through* the *Truth*."
Heb 5:9;12:2 Rev 3:21	"Although He was a Son, He learned obedience through what He suffered and being made perfect He became the source of eternal salvation to all who obey Him."
Heb 7:19 Heb 7:19,28; Heb 2:10	"The (Old) Law made nothing perfect" "On the other hand, a better hope is introduced through which we draw near to God. . .the Word of the oath which came later than the Law, appoints a Son who has been made perfect for ever."

*"LIFE": And he bears fruit as well. "He who abides in Me and I in him, he it is that bears much fruit, for apart from Me you can do nothing" (St. John 15:5).

*"FRUIT OF RIGHTEOUSNESS": "I will not keep Satan in my heart and no folly or sinful deceit shall be heard in my mouth, no lies or cunning shall be found in my lips. The fruit of righteousness (Truth) shall be on my tongue" (Community Rule 10:21-22, Cave I Qumran, D.S.S.).

1 Jn 5:12	"He who has the Son has Life* and he who has not the Son has not Life."
1 Jn 4:6 1 P 1:22	We in turn achieve the perfection the Son demands from us (St. Matt. 5:48) by *obeying* the "Spirit of Truth" so that through "obedience to the Truth" we may bring forth the fruit full of Words of Truth.
2 Th 2:13 1 P 1:2	We achieve "sanctification by the Spirit and belief in the Truth" but we are "sanctified by the Spirit for obedience to" Him: Jesus Christ, and the Truth of His Word.
1 Jn 5:10	His Word abides in us only *if* we believe in Him (St. John 5:38; St. Luke 8:12). "He who believes in the Son of God has the testimony of God in himself."
1 Jn 5:5 1 Jn 4:4	"Who is it that overcomes the world but he who believes that Jesus is the Son of God?" "For He who is in us is greater than he who is in the world."
1 Jn 4:6 1 Co 2:16	And he who is in the world is "the spirit of error" busy sowing the "darnel" of "stumbling blocks." He shall be exposed by those who "have the understanding of Christ" in them.
Rm 12:2	"Do not be conformed to this world but be transformed by the renewal of your *understanding* that you may know what is the will of God and what is good and acceptable and perfect" And what is "darnel" in "His field."
1 Co 14:14 Rm 6:22	If as yet your *"understanding* is without fruit" Be good! that "being made free from sin and become servants to God you have your fruit unto sanctification and the end in life everlasting."
Heb 12:11	Hold fast to His Word and obey His Commandments "For the moment all this discipline seems painful rather than pleasant; later it yields the peaceful fruit* of righteousness to those who have been trained by it." Trained by the "genes" of the Seed: the Spirit of the Word.
Jm 5:7 Jm 5:8	"Behold the farmer waits for the precious fruit of the ground being patient over it." "You also be patient" keep holding fast to the good seed of His Word.
Jm 1:4 Rm 7:4	"Let patience have its full effect that you may be perfect and complete" And "bear fruit for God": the "Farmer" who sowed in you His Word.

*"**SONS OF OBEDIENCE**": The word used for "sons" in I Peter 1:14 is *teknon* which stresses spiritual sonship. The Greek word commonly used to denote natural progeny is *huios.* Other passages that use the word *teknon* for "son" or "sons" may be found in St. Matt. 9:2; 21:28; I John 3:1,2; 2 Tim. 1:2; 2:1.

*"**OUR**": The work of St. John the Baptist who set the first example for us to follow: "There was a man sent from God whose name was John. He came for *witness* to bear *witness* to the Light that all might believe through him. He was not the Light, but came to bear *witness* to the light" (St. John 1:6-8). "John bore witness to Him," (St. John 1;15,32) who is the Truth incarnate (St. John 14:6). "For the Law was given through Moses but *grace* and *Truth* came through Jesus Christ" (St. John 1:17).

*"**GOD** *(El)* God *(El),* the Lord *(Yahweh),* hath spoken" (Ps. 50: I Hebrew Text). "God *(Elohim)* stands in the testimony *(Edah)*[1] of God *(El)*-(Ps. 82: I Literal Hebrew Text). "The Lord said unto my Lord" (St. Matt. 22:42-45; Ps. 110:1).

[1] *Edah* means "to bear witness," "to witness," "to give testimony in behalf" and it also means "testimonies." It is derived from the Word *Ed* which means also "to give witness," "to bear witness," "witness" and "testimony." God is Truth and He bears witness to Himself (Numbers 27:6-7; St. Luke 10:28).

104

Pr 3:13 L.T.	"O the happiness. . .of a man who brings forth Understanding"
Si 37:23	Because "the fruits of his Understanding" bear the seeds of Truth: the "children" of the "Word of Truth" "implanted" in the heart of the "ground."
1 P 1:14	The good seed these are the "**sons* of obedience**" to the Dominion of the Word.
Eph 2:2	Because there is another "spirit that is now at work in the **sons of disobedience**" producing "darnel" "in the midst of the wheat."
Jn 18:37	"For this I was born, and for this I have come into the world, to bear witness to the *Truth.*"
Jn 17:1,4-5	"Father, the hour has come; glorify Thy Son that the Son may glorify Thee. I glorified Thee on earth having *accomplished* the *work* which Thou gavest Me to do, and now Father glorify Thou Me in Thy own Presence with the glory which I had with Thee before the world was made."
	His work was to bear witness to the Truth of the Father (St. John 18:37; Romans 15:8).
Jn 14:13	Our* work is to bear witness to the Truth in Him and in His Words (Acts 1:8) "that the Father may be glorified in the Son"
	And we shall do so the same way He brought forth His Words of Truth: through *obedience.*
Ex 40:33-34	When "Moses *finished* the work *then* the cloud covered the tent of meeting and the glory of the Lord filled the tabernacle" but
Ex 40:16	not before "all that the Lord commanded him" was done. Read how many things Moses had to do before the glory of the Lord came down (Chapter 35-40 Book of Exodus).
Rm 6:17-18	"Become obedient from the heart to the standard of teaching to which you were committed" so that "having been set free from sin you have become slaves of righteousness."
1 P 3:1	"Obey the Word" "because for those who are factious and do not
Rm 2:8,9	obey the Truth but obey wickedness there will be wrath and fury. There will be tribulation and distress for every human being who does evil."
Rm 16:26	Have "the obedience of Faith" that you may continue holding fast to His Word and bear fruit full of Words of Truth bearing witness to Him.
	Never forget that it is the work of the Holy Spirit in you that shall bring forth through you the fruit of righteousness full of the Words of the Holy Spirit (St. John 15:26). For only God can bear witness to God.*
1 Jn 5:7	"The Spirit is the witness, because the Spirit is the Truth"
Ac 6:32	And "the Holy Spirit is given by God to those who obey Him."
Jn 16:14	"He will glorify Me for He will take what is Mine and declare it to you." And what are His and can be declared are His Words of Truth.

*"SANCTIFIED": "That He may grant you from His glorious riches to be strengthened with power through His Spirit *unto the progress of the inner man* and to have Christ dwelling through faith in your hearts" (Eph. 3:16, 17). "The hidden man of the heart" (I Peter 3:4), is the real "you" in you: the child of God you are meant to be. We hold fast so that by "practicing the Truth in charity we may in all things grow into *(eis)* Him who is the head: Christ" (Eph. 4:15 Literal Translation). "Therefore if any man be in Christ, he is a new creature" (*Ktisis*)-2 Cor. 5:17. "The (old) creature (*ktisis*) shall be freed from the bondage of corruption to the freedom (*eleutheria*) of the glory of the children of God" (Rom. 8:21 Literal Translation). "For the seed *(sperma)* of God abides in him" (I John 3:9) who keeps the Word of God in his heart. "The implanted Word which is able to save your souls" (St. James 1:21) is "the hidden man in your heart" (I Peter 3:4 Literally) which is up to you to bring forth by holding fast to "it": the Seed. "He called me. . .to reveal His Son *in* me" (Galatians 1:15,16).

When a man sows a handful of seed is it not that he may reap in bushels?

He sowed Words of Truth to reap Truth abundantly from His field

Rm 3:7   That "God's Truth" may "abound to His glory."

1 Tm 2:4
1 P 1:22
Eph 5:9
Si 37:23
Is 38:19

In the time of the harvest we shall "come to the full knowledge of the Truth" "through obedience to the Truth"
Because through obedience we shall have brought forth the "fruit of light" and "Understanding" full of Words of Truth to "make known His truth."

4 Ezr 9:17   "As is the workman so is the work."

1 Th 2:13
Jm 1:21,18
Jn 17:17

"The Word of God which is at work in you believers" is "the implanted. . .Word of Truth."
The actual work is done in you by "the Spirit of Truth," because the Word "died" in your heart when it "opened" for you.

Jn 17:19
1 P 1:22
1 Jn 5:7
Jn 16:13

We are "sanctified through the Truth" by "obeying the Truth through the Spirit" "because the Spirit is the Truth" and "the Spirit of Truth. . .will *guide* you into all the Truth" of His Word. He will show you the way to be "sanctified."

Jn 14:6

And He will tell you to follow the One who said: "I am the *Way.* and the *Truth* and the *Life.*"

Jn 14:6

"No one comes to the Father, but by Me."

1 Jn 5:7

"The Spirit is the witness" that what He said is true (St. John 15:26).

1 P 1:2

"We are sanctified* by the Spirit for obedience to Jesus Christ"
Because in Him we have the perfect example: the divine plan and complete work of God.

Eph 4:13,14

He is the Person we must constantly aspire to be.
"Until we attain. . .to the measure of the stature and fulness of Christ so that we may no longer be children tossed to and fro and carried about with every wind of doctrine, by the cunning of men and by their craftiness in deceitful wiles."

Jm 3:18

Until we are sanctified through the Truth as He sanctified Himself for us (St. John 17:17-19) and bring forth as He did: "the fruit of righteousness."

Follow Him, for He left us an example that we should follow in His steps (I Peter 2:21).

Ph 1:11
Lk 6:40

"The fruit of righteousness comes through Jesus Christ"
"For a disciple is not above his Teacher but everyone when he is *fully perfected* will be like his Teacher" full of Words of Truth

Ph 1:11

"to the glory and praise of God."

*"THEM": "The humble shall inherit the land and shall delight themselves in the abundance of peace" (Ps. 37:11). It shall be revealed to them because the Lord "teaches the humble" (Ps. 25:9). "To the humble He reveals His secret" (Sir. 3:20 Hebrew Text). "With the humble is Wisdom" (Prov. 11:2) which brings peace to the land (Sir. 47:12-13). "Thus says the Lord, your Redeemer, the Holy One of Israel: 'I am the Lord your God who teaches you profitable things and leads you in the way you should go. O! that you had hearkened to My Commandments! Then your peace would have been like a river' " (Isaiah 48:17, 18). "O! How abundant is Thy goodness which Thou hast laid up for them that fear Thee" (Ps. 31:19). "The Lord hath directed my mouth by His word: and He hath opened my heart (Understanding) by His light: and He hath caused to dwell in me His deathless Life, and gave me that I might speak the *fruit* of His *peace to convert* the souls of them who are willing to come to Him" (Odes of Solomon 10:1-3).

*"REPENTANCE": We are given Understanding in order to bring us to repentance. When we clearly "see" and recognize God in Truth we must turn to Him and depart from all evil or it shall not be forgiven us (St. Matt. 13:14-15; 12:31-32; St. Luke 12:10; St. John 16:13; Hebrews 6:4-6; Prov. 1:22-33). The mercy of God gives us a little time between the appearing of the fruits of Understanding and the reaping of Judgement. The Lord allowed seven days for mankind to repent upon seeing Noah, his family and all the animals *inside* the ark before unleashing the Deluge. It is significant to note that this took place "at the vernal equinox when all earthly things are full of fruits" (Philo, Book 2 on Genesis Q-18 also Q-13 on Genesis 7:10-11).

*"JUSTICE": Justice springs forth when Truth springs forth from the ground for it is Truth that judges falsehood and condemns it. On the day that "Truth shall spring up from the ground" (Ps. 85:11) "The Lord God will look upon the Truth" (2 Macc. 7:6) and execute His judgment on the wicked and their lies. "When Thy judgments are in the earth, the inhabitants of the world *(tebel)* will learn righteousness" (Isaiah 26:9). "The Lord is known by the judgment which He executes: the wicked is ensnared in the work of his own hands. Meditate on this" (Psalm 9:16). "The congregation shall be established in Truth" (Community Rule 8:5, Dead Sea Scrolls). "Truth and peace shall be associated together throughout all the days of the world and throughout all generations of men" (Enoch 11:2), after Justice has been done.

*"WORD OF GOD": Because the Word of God is God (St. John 1:1) and "the beginning of Faith is to cleave unto Him" (Sirach 25:16 Latin Vulgate).

*"REBUKE": "They that forsake the Law praise the wicked; but such as keep the Law contend with them" (Prov. 28:4; Eph. 5:11; I Tim. 5:20). "He who keeps the Law is an understanding *(bin)* son" (Prov. 28:7) heavily armed with the Truth and wielding it with the power of understanding. By "the power of God...we humble the loftiness that exalts itself against the knowledge of God" (2 Cor. 10:5 as quoted in St. Ephrem's Homily I). "Truth abhors the works of falsehood, and falsehood hates all the ways of Truth and their struggle is fierce for they do not walk together" (Community Rule 4:17-18, QI, Dead Sea Scrolls). "I hate and abhor lying: but Thy Law I love" (Ps. 119:163) because Thy Law is Truth and "Thy Word is true from the beginning" (Ps. 119:160). "Hate the evil one thoroughly" (Epistle of Barnabas 19:11) for he is the father of lies.

Ps 85:11,12	"Truth will spring up from the ground. . .and our land will yield its fruit,"
Heb 12:11	"The peaceful fruit of righteousness to those who have been
Is 32:17	*trained* by it."
Jr 33:3,6; Is 66:12 Zc 8:12 Jm 3:18	When the "great and hidden things" shall be made known, there "shall be revealed to them* the abundance of *Peace* and *Truth*" And "there shall be a sowing of peace" for "the fruit of righteousness is sown in peace by those who make peace."
	Peace between brothers and between fathers and their children (Mal. 4:6).
Ml 4:5 Jn 9:4	Understanding comes to bring us to repentance* (St. Matt.13:15), "Before the great and terrible day of the Lord comes," And the "night. . .when no man can work."
1 Co 3:6,7	"God gave the increase" and "God gives the growth." The Lord shall cause to spring up from His field all the Truth He has sown.
Is 60:22 Is 61:11	"I the Lord will suddenly do this thing in its time." "For as the earth bringeth forth her bud and as the garden causes her seed to shoot forth: so shall the Lord God make justice* to spring forth, and praise before all the nations."
	The Lord shall establish Truth And Truth shall bring Peace to the world.
Is 42:3	But tremble and repent Because "He shall bring judgment for the sake of Truth": to *establish* it.
	For there is no Justice without Truth And no Peace without True Justice.
Is 28:21-22 Ml 3:17,18	The day is near when the Lord shall "act" "When once more you shall distinguish between the righteous and the wicked, between one who serves God and one who does not serve Him."
	And between the "wheat" and the "darnel" in His field.
	Hold fast to the Word* of God That you may receive from it light and understanding.
Si 11:3	"*Understand* first, and then rebuke."*
2 Th 2:10	"Love the Truth" first. And you shall hate all lies (Prov. 13:5).
En 10:16 En 93:4	"Let the plant of righteousness and Truth appear!" So that it may expose all the "deceit that shall have sprung up."

*"**NAME**": In Greek the word for devil is *diabolos* which in turn is derived from *diaballo*: "to malign," "to accuse falsely." *Dia*="through," *ballo*="cast": to cast through a "stumbling block."

*"**GROUND**": We are "houses of clay" (Job 4:19) "formed out of the clay" (Job 33:6) and our "foundation is in the dust" (Job 4:19).

*"**FRUIT**": Hebrews 6:1-8 compares those producing good or bad fruits to the ground that produces either good herbs or thorns depending on what it holds. "Whosoever he be on whom the good seed falls, let him not allow the evil one to sow darnel in him" (Aphrahat, c. 337 A.D., *Demonstration* VI Paragraph I).

Mt 13:38   *'The darnel are the sons of the evil one."*
              They are brought forth from the inside of the evil one
              Either as "sons" or evil "seed."

              Darnel is sown as a seed.
              But it is an *evil seed* because it is brought forth from the *"evil one."*

              Evil ones bring forth only that which is evil (St. Matt. 12:34-35).

Mt 13:25   The "Son of Man" sows the *"good* seed" of Truth.
              "His enemy" sows *"darnel":* the *evil* seed of lies.

Mt 13:25,39   Because *"His enemy"* is *"the devil"*
              And by his very name* he is full of slander and deceit.

Jn 8:44   "The devil. . .has nothing to do with the Truth because there is no Truth in him. When he lies he speaks according to his own nature, for he is a liar and the father of lies."

              When "the father of lies" sows his evil seed, you may be sure it is a seed of lies.

              When he sows "darnel" it is because "darnel" is deceitful it looks like wheat.
              Lies masquerade as the Truth.

Mt 13:25   The darnel of lies is sown to cause confusion in "His field."
L.T.   It is scattered "over and in the midst of the wheat"
              To make the "ground" misunderstand the Truth of the "wheat."

Mt 13:19   For "when anyone hears the Word of the Kingdom and does not understand it, the evil one snatches away what is sown in his heart."

              Anyone can "sow" in the field of the world
              But only God and the devil can "sow" in the heart of man.

              When seed is sown in a field
              It is sown in the *ground* of the field.

Mt 13:38   *"The field is the world."*
              We are the *ground** in that field.

              "Wheat" and "darnel" are grown by the ground of a field.
              The ground is needed to bring them forth.
              Without the ground we have no "wheat" *produced* and no "darnel" because we have no "fruit."*

              The "yielding" and the "bearing" of fruit is the "work" of the *ground.*

*"SAVED": "Until now the spirits of Truth and falsehood struggle in the hearts of men. . .the destiny of all the living shall be according to the spirit within them at the time of the Visitation" (Community Rule IV. 24,26, Dead Sea Scrolls. *See also* Rev. 22:11). They "perish because they received not the love of the Truth which would have saved them. For this reason God sends them the operation *(energeo)* of error that they should believe a lie so that they might all be damned who believed not the Truth, but had pleasure (instead) in unrighteousness" (2 Thess. 2:10-12). "Take heed unto thyself and unto the Doctrine, persevere in them for by doing so you will save both yourself and your hearers" (I Tim. 4:16). In the swift judgment of the Visitation "what will be the end of those who do not believe the Gospel of God?" (I Peter 4:17) because in that Day: "where I find you there will I judge you" says the Lord (Ezek. 7:3 Sept. Text quoted by St. Theodore of Studium, c. 799 A.D., in his *Minor Exhortation XXXVI. See also* St. Luke 17:30-33). So "be watchful and stand fast in the Faith" (I Cor. 16:13) and be zealous to preach the Gospel so "that in the sharing of your Faith it may become operative *(energeo)* in you towards the full knowledge of every good *(agathos)* thing in us for (the glory of) Christ" (Philemon v. 6 Literal Translation).

*"EVIL SEED": "For a grain of *evil seed* was *sown* in the *heart* of Adam from the beginning" (4 Ezra 4:30) and this seed was the evil grain of deceit and disobedience which "has produced so much fruit of ungodliness" (4 Ezra 4:31) to the present time. "It is man who engenders *(yolid)* mischief itself"—Job 5:7 (Emended Text).

Pr 10:16 Sept.	"The *works* of the righteous produce life but the fruits of the wicked produce sins."
Jr 21:14	Both the wicked and righteous *work* to produce *fruit*. By their fruits they are known and they are judged "according to the fruit of 'their' doings" Because both the righteous and the wicked are the ground that is sowed upon: in "His field."
Pr 10:16 Sept. Pr 11:30 Ho 10:12 Sept. Pr 11:30 Sept.	"The works of the righteous produce life" because their work is the "fruit of righteousness" bearing the "fruit of life" and "out of the fruit of righteousness grows a tree of Life."
Pr 10:16 Sept. Rm 6:23	"The fruits of the wicked produce sins" because they entice to sinning by their deceitful wiles. And the produce and "wages of sin is Death."
Dt 30:19	"I have set before you life and death, blessing and curse" depending on which seed you shall hold And depending on which fruit you shall eat.
Dt 30:19-20	"Choose Life. . .loving the Lord your God, obeying His voice and cleaving to Him" and His good seed.

The Lord sows Truth commanding obedience to the Law of Truth
The devil sows the lie, planting unbelief, and urging disobedience.

For it is those who believe in the Truth who are saved* (St. Luke 8:12; 2 Thess. 2:11-12).
And it is those who obey the Law who shall live (Lev. 18:5).

The devil wants you dead, body and soul, because he is jealous of what you can become: a son of God.

Ws 2:24	"By the envy of the devil, death came into the world."
Rm 13:12	"The works of darkness" are done in the darkness and on the sly. No one sees the devil sowing except God (St. Matt. 9:4).
Mt 13:25	For the devil sows in the heart of the ground *"while men are sleeping"* and no one is *"watching"* (St. Matt. 26:41; St. Mark 14:38).
4 Ezr 4:30 Eph 2:2; Mt 13:41	His seed is the "evil* seed" of deceit and disobedience. His "sons of disobedience" are those *"who work the lawlessness."*
Ho 10:13 Mt 13:41	They are the evil ground that brings forth the "fruit of lies" full of the "darnel" of *"stumbling blocks."*
Ws 16:19 Sept.	*"The fruits* of the *wicked* ground" *(ge)* are all the evil actions, lies and stumbling blocks it brings forth for the devil who desires them.

*"**HARMLESS**": No part of His field escaped the "oversowing" of darnel by the devil for in this world we are all tempted. It is up to the ground to either reject or accept what the devil sows. "Now good ground produces wheat and expels tares from itself" *(Sayings of the Fathers,* c. 325 A.D., Book II, Sect. 38 Syriac, W. Budge, Edit. Chatto and Windus, London 1907).

*"**DEVIL: HIS ENEMY**": The Lord "knows both the deceiver and him that is deceived" (Job 12:16).

*"**MAN**": Both the Greek and Latin Text of St. Matt. 13:28 preserve the definitive "man" *(anthropos*-Greek), *(homo-*Latin) that is to say "a human being did this": "an enemy *man (echthros-anthropos)* did this" because He has another enemy who is not a man but the devil. The same distinction is appended to the "householder a *man*" in St. Matt. 13:52 because that "man" who was *instructed* was instructed by God the Chief Householder (St. Matt. 10:25). "Christ was faithful over His (God's) house as a Son" (Heb. 3:6). We are our own "house" *holders (idem.)* but our little house is very much smaller than His own. Never forget that God *owns* the building if "you are God's building" (I Cor. 3:9) so be a good housekeeper and keep His building in good order. The meaning of a parable must be found in the Words themselves: *His* Words *not* the "words" of a careless translator. Those who so glibly reject the "man" qualification of the word "enemy" in St. Matt. 13:28 as an Aramaicism in the Gospel according to St. Matthew, should be reminded that we do *not* hear such things as: "a lawyer a man went up to see Him" or "a Pharisee a man came to Him" or "two disciples men were sent by John." When the gospel qualifies by saying: "the Kingdom of Heaven is like a *man,* a merchant" (St. Matt. 13:45) or "a man a householder" (St. Matt. 13:52; 20:1; 21:33) or "a *man* a king" (St. Matt. 18:23) be a "man" and hold fast to His word because His word is eternal and shall remain forever long after all men are gone from this world. Man lives by *all* and *every* word He said so keep His words intact and pray and *wait* for the answer. Light shall come and be given us to understand why those "puzzling" words are there, in the meantime, hold fast. "All things have their season. . .for He has made everything beautiful in its time" (Eccle. 3:1, 11) including His own good Words which were given to us by "a Son, a Man of understanding" (Sirach 47:12): the Son of Man and Son of God—Jesus Christ.

| 1 Jn 3:10 | The "children of the devil" are those "who will to *do* the desires |
| Jn 8:44 | of 'their' father." |

For all that the devil can do in the field of the world is to sow evil desires.
He needs the ground to fulfill them and to act upon them or the darnel stays intact and harmless.*

| Mt 13:39,25 | *"The enemy who sows them is the devil"*: "His enemy"* |

Because only the devil can sow in the heart of the ground hidden and **unseen** "darnel" seed.

| Mt 13:28 | And only *"an enemy man"** can bring forth "darnel" **fruit** for all |
| L.T. | to **see** when it is exposed. |

When it springs forth from the heart of the ground to the surface of His open field where it can be seen.

Any man of the ground bringing forth evil fruit in His field is also His enemy.
Because "darnel" is "darnel" whether in the seed or in the "fruit."

| Ws 14:9 | "For to God the wicked and his wickedness are hateful alike." |
| Mt 13:41-42 | And in the end *"His angels. . .will collect out of His Kingdom all stumbling blocks and those who make (poieo) the lawlessness and throw them into the furnace of fire."* |

Do not rely on the darnel of those who give you their words instead of His.
Do not hold fast to their presumption.

| 1 Co 1:25 | Remember that "the foolishness of God is wiser than men" |
| 1 Jn 3:9 | And "God's seed" must be held fast to give Light to your soul. |

There is no light in the foolish seed of those who give you their own instead of His.
Indeed the light they offer you is darkness.
How great the darkness of those souls whose Faith they have snuffed out.

| 1 Tm 6:20 | Beware of them for they come to you with "godless chatter and the contradictions of what is falsely called knowledge." |
| 2 Co 11:30 | "Such men are false apostles, deceitful workmen, disguising themselves as Apostles of Christ" and often bearing His Name. |

| 2 Co 11:14-15 | "His servants. . .disguise themselves as servants of righteousness. And no wonder, for even Satan disguises himself as an angel of light so it is not strange that His servants disguise themselves as servants of righteousness." |

It is in them that the *"spirit of error"* does the *"working of error"* producing the "wormwood" of the "fruit of lies" (I John 4:6; 2 Thess. 2:11; Amos 6:13; Hosea 10:13).

*"CONCEIVED": Hold fast to the Word of God and you shall "conceive Wisdom in your hearts and have knowledge" (Sibylline Oracles 1:31 quoted by Theophilus, Bishop of Antioch c. 168 A.D. in his *Apol. ad Autolycus* 2:36). Be not like the wicked who "says in his heart, I shall not be moved from generation to generation; for he *conceives evil*" (Psalm 10:6 Syriac Text). Woe to them "conceiving and *uttering* from the heart *words* of *falsehood*" (Isaiah 59:13). Woe to the wicked who "*conceive* mischief and bring forth iniquity" (Isaiah 59:4). For in the end they and their lies shall be cut off by the sword of Truth. The ancient wise men knew that both Truth and lies are "made" in the heart of man and from there brought forth and dispersed through his lips: Happy "the man of understanding...Truth rises to him from his heart fully brewed" (Instruction for King Meri-Ka-Re c.2200 B.C. Leningrad Papyrus No. 1116 A). "How good it is when a son accepts what his father says for thereby fullness (of Truth) comes to him" (Instruction of Ptah-Hotep L. 543, c.2450 B.C. Prisse-Papyrus N.B. Paris). When Wisdom marries Understanding she begets Truth.

*"EXPLAIN": In St. Matthew's gospel the disciples knew about the good seed but not the evil because "the knowledge of wickedness is not Wisdom" (Sirach 19:22).

*"BROUGHT FORTH": The darnel the servants *saw* growing in His field was and is the visible darnel: the seen and heard stumbling blocks *made* by the heart of the ground: darnel "*fruit.*" It is darnel that "appeared" when it was exposed. The servants saw the *false* darnel "fruit," they asked him from where *it* came. Pointing to the *visible* darnel brought forth and sprung up the Lord said: "*An enemy: man did this*" (St. Matt. 13:28) because only man can materialize the lie, utter the falsehood and "create" the scandal. His enemy the devil did the other thing the sowing of the "darnel" no one but God can see: the evil suggestion.

*"EVIL ONE": The darnel are the sons of the evil one. The darnel of lies are brought forth through the "working of error" (2 Thess. 2:11) by the "spirit of error" (I John 4:6) in the heart of the "sons of disobedience" (Eph. 2:2; 5:6; Col. 3:6) who disobey Truth and obey the "spirit of error." In Chapter 10 of the prophet Hosea both in the Hebrew and Septuagint texts we find the same imagery involving the "children of iniquity" (Hosea 10:9) and their "fruits". "Speaking falsely he will make a covenant therefore judgment shall spring up like a poisonous weed in the soil of the field—Sow to yourselves for righteousness gather in for the fruit of life: light ye for yourselves the light of Knowledge; seek the Lord till the fruits of righteousness come upon you—Why have you passed over ungodliness in silence, and reaped the sins of it? ye have eaten false fruit" (Hosea 10:4, 12, 13 Sept.).

*"SOWED": "Woe to those...whose deeds are in the darkness and who say: 'who sees us? who knows us?'" (Isaiah 29:15). The Lord *knows* that "*the enemy who* sowed *them is the devil*" (St. Matt. 13:39).

Ps 7:14	"Behold the wicked man has labored with iniquity And he has conceived* perverseness And has brought forth lies."
Pr 20:17 Pr 4:16,17 Pr 28:21 L.V.	From the darnel of lies is made the "bread of deceit" and because it is offered to "make someone stumble," it is "bread of wickedness." "For a morsel" of this "bread" men "forsake the Truth."
Jn 6:32	They forsake the *True* Bread" made from the "wheat" of His Word.
Is 32:6	Woe to them "who utter *error* concerning the Lord, who leave the hungry unsatisfied" Feeding them the false bread of lies instead of the True Bread of the Word of God (St. John 6:32; St. Luke 4:4; St. Matt. 4:4).
Jn 6:35 Jn 14:6	Whoever comes to the "Bread of Life" "shall never hunger" Because the "Bread of Life" is *"Truth."*
1 Jn 3:9 1 Jn 3:19	Truth begets Truth and lies bring forth nothing but lies. Those who are "born of God" speak the Truth of God because "God's Seed" abides in them and they "know they are of the Truth" And they understand (I Cor. 2:16, 11).
1 Jn 5:18 Jn 13:14 Jn 14:26; Jn 15:13	Because "He who was born of God keeps Him" as well as His Word. He has the "Lord and Teacher" inside of him (2 Cor. 3:14-15). Only God "can teach you *all* things" and "guide you into *all* the Truth."
Mt 13:36	*"His disciples came to Him saying, "Explain* to us the parable of the darnel of the field."*
Mt 13:25	The "darnel" *seed* that is sown inside the heart of the ground is *not seen* neither is His enemy who sows *"while men are sleeping."* The devil is the only one who can sow darnel in the *heart.*
Mt 13:36 Mt 13:28	*"The darnel* of *the field"* is the darnel in the fruit brought* forth by the ground and this is done by *"an enemy: man."* For man is the ground in His field.
	This is *"the darnel* of *the field"* that sprang up and became visible to His servants so that they were able to *see* it and report it to their Lord. It is also *"the darnel* of *the field"* inquired about by His disciples.
Mt 13:38 2 Th 2:7	*"The darnel are the sons of the evil* one"* because it is darnel that has been brought forth from the inside to the outside like a "son." "The lawlessness. . .at work" *in* the evil one brought forth the darnel that is seen.
Mk 7:23	For "all these evil things come from within" the evil one who *sowed** them and the evil one who *brought them forth.*

117

*"*APEITHEIA*": is a Greek word derived from *a* (negative) and *peitho* ("to persuade"), a refusal to believe or to be persuaded towards belief, *i.e.*, "closemindedness." It is impossible to bring forth the "fruit of understanding" if one refuses to hold the Seed of "the Word of Truth" (Eph. 1:3; Col. 1:5; 2 Tim. 2:15).

*"**WHEATLESS**": Those who despise the Word of God: "sow wind and reap the whirlwind their crop has no head it yields no meal" *(qemach)* because it is wheatless (Hosea 8:7).

*"**LIE**": Truth shall never be given to those who "tamper with God's Word" (2 Cor. 4:2) nor to those "who adulterate the Word of God" (2 Cor. 2:17). "He makes void the thoughts of the subtle *(arum)* and their hands do not execute sound Wisdom" *(tushiyah)*—Job 5:12, because they tried to void the thoughts of God through their presumption (Isaiah 55:7-9). "Those who know Thee do not alter Thy Words" (Hymn 14:15 Dead Sea Scrolls). "Grasp hold of Truth and do not add (untruths) to it" (Instruction of Ptah-Hotep Prisse Papyrus N.B. Paris).

*"**CONFOUNDED**": "Every man is confounded, there is no understanding" (Jer. 10:8, 14; 51:17; Jer. 28:17 Sept.).

*"**CONFUSED**": The English translation of the Hebrew Text mistakenly renders the Hebrew word *hobis* as a derivative of *yabesh*, the Hebrew word for "withered," but *hobis* is the Hiphil of *yabash* "to be confounded," "confused," "ashamed"; the same word *hobis* is rightly rendered "ashamed" in Joel 1:17: "the husbandmen are ashamed" *(hobis)*. "Ashamed" or "confounded" or "confused" wine or grain may not make much sense to us if we forget that the *soul* also needs these things allegorically and God gives us His word symbolically in things that are good to eat (St. Matt. 4:4; St. Luke 4:4; 11:11-13). As the Lord said, "I have food to eat of which you do not know" (St. John 4:32). Remember that the Word of God is meant to be taken inside us, it is meant to abide in us and "work" within our hearts. We "see" God in the Truth of His Word and our souls are filled when we "see" God as if we had eaten and drank to our satisfaction. It is written: "They saw God and did eat and drink" (Exodus 24:11; Bereshith 1a B.T.).

*"**MAN**": In the heart of the wicked is the "evil ground" (Wisdom 16:19) that "holds fast to deceit" (Jer. 8:5), "conceiving. . .words of falsehood" (Isaiah 59:13) and bringing forth "the fruit of lies" (Hosea 10:13 Heb. Text).

118

Eph 2:2;5:6; Eph 5:6	It is the "children of **unbelief**" *(apeitheia*)* who produce the "empty words" because they accept the darnel seed of the implanted lie.
1 Jn 4:6; 2 Th 2:11,12	It is in them that the "Spirit of error" does the "working of error" "to make them believe what is false so that all may be condemned who do not believe the Truth." And to make them produce the darnel *fruit* of *uttered* lies, calumnies, stumbling blocks and detractions that obstruct the Truth that He sowed in His field.
Eph 2:2;5:6; Is 32:6 Is 33:11	It is the "children of **unbelief**" *(apeitheia)* who produce the "empty words" full of "error concerning the Lord." "Empty words" because they "conceive chaff and bring forth stubble" and for those who utter and write these wheatless* words is reserved the wrath of God (Isaiah 33:10-12; Eph. 5:6; Hosea 8:7).
Mt 12:37	"For by your words you will be justified and by your words you will be condemned."
Mt 18:7,6	"Woe to that man through whom the stumbling block comes" that "stumbles one of these little ones which *believe* in Me."
2 Co 6:14	"Do not be unequally yoked with unbelievers for what share has righteousness with lawlessness *(anomia)* or what fellowship has light with darkness?"
2 Co 6:15	"What has a believer in common with an unbeliever?"
	Shall the seed of His Word open in the hearts closed to it? Shall the wages of Truth be paid to those who sowed the lie?*
Lk 8:18	"From him who has not, even what he thinks that he has will be taken away."
Mt 24:12	These are the days when it was said that "lawlessness shall abound"
2 Th 2:7 Mt 13:41 Mt 13:41	For "the mystery of lawlessness *(anomia)* is already at work" in the evil ground of *"those doing the lawlessness"* *(anomia)* of bringing forth *"stumbling blocks"* in His field of Truth.
Pr 13:5 L.V.	"The wicked confound and shall be confounded"* Because "the just hate a lying word."
Jl 1:10,12 L.V. Jl 1:17	If "the wine is *confused**. . . and the vineyard is *confused*" it is *"because* the *grain* is *confused"* by the darnel sowed and brought forth in His field.
Jl 1:11 Mt 13:27	"The husbandmen are *ashamed"* and they go to their Lord and say to Him, *"Sir, did you not sow good seed in your field? How then has it darnel?"*
Mt 13:28 L.T.	*"He said to them, "An enemy: man (anthropos) has done this."*
	The devil may sow deceit in the heart of the ground But no devil can bring forth confusion in the field of Truth: Without the help of *"man."**

119

*"SOWING": Rabbi Simeon ben Lakish (3rd Century A.D.) commented that Pharaoh seeking to force intermarriage between the Jews and Egyptians prompted the Lord Himself to speak thus to Pharaoh: "Thou didst seek to *confound* the seed of My beloved Abraham" therefore as a punishment the Lord resolved to send *confusion* (wild irrational acting) among the Egyptians (Midrash Rabbah on Psalm 78 sect. 11). "The sons of darkness tend towards confusion and chaos, they lean on emptiness" (War Rule 16:11; 17:4, Dead Sea Scrolls). The literal term "with confusion of mingling" is found also in the Psalms of Solomon 2:15.

*"MINGLED": It is the mingling of seed which is *tebel* and forbidden (Lev. 19:19). If the field of Truth is confused it is because men added and replaced His inspired Words with their own unwarranted "darnel." Thus Jeremiah 4:22-23 says in the Words of the Lord:
"For My people are foolish they know Me not
Foolish *sons* are they yea they have *no understanding*
They are wise *(chakam)* to do evil
But how to do good they know not
I looked to the earth. and lo
It was confusion *(tohu)* and chaos *(bohu)*
And to the heavens and there was no light" (Jer. 4:22-23 Literal Translation).
How can there be light when His good seed cannot open because it has been cast aside? How can "Truth" *(emeth)* spring forth out of the earth (Ps. 85:11) when the Light that was sown (Ps. 97:11) has been replaced by "darnel"? The Midrash Rabbah brings out the relationship between "being without form" *(tohu)* and "void" *(bohu)* as in Gen. 1:2 and being "confused" or "bewildered" *(tohu)* and "disconcerted" *(bohu)*—See Midrash Rabbah Bereshith on Gen. 2:1 *(See also* Isaiah 34:11; 41:29; for *tohu* as confusion and *bohu* as chaos). "God is not the author of confusion" *(akatastasia)* but "there is *confusion* and every evil work" (I Cor. 14:33; St. James 3:16) when men attempt to do better than God. Hold fast to His Words.

*"CONDEMN": The Word of the Lord that was cast aside shall condemn the presumption of that scribe and his lying pen (Jer. 8:8; 2 Cor. 4:2).

Mt 13:38	*"The field is the world"* and it is confused by all the "darnel."
	When our Lord told the parable He spoke in the Hebrew-Aramaic of the day and the word for "world" was *tebel.* Thus we read in the Hebrew Text the following:
Jr 10:12; 51:15	"He has established the world *(tebel)* by His Wisdom."
Ps 93:1	"He has established the world *(tebel); it shall never be moved."*
Is 13:11	"I will punish the world *(tebel)* for its evil and the wicked for their iniquity."
Ps 9:8	"He shall judge the world *(tebel)* in righteousness."
Ps 33:8	"Let all the inhabitants of the world *(tebel)* stand in awe of Him."
	Whenever the word *tebel* is used for "world" in the Bible it always denotes the habitable and fertile world. The very word for "habitable" is also the word *tebel.* Wisdom speaks:
Pr 8:31	"I (Wisdom) was daily His delight, rejoicing before Him always, rejoicing in His habitable *(tebel)* earth *(erets)* and delighting in the sons of men."
	The word *tebel* is derived from a common root meaning "to flow" *i.e.,* figuratively: "to produce" or "to yield." Akin to it is the word *tebuah* which means "fruits" or "increase," example:
2K 8:6	"all the *tebuah* (fruits) of the field."
	Isaiah prophetically described the "world" as a "field."
Is 24:4	"The world *(tebel)* languishes and withers."
Is 27:6	"Israel shall blossom and put forth shoots and fill the *face* (pannim) of the world *(tebel)* with fruit."
	But besides meaning "world" and "habitable," the word *tebel* also means "confusion," "perversion" and "profanation," especially applied to forbidden "sowing"* of the worst kind:
Lv 18:23	"You shall not lie with any beast and defile yourself with it neither shall any woman give herself to a beast to lie with it; it is perversion" *(tebel).*
Lv 20:12	"If a man cohabits with his daughter-in-law, both of them shall be put to death for confusion *(tebel)* they have made."
	The field is confusion *(tebel)* because men have brought forth "darnel" in the field of the Lord, they have mingled* their words and plucked out His.
Jr 10:12; 51:15	What was established by His Wisdom—as He established the "world" *(tebel)* never to be moved—has been pushed aside and
1 Ch 16:30	oversown by the "darnel" of lies.
	The field is the ordered ornament of the Lord and His Words are meant to be planted there firm as nails (Eccle. 12:11). We must accept (St. John 12:48) and hold fast to them even if we do not fully understand (2 Peter 1:19) until the day comes when
Eph 5:9	they shall bear the "fruit of light."
Jn 10:34	"The scripture cannot be broken," we cannot substitute our words for His own because if anyone does that "profanation" *(tebel),* "the Word that I have spoken will condemn* him on the
Jn 12:48	last day," says the Lord.
Si 37:3 M.T.	"O wicked presumption. . .that fills the face of the world *(tebel)* with deceit" *(tarmith).*

*"**THE FIELD IS THE WORLD**" (St. Matt. 13:38): Even before the time of our Lord the Torah was regarded as a sacred "field." The scribes were enjoined by the Sanhedrin to "make a fence around the Torah" (Pirke Aboth 1:1) to keep it inviolate, and everyone was encouraged to "work much at thy Torah" because for that work (tilling and keeping it like Adam in the garden) "wast thou created" (Pirke Aboth 2:9). There are many references to the Torah as a "field" in the Talmud and Midrash (See Leviticus Rabbah on Exodus 22.1; 34.16; Sanhedrin 102a; Jebamoth 21a; Midrash Rabbah on Exodus 27.9; Rabbi ben Ilai (c.200 A.D.) commentary re. Eccle. 5:8; Ag. Tan. II:265-266).

The comparison was quite apt because the Hebrew word for "word" is *dabar* and the word *dabar* is derived from the Ugaritic word for "fertile field": *dabar* (See Cuneiform Texts of Ras Shamra, Ugarit).

The Words of God are by divine inspiration perfectly placed and arranged in the field of Holy Scripture. They remain there in perfect order as long as we leave them in their proper place. The Scribes knew that the Lord "established the world by His Wisdom" (Jer. 10:12; 51:15; Ps. 104:24) and that He built and founded it with great deliberation (Job 38:4-7), upon a solid foundation (I Sam. 2:8; Job 34:13; Prov. 30:4).

Having been created by Him: "the world is established, it cannot be moved" (Ps. 93:1; 96:10; 1 Chr. 16:30) for "He has set to order the mighty works of His Wisdom" (Sirach 42:21; 16:27; Wisdom 12:15 L.V.) and they are to remain well set for "all His ways are according to His ordering" (Sirach 33:14 L.V.).

The wise men of His time knew that the Torah was given to man by God Himself who is the Author of it: "Whosoever denies the heavenly origin of the Torah will have no part in the world to come" (Sanhedrin 10:1; see also Zebaim 116a; B. Bathra 15a; Shekalim 49a J.T.; Taanith 9a; Nedarim 22b; Lev. R. XIX; Cant. R.5, 11; Sanhedrin 20c J.T.; Megillah 70d J.T.; Pirke de Rabbi Eliezer 2b, 11: 64a, 11: Avodah Zarah 3b, etc.). And since God created in Wisdom both this our visible well ordered world *and* the Torah, the Scribes among themselves began to call the Torah: "the World," and the Master scribes gave strict instructions to the disciple scribes to keep it inviolate and well ordered: "My son, be careful in thy work, because thy work is the work of Heaven: if thou omittest a single letter or addest a single letter thou dost as a consequence destroy the whole world" (Sotah 20a B.T. quotation of Rabbi Ismael c. 130 A.D.). Even to change one "tittle" from a single letter in Sacred Scripture was to destroy as a consequence "the whole world" (Midrash Rabbah on Lev. XIX.2). In the Dead Sea Scrolls the "sons of light" are promised the final vindication of "the Truth *(emeth)* of the world" *(tebel)* from the errors that had crept in and polluted it (Community Rule 4:19-20). Those among the scribes who faithfully occupied themselves with the study of the Torah were said to be building up the "world" through their wise deliberations: "the disciples of the wise are engaged all their days in building up the world" (Shabbath, fol. 114 col. I.B.T. *See also* Berakoth 64 col. 1 and the Targum on the Song of Songs 4:1). In the first edition of the Pirke of Rabbi Eliezer (Sect. 21 A.1), Rabbi Ismael (c. 130 A.D.) took to task St. Paul's statement that "the wisdom of this world is foolishness with God" (1 Cor. 3:19) by saying it could not be so for the "wisdom of this world" is "this *(zoth)* world: the Torah" (which was given by God Himself).

A scriptural text that had precedence over another text was called the "father" of the text in question. The word "father" was also used as a term of respect for anyone who was an expert in his field of work. Thus esteemed rabbis were often called "father" *(abba)*, viz., Abba Saul, Abba Gurjan, Abba Joses ben Chanan, Abba Joses ben Dosai, Abba Judah, etc. (See Peah 8:5; Kidd. 4:14; Middoth 2:6; Tosefta 23:4; 259: 18 etc.). And since the Scribes were experts in the Law (Torah) which was also called "the world" *(tebel)*, scribal sages were referred to as "fathers of the world" (Bereshith Rabbah 1:15). When Ben Sirach commented on the disadvantages of being an artisan instead of a scribe he nevertheless gave solace to the artisans by saying that they also in common with the scribes: "strengthen the state of the world, and their prayer shall be in the work of their craft applying their soul and searching in the Law of the Most High" (Sirach 38:39 L.V.). Therefore: "everyone who is occupied with the Torah for its own sake: the whole world, all of it is his" (Pirke Aboth 6:1) and rightly so, for is not "the whole world only 1/3200 part of the Torah?" (Erubim 21a B.T.), i.e., the Torah that is to come in the Days of the Messiah because then "all the Torah learnt in this world will be vanity compared with the Torah of the world to come" (Midrash Rabbah on Eccle. II.I. see also Targum on Isaiah 12:3). For in the coming days of the "new world" the Torah itself will also be restored again as a "new world" in all its pristine glory (See Sanhedrin 97a; Midrash Rabbah on Song of Songs 2:13; Genesis Rabbah 98; Targum on Song of Songs 5:10; Yalkut on Isaiah 26; Numbers Rabbah XIX. 6. Strack Billerbeck vol. IV p.2.N.9.).

"The field is the world": This world of ours that has been sown throughout with the seeds of the Gospel.

"The field is" also "the world" of His Teaching: the Torah.

For early Christian interpretation of the "world" *(kosmos)* as being the Torah and the "rudiments *(stoicheia)* of the world" (Col 2:8, 20; Gal. 4:3,9; Heb. 5:12) as being the elementary principles of the Torah, please see Tertullian in Adv. Marc V.4; 19:7 and St. Jerome in Com. on Gal. 4:2,8,9.

"OIKOUMENE", is the common Greek word for habitable "world." Thus the Hebrew word *tebel* is rendered *oikoumene* in the Greek Septuagint and New Testament. But in St. Matthew 13:38 another Greek word: *kosmos* is used for "world" instead of the usual word: *oikoumene* because *kosmos* implies the order manifest in the world. The word *kosmos* primarily means "adornment" or "ornament" and besides meaning "world" as well, it also means "honor," "good arrangement" and "order": "the essence of *kosmos* is order" (Corp. Herm. Lib. XI.2). Inasmuch as the Hebrew-Aramaic word play between *tebel* ("world") and *tebel* ("confusion") could not be brought forth in Greek by using the word *oikoumene*, the evangelist used *kosmos* to evoke the "orderly" *(kosmos)*, "beautiful" (kosmos), "well arranged" *(kosmos)*, "ornament" *(kosmos)* of the Lord: His field—the "world" *(kosmos)* before it became corrupted by the darnel "strewed" by the evil one.

122

Mt 13:38	*"The Field* is the world"* (kosmos)
Pr 28:17 Sept.	The Greek word *kosmos* means many things: it signifies "honor": "Give honor *(kosmos)* to thy soul" and it also means "ornament":
Pr 20:29 Sept.	"Wisdom is the ornament" *(kosmos)*, and if an ornament is gloriously beautiful it is because the jewels in it are "well set":
Si 35:5 Sept.	as "a signet of carbuncle well set *(kosmos)* in gold."
Gen 2:1 Sept.	The "order" *(kosmos)* of heaven "is the beauty *(kosmos)* of it" and He has placed it above us as an example for us to look up to.
Jdt 1:14 Sept.	For He has "appointed man. . .that he should order *(kosmos)* the
Ws 9:2,3 Sept.	world according to equity and justice" to His glory and praise:
Si 26:16 Sept.	"as the sun when it arises in the high heaven: so is the beauty *(kalos)* of a good *(agathos)* wife in the ordering *(kosmos)* of her house." So be good inside out and you will order His things well.

Pr 20:29 Sept.	"Wisdom is the ornament" *(kosmos)* of the "world" *(kosmos):* His field. He sowed His Words into the ground in perfect "order" *(kosmos)* for us to hold them fast and bring forth praise to His "honor" *(kosmos).* In the field is the "setting" *(kosmos)* and "ordering" *(kosmos)* of all His Words.

The "beauty" *(kosmos)* of His Wisdom is found in His field.
The "order" *(kosmos)* of heaven is sown on earth for us to behold and marvel.
If we hold His Word fast in our hearts.

	Have respect for His Words and leave them intact in His field.
Ws 9:9 Sept.	For "Wisdom. . .was present when He made the world" *(kosmos)* and His Understanding was there when He sowed it.

Ws 7:17 Sept.	"He hath given us certain knowledge. . .to know how the world *(kosmos)* was brought together." The "world" *(kosmos)* was "brought together" "by his Wisdom" (Ps. 96:10; Prov. 3:19; Jer. 51:15 Sept.).
Ws 16:17 Sept.	"The world *(kosmos)* fights *for* the righteous."
Ws 5:20 Sept.	"The world *(kosmos)* shall fight with him *against* the *unwise"* who deny Him the Words that are His (Sirach 4:28).
Ws 6:24 Sept.	"The multitude of the wise is the welfare of the world" *(kosmos)* Because they know how to till the "field" and clear away the "darnel."
Jb 12:8	"Ask the earth and it shall teach you." Teach you why St. Matthew used the word *kosmos* for "world" instead of the more common and usual word for "world" in Greek: *oikoumene*.*
Si 1:23 Sept.	"He will hide His Words for a time and the lips of many shall declare His Wisdom,"
2 Esd 6:28 RSV	"When Truth which has been so long without fruit, shall be revealed,"
Ps 85:11	Because "Truth shall spring out of the earth," when the time comes for His exaltation.
Ps 97:11	"Light is sown for the righteous"
Eph 5:9 L.T.	And it is up to them to bring forth "the fruit of light."

*"BREAK OPEN": "Trust in God with all your heart and do not rely on your understanding" (Prov. 3:5). "In all thy methods get to know Wisdom that she may rightly divide your ways" (Prov. 3:6 Sept.), and show you which way is right and which way is wrong. Know Wisdom and you shall know how to go about "rightly dividing the Word of Truth" (2 Tim. 2:15) so that you may see and reveal to others the goodness inside of it. By "breaking" the Bread of His Word we "interpret" it: "when Gideon heard the telling of the dream and its interpretation (sheber-"breaking") he worshipped" (Judges 7:15; St. Luke 24:30-31).

*"TEST": "All these things therefore I proved...and I wandered not from the Truth of the Lord" (Test. of Asher 5:4). "Look unto the thing that is really good and keep it" (Idem. 6:3).

The field is the world and it is sown throughout, for all the nations are meant to receive the good seed of His Word (St. Matt. 28:18-20).

In the Sower parable we learn about the types of "ground" in His field.

Mt 13:36 In the *"parable of the darnel"* we learn that there are two kinds of seeds sown in His field: good and evil seed.

Let us remember that we have four types of soil in the world:
The hard ground that is impervious to His Word;
The superficial ground that is too shallow to hold on to it;
The untilled ground that accepts and holds fast to all kinds of seed;
And the good ground that accepts and holds fast to that which is good.

But only to that which is good *(agathos)* inside.
Because evil seeds look good *(kalos)* on the outside but are evil within.

Mt 13:24,27,37 The *"good (kalos) seed"* that is sown is not only "beautiful" *(kalos)* on the outside but "good" *(agathos)* inside because we

Mt 13:25,30 know that it is *"wheat"*
Lk 1:53 "He *fills* the hungry with good *(agathon)* things" such as "wheat."

Heb 6:5 "Have you tasted the good *(kalos)* Word of God?"
Try it, but first rub off the beautiful *(kalos)* husk (St. Luke 6:1) for only then will you know that it is also "good" *(agathos)* inside to eat.
Break* open the Bread
And you shall know

Jn 6:32 Whether it is *"True* Bread" or "bread of deceit."
Pr 20:17

Pr 30:5 Test* all things by *Wisdom* (Eccle. 7:24) and by *Fire*.
For "every Word of God is fire-tried"
By the same fire that consumes the chaff (1 Cor. 3:13-15).

Ps 12:6 "The Words of the Lord are pure Words: as silver tried by the fire, purged from the ground, refined seven times."

Pr 30:6 Do not oversow "darnel" among the wheat.
"Do not add anything to His Words lest thou be reproved and found a liar," nor subtract and deny Him the Words that are His.

The very same ones that do so, also tell you that the "good seed" are the good people and the "darnel": the bad ones in the world. You tell them that what is *sown* in His field is sown into the ground and so their good and bad people are both buried.

Tell them that we are the ground in His field
And we *become* either good or evil
Depending on which seed we hold.

*"TRUTH": Although it was required by the Oral Law that barley and lintels be sown with their husks on, it was customary to sow the wheat "bare" of its own husk (Sanhedrin 98b, Kethuboth 119b; Bacher's Tan. II.69) as St. Paul said: "what you sow is. . .a bare kernel" (I Cor. 15:37). Thus when our Lord likened Himself and us to a grain of wheat that must die before it can bear fruit, He spoke of a bare kernel (St. John 12:24). But there were exceptions to the custom of sowing bare kernels of wheat (Hullin 117b, 119b; Terumoth 9:7) and so when our Lord spoke of His *Word* being sown as a seed it is always sown as covered wheat. Because the Truth of His Word is always to be **kept** either in the sac of the sower, the husk or body of the grain or by the ground of His field. Even when the children seeds of the full ear are gathered they are stored, *i.e.,* **kept** in His barn where the Lord "keeps Truth" *(emeth)*-Ps. 146:6, for Truth must always be kept and held within our hearts. The naked Truth is a terrible weapon entrusted only to those who can temper it with "mercy, goodness, sincerity, peace, loving kindness, meekness and light." Thanks be to God, Truth is always found in the company of mercy (Gen. 24:27; Exod. 34:6; Josh 24:14; 2 Sam. 2:6; 15:20; I Kings 20:19; Esther 9:30; Ps. 25:10; 40:11; 43:3; 45:4; 57:3, 10; 61:7; 85:10, *etc.).* "Sow for yourselves in righteousness" but "reap in mercy" (Hosea 10:12) because the naked Truth hurts.

*"EARS OF THE GOOD SEED": It is the seed (of the fruit) *from* the seed (that was sown) which is the "seed of Peace" (Zech. 8:12) and which shall then be "sown in peace by those who make peace" (St. James 3:18). But never forget that the glorious seed of peace springs forth from the humble seed that was sown and held fast by the good ground.

*"TRUTH. . .SET FREE": "In the Mysteries of His Understanding and in His glorious Wisdom God has ordained an end for falsehood, and in the time of His visitation He will destroy it forever. Then the Truth *(emeth)* of the World *(tebel),* which during the dominion of falsehood has been sullied in the ways of wickedness until the appointed time of judgement, shall appear in triumph forever. God will then purify every deed of man with His Truth" (Manual of Discipline IV. 18-20, Dead Sea Scrolls). For the Lord has promised "for His righteousness' sake, to magnify His Teaching *(torah)* and make it glorious" in the end (Isaiah 42:21. *See also* Isaiah 29:18-20; 52:15; Dan. 10:21; Jer. 23:20; 30:24;31:33-34; Heb. 8:10-11; 2 Peter 1:19; St. Mark 4:22; Midrash Rabbah on Eccle. II.1; Idem, Song of Songs 2:13 and Gen. 98; Yalkut on Isaiah 26; Numbers Rabbah XIX. 6 etc.). Rejoice! for "ye shall receive new instruction with joy from the chosen of righteousness" (Targum on Isaiah 12:3; St. Matt. 26:29; Mal 4:5-6, and marginal notation of Sirach 40:18 Hebrew Text).

Jn 4:23-24   "The hour is coming, and now is, when the true worshipers will worship the Father in spirit and Truth, for such the Father seeks to worship Him. God is Spirit and those who worship Him must worship in spirit and Truth."

The Truth that is found *in* His Word.

Mt 13:24,27,37   The "beautiful *(kalos)* seed" when *sown* is covered
So that we, the ground, may act upon it
And uncover the "wheat" of His Truth.*

Is 65:16   "The God of Truth" is recognized in the unfolding of His good seed and in the breaking of the True Bread of His Word (St. Luke 24:30-31).

Rev 21:5   His Words are "trustworthy and true"
Because they are consistent and do not deviate (Mal. 3:6).

What is sown as His Word in one parable (St. Mark 4:14; St. Luke 8:5, 11) is not sown as a man in another.
Because the "good seed" that was sown bore fruit
And for that you need the ground.

Truth may be sown and lies may be scattered
But good and evil men are *made* in the ground.

And they are made by the kind of seed they hold fast in their hearts.

4 Ezr 4:30   "For a grain of *evil seed* was *sown* in the heart of *Adam* from the beginning, and how much *fruit* of *ungodliness* has it produced unto this time, and shall yet produce until the threshing floor come!"

4 Ezr 4:31-32   "If a grain of *evil seed* has *produced* so much *fruit of ungodliness* when once the *ears** of the *good seed* shall have been *sown* without number, how great a floor shall they be destined to fill?"

Jm 3:18   The ears of the good seed are found in the fruit of righteousness and from it Truth "is sown in peace by those who make peace."
But before Truth can be sown it must first be understood and then brought forth by effort.

Only then shall we be freed to merit Truth as a wage
And as a binder to tie up all the darnel plucked from His field.

Before stumbling blocks can be bound
Truth* must be set free to spring forth from the ground.

The lie is exposed when the Truth appears,
To make us understand and see the difference
Between the good and evil sown in His field.

*"**CUT OFF. . .DECEIT**": "A sword is on the lies (*baddim*)[1] that they may become foolish" (*yaal*)—Jer. 50:36.

[1] *Baddim* is the plural of *bad:* "a lie," "a deceit" or "a vain boast" (*See* Job 11:3; Isaiah 16:6; Jer. 48:30) and it also means "vain boasters."

*"**THE FIELD**": The field is meant to be the new world where Truth shall reign and everyone shall worship the Father in Spirit and in Truth (St. John 4:23-24). Then the seeds of Truth from the fruit of righteousness shall be sown in peace by those making peace because in that time the new field shall have been cleared of all the darnel. "The new world comes which does not turn to corruption. . .and leads not to perdition those who (shall) live in it" (2 Baruch 44:12).

The world was created to be a Paradise for man or in other words a glorious "field" because the very word *eden* is derived from the Babylonian word for "field": *edennu.* This is also true in Sumerian where the word for "plain" or "field" is *edin* and in Akkadian where "field" is *edinu.* Truly "the field" of the "world" was meant to be a delight to Man, the word *eden* in Hebrew has a homophonous root meaning "delight":

"How precious is Thy steadfast love, O God.
The children of men take refuge in the shadow of Thy wings.
They feast on the abundance of Thy house
And Thou givest them drink from the river of Thy Delights" (*eden* pl.)—Ps. 36:8

Nothing delights the understanding of the sons of men more than to see how the Lord in His wonderful Wisdom fitted perfectly His Words one to another. It must be the reason why the wise Jews call a "socket": *eden.*

*"**PS. 149:5-9**":"Let the faithful exult in glory; let them sing for joy in their couches. Let the high praises of God be in their mouth and a two-edged sword in their hands, To execute vengeance upon the nations and chastisements among the peoples, to bind their kings with chains and their nobles with fetters of iron, to execute upon them the judgment that is written! This honor have all His saints."

128

T.L. 13:6a	"*Sow good things* in your soul that you may reap them in your life."
T.L. 13:6b	"If you *sow evil things* you shall reap every trouble and affliction."
Ps 54:5 L.T.	"Turn back the *evil thing* to mine enemies, and in Thy *Truth cut* them off."
Qo 8:5	"A wise man's understanding discerns Time and Judgement."
En 93:4	When the harvest time comes Truth is released from its sheath like a sword
Jr 50:36	To cut* off all the "deceit that shall have sprung up."
Mt 13:27,28 Rm 8:13-19,23	When the "bondservants" *(doulos)* are freed from their voluntary bondage they obtain from the Spirit "the glorious liberty of the children of God"

And they share the inheritance of His children and Son (Rom. 8:17; Rev. 21:7).

The inheritance is the gift of understanding the Truth of His Word (I Peter 1:4-5, 7) and discerning the lie of the evil one (I John 2:20-21, 26-27).

Until Truth is released the lie cannot be bound.
And no one is "sent" to collect darnel until he has brought forth fruit of righteousness and earned the seeds of Truth inside (2 Cor. 10:5-6).

Mt 12:34	We "speak good *(agathon)* things" only after we have become good *(agathos)* inside (St. Luke 6:45).

We bind the darnel in bundles to be burned only after we are loosed from our bondage
And not before the fruit is ripe and the measure made full.

4 Ezr 4:29	"Unless therefore that which is sown be reaped and unless the place where the evil is sown shall have passed away, the *field* * where the good is sown cannot come."
4 Ezr 4:35, 36,37,40 Mt 13:29-30	"When cometh the fruit upon the threshing floor of our reward?. . .when the number like yourself is fulfilled for. . .He will neither move nor stir things until the appointed measure be fulfilled. . .Go ask a woman who is pregnant, when she has completed her nine months if her womb can keep the birth any longer within her? Then said I: No, Lord, it cannot."
4 Ezr 4:28	"Evil is sown but the destruction of it is not yet come."

Until the sword of Truth is given to the harvestmen who are "sent" to reap His field.

Before the Lord shall bind all evil on earth (Rev. 20:1-6), He shall set free "His own that are in bonds" (Pss. 69:33;72:13,14;89:48; 97:10-12; 102:20, 21, 28; 129:4; 142:7; Isaiah 42:6-7, 49:9-10, 58:6; 61:1; Zech. 9:11-12).
To execute His Justice (Ps. 105:22 Hebrew Text Ps. 141:10; Ps.* 149:5-9; 2 Cor. 10:5-6, 1 Cor. 6:2).

2 Ba 70:2 (c.70-90A.D.)	"The time of the age has *ripened*. . .the *harvest* of its evil and *good seeds* has come."
	The lie is bound when Truth is released.
Ml 4:2	The dawn of Truth arises before it blazes as the "sun of Justice" at noon, Because the Lord promised He would open our understanding before the end.
Is 8:16,20; Mk 4:22,34, 2 P 1:19	"Bind up the testimony, seal the instruction among my disciples"—until the coming of the "dawn." "We have the prophetic Word made more sure. You will do well to pay attention to this as to a lamp shining in a dark place until the day dawns and the morning star rises in your hearts."
Dn 12:4,9	"Shut up the words, and seal the book until the time of the end. . .for the words are shut up and sealed until the time of the end."
En 104:12-13; Rev 11:11	"Books shall be given to the righteous and wise to become a cause of joy and uprightness and much Wisdom for to them shall the books be given and they shall believe in them and rejoice over them."
En 100:6	Because "they shall understand all the words."
Jm 3:18	Understanding is given to the righteous because it is they who bring forth the "fruit of righteousness" full of the seeds of Truth. They are the ground and the fruit they produce bears witness to the Truth of the implanted Word.
Jm 5:7	For this "precious fruit" dedicated to His praise: the righteous are rewarded with the wages of Truth. They are set free and given a share of the crop to bind all the stumbling blocks in His field.
Mt 13:30	*"In the time of the harvest I will say to the harvestmen, Collect first the darnel and bind them into bundles to be burned."*
Ps 31:18 (19)	"Let the lying lips be dumb *(alam)* which speaks insolently against the righteous in pride and contempt."
Ps 31:18(19)M.T.	"Let the lying lips be bound" *(alam)*.
	The Hebrew-Aramaic word for "dumb" or to "be made dumb" is *alam* and it is also the word for "bound" or to be "bound" in tongue. From the word *alam* is derived the word for "bindings" or "sheaves": *alummah*.
Gn 37:7	Thus we read: "For behold, we were binding *(alam)* sheaves *(alummah)* in the midst of the field" (Literally "we were binding bindings").
Ezk 3:26	"Thou shalt be made dumb" *(alam)* said the Lord to Ezekiel until the time comes when: "Thou shalt speak and be no more dumb"
Ezk 24:27	*(alam)* or "bound" *(alam)*.

131

"HOLY ONES": Blessed are the righteous in the time of "the regeneration when the Son of Man shall sit in the throne of glory, ye also shall sit upon twelve thrones judging" (St. Matt. 19:28). "Know you not that the saints shall judge the world?". . .(I Cor. 6:2. *See also* Wisdom 3:8; Sirach 4:15; Dan. 7:22). "God will place the judgement of all nations in the hands of His elect" (Habacuc Commentary 5:4 f. Dead Sea Scrolls). "For the weapons of our warfare are not wordly but have divine power to destroy strongholds casting down imaginations and every high thing that exalts itself against the knowledge of God and taking captive every thought to the obedience of Christ, being ready to punish every disobedience when your obedience is complete" (2 Cor. 10:4-6). In that day: "the strong shall become tow and his work a spark, and both of them shall burn together, with none to quench them" (Isaiah 1:31).

To be "dumb" was to be "tongue-bound" or tongue-tied. We find an echo of this Aramaicism in St. Mark 7:35: "and his ears were opened, and immediately the bond *(desmos)* of his tongue was freed *(eluthe)* and he spoke correctly" *(orthos)*.

Holy Scripture warns that those who work iniquity and speak falsehood meet their just retribution by being cut off, silenced and bound.

Thus the Psalmist ironically asked the wicked liars:

Ps 58:1-3,11 M.T. "Is it true, O dumb *(alam)* one, (or "bound" one) that you speak righteously?
And judge uprightly, O sons of men?
Nay, even in your *hearts* ye *work iniquity*, your hands deal out violence on earth.
The *wicked* go *astray* from the womb, they have *erred* from the belly *speaking lies*. . .
Truly, fruit *(peri)* is for the *righteous*, *Truly*, there is a God judging in the earth."

Jb 17:8-9,10 In the hidden words of the wise, Job says:
"The innocent stirs himself up against the *godless*
And the righteous holds to his way
And he that has clean hands grows stronger and stronger
And—*dumb* are they all" *suddenly* because they are "bound" by the innocent, righteous and clean when the time comes.

Ho 10:10 The Lord promised through the prophet Hosea:
"When I desire *then* do I *bind* them and the nations shall be gathered against them when they are *bound* for their double iniquity."

Ho 10:9 Those who are "bound" are the "children of perversity" *(alvah)*
Ho 10:4 the ones who are "swearing falsehood."
Ho 10:13 They are the ones who "have ploughed wickedness. . .reaped perversity" and "eaten the fruit of lies."

Ho 10:4 To them it was decreed that "judgment shall spring up like a poisonous herb on the furrows of a field" they have sowed.

Pr 2:22 "The wicked will be cut off from the land and those who deal treacherously shall be rooted out of it."
En 92:11 "Blasphemers shall be cut off in every place."

En 1:9 When "He comes with ten thousands of His holy* ones to execute judgment upon all and to destroy the ungodly and to convict all *flesh* and the *works* which the ungodly committed and all the hard things which ungodly sinners have spoken against Him."

Ws 14:9,10 "For equally hateful to God are the ungodly man and his
Mt 13:41-42 ungodliness—
What was done will be punished together with him who did it."

*"**NUMBERS 15:31**" reads: "Because he has despised the *Word* of the Lord and has broken His Commandments, that person shall be cut off; *his iniquity* shall be *upon him.*" So let the scoffers and deceitful ones beware for He also said: "Woe to those who call evil good and good evil, who put darkness for light and light for darkness, who put bitter for sweet and sweet for bitter. Woe to the wise in their own eyes and intelligent in their own sight. . .who acquit the guilty for a bribe and deprive the innocent of their rights. Therefore as the tongue of fire devours *stubble* and as *straw* falls into the *flames* so their root will be as rottenness and their blossom go up as dust for they have *rejected* the *teaching (Torah)* of the Lord of Hosts and have *despised* the *Word* of the Holy One of Israel" (Isaiah 5:20-21,23-24). "He that sows good, reaps good; and he that sows evil, his seed returns upon him" (Test. of Levi 13:6 Cambridge Aramaic fragment). "Evil shall slay the wicked" (Ps. 34:21) but "call to mind now! what innocent man ever perished? and where (or when) were the righteous cut off?" (Job 4:7) Never! for "never have I seen the righteous forsaken" (Ps. 37:25; Sirach 2:10-11).

*"**JUSTICE**": Our Lord excoriated against those who "bind together burdens heavy and grievous to be borne and lay them upon the shoulders of men, but with their finger they will not move them" (St. Matt. 23:4; St. Luke 11:46). These Words He directed at the "lawyers," "scribes" and "Pharisees" who made up the Oral Law (Mishnah) with all its many burdens clothing all its ordinances with the authority of Mosaic Law and even more. All those who tried to bind the Truth to make it ineffective through their restrictions were to be bound themselves in the end (St. Jude 6; 2 Peter 2:9).

*"**FROM THEIR LIPS**": And from their unbridled tongue as well (*See* St. James 3:5-8). "Death and life are in the power of the tongue" (Prov. 18:21), "for by thy words thou shalt be justified and by thy words thou shalt be condemned" (St. Matt. 12:37). "He that keeps his own mouth (shut) keeps his own life" (Prov. 13:3).

*"**BOUND**": Commenting on Psalm 31:18 the Rabbis said: "Let the lying lips be bound" *(te'alammah)*; this means, let them be bound, made dumb and silenced. It means "Let them be bound" as in the verse (Gen. 37:7): "For behold we were binding sheaves" *(me-allemim, allumim)*; "Let them be dumb" as you read in Exodus 4:11: "who made a man dumb" *(illem)* etc. (Midrash Rabbah Genesis I.I) Even the ancient Akkadians of Mesopotamia knew that: "the tongue that was bound was unable to function" (Sippar Text No. 55 Line 26 Section III).

*"**WEEPING AND GNASHING OF TEETH**" (St. Matt. 8:12; 13:42; 22:13; 24:51; 25:30; St. Luke 13:28): The physiological reaction of envy and impotent rage is weeping and gnashing of teeth (Ps. 112:9-10). It is also common for mourners in great anguish to be struck dumb (Baba Bathra 16b; Gen. Rabbah 62:14).
In Holy Scriptures the wicked gnash their teeth at the righteous while doing evil towards them (Ps. 35:16; 37:12; Job 16:9; Lam. 2:16; Hymn I.39, Dead Sea Scrolls) and in the end the wicked shall still "gnash" their teeth from force of habit but that is all they shall be able to do when they shall be bound and gagged. In their desolation the wicked shall see: "light rising in the darkness for the upright" (Ps. 112:4) but not for them. St. Matthew wrote the gospel for the Jews who knew that the particular facultative punishment of the wicked was to be struck dumb: "after death as regards to the faculties there is no difference between the righteous and the wicked except the power of speech" (Midrash Rabbah on Eccle. IX.2). The power of speech is given us to praise God, the wicked in Sheol are no longer able to exercise that function for "the perverse tongue shall be cut off" (Prov. 10:31). In the Testament of Abraham (a Jewish Apocryphal work, c.20 A.D.) the mouth of the condemned soul is forcibly closed. So hold fast to His Words or "thou shalt gnash thy teeth in the end" (Sirach 30:10; *See also* Pss. 112:5-10; 115:17; 6:5; 30:9; 88:12-13; 142:8; 63:12). For in the end "the upright see and rejoice, and all wickedness closes its mouth" (Ps. 107:42).

*"**TRUTH**" "O God. . .in Thy Truth *(emeth)* cut them off" (Ps. 54:15).

*"**UNDERSTANDING**": "To whom has the understanding of Wisdom been revealed?" (Sirach 1:7 Syriac and Sahidic Texts). "A wise man's *understanding (leb)* is at his *right hand*" (Eccle. 10:2). We are given Understanding to understand hidden Wisdom and to reveal the Truth. According to the ancients, the understanding of a man resides in his "heart" *(leb)*. Thus in Holy Scripture the word *leb* ("heart") is synonymous with "understanding" (*See* Proverbs 6:32; 7:7; 9:4; 10:13; 12:11; 15:32; 17:18; 24:30 etc.) As Jeremiah (5:21) said: "O foolish people without understanding" *(leb)*. The wise men knew that the understanding of the heart is made manifest in the power and skill of the right hand: "Awake! Awake! put on strength, O! Arm of the Lord. . .was it not Thou (O Arm of the Lord) that aidst cut Rahab in pieces?" (Isaiah 51:9). For God "by His power stilled the sea and by His *Understanding (tebunah)* He smote Rahab" (Job 26:12). When the Lord said: "My *right hand* has stretched out the heavens" (Isaiah 48:13), it was the same thing as saying: "He. . .has stretched out the heavens by His *Understanding*" (Jer. 10:12; 51:15; Prov. 3:19; Ps. 136:5). And since it is the right hand which is powerful the Targum paraphrased Isaiah 48:13 by saying: "By My *Power* I have stretched out the heavens." Again, we have Job saying: "in length of days: Understanding" (Job 12:12) and knowing that Wisdom's Understanding is in her right hand we can say as the wise man did that: "Length of days are in the right hand of Wisdom" (Prov. 3:16).

134

"The righteousness of the righteous shall be upon himself and the wickedness of the wicked shall be upon himself" (Ezekiel 18:20; Numbers* 15:31).

Pr 5:22 Sept.
Lm 1:14

The liars are bound with their own lies for "everyone is bound in the chains of his own sins"

2 Tm 2:9

But "the Word of God is not bound."
It is freely gathered when the "bond servants" have become "harvestmen."

Mt 13:24,30
Ps 146:6

In the time of the harvest Truth is revealed to expose the lie.
The sown *"good seed"* is gathered as uncovered *"wheat"* into His barn where the Lord "keeps Truth *(emeth)* forever."

The darnel is bound into bindings so that it may never be disseminated again.
Justice* demands that the lies be bound when they are "collected" because they were unrestrictedly scattered when they were sown.

Liars shall also be dumb-bound because the bundle of lies came from* their lips.

Ps 31:17,18

"O Lord, let me not be put to shame
for I call on Thee.
Let the wicked be put to shame.
Let them go dumbfounded to Sheol.
Let the lying lips be bound"* *(alam)*.

Is 2:9
Ex 15:16

"The wicked shall be silent *(damam)* in the darkness."
They shall be "still *(damam)* as a stone."

Mt 13:42

All they shall be able to do is "weep* and gnash their teeth,"
Because they shall be bound, chained and dumbfounded.

Jr 8:14

They shall ask themselves in their "minds": "Why do we sit still?. . .we are silent *(damam)*. . .because the Lord our God has put us to silence" *(damam)*.

Ex 23:7
Jr 49:26;50:30
Jr 48:2

So be good and hold fast to His Words.
"Keep away from all that is false" or else
"You shall be cut off" *(damam)*, because
"the sword shall pursue you, and you. . .shall be cut down" *(damam)*.

Is 29:21

"All who watch to do evil shall be cut off, who by a word make a man out to be an offender. . .and with an empty thing turn aside him who is on the right."

Pr 10:31

"The perverse tongue will be cut off" by the sword of Truth*
Which is handled by the right hand of Understanding* (2 Tim. 2:15).

135

*"CUT": "Every false speech clothed in untruth will be cut off by the sword of death" (Secrets of Enoch 63:4). For Truth is life to the righteous but death to all falsehood. "In those days violence shall be cut off from its roots, and the roots of unrighteousness together with deceit and they shall be destroyed from under heaven" (Enoch 91:8). "Sin when it is fully grown brings forth death" (St. James 1:15; Joel 3:13; Apoc. 14:15-16). For in the time of the harvest all "falsehood and iniquity will be cut off" (Apostrophe to Zion, line 7 Psalm Scroll, Cave 11, Quamran).

*"BINDINGS": Epiphanius (c.315-400 A.D.) quotes St. Matt. 13:30 in the idiomatic: "bind (desata) them (auta) into bindings (desmas) bindings" (desmas) or in other words double bind them and tie them up for good. The repetition is a typical Aramaicism comparable to St. Mark 6:39 which literally reads: "and He instructed them to recline all companies, companies, on the green grass". Has this not been "told, told" (Ruth 2:11 literally) you before? Through the jawbone of an ass you shall see "heaps upon heaps" (Judges 15:16) as a lesson. The Hebrew way of learning was through repetition. Thus the Hebrew word shenah literally means "to repeat" it also means "to study," "to learn" and "to be taught." The word Mishnah (Oral Law) is derived from shenah ("to repeat"). The final rulings decided by the Rabbis as regards the Oral Law are known as the halakoth. These legal norms of the Pharisees through which the Law was circumvented to win popular favor, were derisively called halaqoth ("smooth things") by the stricter Essenes who in turn called their own legal decisions on matters of the Law: mishpatim, i.e., "judgments" instead of the usual Rabbinic term (Manual of Discipline 5:15 fol. Dead Sea Scrolls).
The number of halachic decisions grew to such proportions that the Rabbis themselves referred to the halakoth as the tille tillim which literally means "piles upon piles" (Midrash Rabbah on Song of Songs 5:11 and Lev. R.19:1). The people in His time were bound by these "piles upon piles" of legal burdens which were often difficult to observe (St. Matt. 23:4; St. Luke 11:46). However in our day we have gone to the opposite extreme of not only loosening all legal restrictions but also denying the very Truths which are meant to bind us fast to God. "Now therefore do not scoff lest your bonds be made tight" (Isaiah 28:22) and you be relegated to the furnace with the "piles upon piles" to be burned.
Hold fast to His Word that you may bring forth fruit from His Seed and produce "bundles upon bundles of merits" (Midrash Rabbah on Lev. 21 Sect. 6).

*"GO": "There shall be no more lies and all the works of falsehood shall be put to shame" (Community Rule 4:23, Dead Sea Scrolls). For then "He shall no longer allow unrighteousness to dwell anymore in their midst" (Ps. of Solomon 17:29). "When they (the wicked) are given over to those who shall condemn them, then they shall learn that the Word of the Lord is true" (Ps. 141:6 Psalm Scroll, Dead Sea Scrolls).

*"ESTABLISHED": "Slay the ungodly from before the King and his throne shall prosper in righteousness" (Prov. 25:5 Sept.). "As for those enemies of Mine who did not want Me to reign over them bring them here and slay them before Me" (St. Luke 19:27).

*"REMOVED": Before they are removed they are bound, the Hebrew—Aramaic word ud means "to turn" or "to bind" by winding. From ud is derived the Hebrew word udhe which is the Talmudic word for "bundle." The same word ud means "to bind fast" or "ensnare" as in Ps. 119:61. It also means "to testify against" as in Amos 3:13 or "to record against" as in Deut. 30:19, "to protest against" as in Genesis 43:3, "to admonish" as in Zech. 3:6 and "to rebuke" as in Neh. 13:15. So, when you see those bundles (udhe) "know certainly that 'we' have admonished (ud) you this day" (Jer. 42:19) to hold fast to the Truth. Another word for "to bind" is amar (as in Ps. 129:7) which is pronounced the same way as the word for "to answer back," "to refute" and to forcibly "confute" by superior argumentation—amar.

*"WITNESSES": They shall bear witness and declare that "all His works He established in Truth forever and in Truth they are all of them praised" (Syriac Text of Sirach 42:22. Vide St. John 4:23-24).

The work of the harvestmen is to cut* and bind.
In the Hebrew-Aramaic the reapers "silence" *(damam)* when they "cut off" *(damam)* and also when they "bind" *(alam)* because they make "dumb" *(alam).*

"Dissemblers" *(alam)* are "dumbfounded" *(alam)* when they are "bound" *(alam)*

Mt 13:30   And even more so when you *"bind them into bindings of bindings"**

Ho 10:10   "for their *double* iniquity."

Ps 26:4 M.T.   "I have not sat with men of lies *(shav)* nor do I go with dissemblers" *(alam)*

Is 59:4   For "they trust in worthless things and speak lies" *(shav).*

Pr 6:16,17,18,19 "The Lord hates. . .a lying tongue. . .a heart that devises wicked plans. . .a false witness who breathes out lies and a man who sows discord"

Jr 28:15   For "they cause His people to err by their lies" by making them
Jr 29:31   "trust in a lie" and stumble by their "stumbling blocks."
Mt 18:7   "Woe to the man through whom the stumbling block comes."

Pr 19:5   "He who utters lies will not escape."
Pr 19:9   "He who utters lies will perish."

In the time of the harvest "the righteous will never be removed but the wicked will not dwell in the land" (Prov. 10:30) because

Pr 10:24   "What the wicked dreads will come upon him."

Ps 101:8   "Morning by morning I will destroy all the wicked in the land, cutting off all the evil doers from the city of the Lord."

Mt 13:24,41   Before *"His field"* can become *"His Kingdom"* all the evil ones must go.*
And all their "stumbling blocks" with them.

Pr 25:5   "Take away the wicked before a King and his throne is established."*
Take away the "darnel" first and the glory of the wheat shall be seen by all.

Before Truth can be established all the lies must be removed.*
Wisdom is established by Understanding,
Truth: by the sword of His Word (Rev. 1:16; 2:12, 16; 19:13, 15; Eph. 6:17).

And the sword of His Word is a sword of fire (Rev. 11:3-5),
That shall consume all the chaff (I Cor. 3:10-15).

Lk 22:38   "Behold, Lord, here are *two* swords"
And He said to them, "It is enough."

Because Truth is established by *two* witnesses* (St. John 8:17).

*"*DAMAM*" also means "to weep" in Ugaritic.

*"**TODAY**": Ancient Aramaic still survives and is spoken today in the isolated Christian villages of Maloula, Bakhi and Jubb Adin in Syria.

*"*TSARAR*" is the word for "enemy" in Psalms 6:7; 7:4,6; 8:2; 10:5; 23:5; 31:11; 42:10; 74:4,23; Esther 3:10; 8:1; 9:10, 24. It is derived from *tsar* ("enemy" or "adversary").

In the Hebrew-Aramaic spoken by the Lord we note the word relationship between "cutting" *(damam)* and "silencing" *(damam*)* and between "binding" *(alam)* and "making dumb" *(alam)* the "dissemblers" *(alam)* and their lies.
Thus the act of harvesting would result in "doubly silencing" the "double iniquity."

Mt 13:30   But *"collect first the darnel"* before you double bind it.

The Hebrew-Aramaic word for "to collect" or "to heap up" is *tsabar.*

Ex 8:10
Jb 16:3-4
Remember *tsabar* is the word used when unpleasant things are "collected" such as "dead frogs" and "windy words."

Tsabar also means "to babble," "to prattle," "to chatter" or talk about empty things.
It retains this meaning in the Aramaic and Syriac of today.*

Tsabar originally meant "to bind together" and in Arabic it retains this sense.
The Hebrew word *tsabath* which means "to join by binding together" is derived from *tsabar.* The plural of *tsabath* is used once in Holy Scripture:

Rt 2:16
"Pull out some from the bundles *(tsabathim)* for her, and leave it for her to glean."

Thus in "collecting" *(tsabar)* the darnel the harvestmen would already be thinking about "binding together" *(tsabar)* the "foolish words" *(tsabar)* to the ones who uttered them.

The Hebrew-Aramaic word for "bundle" *(tseror)* is derived from *tsarar* which is another word meaning "to bind" but especially in a figurative sense: "Bind up *(tsarar)* the testimony, seal the teaching"—

Is 8:16

Ho 13:12
"The iniquity of Ephraim is bound up *(tsarar)* and his sin is kept in store."

It is not a pleasant experience to be bound up so that the Hebrew word for "to bring to distress," "to afflict," "to straiten" or "to be in trouble" is the same word *tsarar:*

Jg 11:7
"Did you not hate me, and drive me out of my father's house? why have you come to me now when you are in trouble" *(tsarar)?*

The good ones were frequently bound by the evil ones but in the time of the harvest the tables are turned.
The righteous shall then be given power "to bring to distress" *(tsarar)* His "enemies" *(tsarar)* by "binding" *(tsarar)* them into "bundles" *(tseror)* to be burned.

Ps 74:1,4
Tsarar is also the word for "enemy."*
"O God. . .Thy enemies *(tsarar)* have roared in the midst of Thy Holy place."
But they shall roar no more when they are bound and dumbfounded.

*"STUMBLING STONES": They are praised for their "deceitful *(mirmah)* stones" *(eben)*—Micah 6:11.

*"FLUNG AWAY": Both the stumbling block and the worker of lawlessness shall be cast away. "The lives of your enemies He shall sling out as from the hollow of a sling" (I Sam. 25:29).

*"BURNED": Truth "kindles falsehoods" (Prov. 14:5 Sept.).

*"BOUND": The only way to keep the devil from roaming about (I Peter 5:8) is to bind him. This tradition is very ancient among the Semitic peoples, the Aramaic Incantation Texts from Nippur (T. 52) give specific instructions on how to "bind" one. The Lord said to Raphael: "Bind Azazel hand and foot and cast him into the darkness" (Enoch 10:4).

*"EARLY GREEK TEXT": As quoted by St. Basil (c.370 A.D.) Sermon on Humility. *See also* Cassian (*c.* 495 A.D.) Conf. VII Chapter 4 and Conf. XVII Chapter 14 for the same quotation.

*"HE COMES": "Then the Lord your God will come and all the holy ones with Him" (Zech. 14:5), "to wreak vengeance on the nations and chastisements on the peoples, to bind their kings with chains and their nobles with fetters of iron, to execute on them the judgement written. This honour have all His faithful ones" (Psalm 149:7-9). This glorious task have all His "harvestmen" *(See also* Daniel 7:22 Sept., Latin Vulgate and Syriac Text; Wisdom 3:8 and Ps. of Solomon 8:40). "Then transgression will be finished and sin come to an end and iniquity be abolished and everlasting justice be brought in" (Daniel 9:24).

*"LIARS": Both the devil who is a liar and the father of lies and those who are "of" their father the devil shall be bound and their stumbling blocks with them. They shall be kept bound in "His field" until "the world" becomes "His Kingdom" (I Cor. 15:23-28).

140

Pr 10:18 M.T.	"He who utters a slander is a fool."
Pr 26:8	"Like one who binds the stone in a sling is he who gives honor to a fool."

Because fools are often honored for their stumbling* stones.

Is 34:11   Their "stones *(eben)* of emptiness" which they offer to the hungry as bread (St. Matt. 7:9; St. Luke 11:11).

Rm 16:18   "And by smooth speech deceive the hearts of the simple-minded."

Those who honor fools for their stumbling stones
Are a stumbling block themselves
For by their praise they give weight to the slander.

A stone is placed on a sling pouch not to be kept there but to be flung* away.

Mt 13:25,41   The *"darnel"* of *"stumbling blocks"* are bound in bundles to immobilize and silence them forever

Mt 13:42,30   And also to make it easier for the angels to *"throw them into the furnace of fire"* when the time comes for them *"to be burned."**

En 54:4,5   "For whom are these chains being prepared? And he said to me: 'These are being prepared for the hosts of Azazel, *so that* they *may take and throw them* into the abyss of complete condemnation, and they shall cover their jaws with rough stones'"—
To shut them up for good.

T.L. 18:12   "Belial shall be bound by Him"— "Belial the spirit of deceit
T.J 25:3   shall be cast into the fire forever."
Tb 8:3   "The demon fled...but Raphael went and bound* him and promptly shackled him."

En 69:27   "Those who have led the world astray shall be bound with chains"
Together with their stumbling blocks (Prov. 5:22 Sept.).

Zp 1:3 M.T.   "I will destroy...stumbling blocks together with the wicked."
Si O 3:618   "The works of men's hands shall fall into the flames of fire."

Is 66:18 Early*   "I come to gather together their works and their thoughts."
Gk & L.V.

En 1:9   "Behold, He* comes with ten thousands of His holy ones to execute judgement upon all and to destroy all the ungodly...and all the works which the ungodly committed and all the hard things which ungodly sinners have spoken against Him."

For Truth established will not tolerate the scandal of lies nor the liars* who sowed and brought them up in His field.

*"*PAQAD*" means "punished" and also "judged" as in Jer. 51:47,52 (English Version of Hebrew Text).

*"TARTARUS" is the darkest of the dark places of the Abyss of Sheol. All who are taken there are first bound up (Enoch 10:4, 10-14; 20:2, Sibyline Oracles 4:186, Philo on Exec. 6 and on Cherub. 1). In this pit of Sheol fallen angels are kept in chains together with the wicked until the great and terrible day of universal judgement. The Latin Vulgate Text of 2 Peter 2:4 also emphasizes the "binding": "God spared not the angels that sinned but delivered them drawn by ropes of darkness into Tartarus." The best Greek Texts (Vaticanus, Alexandrinus, Sinaiticus and Ephraemi) also render it "chains of dungeons" or "pits." "With one chain of darkness were all bound" (Wisd. 17:17). "The wicked are darkness, Gehinnon is darkness, the depths (Tartarus) are darkness" (Genesis R. 33:1). The book of Job also brings about the relationship between being captive in the darkness and being in Tartarus: "He makes the deep to boil like a blazing cauldron and the lowest *(Tartarus)* part of the *deep* as a *captive*" (Job 41:23 Sept.). In Tartarus light shall be withheld from the wicked (Job 38:15) and all they shall "know" in the pit of hell is the darkness (2 Peter 2:17; Isaiah 65:13). "Gehinnon is black like the night" (Yebam. 109b. B. Talmud). "I tremble and weep for I am about to be led to the King of Kings, the Holy One, blessed be He, whose chains are chains forevermore" (Reply of Rabbi Jochanan ben Zakki c. 10-50 A.D. in Berakoth 28b. B. Talmud on being asked why he wept on his death bed).

*"SEEING": For they shall see the Lord gather the "bundle of the living" or the "good bundles." As Abigail said to David: "the life of my lord shall be bound *(tsarar)* in the bundle *(tseror)* of the living in the care of the Lord your God" (I Sam. 25:29). "I thank Thee, Lord, for Thou hast placed my soul in the bundle of the living" (Hymn 2:2, Dead Sea Scrolls). The righteous shall be fed with knowledge and understanding (Jer. 3:15) but the *deceitful* soul shall suffer hunger" (Prov. 19:15) for "their heart prepared deceit" (Job 15:35) their punishment is having to eat their "bread of deceit" (Prov. 20:17) thus their own "mouth shall be filled with gravel" (Prov. 20:17), with the gravel of their stumbling stones. "Scoffers" and "fools" "shall eat the fruit of their own way" (Prov. 1:22,31), the fruit of their own devices (Jer. 17:10). "Their fruits shall be unprofitable and sour to eat and fit for nothing" (Wisdom 4:5) because their own fruit is a "fruit of lies" (Hosea 10:13). "The mouth of fools feeds on foolishness" (Prov. 15:14) for they have to eat their own words, but "the lips of the righteous shall feed many" (Prov. 10:21) with the bread of His Word.

*"GLORY": "All iniquity and wickedness You will destroy forever and Your uprightness will (then) be manifested before the sight of all whom You have made" (Hymn 14:16, Dead Sea Scrolls). "Iniquity shall depart from uprightness, as darkness departs from the light" (Liturgical Frag. Q 1, Dead Sea Scrolls). "When the wicked are cut off, you shall see. . ." (Psalm 37:34 Literal Translation).

*"WAY OF TRUTH": "With the remnant which held fast to the Commandments of God, He made his covenant with Israel forever, revealing to them the hidden things. . .He unfolded before them. . .the testimonies of His righteousness and the ways of His truth" (Community Rule 3:12-15, Dead Sea Scrolls.)

142

Is 24:21,22-23.   "The Lord will punish. . .the Kings of the earth on the earth *(adamah)* they will be herded together as bound ones *(assir)* in a pit, they will be shut up in a dungeon and after many days they will be judged *(paqad*)*.
And the moon shall be confounded and the sun shall be ashamed when the Lord of Hosts shall reign in Mount Zion, and in Jerusalem, and He shall be glorified in the sight of His elders."

2 P 2:9   "The unrighteous shall be kept in bonds until the day of judgment."

2 P 2:4   "For if God did not spare the angels when they had sinned but cast them into Tartarus* and delivered them to chains of darkness to be kept until the judgment," you may be sure He shall keep

Jd 6   the evil ones and their stumbling blocks bound "in eternal chains in the nether gloom until the judgment of the great day."

And the great day of the Lord comes *after* the day He shall *act* (Mal. 3:17-18; 4:5).

2 P 3:8;   "But never forget that with the Lord one day is as a thousand
Rev 20:1-5   years, and a thousand years as one day."

The "bundles" shall remain bound up in His·field until the great day when they shall then be collected out of His Kingdom and cast into the furnace of fire.

But before then, they shall remain to see the righteous ones exalted with their Lord (St. Luke 14:14; Wisdom 4:17; Rev. 20:5; 2 Bar. 51:5-6).
And reigning with Him in "the world": "His Kingdom" (St. Matt. 8:11-12; Rev. 20:4; 11:15-18; Daniel 7:25-27).

Seeing* they shall weep and gnash their teeth in bitter anguish.

When St. Matthew wrote the gospel in Greek he used the word *deo* for "bind" and *desmas* for "bundles."
Deo also means "to imprison" and *desmas* bears a close relation to *desmos* which means "bonds" or "chains."
A *desmios* was "one bound" or a "prisoner" and he was put in a *desmoterium* where they "hold" *(tereo)* "keep" *(tereo)* "watch" *(tereo)* and "observe" *(tereo)* those in "bonds" *(desmos)* and their "bundles."

The "darnel" is collected first in order to clear the field
So that everyone may see the glory* of the unobstructed wheat.

The lies must first be bound and silenced,
That the Truth may be heard by all.

The stumbling blocks must first be removed,
2 P 2:2   Before "the way* of Truth" can be freely followed.
Ps 119:30

143

*"**MY BARN**": Our Lord was a carpenter, thus He could say: "My yoke," "My barn" and "My house" (St. Matt. 11:29-30; 13:30; 21:13; St. Luke 14:23). "If thou art pure and upright surely now He awakes for thee and has completed the habitation of thy righteousness" (Job 8:6 Literal Translation. *See also* St. John 14:2-3). God "builds" *(banah)* houses for those who fear Him (Exodus 1:21; I Sam. 2:35; 2 Sam. 7:11,27; I Kings 2:24; 11:38; Psalm 127:1).

*"**LEFT IN THE BRANCHES**": "He who sows the earth but does not reap its fruit in its season does he not lose everything?" (2 Baruch 22:5). "Through His Teaching (the Messiah's) peace will abound for us and by our gathering of His Words our sins will be forgiven us" (Targum Jonathan on Isaiah 53:5).

*"**GATHER WHAT THEY BROUGHT FORTH**": "If in thy youth thou hast not yet gathered Wisdom how wilt thou find her in your old age?" (Sirach 25:3 Syriac Text. *See also* Aboth de Rabbi Nathan Chapter 24). Hold fast to the Word of God. "Conceive Wisdom in your hearts and have Knowledge" (Sibylline Oracles 1:31 quoted by Theophilus, Bishop of Antioch, 168 A.D., *ad. Autol.* 2:36).

*"**PORTION**": The inheritance of the righteous is Truth and the Knowledge of Truth (I Peter 1:4). "Thou wilt increase his portion in the knowledge of thy Truth" (Hymn 10:29 Dead Sea Scrolls). "Abundant delights. . .Thou wilt give to the children of Thy Truth" (*ibid.*), "for Thou art a Father to all the sons of Thy Truth" (Hymn 9, Dead Sea Scrolls). "To the repentant and to those who persevere He hath appointed the lot of Truth" (Sirach 17:20 Latin Vulgate).

*"**FEAR**": "Is the seed yet in the fear *(megurah)*? yea, is the vine and the fig tree and the pomegranate and the olive tree not yet exalted *(nasa)*? from this day will I bless you" (Haggai 2:19 Literal Translation). The word *megurah* means "fear" in Hebrew. In the two other instances where it is used in Holy Scripture it also denotes "fear": "I sought the Lord and He heard me and delivered me from all my fears" *(megurah)*—Ps. 34:4. "I will choose their delusions and will bring their fears *(megurah)* upon them; because when I called none did answer and when I spoke they did not listen" (Isaiah 66:4). *Megurah* is closely related to *megorah* which also means "fear": "the fear *(megorah)* of the wicked it shall come upon him" (Prov. 10:24). Both words are derived from *magor* ("fear") and *magar* ("terror"). In turn the word *nasa* which is used in Haggai 2:19 means "to lift up," "to exalt," *i.e.*, "to bear high" upon the shoulders. *Nasa* does *not* mean "to bring forth" in the sense of fruition; the Hebrew words for that process are *yatsa* and *asah*. Wisdom, Knowledge, Truth and Understanding in Holy Scripture are often referred to in an allegorical manner as "fruits" (Psalm 1:3; Prov. 8:19; 13:2; 18:20; Isaiah 4:2; Jer. 11:16; Hosea 3:15; 14:8; Amos 6:12; Sirach 1:22; 11:3,24; 24:23; 37:25, etc.). In the enigmatic words put forth by the prophet Haggai concerning those who have finally kept the Seed of His Word in reverential fear, that He will bless them the moment they then begin to attempt to sing in exaltation the praises of His Truth, Wisdom, Knowledge and unsearchable ways. The Lord Himself at that very moment will perfect His praise, He will come to their aid and inspire them to praise Him properly. There is also a hidden word play in the expression: "is the Seed yet in the fear?" because the Hebrew word for "wheat" or "grain" is *chittah* and the Hebrew word for "dread" or "fear" as in Genesis 35:5 is also pronounced the same way: *chittah*. The moral is that we shall not be able to exalt His Truth in praise unless we have gathered His words and kept them with reverence in the barn of our holy fear.

144

Mt 13:30

Collect first the darnel—
"But gather the wheat into My* barn."

When the fruit is ripe shall it be left* in the branches?
When the grain is full shall it remain in His field?

Ho 2:9

"I will take back My wheat in its season."
Because in its season it has become fully matured
And all growth has ceased in the heart of the ground.

What is fully grown in the time of the harvest has become either good or bad.
Irrevocably (Rev. 22:10-11).

Jn 15:16
Jn 4:36

Those who have kept the Word "bring forth fruit" "unto life everlasting."
They bring forth Truth: the fruit of life (Prov. 11:30).
And in the end they gather* what they brought forth.

Rm 7:5
Jm 1:15
Rev 21:8,27

But those who have despised His Word "bring forth fruit unto death."
"Their portion* is in the lake" of "fire."

Hg 2:19

"Is the seed yet in the fear?"*
In the fear of the Lord.

Is 33:6
L.T.

Because "the fear of the Lord is His treasure" *(otsar)*
It is the "barn" *(otsar)* where He keeps His Truth, Wisdom and Knowledge (Isaiah 33:6).

The fear of the Lord is His "treasury" *(otsar)* where He keeps the "treasures" *(otsar)* of His Word *(otsar* in Hebrew means "garners," "storehouses," "treasure," "treasury").

Jb 28:28

"Behold the fear of the Lord, that *is* Wisdom."

Dt 17:19

Reverence the Word of God that you "may learn to fear the Lord."
Keep His Commandments and *prove* that you really love Him (St. John 14:15, 21, 23, 24; 15:10; St. Matt. 7:21).

True love of God is born of perfection
And perfection is the child of those who have obeyed.

Gold is proven when the dross has been burned away.
But never forget that before it is proven it must be tried in the fire.

Before the wheat is gathered it is reaped
It is threshed, winnowed, shaken and searched thoroughly in the sieve of His holy fear.

The fan in His hand that cleanses the wheat (St. Matt. 3:12; Jer. 4:11)
Shall scatter the chaff into the furnace of fire.

145

*"SOUL": Cherish the Word of God because it is precious to Him who uttered it (St. John 14:23). Never forget that "the utterance of His (God's) mouth is His treasure" (Literal Translation of Sirach 39:17 Hebrew Text), and He treasures His word. In turn the Word of God shall keep them who have kept His Word in the treasury of their hearts (St. Matt. 12:35; 2 Cor. 4:7). "If ye keep the Law ye shall be kept" (2 Baruch 84:2), in the day when "all who cleave to the mysteries of sin shall be no more" (Liturgical fragment Q.1., Dead Sea Scrolls).

*"BAR" is a Hebrew word with many meanings. Thus bar means "son" (Prov. 31:2; Ezra 5:1,2; 6:14; Dan. 3:25; 5:22; 7:13), "wheat" (Gen. 41:35,49; 42:3,25; 45:23; Job 39:4; Psalm 65:13; 72:16; Prov. 11:26; Jer. 23:28; Joel 2:24; Amos 5:11; 8:5,6), "pure" (Psalm 19:8; 24:4), "clean" (Job 11:4; Prov. 14:4) "clear" (Song of Songs 6:10), "choice" (idem. 6:9) and "field" (Dan. 2:38; 4:12, 15, 23, 25, 32). In the book of Daniel, bar is the word used for "son (bar) of man" and "son (bar) of God" (Daniel 7:13; 3:25). The Hebrew word bar is derived from the Akkadian word bararu="to shine" hence barar in Hebrew means "to purify" to be found "pure". In the end the "righteous" sons (bar) "shall shine like the sun in the Kingdom of their Father" (St. Matt. 13:43).

*"IN THIS WORLD" God is hidden from us (Isaiah 45:15) but He reveals Himself to us in His Word: the Truth (Isaiah 45:19). "But the seed of man did not understand all that Thou hast caused them to inherit, they did not discern Thee in all Thy Words and wickedly turned aside from every one of them" (Liturgical Fragment Q.I., Dead Sea Scrolls).

*"THRESHED": Wheat is gathered into the barn for storage after it has been threshed: "Whose fan is in His hand and He will thoroughly cleanse His threshing floor and gather His wheat into the barn" (St. Matt. 3:12). He will store His grain after the threshing that shall separate the wheat from the chaff. The threshing floor is the place where the wages (a share of the crop) are paid to the harvestmen (4 Ezra 4:35). We shall all undergo the tribulation of the threshing, and there in the threshing floor of the Lord we shall be cleansed and gathered if we have remained cleaved to His Word. The prophets knew that we are to be proven in the great threshing that shall surely come: "O my threshing and the son (ben) of my threshing that which I have heard from the Lord of Hosts the God of Israel, I have declared (nagad="to set forth plainly," "to expound") to you" (Isaiah 21:10). After the threshing all things shall be clear to those who shall survive it for those who shall survive it are the "bright" (barar) "sons" (bar) who are "pure" (bar-barar) as the "shining" (bar-barar) "wheat" (bar) in the threshing floor.

*"NOT SURVIVE": When "Knowledge shall fill the world, folly shall no longer exist" (Liturigcal Fragment Q.I. Dead Sea Scrolls) because "wickedness shall then be banished by righteousness as darkness is banished by the light" (idem). "There was no Satan nor any evil in the days of the life of Joseph" (Book of Jubilees 46:2) for when Joseph ruled Wisdom also reigned throughout the land. "I, Solomon. . .prayed to the Lord to cause the demons that hamper humanity to be bound. . .and I, Solomon, had much quiet in all the earth and profound peace" (Testament of Solomon 107, 108) because again in Solomon's time Wisdom reigned.

*"THOSE WHO FEAR HIM"—"otsar": Precious things and secret or confidential documents are kept in security within a "treasury": treasuries are built to hold treasures and treasures are kept in treasuries, thus the Hebrew word otsar means both "treasure" and "treasury."
We value our valuables: "where your treasure is there will your heart also be" (St. Matt. 6:21). It will be alongside your treasure within your treasury.
"The Lord loves the just" (Psalm 146:8) "for the righteous Lord loves righteousness" (Psalm 11:7; 33:5) He loves the righteousness within the hearts of those who are just. God loves those who reverence Him and do His Will (Deut. 7:13; St. John 8:29; 14:15, 21, 23) it is they who are His "friends" (St. John 15:14) and to whom He confides His innermost thoughts (St. John 15:15). The righteous become in a way the "treasury" of the Lord just as our Lord Himself is the "treasury" (of the Father) "in whom are hid all the treasures of Wisdom and Knowledge" (Colos. 2:3). He confides His precious thoughts to the righteous and they in turn treasure them in their hearts.
Reverential fear of the Lord is basically the foundation upon which our friendship with the Lord rests, and since it is through our friendship with Him that we become the recipients of the treasures of His confidences, Isaiah (33:6) rightfully said, that "the fear of the Lord is His treasure" (otsar) or "treasury" (otsar). Thus King David in Psalm 25:14 literally said: "the secret counsel (sod) of the Lord is for those who fear Him to make them know" (yada) for by disclosing to them His secret designs He brings them into His confidence to their benefit (See also Malachias 3:16-17). So let us have reverential, filial fear of the Lord for: "the fear of the Lord is the beginning of Wisdom" (Prov. 1:7) and as we persevere in this holy fear we shall begin to understand that "to fear the Lord is Wisdom's full measure" (Sirach 1:17) indeed we shall know that "the fear of the Lord that is Wisdom" (Job 28:28) and even more so "the fear of God is the beginning of love" (Sirach 25:16 L.V.)—the love of God which surpasses all Wisdom and Understanding. So have faith and hold fast to His words for "faith is the beginning of love and the end of love is knowledge of God" (Evagrius the monk, c. 370 A.D.).
Besides meaning "treasury" or "treasure" the Hebrew word otsar is also used in the sense of a "storehouse" viz., "the garners (otsar) are ruined" (Joel 1:17), "the storehouses (otsar) of food, oil and wine" (2 Chr. 11:11). In those days anything man valued was kept in an otsar, viz., the "treasuries (otsar) for silver, for gold, for precious stones" (2 Chr. 32:37).
When we disdain the treasures of His Wisdom and do not keep the wheat of His Truth we begin to fill up our own treasuries with foolish things just as King Zedekiah was found to have done when the men went into "the house of the King and the place of the treasure (otsar) and took from there (the treasury) old worn out clouts and rotten rags" (Jeremiah 38:11, Literal Translation). Foolish Zedekiah did not hearken to the good counsel of Jeremiah the prophet (Jeremiah 37:1-2) but listened instead to false advisors (Jer. 37:19; 38:4-5).
The lesson of the treasury is that we must listen to good "counsel" (melak) or we shall end up as King Zedekiah did (Jer. 39:4-7) who kept "rotten rags" (melachim) in his "treasury."

146

Cherish the Word of God because it is the grain and sustenance of your soul.*
Keep His Word inside of you and cleave to it as the husk cleaves to the seed.

Do not exchange the Truth of His Word
For the empty darnel of lies.

Jr 23:28

For "what is the chaff to the wheat" *(bar)* of His Word?

Ps 2:12 M.T.

"Kiss the wheat *(bar*)* lest He be angry and ye perish in the way when suddenly His wrath is kindled."

Kiss the "choice" *(bar)*, "pure" *(bar)*, "clean" *(bar)*, "clear" *(bar)*, "chosen" *(bar)* "wheat" *(bar)* of His "field" *(bar)*
For there is nothing like it in* this world.

If the Word which was sown as "good seed" is stored as uncovered "wheat" it is because it has been threshed.*
Hidden Truth becomes revealed after the threshing that shall scatter all lies to the wind.

Mt 24:21,29

The "great tribulation" of the threshing shall come in the time of the harvest.

Is 38:19,18

"The living. . .the living shall make known Thy *Truth*. . ." but "those going down into the pit have no hope for Thy Truth."
Because the wicked shall not* survive the threshing.

Pr 12:19
Qo 9:11

In the day "the lip of Truth is established forever": "the righteous and the wise and their works are in the hand of God": safe and sound.

For the special treasure of the Lord are those* who fear Him (Mal. 3:16-17).
It is they who really are: His "barn."

Pr 2:7
Is 33:6

"The Lord stores up Wisdom for the upright" *in themselves.*
For *"His"* "treasury" *(otsar)* or "storehouse" *(otsar*)* is "the fear of the Lord" and it is the upright who possess this holy fear.

Si 1:21
L.V.

The storehouses of Wisdom are the righteous.
Of them it is said that "Wisdom shall fill all her storehouses with her treasures"—*in the time of the harvest.*
Because it is *then* that all storehouses are *"filled."*

Si 1:26

"In the treasures of Wisdom is understanding and knowledge"
For those who have held His Word fast to the very end.

Si 1:24

In the end it is through the lips of the righteous that "Wisdom shall distribute knowledge and understanding."

En 5:8

"Wisdom shall be given to the upright,"
That they may turn all hearts to one another and all souls to God (Prov. 11:30 L.V. and A.V.).

147

*"NOON": As it finally rises to light up the darkness of the world, the rising sun is then allegorically called the "sun of Understanding" (Wisdom 5:6 Latin Vulgate and Old Latin Texts) for it is the "sun" that shall bring the "dawn" of understanding into the hearts of the righteous who have held fast to His Words (2 Peter 1:19). Hence this sun is also called the "sun of righteousness" (Wisdom 5:6 Greek Text). When the eyes of our hearts shall see the light it is time to "wake up" and repent because the "sun of understanding" inexorably continues on its heavenly course to become the blazing "sun of justice" (Malachias 4:2,1) at noon. "He will bring forth thy judgment as the noon" (Ps. 37:6).

148

Ps 43:3	If we do not live according to the Truth, we walk in the darkness (I John 1:6,7). "Send forth Thy Light and Thy Truth."
1 Jn 1:5	"God is Light." He is our light and our salvation (Psalm 27:1), In His light we see light (Psalm 36:9).
	If we follow Him we shall walk unafraid, For His Word is a lamp to our feet and a light to our path (Ps. 119:105).
	Those who keep His Word have light in themselves (St. John 8:12), A light enkindled by obedience to His precepts.
T.Z. 9:8	"The Lord Himself is the light of the righteous" For He abides in those who keep the Word of God (St. John 14:23; 2 Cor. 4:6).
Jn 1:9	He is "the true light that enlightens every man coming to the World."
Jn 12:36	"Believe in the light that you may become children of light."
Ps 97:11 Eph 5:9 L.T.	"Light is sown for the righteous." For it is they who hold fast to the seed of His Word and bring forth "the fruit of light" *(photos).*
Ho 6:5 Lk 17:24	"His judgments shall go forth as a light." "As the lightning flashes and lights up the sky from one part of the heavens to the other."
Mt 24:27 Zp 3:5	And "as the lightning which comes from the east and shines as far as the west": "He will bring His judgment to light"
	Suddenly.
Ps 85:11 Ho 10:4 Sept. Is 61:11	When "Truth shall spring out of the earth": "Judgment shall spring up" *also.* "The Lord shall make justice to spring forth" from the "ground" in His field.
Si 32:20 L.V.	"They that fear the Lord shall find just judgment and shall kindle justice as a light."
Ps 37:5,6	"Trust in Him. . .He will do it. He will bring forth your justice as a light and your judgment as the noonday" if you have been righteous, otherwise you shall not see the glory of His light.
Ws 5:6 L.V.	And you shall cry: "We have erred from the way of Truth and the light of justice has not shined upon us and the sun of understanding has not risen upon us."
	Repent! Repent! Because the rising sun of Understanding brings judgment at noon.*

*"SEED": Do not adhere to the darnel of lies. Be determined like David who said: "I will not set before my eyes any worthless thing. I hate the work of those who turn aside (setim=to apostatize) it shall not cleave to me" (Psalm 101:3) because the doings of those who rebel against God are a work of lies. We cleave to what we love. "Hate evil and love good" (Amos 5:15); "abhor what is evil and cleave to what is good" (Romans 12:9). In other words stick to the "good Word of God" (Hebrew 6:5) discard all lies so that you may say to Him in the end: "I have chosen the way of Truth. . .I have adhered to Thy testimonies" (Psalm 119:30,31).

*"CHILDREN SEEDS": The seeds that are found in the fruit are identical and true to the seed that was sown. The reward of the patient holding fast of the seed by the "ground" is the tasty fruit brought forth from it: the glorious fruit of understanding bearing within it the well arrayed children seeds of Truth. It is the orderly marshalling of the grains of Truth in the full ear that confronts and scatters the disarrayed fruit of lies.
"With whom wilt thou find the fight for the Law? with him in whose hands are bundles of laws of the Mishnah" (Midrash Rabbah on Leviticus 21, Munich MS.) The convincing rebuttal that will convict deceit shall be found in the lips of the righteous bringing forth the ripe ears of grain full of well ordered seeds of Truth. This is the hope of the just towards the day of "the acknowledging of the Truth" (Titus 1:1) by all men (Coloss. 2:2-3; 2 Tim. 2:25; Philemon 6). The perfect reign of God in the heart of man shall be made manifest through the power of a well ordered Understanding and not in mere empty loud words (I Cor. 4:19-20).

*"ISAIAH 21:10": "O my threshing and the son (ben) of my threshing, what I have heard from the Lord of Hosts, the God of Israel, I declare to you" (Literal Translation). Ben means "son" not "corn" or "grain". Isaiah could have used the Hebrew word bar and meant both "grain" and "son" but he elected to use ben so that there would be no misunderstanding that the survivor of the travail of threshing is a true "son" (ben) ready to understand.
The "threshing" is a testing time that both the good and the bad have to undergo. For "the Lord tests the righteous and the wicked—on the wicked He will rain coals of fire and brimstone; a scorching wind shall be the portion of their cup. Because the Lord is righteous. He loves righteous deeds; the upright shall behold His face" (Ps. 11:5, 6-7). The upright shall see God for they shall have been purified by the threshing, the portion of their cup is not a scorching wind but the spirit of Understanding. "When His anger burneth but a little, O the happiness of all trusting in Him" (Ps. 2:12 Literal Translation). Happy shall they be indeed for "they that trust in Him shall understand Truth" (Wisdom 3:9). "O the happiness of a man" who understands Wisdom (Prov. 3:13) and has knowledge of the Truth within.
The time of the threshing is also the time the wheat of His Word is bared, i.e., "revealed", it is also the time of the flailing when we shall learn that the "rod for the back of him who is void of understanding" (Prov. 10:13) is the same "rod and reproof that give Wisdom" (Prov. 29:15) to those who understand. The threshing floor is the place of admonishment. Thus in the time of our Lord the chamber where the Sanhedrin sat to deliberate and to judge was known as the "threshing floor of admonishment" (See Sanhedrin 36b B.T. and Midrash Rabbah on Canticles 7:3). When we are "admonished" (zahara) we shall see the "light" (zahara).

*"HIS BARN CALLED: THE FEAR OF THE LORD": "We are His houses" (Hebrews 3:6) and we "are God's building" (1 Cor. 3:9) if we hold fast to His Word. The same thought is found in the Dead Sea Scrolls: "He has joined their assembly to the sons of heaven to be a Council of the Community, a foundation of the building of Holiness" (Community Rule 11:8, Dead Sea Scrolls). Thus the congregation of the righteous are His "barn" or "storehouse." "When the righteous shall appear. . .and when the Righteous One shall appear before the eyes of the righteous. . .the righteous and Elect One shall cause the house of His gathering to appear" (Enoch 38:1-2; 53:6).

The righteous are good because they obey and keep the Word of God.
They cherish the "wheat" of His Word and cleave to it as the husk adheres to the seed.*

1 Co 3:9 The righteous are the ground that holds fast to the seed that was sown.
They are "God's tilled field" *(georgion)*.
It is they who bring forth the fruit full of children* seeds.

The roots of His standing grain are set firm in the hearts of the righteous.
The heavenly plant springs forth from within themselves.

The time of the harvest comes when some of the grain is released to seal and sanctify the ground that bore it.
The ground that held fast to the Word and brought forth the glory of His Truth.

There comes a time when the standing grain must be gathered because it has become fully matured.
Then the righteous souls who have cleaved to Him (Ps. 63:8) shall no longer remain bound to the ground.

1 S 25:29 His faithful ones shall be gathered (Ps. 50:5) into "the bundle of the living" and taken to the threshing floor to prove their worth.
And also their right to be called: His children (Isaiah* 21:10).

As gold is tried in the fire so is the wheat tried in the threshing that separates it from the stubble and chaff (St. Matt. 3:12; St. Luke 3:17; Amos 9:9).
The threshing floor cleanses, and reveals those who have endured to the very end.

It is after the great threshing that Truth shall be made manifest to all.
Because there in the threshing floor shall the bare wheat be revealed.

The great tribulation of the threshing shall come so that we may learn to fear God again
And truly love Him as our Saviour.

From the threshing floor the choice wheat is gathered into His* barn called: "the fear of the Lord", to remind us of the threshing.

Not forever shall He thresh His finest grain (Isaiah 28:28)
For the sake of the chosen those days shall be shortened (St. Matt. 24:22).

1 Co 3:9
Mt 13:30
And for the sake of the pure, clear, choice, and chosen wheat of His field, Truth shall be kept forever in "God's building"· His *"barn":* the *righteous* themselves.

*"ARK": "Just as there was a flood of water. . .there will be a flood of fire and the earth will be burnt up together with its mountains. . .and the just shall be delivered from its fury as their fellows in the ark were saved from the waters of the Deluge" (St. Melito, Bishop of Sardis, c. 150-170 A.D.).
In the Day "when the wicked are burnt up, God makes a tent in which He hides the just" (Siphra, fol. 187 B. Talmud). When tribulation comes, the just seek refuge in Truth, they are not like the wicked, who make lies their refuge and seek shelter in falsehood (Isaiah 28:15, 17). Hence "the son that keeps the Word shall be free from destruction" (Prov. 29:27 L.V.), he shall be safe because the Word shall keep him in the end (Rev. 3:10). For "the mercy of the Lord is upon them that love Him in Truth" (Ps. of Sol. 10:4).

*"REFINE": The prophets foretold about the coming "fire" that is to consume the wicked and refine the just: "In the whole land says the Lord, two thirds shall be cut off and perish and one third shall be left alive. And I will refine them as silver is refined and test them as gold is tested" (Zech. 13:8, 9. See also I Peter 1:7; 2 Peter 3:6-7, 10-11; 1:19; I Cor. 3:13-15). The refining is to take place in the time of the glorious coming of the Lord: "Who can endure the day of His coming and who can stand when He appears? For He is like a refiner's fire and. . .He will sit as a refiner and purifier of silver and He will purify the sons of Levi and refine them like gold and silver" (Mal. 3:2,3).
The Lord will indeed refine them through the cleansing fire. There is a parallel in Holy Scripture between being "clean" and being "holy" (See Lev. 10:10; Ezek. 22:26; 44:23, etc.) and invariably this cleansing is done by "fire." "God hath tried them. . .in the time of their Visitation they shall shine forth" (Wisdom 3:5,6,7; St. Matt. 13:43). "Then shall they be known, who are My chosen; and they shall be tried as the gold in the fire" (2 Esdras 16:73). "When He has tested me I shall shine as gold" (Job 23:10).

*"HOLINESS": The aim of righteousness is holiness for "without holiness no one shall see the Lord" (Hebrews 12:14). Only "the pure in heart. . .shall see God" (St. Matt. 5:8) for "who shall stand in His holy place? He who has clean hands and a pure (bar) heart" (Ps. 24:3,4). We 'perfect holiness in the fear of the Lord' (2 Cor. 7:1) and fulfill the Law so that we may thereby become holy before the Lord and be "renewed. . .and put on the new nature created after the likeness of God in true righteousness and holiness" (Eph. 4:24). Thus "having been set free from sin we. . .become slaves of righteousness" (Rom. 6:18) "obedient from the heart to the standard of Teaching" (Rom. 6:17) in that "obedience which leads to righteousness" (Rom. 6:16), a "righteousness unto holiness" (Rom. 6:19). The reward of the righteous is the fruit of holiness (Rom. 6:22) full of the seeds of understanding and Truth so that they may be able to praise Him well.
The true children of God are the holy just ones and it is they who "shall shine like the sun in the Kingdom of their Father" (St. Matt. 13:43). They shall shine "then" because to be "holy" is to "shine". The Hebrew word for "holy" is qadosh, derived from the Akkadian word qadashu which means "bright" or "shiny." Thus the brightness of fire is strikingly and most frequently associated with the holiness of God. In Holy Scripture the most characteristic Theophany is a manifestation through the brightness of fire (Exod. 3:2-3; 19:18; 24:17; Deut. 4:12, 24; 5:22-27; Ps. 18:8-14; 2 Sam. 22:9-15; Ezek. 1:4-28; Heb. 3:3-4 etc.). With particular emphasis on the eschatology of St. Matt. 13:40-43, the Visitation in the Day of the Lord is associated with great light and an avenging fire (Isaiah 30:26-28; 5:24; 9:18-19; 34:8-10; 47:14; Zeph. 1:18; Joel 2:3-5 etc.). The same imagery is found in the New Testament (St. Luke 12:49; 17:24; St. Matt. 3:11; 24:27; Acts 2:1-4; Heb. 12:26-29, etc.). The same fire that clears the field of all the weeds chaff and stubble also enriches the field for the time of the re-seeding and the glorious new growth (Joel 2:3, 19; Ps. 72:6; Amos 7:1).

Things are stored in order to preserve them.

The fear of the Lord is a barn built like an ark*
To shelter the righteous from the storm of fire (2 Peter 3:7).

Ps 72:6 AV
4 Ezr 4:29

Because after the wheat is gathered, the field is burned.
It is set on fire to clear it thoroughly of all the weeds and
make it "new" again.

Lk 12:49

He "came to cast fire upon the earth"
And if He longs that it be kindled it is because His fire purifies
(Jer. 23:29).

1 Co 3:13

It reveals all things by its brightness and it "tries what sort of
work each one has done."

Is 1:25 L.T.

"He shall refine* *(tsaraph)* as purity *(bor)* thy dross,"
And that kind of refining is done by fire.

Pr 30:5

The sword of His Word unsheathed, is a sword of fire.
"Every Word of God is fire-tried" *(tsaraph)* no lie shall stand
beside it.
Every deceit shall be consumed.

Dn 12:10

And everyone holding His Word fast on the Day it is unsheathed
shall be "purified *(barar)*,. . .and tried" *(tsaraph)*
Only the "sons" *(bar)* holding His "wheat" *(bar)* shall survive the
fire of the Lord (I Cor. 3:14-15).

Sg 6:11

They shall be cleansed and they shall be resplendent in holiness.*
"Fair as the moon and bright *(bar)* as the sun."

But all the stumbling blocks of the "foolish" *(baar)* shall be
"burnt" *(baar)* away.
The foolish ones bound to them shall not be around when all
things are "made plain" *(bah-ar)* to the righteous
When all things are made "clear" *(bar)* to the "sons" *(bar)*.

Mt 13:43

"Then shall the righteous shine forth as the sun in the Kingdom
of their Father.
He who has ears to hear, let him hear,"

And let him depart from evil that he may understand (Job
28:28).

Pr 30:1 Sept.

"My son reverence My Words, receive them and repent"
For those who understand and do not repent—it shall not be
forgiven them (St. Matt. 13:15; 12:32; St. Luke 12:42-48; St.
John 9:41; Romans 1:32; Heb. 6:4-6; 10:26-29; 2 Peter 2:20-21;
Ep. of Barnabas 5:4; 4 Ezra 7:71; Sirach 4:18-19 H.T.; 26:28
Sept.; Prov. 21:15-16).

Those who despise the Light shall sit in the darkness forever,
There to weep and gnash their teeth in vain.

153

*"**SHINE**": In the intertestamental era, an instruction that gave insight was said to "shine," *i.e.*, make things lucid. Thus in the Psalm Scroll recovered from Cave 11 (Quamran) the preface to Psalm 140 states that "David the son of Jesse was wise and a light" (See 2 Sam. 23:3-4), and that his compositions (the Psalms) are "like the light of the sun, well written." In another Psalm the Word of God is likened to the sun running its course (Ps. 19:2-7; 2 Thess 3:1).

*"**WISDOM AND UNDERSTANDING**": We may be aware of the wise and be acquainted with them and hear or read their wise sayings and be able to repeat them but only those who are good can fully understand Wisdom and bring the Knowledge of Wisdom to light. Because those who are good have departed from evil and having done so they are the ones who truly understand (Job 28:28).
   Those who understand Wisdom possess her in righteousness. Thus it is that: "the mouth of the righteous brings forth Wisdom" (Prov. 10:31) and "on the lips of him who has understanding Wisdom is found" (Prov. 10:13) for he who has understanding is righteous. "The knowledge of the righteous is Understanding" (Prov. 9:10 Syriac Text) and so is "the counsel of the holy ones" *(idem.,* Sept.) because in the words of Daniel 2:21: "God. . .gives Knowledge to those who really understand"—the righteous ones.

*"**LIGHT**": "Wisdom excels folly just as light excels darkness" (Eccle. 2:13) for "Wisdom is more beautiful than the sun. . .being compared with light she is found to be before it for light is succeeded by night but against Wisdom evil does not prevail. Wisdom reaches mightily from one end of the earth to the other" (Wisdom 7:29-30; 8:1). "I chose to have Wisdom rather than light because her bright shining never sets" (Wisdom 7:10). "Wisdom is radiant and unfading" (Wisdom 6:17) and so "Wisdom shines in the face of the wise" (Prov. 17:24 Latin Vulgate).
   The righteous are the ones who will shine and they are the ones who shall "bring the Knowledge of Wisdom to light" (Wisdom 6:24 L.V.) because those who are good revere the Word of God and they "Will not pass over the Truth" *(idem.).*

*"**UNDERSTAND**": Only the good can truly understand the Wisdom of God. Thus St. Paul says: "Wisdom we speak among the perfect" (I Cor. 2:6) for "Wisdom will not enter a deceitful soul, nor dwell in a body enslaved to sin" (Wisdom 1:4).
"Wisdom goes about seeking them that are worthy of her" (Wisdom 6:16) and have proven that they love her. "Love for Wisdom is the keeping of her laws" (Wisdom 6:18; St. John 14:15, 23). Thus "he who holds to the Law will obtain Wisdom" (Sirach 15:1; Deut. 4:6, 9-10) because Wisdom "goes for" those who are good.

*"**LAW**": In the reverent observance of doing what He commands, we "keep" His Law i.e., His "Teaching" *(torah).* In the faithful keeping of His Law we shall continually remember Him (Deut. 5:12; Exod. 20:8).
True Wisdom and Understanding are a reward from God to those who are faithful to His Commandments (Deut. 4:6, 9-10). Keep this in mind and "meditate in the fear of the Most High and think upon His Commandments continually then He will instruct thine heart and thy desire for Wisdom shall be given unto thee" (Sir. 6:37).
"To the man who is good in His sight He has given Wisdom and Knowledge and joy" (Eccle. 2:26). Truly "Thou. . .revealest what is hidden to the pure who in faith have submitted themselves to Thee and Thy Law" (2 Baruch 54:5). Truly "Thou, O Lord my God, hast revealed to the ear of Thy servant" (2 Sam. 7:27 L.V.) that there are few things hidden from those "who in the fear of the Lord are wise and understanding" (2 Bar. 46:5).
"What is the greatest Wisdom of all?
The Wisdom of being good and doing good" (B. Talmud. *See also* Wisdom 8:7).

*"**THOSE WHO KNOW**" are the children of His Truth for "all the children of His Truth shall rejoice in eternal knowledge" (War Rule 17:8 Dead Sea Scrolls) and knowing they shall shine because they possess the "light of Knowledge" (Test of Benjamin 11:2) and "a man's Wisdom makes his face to shine" (Eccle. 8:1).
Furthermore "all the children of righteousness are ruled by the Prince of Light and walk in the ways of light but all the children of falsehood are ruled by the angel of darkness and walk the way of darkness" (Community Rule 3:20-21, Dead Sea Scrolls). Thus the "children of His Truth" are the "children of righteousness" *i.e.,* those who espouse the cause of Truth—His righteous ones.

154

Si 1:1 En 5:8 Pr 2:7	"All Wisdom comes from the Lord." "Wisdom shall be given to the righteous." For they have departed from evil and are able to understand it. (Job 28:28).
Si 16:25 L.V.	Wisdom is given to those with understanding so that they may teach and "show forth in Truth His knowledge."
Si 24:32,34 Si 24:27	The righteous who understand shall "make instruction shine* forth like the dawn. . .shine afar. . .for all those who seek instruction." They shall "make instruction shine forth like light,"
	Because they shall instruct with Wisdom* and Understanding.
Ws 7:26	"Wisdom is the brightness of eternal light*. . .the unspotted mirror of God's majesty and the image of His goodness."
Ba 4:2 Ws 6:23 L.V. Qo 8:1	"Walk towards Wisdom shining in the presence of her light" and bask in the "light of Wisdom." For "a man's Wisdom makes his face to shine. . .his face is changed to brightness."
Pr 14:33	If you want to be truly wise be righteous first so that you may understand* His Wisdom. "Wisdom rests in the heart of him that has understanding" because Wisdom rests only in the hearts of those who are righteous, compassionate and pure.
Si 33:3	No one is given true understanding unless he departs from evil. "A man of understanding is faithful to the law* of God." A righteous man is faithful to His Word.
Pr 6:23	He knows "the law is a light" and the Word of God is a light, a light to his path and a lamp in his hand to find Truth (Ps. 119:105).
	Because Truth is the glory of Wisdom.
Ws 5:6; 2 P 2:2	The truly wise walk "the way of Truth" and are guided by His Commandments. Having departed from evil they understand (Job 28:28).
Si 18:28 Jn 8:31-32 Ws 3:9	"Every man of understanding knows Wisdom." He knows that those who hold His Words fast "shall know the Truth" and "they that trust in Him shall understand" it.
	It is those* who know and understand the Truth who shall shine. For Truth is the Light that shall banish the darkness (I John 1:6; St. John 14:6; 8:12).

155

*"ARISE": The word "arise" has many eschatological connotations in Holy Scripture, e.g., "arise, shine, for thy light is come and the glory of the Lord is risen upon thee. For behold, the darkness shall cover the earth and thick darkness the people but the Lord shall arise upon thee and His glory shall be seen upon thee. . .the Lord shall be thine everlasting light" (Isaiah 60:1-2, 19; See also Isaiah 2:19; 26:19; 31:2; Psalms 12:5; 76:9; 82:8; 132:8; 149:4-5; Mal. 42:2; Eph. 5:14; Enoch 58:4-5,6; Eth. Secrets of Enoch 39:7; Asc. of Isaiah 8:22, etc.). Whenever the Lord is said to "arise," He arises to judge and punish the wicked, and to give "light" to the just for "unto the upright there arises light" (Ps. 112:4; Wisdom 18:1). Not so for the wicked who shall cry out: "we have erred from the way of Truth and the light of righteousness has not shined unto us nor has the sun of understanding risen upon us" (Wisdom 5:6 L.V.). The Midrash Rabbah on Ps. 11:7 states that: "as for the upright their faces shall shine" because "the upright shall behold his face" (Ps. 11:7; Dan. 2:22).
Remember that "light is sown for the righteous" (Ps. 97:11), the "light" that is found within the Seed of His Word which the righteous hold in the ground of their good hearts and which "unfolds" in them to give them "light and understanding" (Ps. 119:130). If it is "His Word that makes His mighty servant (the sun) brilliant" (Sirach 43:5 Hebrew Text) shall it not also make His other servants to shine? "As the sun and the moon give light in this world so the righteous will give light in the world to come" (Midrash Rabbah on Ps. 72:5). "In the future the righteous will shed light" (Pirke de Rabbi Eliezer, Chapter IV), thus the great Rabbi Gamaliel who led an exemplary life and was full of wisdom and understanding was referred to by later Rabbis as "that sun in Israel" (B. Talmud) for he not only instructed but gave light by his good example. So keep the Seed of His Word for "what will happen to those who have kept the Words of the Torah? It is to them that Scripture says: 'arise, shine for thy light is come' " (Midrash Rabbah on Ps. 119:88 Sect. 34; See also Job 11:13, 17; Ps. 37:5,6). Indeed "the holy and wise man is as unchanging as the sun" (Sirach 27:11 L.V.). Be good then and "He will bring forth thy righteousness as a light" (Ps. 37:6).

*"WISE (maskilim)": in Holy Scripture the usual word for "wise man" is hakam (hakkim, plural) derived from hokmah the Hebrew word for "wisdom." The word maskilim (plural of maskil) is rendered the "wise" in Daniel 12:3 (AV. RV., RSV, NEB.) but it means more than that. Maskil is derived from the verb haskil which means "to teach" or "to make to understand." From the same verb we have the related Hebrew word sakal and sekel which mean "good understanding" and also "to teach expertly." The maskilim are those who possess sakal so that they can haskil well.
Sakal ("good understanding") is a gift from the Holy Spirit and it brings along with it haskil, the ability to teach well so as to give the well disposed hearer perfect understanding in a matter. Sakal is possessed only by those who are good for it is a reward of righteousness (Prov. 1:3; 3:4; Deut. 29:9; Josh. 1:7,8; I Kings 2:3). Thus a maskil is a righteous man, a master of instruction who teaches both by example and by word. The Dead Sea Scrolls reveal that the Essenes had three types of teachers: the mebaqqer, the Levite Priest and the maskilim, The mebaqqer instructed on biblical history, the Levite Priest taught the Precepts of the Law but it was to the maskilim that the instruction of the finer points of the Torah: the secret spiritual meaning of the texts and the interpretation of prophecies was delegated to. The maskilim held the highest rank and spiritual prestige in the Community because they possessed the gift of sakal, i.e., the ability to bring to light the true meaning of an obscure text and the correct interpretation of an enigmatic one. They were held in high regard because Essenes judged the spiritual worth of a man according to the measure of "fine understanding" (sakal) that he was endowed with by the Lord: "A good understanding (sakal) have all those that do His Commandments" (Ps. 111:10. See Community Rule 5:23-25; Zadokite Document 12:21; Manual of Discipline 9:12-14, 18, 21; Thanksgiving Hymns 1:29-33; 12:22,23). Thus it was the maskil "who guided them with Knowledge and instructed them in the wonderful mysteries of His Truth" (Manual of Discipline 9:12,18-19) and "opened their eyes to see and understand how God acts" (Zadokite Document 2:14) because the maskil possessed sakal and it is sakal that gives us "to understand (sakal) His ways" (Job 34:27), and "to understand (sakal) His doings" (Ps. 64:9) and "to understand" (sakal) His "wonders" (Ps. 106:7) and "to understand" (sakal) the "writings" of the Lord (I Chr. 28:19). We must not forget that these things of the Lord are only understood by those close to Him whom He takes into His confidence. For "who has stood in the counsel of the Lord?" (Job 27:18). Have you heard "the secret counsel of God?" (Job 15:8). Let us be good for "the secret counsel of the Lord is with those who reverence Him, He will make them know". . .(Ps. 25:14) for "His secret is with the righteous" (Prov. 3:32; Amos 3:7). In turn it is left to the righteous maskilim to convincingly refute error and exalt the Truth and by their excellent understanding to winningly exhort sinners to return to the Lord. "By His knowledge shall My righteous servant make the many righteous" (Isaiah 53:11) by "speaking the fruit of His Peace to convert the souls of them who are willing to come to Him" (Odes of Solomon 10:33) and teaching well "to show forth in Truth His Knowledge" (Sirach 16:25 L.V.) so "that we might turn from our iniquities and understand his Truth" (Daniel 9:13). Truly it is "they that are understanding (maskilim) among the people who shall make many to understand" (Daniel 11:3) for being "wise in understanding" (2 Baruch 66:2; 46:5) they shall be able to convince their hearers that it is worthwhile "to depart from evil" and thereby understand (Job 28:28; Dan. 9:13). Above all, the instruction of a maskil is effective because he teaches by good example for "whosoever teaches noble things and does them" (Testament of Levi 13:9) lives what he preaches (Acts 1:1). "Truth comes to those who practice it" (Sirach 27:9 Sept.) As the Rabbis said: "when is the teaching of the Lord trustworthy? when it comes from the mouth of a faithful man" (Midrash Rabbah on Ps. 19:8 Sect. 14) for they knew that "Wisdom shall be made plain in the mouth of the faithful" (Sirach 34:8 L.V.; Prov. 10:31). For God has given "understanding into the knowledge of the Most High to the upright and the wisdom of the sons of heaven to the perfect" (Community Rule 4:22 D.S.S.; 1 Cor. 2:6) so that it is these "righteous" ones who "shall shine like the sun in the Kingdom of their Father" in heaven. They shall "shine" (zahar) then for they shall "teach" (zahar="to teach" also as in Exod. 18:20) and throw light on difficult subjects when the time comes for all to understand the glorious Truth of His Word.

T.J. 24:1	"A man shall arise* from my seed (Judah) as the sun of righteousness."
T.L. 18:4	"He shall shine forth as the sun on the earth and shall remove all darkness from under heaven and there shall be peace in all the earth."
T.Z. 9:8 Ml 4:2	"The Lord Himself is the Light of righteousness and healing and compassion shall be in His wings."
T.L. 14:3,4	"The lights of Israel shall be as the sun and moon; bright and pure before the Gentiles."
2 Esd 7:125 RSV	"The faces of those who have practiced self control shall shine more than the stars."
2 Esd 7:88,97	"Those who have kept the ways of the Most High. . .their face is to shine like the sun."
	The Wisdom of God always bears the seal of Truth.
Dn 12:3	The "wise" *(maskilim)* * who "shall shine like the brightness of the firmament" are the *righteous wise:* His holy ones (Ps. 11:7).
Mt 13:43	For He said it is *"the righteous"* who *"shall shine forth like the sun in the Kingdom of their Father."*
Jm 1:17	It is they who are the children of "the Father of lights, with whom there is no change, nor shadow of alteration."
Jn 12:36	"The children of light" are those who believe and hold fast to His Word.
Jn 8:12	The Word of "the Light of the world."
Is 15:29	"The Glory of Israel will not lie" Because the Lord is Light and Truth (1 John 1:5; St. John 14:6).
Jm 1:18 2 Esd 14:25	It is in the hearts of those who hold fast to His "Word of Truth," That He shall come to light "the lamp of Understanding": the Truth of His Word (Wisdom 3:9).
	Hold fast to the Truth.

*"**SEED PIPE**": A good illustration of this type of plow is found in a 7th Century obelisk of King Essarhadon of Assyria (See the Biblical Archaeologist Vol. XVIII Sept. '55, Fig. 1.). The Ugaritic tablets recovered at Ras-Ash Shamrah mention "the wheat in furrows" (Legend of Keret 2.3.5.) and again in another tablet: "sweet to the wheat in the furrow, to the spelt in the tilled row" (U.T. 126 III: 9-10).
In the Enuma Elish epic a god is described as the "Irrigator of heaven and earth, who establishes seed rows and plows land. . .who delineates the furrow" (U.T. VII fol. 60). This system of sowing was prevalent in later times as seen in the Targum to Isaiah 28:25: "bring them near, families by families to their tribes, even as the seeds of wheat in rows and barley in the appointed places."

"*SUM*" means "to put in a proper place," the El-Amarna tablet 155:20-21 verifies this early usage of the word. *Sum* also means "to appoint" for a specific purpose. *(See* Exod. 9:5; Num. 4:19; I Sam. 8:11,12; Jer. 33:25, etc.).

*"**DIRECTS HIM**": The twenty-eighth Chapter of the Book of Isaiah from which this verse is taken concerns the "scoffers" and how they are to be humbled by someone who shall do it competently because he has been taught by God. Thus in Chapter 28 Isaiah excoriates the "proud," "the priest and (false) prophet" who "are confused with wine" and "reel with strong drink" and who "err in vision and stumble in giving judgment" because they have become "scoffers" "making lies their refuge and falsehood their shelter" (Isaiah 28:1,7,14,15). Isaiah castigates them for having become derelict in their duties of counseling the people, feeding them with knowledge and understanding (Jer. 3:15) doing justice in their behalf and interpreting the Law for them (2 Chr. 19:8-10; Neh. 8:8; Mal. 2:6-7). In the same Chapter Isaiah exhorts the listener: "now, therefore do not scoff" for when the time comes the Lord "will teach knowledge and. . .explain the Message" (Isaiah 28:22,9) to the little ones who trust in the Lord and are better disposed to receive instruction from Him than are the proud scoffers who arrogantly rely on their own judgment. His instruction is always for the little ones (St. Matt. 11:25) who hunger and ask the Father for food as children do "who are weaned from the milk" and are "taken from the breast" (Isaiah 28:9). Having been deprived of the "milk" of His Word (I Peter 2:2; Heb. 5:12) through the laxness of their "mother" (priest and prophet source of the Word), the famished little ones cry out to the Lord and thus it is to them that He shall apportion the bread of judgment (Heb. 5:12). From among the little ones shall arise the "mighty and strong one" (Isaiah 28:2) who shall humble the proud and excoriate the "scoffers" with "precept upon precept, precept upon precept; line upon line, line upon line; here a little, there a little" (Isaiah 28:13) using "the Word of the Lord" as a rod of instruction methodically and unremittingly until they "go and fall backward, and be broken, and snared and taken" (*idem.*) through superior argumentation. Just as "the plowman" in Isaiah 28:24-28 knows how to plant things well because "he is instructed aright" so will the chosen one of the Lord know how to place His Words well "for his God does instruct him—and does teach him" for "judgment" (*mishpat*)—Isaiah 28:26.
When the Wisdom and Power of the Lord shall be made manifest in the process of humiliating the proud, the people shall then praise the Lord and say wholeheartedly of Him: "He hath made counsel wonderful, He hath made Wisdom great!" (Isaiah 28:29).
The Wisdom of God is made manifest in the wonderful ordering of His Words in the field of Scripture. Thus in Isaiah 28:24,25 "the plowman" "places *(sum)* in the ordered *(sorah)* wheat and the appointed *(saman)* barley and rye in their proper *(sorah)* place." We know that *sum* means "to place properly." In turn *sorah* and *saman* are unique words found only in Isaiah 28:25. The Hebrew word *sorah* denotes "distinctness," "choice separatedness," a thing carefully set apart. *Sorah* is related to two other rare words *soreq* and *soreqah* that are found only in Genesis 49:11; Isaiah 5:2; Jeremiah 2:21 where again these also evoke the sense of "selectedness," "choiceness" and "nobility of stock" in all three instances they denote the Lord's own planting which He rightly implants. Thus it is no ordinary "wheat" *(chittah)* that the particular "plowman" in Isaiah 28:24 sows *(zara)* but "choice" *(sorah)* or "special" *(sorah)* "ordered *(sorah)* wheat" *(chittah)* which he "places" *(sum* not *zara)* "properly" *(sorah)* in His field. The "barley" *(seorah)* is no ordinary "barley" but "the appointed *(saman)* barley *(seorah).*"
Saman is related to *zaman:* "appointed" *(See* Ezra 10:14; Neh. 10:34; 13:31).
These grains are excellent analogies to His Word and the testimony in its behalf. Wheat is symbolic of His Word (Jer. 23:28; Isaiah 55:10, 11; St. Luke 8:11; St. Matt. 4:4 etc.) and barley of the championing and peace offering of the Word and judgment: the "barley that makes peace between husband and wife" (Midrash Rabbah on Lev. 28:4-6 re. Lev. 23:10; Numb. 5:15) the barley of judgment *(idem.),* the powerful barley that tumbled the tents of the wicked (Judges 7:13) and "the appointed barley" coupled to the "rye" for it takes two to bear witness to the Truth.
(See Pirke Aboth de Rabbi Nathan Chapter 18 *re* Rabbi Akiba's arranging of the "wheat," "barley," "spelt" and "lentils" of the Torah—Isaiah 28:25,27).

In His time when grain was sown it was placed in the furrows by hand or through a seed* pipe, a kind of funnel fixed to the plough. Wheat and barley were sown in an orderly manner the same way His Words have been placed by Him in His field. Other seeds may have been scattered but not wheat.

Is 28:25,26

"Does He not scatter dill, sprinkle *(zaraq)*, cummin, and put *(sum*)* in the principal *(sorah)* wheat in rows and the appointed *(saman)* barley in its proper place?...For he is instructed for judgement *(mishpat)*; his God directs* him."

Is 28:29
Is 52:15

He directs him how to sow His Words properly
For counsel to be made wonderful
And Wisdom to be made great.

Is 28:17

On that day those who have strewed darnel shall be scattered
"And hail shall sweep away the refuge of lies."

Is 28:13

"For the Word of the Lord will be to them
precept upon precept, precept upon precept,
line upon line, line upon line,
here a little, there a little; that they may go and fall
backward and be broken, and snared and taken"

By the Truth of His Word.

Mt 13:36

The *"parable of the darnel of the field"* is found only in St. Matthew who wrote the Gospel for the Jews, because only they would understand about "his field" and know that when grain became ritually unclean it had to be destroyed as it could no longer be offered, consumed or sold by them.

However the Oral Law (Terumoth 9:7, Mishnah) provided a way out of this unwelcome and disheartening task; it decreed that if the unclean grains were sown instead, it was then possible to redeem it, as the new crop that sprung from it was legally clean and free from taint. Thus in a way the "ground" had redeemed the unclean grain making it once more acceptable before the Lord in its own "children" seeds. For the good ground accepted what

Mt 11:19
Lk 7:35

was rejected and brought forth from it the pure and glorious fruit of light,

The fruit of the full ear of grain
With all the kernels of wheat within it in perfect arrangement,

Giving glory to the order manifest in all the wonderful works of God.

CHAPTER 6

THE PARABLE OF THE SECRETLY GROWING SEED

St. Mark 4:26-29

[26] And He said, "Thus the Kingdom of God is as if a man should cast the seed upon the ground [27] and should sleep and rise night and day and the seed should sprout and lengthen, he knows not how. [28] For of itself the ground bears fruit, first the blade, then the ear, then the full grain in the ear. [29] But when the fruit delivers itself, immediately he sends forth the sickle that stood by the harvest."

Literal Translation from the Greek.

*"ONE SEED": The Greek text of St. Mark is very specific about the singularity of the seed, it states that a man cast "the seed" *(sporon*=singular) upon the "ground" *(ge)*. The Lord phrased it that way to draw our attention to the one Seed which was cast upon the ground. We shall miss the point of the parable if we arbitrarily change "the seed" into "seeds" and the "ground" into his "field."

*"DELIVERS" (paradidomi): The Greek word *paradidomi* means "to deliver up to", "to give over to," "to surrender to," "to offer up to," "to consign to" or "to present to." In the 140 times the word *paradidomi* is used in the New Testament it is always employed in the context of being "delivered up to" or "presented to." St. Mark uses the same word 19 other times (1:14; 3:19; 7:13; 9:31; 10:33 (twice); 13:9,11,12; 14:10,11,18,21,41,42,44; 15:1,10,15) always in the sense of being "delivered up to." The same holds true for the many times it is used in the Septuagint and by Josephus and even in the Classical Greek of Herodotus, Xenophon, Polybius, etc. The word *paradidomi* does not mean "ripe." The Greek words for "ripe" are *akmazo* as in Rev. 14:18: "her grapes are fully ripe" *(akmazo)* and *pepeiros* as the "ripe *(pepeiros)* grapes" found in Genesis 40:10 Sept. The distinction is important because in this parable the "fruit" is "the full grain in the ear," the man knows that the fruit is ripe when he sees that it "delivers itself" of some of the ripe grains within the golden ear.

Mk 4:26	The parable of the Secretly Growing Seed deals with the "*Kingdom of God*."
Mk 4:26	Thus only one* seed is said to be sown and "the seed" is "*cast. . .upon the ground,*" not into a wide field.
Mk 4:29	There are no servants and no harvestmen in this parable And when the time of the harvest comes, only "*the sickle*" is sent to reap the fruit of that one seed.
Mk 4:27 Mk 4:28 Mk 4:29	The growth of the seed is gradual "*night and day*" it continues to grow from the time it sprouts. First comes "*the blade, then the ear, then the full grain in the ear*" until all the growth stops and "*the fruit delivers* itself*" because it has become fully matured.
Mk 4:29	Then, "*immediately he sends forth the sickle that stood by*" Because the harvest has come for the fruit of that one seed.
Mk 4:28	Even the earth that bore it is dealt with personally For it is written that "*of itself the ground bears fruit.*"
1 P 1:23 1 Jn 3:9	Because the Kingdom of God is a personal thing Between the heart of the ground and His seed.
Lk 17:21	"The Kingdom of God is within you" And within me waiting for us to bring it to fruit.
Lk 8:15	We do not know how it grows But we do know that it grows within us If we love and hold fast that one seed of His Word: "with patience."

Until it has fully transformed us
And brought forth from the ground of our hearts:
The fruit of Understanding, full of His Words of Truth.

This is the work of the Kingdom of God within us
A work done by the seed of His Word.

The Word we must believe and hold fast to
Even though we may not fully understand it.

So persevere and have faith
For His Word is sown as a seed
And all seeds bear fruit in their season
If the ground remains good.

*"FIRST FRUITS": *See* Exodus 13:11-16; 22:29-30; 23:19; 34:19-20,26; Leviticus 19:23-25; 23:10-11; 27:26; Numbers 15:20-21; 18:12-17; Deuteronomy 14:23; 15:19; 18:4; Nehemiah 10:37.
We also are to render to God our spiritual fruits: "Honor the Lord with thy just labours and give him the first of thy fruits of righteousness" (Prov. 3:9 Sept.).

*"LORD": "The Lord's hallowed portion, His first fruits of the increase" (Jer. 2:3) from "the seed which the Lord has blessed" (Isaiah 61:9).

*"DELIVERED": When something was set apart for the Lord it was customary to bind or tie a string around it thus differentiating it from the rest.
The stem of the "first fruit" was tied up with a rush and days later it was cut at the time of the solemn dedication. While tying up the stems of the particular chosen sheaf the proprietor would pre-dedicate it saying: "Lo, these are the first fruits" thereby asserting the covenant relationship. The same formula would be repeated a few days later at the time of the actual cutting or solemn dedication of that sheaf which was the Lord's first fruits.
There are two distinct grain harvests in the Holy Land: the barley harvest and the wheat harvest. The barley matured before the wheat and thus it was harvested beforehand usually during Passover week. The "omer of the first fruits" (Lev. 23:10-11) was taken from the barley and the ceremony of the solemn dedication took place in the barley field. The solemn dedication of the "sheaf" or "omer" was a time of great rejoicing and large crowds would gather in that particular field to watch "one man with one sickle" put the sheaf of the first fruits into "one basket" (Menahoth 10:1, Mishnah). The "omer of the first fruits" was then taken to the Temple followed by the procession of jubilant people (*See* Pesikta 8, 70d; Megillah 20b; Menahoth 65b, 68; Meg. Ta'an 1). Needless to say the farmer chose the best of the crop to be the "omer," "never was a defect found in the omer" (Pirke Aboth 5:5).
Since this parable deals with the mystery of the Kingdom of God our attention is drawn towards one thing at a time from the beginning to the end. Thus it deals with one sower, one seed, one blade, one ear, one full ear, one sickle to be applied by one man who shall put the one sheaf into one basket.

The first fruits* of the field belonged to the Lord as did the firstborn and firstlings of the Israelites.

Only the best might be presented to the Lord so that when a man planted his field he kept watch over the best portion of the yield for a particularly exceptional plant to be offered in solemn dedication to the Lord as His choice first fruits.

Jm 5:7

All attention was then directed towards that particular plant or fruit which belonged exclusively to the Lord* because until it matured and was cut and solemnly dedicated to Him, the owner could not harvest his field nor partake of any of its fruits.

The determiner of the entire crop was the chosen and dedicated fruit: "the precious fruit of the ground" which the farmer waited on "being patient over it" until it was ripe and ready to be delivered* and cut at the solemn dedication to the Lord. When the time arrived the sickle was sent to that particular plant with much ceremony and the stalk was cut in an individual manner by "one man with one sickle and one basket."

Men 10:1
(Mishnah)

The sheaf of the Lord had to be reaped first and taken to the Temple, only after that was done could the rest of the field be harvested.

Thus in the parable of the secretly growing seed the man is concerned with the progress of that one plant from its early growth until full maturity at which time the sickle is sent to it.

In contradistinction to the parable of the darnel, the eschatology of this parable is personal for it deals with the Kingdom of God. The harvest is the harvest of that one fruit from that one seed although there is the intimation that the rest of the field shall also be reaped.

The patient man that sleeps and arises night and day is not stuporous as the sleeping men were in his field. The patient man watches the progress of the seed that was sown. He watches it "sprout and lengthen" into "the blade," "the ear" and "the full grain in the ear."

Mk 4:27
Mk 4:28

He is indeed very patient

Mk 4:29

But "when the fruit delivers itself"
He is no longer patient

Mk 4:29

Because "immediately he sends forth the sickle"—

For the time has come for that fruit to be reaped
And that field to be harvested.

*"CAST": In the parables of the Sower and the Mustard Seed as preserved in the Gospel according to St. Mark, the usual Greek word for "to sow": *speiro,* is used but in this parable *ballo* which means "to cast" is used instead. *Ballo* corresponds to the Hebrew-Aramaic word *yarah* which means "to cast" but it also means "to teach." Our Lord told the parable of the Secretly Growing Seed to His disciples *after* he had explained to them that "the Seed is the Word of God" and that "he that sows, sows the Word" (St. Luke 8:11; St. Mark 4:14). Indeed He sows the Word when He teaches the good ground.

*"LENGTHEN" (mekunomai): The Greek word *mekunomai* means "to lengthen," "to extend" or "to make long." It is derived from *mekos* which means "length." The word *blastano* means "to sprout," or "to put forth shoots." *Blastano* is derived from *blastos:* a "sprout" or "bud." A seed placed in a saucer containing some water soon starts to "sprout and lengthen" but it shall never bear fruit in that saucer.
However, if the seed is implanted "into" *(eis, en)* the good ground it "grows up" *(anabaino)* and if the ground continues to hold it fast, the seed "increases" *(auxano)* it becomes many seeds inside the fruit brought forth by the heart of the good ground (St. Mark 4:8; 2 Kings 19:30).
In the parable of the Secretly Growing Seed the man "casts" *(ballo)* the seed, he does not "sow" *(speiro)* it. Thus the seed falls "upon" *(epi)* and not "into" *(eis, en)* the ground. The seed stays upon the ground until it is "received" *(lambano)* and "gladly welcomed" *(paradechomai)* inside the heart of the ground. Once the seed is received within and held fast enduringly it only takes a matter of time before it shall open up and teach the ground how to bear fruit of itself.

*"SICKLE": The special sickle (Isaiah 54:16-17) with which the servant of the Lord shall reap the fruit of righteousness: Understanding. With the same sickle all falsehood and deceit shall be cut off from His field. The powerful instrument of Understanding which is "the heritage of the servants of the Lord" (Isaiah 54:17) is the peerless weapon of Wisdom and Knowledge against which no argumentation of the scoffers shall stand (St. Luke 21:12-15) for it shall be to them "the ravager to destroy" (Isaiah 54:16) their pride. The wise men of the era just before the time of our Lord rightly interpreted "the instrument for His work" (Isaiah 54:16) to be a scholar and lawgiver (Zadokite Fragment 8:7-8).

*"STOOD BY" (paristemi): The Greek word *paristemi* is made up of two words: *para* ("beside") and *histemi* ("to stand"). In all the thirty-nine times the word *paristemi* is used in the New Testament, it is used in the context of "standing by" or being "present." St. Mark uses the same word five other times (14:47,69,70; 15:35,39) and always in the context of "standing by."
In His time the sickle *did* stand by the harvest because the day of the solemn dedication of the first fruits invariably fell on one of the days of Passover week. The first and the last day of Passover week were strictly observed as Sabbaths and the intervening days were considered *Moed Katan, i.e.,* "minor festivals" and as such they were also subject to the restrictions as to the kind of work and carrying of utensils allowed on such days. *(See* Mishnah Moed Katan, Chapters 1-3). Yet notwithstanding all the Passover week restrictions, the Oral Law permitted the cutting and taking of the omer of the first fruits to the Temple on the day of solemn dedication even if that particular day fell on a Sabbath or Passover (Menahoth 10:1-3; Josephus Antiq. 3:10,5,6; Philo Op. 2:294). But although the Oral Law allowed the sheaf of the first fruits to be harvested any day of the Passover week it forbade carrying to the field in that week the instruments and utensils used for the purpose of harvesting. Thus it was customary to leave the "one sickle and one basket" standing by the first fruits days before the actual cutting. That particular sickle was of course: "the sickle that stood by the harvest."
Note that the man who cast the seed and patiently waited for it to bear fruit suddenly acts with alacrity the moment the "fruit delivers itself" for *"immediately* he sends forth the sickle" then, swiftly and decisively. The humble sower *orders* at the time of the harvest: "he sends forth *(apostello)"* just as the "harvestmen" are sent forth to collect the darnel and gather the wheat when the time is ripe (St. Matt. 13:30). Because in the time of the harvest the humble sower returns as King to "his field" to claim it as "His Kingdom" (St. Matt. 13:24,41) for He comes then as Lord of the Harvest to command and to be obeyed (Joel 3:12-13). Truly in the end "a *wise King* winnows *(zarah=*"to winnow") the wicked and brings the (threshing) wheel over them" (Prov. 20:26. *See also* St. Matt. 3:11-12; Prov. 20:8; Isaiah 28:27-28; Ps. 101:3-5; 18:27; Prov. 6:16-19). Truly all lies shall be scattered in the end when "He makes understanding to abound. . .*in the time of the harvest"* (Sirach 24:26).

*"HARVESTED": "He that gathers in the summer is a wise son" (Prov. 10:5) who has learnt from the "exceedingly wise" ants (Prov. 30:24-25; 6:6-8).
"Let there be among you a man of Understanding who when the fruit has ripened comes quickly with his sickle in his hand and reaps it." *(The Gospel According To Thomas,* Logion 22:15-18, Harper Bros., N.Y. 1959)

166

There are three workers in the parable of the Secretly Growing Seed.
They are: the man, the seed, and the ground.

Mk 4:26   The work of the man is to "*cast* the seed upon the ground*"
And to watch and wait—
For the seed to start to work.

Mk 4:27   The work of the seed is to "*sprout (blastano) and lengthen*"*
(mekunomai).
The seed can sprout and lengthen anywhere there is a little moisture.

But to bear fruit the seed needs the ground.

The man casts the seed upon the ground
Because he wants some fruit.

After the ground has accepted it, and the seed has done its work
Mk 4:28   The ground then works "*of itself*" to bear fruit
Mk 4:28   "*First the blade, then the ear, then the full grain in the ear.*"

The ground keeps working until the fruit is ripe
Mk 4:29   Then the fruit "*delivers itself*" of some of its seeds
To let the man who is watching know

That it is time to send the sickle*
Col 1:5-6   To the fruit of that one seed.

Mk 4:29   "*The sickle that stood* by the harvest*" is wielded by the one
Rm 8:23   bringing forth the first fruit.

1 P 1:22-25 It belongs to the harvestman risen from the ground sanctified by His Word.
The "ground" sealed by the Truth delivered from the fully perfected fruit.

Lk 8:11   "The Seed is the Word of God"
The fruit is Understanding the Truth of His Word.

Si 10:4 Sept. "The power of the ground is in the hand of the Lord and in due time He will set over it one that is right for the time."

Repent!
Repent!

For when that precious fruit is harvested*
The Reapers are sent.

167

*"TRIBULATIONS": we are made "perfect through suffering" (Hebrews 2:10).

The Kingdom of God is within us
And it becomes established in the perfect doing of His will.

The Kingdom of God is a Reign.
It is a dominion over us that calls for obedience.

The perfection of His rule within us is achieved in proportion to our submission to it.

The perfect example of the unimpeded Reign of God in the heart of man is the Lord Himself.
He *is* incarnate Kingdom of God,
The true model of absolute obedience to His holy will.

The Kingdom of God shall be established in the world
When everyone shall perfectly fulfill all His Commands.

In the meantime the Kingdom of God is within you,
A personal thing between God and you
Between His willing and your doing.

He wills that you become truly His son.

It takes a lot of doing
A lot of patience, perseverance and endurance to the very end

To have you become like Him.

Ac 14:22 It is "through many tribulations* that we must enter the Kingdom of God,"
For it is a struggle to do His will on earth faithfully as it is done in Heaven.

No one enters the Kingdom of God unless he has died to himself
And dying to oneself is not an easy thing to do,

Yet we must if we are to be born again in Him.

A child is born only after much labor
And a seed must die before it bears the fruit

Shall there be bread without crushing the grain?

Upon whom the Reign of the Lord shall fall,
Mt 21:44
Ph 3:21 It shall grind him to powder
And mould him again to the image of God.

169

*"**WILL**": The Kingdom of God is *achieved* through Him in obedience to His will. The Kingdom of Heaven is *received* through Him (1 Cor. 1:24,30; 2:16).

*"**COMES FROM HIM**": True understanding of the wisdom of His words is a precious gift from God. "The Lord gives Wisdom" but it is from "His mouth" that we receive the greater gifts of "knowledge and Understanding" (Prov. 2:6). We "**hear** *Wisdom*" but we "**receive** *Understanding*" (2 Bar. 51:3). "Teach me, O Lord. . .and. . .make me to understand," "O Lord, give me Understanding according to Thy Word" (Ps. 119:33,34,169). "Bless the Lord who has given me Understanding" (Ps. 15 (16): 7 Latin Vulgate).
The Lord gives Understanding that we may instruct and restore all things in their proper order to His glory. But to receive Understanding we must be good and ask Him for this great gift. Why grapple violently to "take" Wisdom and "know" her when you can receive her understanding from the Lord? (St. Matt. 11:11-15; St. Luke 24:27,45). "Ask and it shall be given unto you" (St. Matt. 7:7). The Heavenly Father gives the Holy Spirit to those who ask Him (St. Luke 11:13), "the Spirit of Wisdom and Understanding" (Isaiah 11:2), "the Holy Spirit. . .who will teach you all things" (St. John 14:26). For the Holy Spirit is "the Spirit of Truth," who "will guide you into all the Truth" (St. John 16:13), and that is Understanding. So if you want to understand, be poor and little before him and you shall be a "*poor* wise child" (Eccle. 4:13) rich in understanding. For who does the most asking in this world and expects the most receiving? The little ones of course! (Isaiah 8:9; St. Matt. 11:25) especially if they are "*poor*" *(misken)* "empty" *(miskenuth)* and hungry because mama has run dry. To these little children of the Lord, "it is *given* to know the Mysteries" (St. Matt. 13:11; St. Mark 4:11; St. Luke 8:10) and it is they who shall receive the "bread of Understanding" (Sir. 15:3) from God.

*"**REVEALED**": "To whom has the Understanding of Wisdom been revealed?" (Sir. 1:7 Syriac Syro-Hexaplar Text and Sahidic Text). "Awake, awake, put on strength, O arm of the Lord. . .was it not Thou that didst cut Rahab in pieces?" (Isaiah 51:9). The Lord "by His Understanding He smote Rahab" (Job 26:12). Indeed the arm of the Lord is Understanding by which He smites the proud. "What is His name and what is the name of His Son? surely you know!" (Prov. 30:4) by now. If "a wise man's understanding is at his right hand" (Eccle. 10:2) so is his soul who understands.

The Kingdom of Heaven is the Reign of Understanding the holy things of God,
The holy mysteries of the things to come and the holy reasons for the things that have happened.

The Kingdom of Heaven reigns when we understand the mysteries of His Wisdom
And have knowledge of His marvellous Truth.

The Kingdom of *God* is established in the perfect *doing* of His will*.
The Kingdom of *Heaven* is established in the perfect *knowing* of His will,

His will towards all and each and everyone of us.

When we shall see and understand the works of God
We shall have entered into the Kingdom of Heaven.

We know through the Understanding that comes* from Him
And is given to those who are willing to receive it: the little ones.

It is given to the humble righteous ones
Who are able to be taught by God

Because they are merciful and can understand Him
And want to bear fruit for Him in the ground of their good hearts.

God teaches the pure because they know where to find Him
And the meek because they know how to ask.

Ws 3:9
Heb 11:3
Those who believe in Him shall understand His thoughts
Because they have faith and hold fast to His Words

It is the Word of God who reveals Him to us
That we may worship Him in spirit and in Truth

Jn 4:24
For "God is Spirit, and they that worship Him must worship Him in spirit and in Truth,"

The Truth revealed to us by His beloved Son.

Is 53:1
"To whom has the arm of the Lord been revealed?"*

If the Father is Wisdom
The Son at the right hand is Understanding.

*"TEARS": Sowing time is the laborious time of plowing and tilling the field. It is a time fraught with uncertainty as regards the final outcome of the sowing for there are many things to fear: drought, locusts, mildew, cankerworms, hail, frost, fire, birds, rodents and floods, any and all of which can bring the family dependent on the crop to misery and starvation. The poor farmer had oftentimes to go into debt to obtain the seed upon which his livelihood depended and so he sowed in tears desperately hoping for a bountiful crop so that what was "sown in dishonor" be "raised in glory" and what was "sown in weakness" be "raised in power" (I Cor. 15:43).

*"UNDERSTANDING": *Sunesis* in the Greek of Sirach 1:23 means "understanding." For a man who truly understands is a humble and patient man, slow to anger, unassuming, not taking credit to himself but leaving it for others to praise him (St. John 7:6; Isaiah 53:13-15; Sirach 1:22-23). A man of understanding is long suffering for "he that is slow to wrath is of great understanding" *(tebunah)*, he knows that "he that refraineth his lips is understanding" *(sakal)*, and "he that hath knowledge spares his words" and "he that shuts his lips is esteemed a man of understanding" (Prov. 10:19; 17:27; Dan. 2:21; Prov. 17:28). An understanding man remembers that there is "a time to keep silence and a time to speak" (Eccle. 3:7) and so "the understanding *(sakal)* shall keep silence" (Amos 5:13) until the time is ripe for words. The best answer to a riddle is another riddle with the answer (Judges 14:13,18).

*"NO UNDERSTANDING": Wise men may fear the Lord but if they do not depart from evil their fear is in vain and they are without understanding (Job 28:28). "O! Solomon, how wise you were in your *youth* and as a flood full of *understanding" (sunesis)* but not in your old age when "you did stain your honor and pollute your seed" (Sirach 47:14, 20 Sept.), for then you did not depart from evil and so you no longer understood. "There is a wisdom that abounds in evil and there is no understanding" (Sirach 21:15 Latin Vulgate) because evil abounds. But "here is the understanding that has Wisdom" (Rev. 17:9), if you want to be truly wise, *be good*, for "wine and women make wise men fall off" (Sirach 19:2 Latin Vulgate; 1 Kings 11:1-8).

*"THING": Both St. Matt. 12:42 and St. Luke 11:31 use the Greek neuter: *pleion* for "greater" rather than the Greek personal *meizon*. God does not compare anyone to Himself. The comparision is between Solomon's wisdom and the Lord's understanding. Thus He says that the Queen of Sheba "came out of the limits of the earth to hear the wisdom of Solomon and, behold! a greater thing *(pleion)* than Solomon is here," *i.e.*, a greater thing than "the wisdom of Solomon" which drew the Queen of Sheba to visit him, is the Understanding of our Lord which encompasses all wisdom.

*"MAN": "The husbandman that labours must be first partaker of the fruits. Understand *(noeo)* what I say and the Lord will give you understanding *(sunesis)* in all things" (2 Timothy 2:6-7). "It is one man that sows and it is another man that reaps" (St. John 4:37). "God sows" (Hosea 2:22), man tills the ground of his own heart keeping it clear of weeds and tending His Word. The faithful husbandman that continues in this work to the very end shall, in the time of the harvest, partake the fruit of understanding the Truth within the kernel of the Word He sowed.

*"HARVEST": His Word is sown as a Seed (St. Mark 4:14; St. Luke 8:11). Those who receive, keep, obey and attend to the Word bear the fruit of understanding it. The time of understanding is the time of the "fruits": harvest time. Thus: "He fills all things with His Wisdom. . .in the time of the harvest. . .He sends forth the teaching of knowledge to appear as a light. . .in the time of the vintage" (Sirach 24:25,26,27 Sept.). In the time of the harvest "whosoever understands shall then be wise" (2 Bar. 28:1) *really* wise. In the meantime. . ."come to Wisdom as one that plows and sows and wait for her good fruits. For in her service you will toil a little while and shall quickly eat of her fruits" (Sirach 6:19) and say to her then: "Even from the time of the flower till the grape was ripe, my heart delighted in Wisdom" (Sirach 51:15 Sept.). "If in thy youth thou hast not gathered Wisdom, how shalt thou attain Wisdom in thine old age? O! how comely a thing is judgment for gray hairs and for ancient men to know counsel" (Sirach 25:3 Syriac Text).
"God gives to a man that is good in His sight, Wisdom and Knowledge and joy but to the sinner He gives travail to gather and to heap up, that He may give to him that is good before God" (Eccle. 2:26). Among the Rabbis the Torah was a "field" wherein the scribes, Mishnah teachers, and disciples "laboured" (*See* Midrash Rabbah on Lev. XXXIV. 16). It is by caring for His Words and "doing" them that we are sanctified and merit to understand them. "Through His Teaching peace will abound for us and by our gathering of His Words our sins will be forgiven us" (Targum Jonathan on Isaiah 53:5; St. John 17:17, 19; St. Luke 2:46-47,52; St. Matt. 13:54; St. Mark 6:2). "He that seeks the Teaching shall be filled therewith" (Sirach 35:15 Sept.; Jer. 15:16).

*"ATTENTION": "If you will incline your ear you shall receive instruction and if you *love* to hear you shall be wise" (Sirach 6:34 Latin Vulgate). Where else do we love but in the heart? Therefore, "listen to me, my son, and acquire knowledge and pay close attention to my words with your heart" (Sirach 16:24). "Desire" to hear the Word of God (I Peter 2:2) and "be meek to hear the Word of God that you may understand and return a true answer with wisdom" (Sirach 5:13 Latin Vulgate).
"Be meek" for it is to the humble that He gives instruction (Ps. 25:9, 14). "Hear me and I will instruct thee," "Hear ye and understand" (4 Ezra 7:49; St. Matt. 15:10). "If you now have understanding, hear this: hear the *voice* of my *words*" (Job 34:16) and pay close attention for it is according to your attention that you shall receive the understanding of His Words (St. Mark 4:24,25).

172

Ps 126:5	"They who sow in tears* shall reap in joy."
Si 1:22	"A long suffering man will endure for a season and afterward joy shall spring up unto him" as a bountiful harvest from his seeds.
Si 1:23 Sept.	"He will hide his words for a season and the lips of many shall declare his *understanding*" when they partake of his fruits.
	They shall then know that a man of Understanding Can put a hundred wise men of this world to shame.
Pr 10:23	For sometimes those who are wise have no* Understanding "But a man of Understanding has Wisdom."
Si 18:28 Sept. and L.V.	"Every man of Understanding knows Wisdom" And understands that the one who expounds a riddle is far wiser than the one who propounded it.
Mt 12:42 Lk 11:31	A greater thing* than the wisdom of Solomon is the Understanding of God.
Lk 11:31 Col 1:27 1 Co 2:16	And the Understanding of God "is here" In the heart of everyone who believes in the Lord.
Pr 28:11	"A rich man is wise in his own eyes but a poor man who has understanding will search him out."
Pr 20:5	"A man of Understanding will draw it out."
Mt 25:24,26 Mt 13:25	It is the man* of Understanding who gathers what is good in His field and collects the foolishness that was scattered to confound it.
Lk 19:21-22	It is the one who understands who shall reap because he watches and knows when the time is ripe.
Jr 9:12 Dn 12:10	"Who is the man so wise that he can understand this?" "The wise shall understand" at the time of the harvest.*
Pr 4:7 L.T.	So "with all thy getting get Understanding" And you shall then be truly wise.
Pr 5:1 Pr 5:1 Pr 2:2 Si 6:35 Sept.	"My son be attentive to my Wisdom" But if you also want "my Understanding": "incline your ear" and "bow your heart" and listen very closely. "Let not the parables of Understanding escape you."
Pr 4:1	For you have "to give attention* to know Understanding" And you really have to work to bring it forth from you.
Pr 3:13 L.T.	But "O the happiness...of a man who brings forth Understanding."

The Hebrew-Aramaic words used to describe the various stages of development in man from conception to adulthood, closely parallel the growth of a seed into the fully matured fruit bearing plant.

Thus man commences as a "seed" *(zerah)* that bears "fruit" *(peri)*.

Gn 1:29
Jr 31:27
Dt 7:13

"The fruit *(peri)* of a tree yielding seed" *(zerah)*.
"The seed *(zerah)* of men" and "the fruit *(peri)* of thy womb."

The fruit of the womb is brought forth as a *yeled* ("a newborn babe").
The word *yeled* is derived from *yalad* ("brought forth," "delivered," "hatched").
At this stage the child "howls" *(yalal)* and "yells" *(yelel)*.

The "newborn babe" *(yeled)* becomes a *yonek* ("suckling child") for it soon "sucks" *(yanak)* at the mother's breast.

Is 53:2
Jb 14:7

At this stage the "suckling child" *(yonek)* is like a very young and tender plant that is entwined about: "He grew up before Him as a tender plant" *(yonek)* with "tender branches" *(yoneqeth)*.

Like a young tender plant the suckling child soon begins to grow upwards or "ascend" *(olah)* in height. Thus the *yonek* becomes an *olal* ("a growing child").

The *olal* continues nursing until it becomes "perfected" *(gamar)* as in Ps. 138:8, that is to say until it acquires its own teeth.
The child is then taken off the breast and known as a "weaned *(gamal)* one."

Is 18:5

The "weaned child" *(gamal)* is "complete" and a perfect although very immature replica of a man.
At this stage it is like the young plant bearing the tiny fruit buds just like "the sour grape is ripening *(gamal)* in the flower."

"Weaned children" *(gamal)* start walking and wander about in all directions often stumbling and going into the wrong places.
These wandering little ones are known as *taph* ("little ones") which is a word derived from *taah* and means "to wander" or "to cause to err."

At this stage the "little ones" *(taph)* are like young plants bearing small immature fruit. These plants are "complete" but their roots are very fine and bushy spreading out in all directions and often intertwining with the roots of their neighboring plants. The roots of these young plants are not yet firm and fully directed downwards. It is unwise to pull up their neighboring plants even though they may be weeds:

Mt 13:29

"Lest in collecting the darnel you should uproot with them the wheat."

*"WAIT": As in the parable of the Good Seed and the Darnel, the immature are often anxious to be of help just as the zealous "bondservants" *(ebed* in Hebrew) were who wanted "to bear witness" *(ed)* to the Truth although they were still "green" *(eb)* about it. They had to wait and remain bound to the ground until the time was ripe. "It is good for a man to bear a yoke in his youth" (Lam. 3:27) lest he upset the cart. "As long as the disciples are small, cover up for them the words of the Torah (*i.e.*, hide the meaning of the words) but when they are grown up and have become strong as rams, then lay open to them the secrets of the Torah" (Rabbi Simeon ben Halafta in the name of Rabbi Samuel ben Nahman—3rd century A.D. *See also* Jer. Abodah Zarah 2, 41c; cf. Hagigah, 13a. *See* Dikduke Soferim *ad* Prov. 27:26 and Yalkut to Proverbs Sect. 961).

*"ELEM": The word *elem* ("young man") is closely related to another Hebrew word: *elim* which means "trees." "Young men" *(elem* pl.) and "trees" *(elim)* are both firm and erect when they are fully grown. Thus "trees *(elim)* stand up" (Ezek. 31:4) as good "young men" *(elem)* do when they have become "trees *(elim)* of righteousness" (Isaiah 61:3).

*"NAAR": Another Hebrew word for "young man" is *naar* which is derived from the verb "to shake off" *(naar)*. A *naar* is a mature young man strong and ready to set off on his own without restraint. The strength and freedom implied in the word *naar* is evident in the early inscriptions found in the Hebrew seals known as the *ebed* seals. In one of these is inscribed: "belonging to Eliakim *naar* of (king) Jehoiakim" (Tell Beit Mirsim-Kiryath-*Sepher*-seal impression). Obviously this *naar* or king's man was a free man possessing his own seal.
The Hebrew language is rich in word plays. Thus *nata* means "plant" (botanical) and also "fixed." Again *gadal* means "to rear up" also to be "exalted" and to be "great." In Psalm 144:12 there is a beautiful wish: "May our sons be as plants *(nata)* becoming great *(gadol)* in their youth *(naar)*." Let them be bound to the earth and they shall reach for the sky.

*"CLEANSING WITH FIRE": When the ears of the "omer of the first fruits" were brought to the Temple they were taken to the Court of the Temple where they were thrashed with slender canes so as not to injure the grain freed from the chaff. The uncovered grain was then parched on a specially perforated pan that enabled each grain to be touched by the fire and thereby purified and rendered acceptable before the Lord. The parched grain was then spread out in the Temple Court so that the wind might blow over it in fulfillment of the Law in Leviticus 2:14 (*See* Mishnah Menahoth Section 10:4; Kelim 2:3).
All things acceptable to God are tried and proven as were the offerings to the Lord called the "fire offerings" (Exod. 29:18,25,41; Lev. 2:16; 3:3,9,14; 7:5,25; 8:21,28; 22:27; 23:8,13,25,27,36,37; Numb. 15:3,25; 28:2,3,6,19; Deut. 18:1; Josh. 13:14, etc.).
As the Archangel Raphael said to Tobias: "because you were acceptable to God there had to be some trial to test you" (Tobit 12:13. *See also* Dan. 11:35; 12:3,10; Sir. 2:1-5; Judith 8:21f. L.V.; 1 Cor. 3:13,15; 1 Peter 1:7 etc.).

Mt 13:26-29

So Father's little helpers His "small ones" *(taph)* have to wait* until they have become mature and are no longer bound "to cause to err" *(taah)* in attempting to pull out darnel words from His field.

Nevertheless their Father is encouraged for by their own little fruits they are able to tell the difference between His good things and the foolishness belonging to the "father of lies."

As times goes by the "little ones" *(taph)* become stronger and grow up to be "young men" or "mighty" *(elim)* "youths" *(elem)* like sturdy vigorous plants with firm roots and rapidly maturing fruit.

At this stage the strong "young men" *(elem)** are eager to "shake off" *(naar)* restraint. They are ready to strike out on their own and they desire to be free as harvestmen making their own wages. They are now called *naar* ("young men") like "Jeroboam mighty in valour, Solomon saw this young man *(naar)** working hard and appointed him over all the burden *(sebel)* of the house of Joseph,"

1 K 11:28

And no doubt over all the bundles as well.

When the *naar* (young man) has fully matured and is considered eligible to make his own way and do his own sowing, he is called a *bachur* ("choice young man") for he has been "proven" *(bachan)* and found "acceptable" *(bachar)* "excellent" *(bachar)* and "chosen" *(bachar)* among all others in His field.

Who is the wise and faithful *bachur* whom the Lord and Master shall place over all His fruits?

Jr 4:31
Ezk 47:12

He is the one who shall "first bring forth" *(bakar)* out of the good ground of his heart: the "first of the first fruits" *(bakkurah)*.

Then after the reaping comes the threshing that uncovers the grain and the cleansing* with fire that shall bare the "clean" *(bar)*, "pure" *(bar)*, "clear" *(bar)*, "choice" *(bar)* "wheat" *(bar)* of His "field" *(bar)*,

The wheat of Truth borne to His barn by His "bright" *(bar)* "son" *(bar)*:

The fruit of His seed.

177

*"**THE FIRST MONTH**": The first month of the Hebrew calendar is the month of *Nisan* which corresponds to March-April. Before the first month was called *Nisan* by the Jews, it was known to them as the month of *Abib* which means "ears of corn" *i.e.*, "ear month" (*chodesh Ha Abib. See* Exod. 13:4; 23:15; Deut. 16:1). They called it *Abib* because at that time of the year (March-April), the wheat is in the ear and the more rapidly maturing barley ears of grain are ready to be harvested. In Israel the barley is harvested in April and May and the wheat in June or July.

There are two rainy seasons in the Holy Land: the late fall rain and the spring rain. The fall rain commences in mid-October to the end of November and it comes after the long hot summer to soften the hard dry ground for plowing and sowing. The spring rain falls between March and April, just before the harvest, to help bring the grain to maturity. Since the *agricultural* year begins at the time of plowing and sowing, the fall rain is called the "early rain" or "former rain"—*yarah*. The spring rain which in turn falls in the latter part of the agricultural year, is called the "latter rain"—*malqosh*.

In the wonderful Hebrew language as previously noted, the word *yarah* ("early rain" or "former rain") also means "to cast," "to teach" and "teacher":
"I may cast (*yarah*) lots for you here" (Josh. 18:6), "I will make thee to understand and teach (*yarah*) thee" (Ps. 32:8). "Your teachers (*yarah* pl.) shall no longer be hidden, your eyes shall see your teachers" (*yarah* pl.)—Isaiah 30:20.
Malqosh ("latter rain") in turn, is closely related (through the common root *laqosh* to the Hebrew word *leqach* which means "learning" and "doctrine": "teach a righteous man and he will increase in learning" (*leqach*)—Prov. 9:9. "My doctrine (*leqach*) shall drop down as the rain" (*malqosh*)—Deut. 32:2 Targum Onkelos and Jerusalem.
The prophets knew that both these words provided a wonderful medium of allegory for their prophecy concerning the coming of the Messiah as a marvellous Teacher:
"He shall come down to us as rain, as the latter rain (*malqosh*) and the early rain (*yarah*) unto the earth" (Hosea 6:3). "Be glad then, ye children of Zion, and rejoice in the Lord your God; for He has given you a Teacher of righteousness (*yarah litsedaqah*) and He will cause to come down for you the rain, the former rain and the latter rain in the first month" (Joel 2:23). In other words the "Teacher of Righteousness" will cause the "Teaching Rain" (*yarah*) and the "Learning Rain" (*malqosh*) to come down simultaneously upon the ground of our hearts to make the Seed of His Word suddenly spring forth to light so that we may truly understand it.
"For when God chooses to teach, He first gives His disciples the power of understanding, without which no man can learn Divine Knowledge" (St. Augustine Commentary on Ps. 119 (118):66).
"Behold, I will do a new thing; now it is springing forth; shall you not know it?" (Isaiah 43:19). Of course, "you shall know it" (*idem.* Septuagint) for "now it shall be revealed" (*idem.* Targum on Isaiah 43:19).
The prophets Isaiah, Hosea and Joel knew that the "Teacher of Righteousness" would not only "teach" (*yarah*) but would enable us to understand (St. Luke 24:45) and "learn" (*malqosh-leqach*) His "doctrine" (*leqach*). He would do this simultaneously when the time is ripe for the Word to bear the fruit of light, *viz.*, "in the first month" (*Nisan-Abib*) which is the month close to the time of the harvest. He shall then concomitantly teach and make us learn because "He makes understanding to abound. . .in the time of the harvest" (Sirach 24:26). As Jeremiah (23:20; 30:24) said: "in the *latter days* ye shall understand (*bin*) with understanding (*binah*)."
So "ask ye of the Lord rain in the time of the latter rain" (Zech. 10:1) when all the fruits both good and bad are visible in His field. For the time to ask for understanding is when lies abound because the shepherds are delinquent (Zech. 10:2) and they no longer understand (Jer. 50:6; Isaiah 28:6; Ezek. 34:5-16; Jer. 3:15; St. Mark 6:34). Ask then, and "the Lord shall make lightnings and give. . .torrential rain (*matar-geshem*) to everyone" (Zech. 10:1). He will enlighten and give us the teaching and learning rain *together* at the same time as a "torrential rain" (Zech. 10:1; Joel 2:23) to make us understand.
Also repent!: "break up (*nir*) your fallow ground (*nir*); light up (*nir*) your lamp (*nir*), for it is time to seek the Lord till He come and rain (*yarah*) righteousness upon you" (Hosea 10:12) and "teach" (*yarah*) you to be good.
Watch and be ready for "He shall come down like rain upon the mown grass, as showers sprinkling the earth. The righteous shall flourish in His days and there shall be abundance of peace till the moon is no more" (Ps. 72:6-7). Then shall "the fruit of righteousness" be "sown in peace by those who make peace" (St. James 3:18). In the meantime hold fast and be patient, "for the moment all discipline seems painful rather than pleasant; later it yields the *peaceable fruit of righteousness* to those who have been trained by it" (Hebrews 12:11). Truly, "Thou, O God, didst send a plentiful rain whereby Thou didst confirm (*kun*) Thine inheritance when it was weary" (Ps. 68:9; Yalkut Deut. 863). Truly, O Lord, "Truth (*emeth*) shall spring out of the earth" (Ps. 85:11) when You shall send upon it the Teaching and Learning Rain.
"Thou, O my God hast put in my mouth as it were an abundant rain for all and a spring of living waters which shall not run dry. . .they shall become an unleashed torrent over all the banks and shall go down to the fathomless seas" (Thanksgiving Hymn 8:16, 17, Dead Sea Scrolls. *See also* Isaiah 58:10-11; Sirach 24:29-33; Isaiah 11:9; Habakkuk 2:14; B.T. Berakoth 1:24a *re* Hosea 10:12; Sifre Deut. Ha'azinu 306,f. 131b). Blessed be the Lord who has "rained down skill (*epistemon*) and knowledge of understanding" (Sirach 1:19).

Jl 2:23	May the Lord "rain the former rain and the latter rain in the first month,"* Before He sends His harvestmen to reap and to bind.
Ps 72:16 M.T.	"May He be as a rich cornfield in the land" When He comes to gather what is His.
Jl 3:24 Is 21:10	May "the floors" of His barn "be full of pure wheat" (*bar*): The proven sons of His threshing.
	And may His loving kindness and mercy be there The Day His Truth is revealed.
	He tarries along with His seed until the fruit is ripe But in the Day He shall act the reaping shall be swift And the winnowing soon over.
Jn 4:35 Ps 126:5 Am 9:13	"Behold! lift up your eyes and look on the fields for they are white and already to harvest." The day is near when Sower and Reaper shall both rejoice.
Ps 96:12 Ps 96:13	"Let the field be glad and all the things that are in it. . . Because He comes, because He comes to judge the earth" To "judge the world with righteousness and the peoples with His Truth."
Is 45:8 Is 45:8 Sept.	"Drop down, O heavens, from above and let the clouds rain down righteousness." "Let the earth bring forth and blossom with mercy and let righteousness spring forth as well."
Dn 3:76 L.V. Lk 10:2	"O! all things that spring up in the ground bless the Lord": "The Lord of the Harvest."
	Repent! Repent! Return to Him with all your hearts
Jm 5:8	"For the coming of the Lord is at hand."
Jm 5:9	"Behold, the Judge is standing at the doors" And the books that were sealed are now open.
Hab 2:2	Read this And understand. Then quickly run to Him.

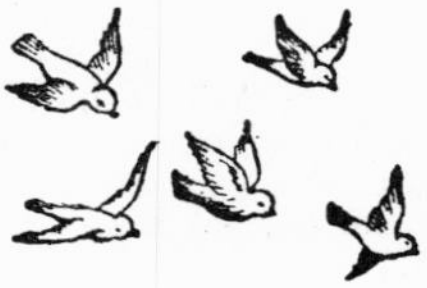

CHAPTER 7

THE PARABLE OF THE MUSTARD SEED

According to St. Matthew 13:31-32

[31] Another parable He set before them saying, "The Kingdom of heaven is like to a grain of mustard which a man took and sowed in his field. [32] It is the least indeed of all the seeds but when it may be increased it is greater than the vegetables and becomes a tree so that the birds of heaven come and shelter in its branches."

Literal Translation.

*"**THREE DIFFERENT WAYS**": Each way with its own "pattern of sound words" (2 Tim. 1:13) to have the same parable convey a different "form of teaching" (Rom. 6:17) according to a "pattern of knowledge" (Rom. 2:20). Thus He told the parable of the Mustard Seed (St. Matt. 13:1-2,31; St. Mark 4:1, 30-32) **twice** in the **same place**: "beside the sea" but on **different occasions** there (St. Mark 4:1 says: "when He began **again** *(palin)* to teach by the sea side"). On these two different occasions our Lord illustrated by the simile of the Mustard Seed two distinct concepts: "the Kingdom of Heaven" (St. Matt. 13:31) and "the Kingdom of God" (St. Mark 4:30-31). St. Mark preserves the parable of the Mustard Seed as told by our Lord to bring to the fore the relationship between the Kingdom of God and us, describing its effects upon us. On yet another occasion and in a different place (close to a synagogue), our Lord ingeniously contrived for the **third** time to tell the same parable in a special way again but this time to describe Himself: the incarnate "Kingdom of God." St. Luke (13:10,17-19) tells us that He "**therefore**" told it then in response to the acclamation of the crowd that was gathered there at the time "when all the people rejoiced over all the glorious things that were done by Him." "If you have faith as a grain of mustard" (St. Matt. 17:20) you shall understand and be able to tell the apparently same parable apart, through the little variations that make all the difference in meaning. You shall also remember that immediately after telling the parable of the Mustard Seed, St. Mark (4:33) states that "many such *(toioutos*="of such a sort") parables He spoke to them," i.e., many such parables as the parable of the Mustard Seed, etc., He spoke to them. On "that day" St. Mark 4:35-41 tells us that He crossed the sea of Galilee in a boat during a storm. This episode is recorded in St. Matthew 8:16-27 but not in St. Matthew Chapter 13 the "day" when He told the version of the parable of the Mustard Seed retained by St. Matthew.

*"*LAMBANO*": The Greek word *lambano* means either "to take" or "to receive." It is used one hundred and four times in the former context and one hundred thirty-five times in the latter context in the New Testament. When the New Testament Greek was translated into Latin by St. Jerome he chose the Latin word *accipio* to render *lambano* into the Latin Vulgate. *Accipio* also means either "to take" or "to receive." Both the Greek and Latin texts render correctly the Hebrew word *laqach* which means both "to take" and "to receive." The understanding of wisdom can be "taken" through assiduous effort but it can also be effortlessly "received" as a reward of obedience to His Word. Those who possess understanding of the wisdom of His Word can in turn take from themselves Seeds of Truth to sow, and as His children they can also draw upon and sow those Seeds of Truth which they have received as a reward from their loving Father.

The Kingdom of Heaven is the Reign of Understanding the Wisdom of God.
And it is established in our hearts when we come to the knowledge of His marvellous Truth.

The great Wisdom of God is found hidden inside the smallest things,
The little things reserved for the little ones.

Mt 13:24,31 — St. Matthew uniquely says that "He set *(paratithemi)* before them" His parables,
Because the gospel according to St. Matthew stresses the Wisdom of God,

Dt 8:3
Jr 15:16 — The Wisdom given to those who know that the Word of God is "bread" set before us.

Pr 9:5 — "Come, eat of my bread," says Wisdom.

Si 15:3 M.T. — The bread of Wisdom becomes to us our "bread of Understanding" once we have partaken of it.

Ps 51:6 — Once we have been nourished by the Truth within it which is the life of our souls.

Si 6:35 Sept. — The parable of the Mustard Seed is a "parable of Understanding," To those who really listen and partake of each and every Word.

Si 6:35 Sept. — Only to those who accept and hold fast all His Words,
Do the "parables of Understanding" open to reveal His Truth,

The wonderful Truth found inside the seeds that He sowed.

The parable of the Mustard Seed was told by Him in three* different ways,
To teach us about three distinct things:

Mt 13:31-32 — The Kingdom of Heaven.
Mk 4:30-32 — The Kingdom of God and Us.
Lk 13:17-19 — The Kingdom of God: Himself.

Jb 11:6 Sept.
& M.T. — "Oh, that the Lord would speak to thee and open His lips with thee
Then shall He declare to thee the secrets of Wisdom: that there are two sides to Wisdom."

Mt 13:31 — *"The Kingdom of heaven is like to a grain of mustard which a man took (lambano)* and sowed in his field."*

Mt 11:11-15 — The Kingdom of heaven can either be "taken" *(lambano)* or "received" *(lambano)* and then sowed.

Wiser are the little ones who ask and receive Understanding from God.

Is 45:11 M.T.
Ps 51:6 Sept. — For He said: "Ask Me of the things that are to come" and receive the Kingdom of Heaven: "the secret and hidden things of His Wisdom."

183

*"**THING**"=*Dabar* which means "word" or "matter": "It is the glory of God to hide a word *(dabar)* but the glory of kings is to search out a word" *(dabar)* or "matter" (Prov. 25:2) until "He brings forth the thing that is hid *(taalumah)* to light" (Job 28:11) and "the thing that is hid" *(taalumah)* are the "secrets *(taalumah)* of Wisdom" (Job 11:6).

*"**LEAST**": The smaller a thing is, the easier it is to conceal it. When God hides His Wisdom He conceals it inside little things as a word, letter, jot or tittle small as a grain of mustard. He then sows or caches it in the field of Holy Scripture.
A wise man is judged by his ability to disguise profound thoughts in simple and appropriate analogies. The classic test of the wisdom of another is the challenge by riddle and the questioning that fathoms his knowledge (I Kings 10:1-8). The riddles and questions are devised to test the competence behind the response.

*"**VEGETABLE**" (lachanon): In the parable of the Mustard Seed both St. Matthew and St. Mark use the Greek word *lachanon* which is commonly rendered "herbs" in English translations, however, it really mean**s** "vegetable" and is distinct from the common Greek word for "herb": *botane.* The word *lachanon* ("vegetable") is derived from the verb *lachaino* which means "to dig" because "vegetables" *(lachanon)* are harvested by digging them out. Thus when St. Jerome translated the Greek bible into Latin he rendered *lachanon* into the Latin word for "vegetable": *holus.* St. Jerome did not use the common Latin word *herba* because it means "herbs" but a "vegetable" is a "vegetable" *(holus).* Vegetarians do not live on "herbs" but they do live on "vegetables" and they know that "better is a meal of vegetables *(lachanon)* with friendliness and kindness than a feast of calves with enmity" (Prov. 15:17 Sept.). As St. Paul said to the Romans (14:2), "do not despise the weak man who eats only vegetables" *(lachanon)* and do not hide the "vegetables" behind the word "herbs."
Among all the seeds that are sown to produce an annual crop the grain of mustard is the least in size. Yet although it is the least in size as a seed it produces the largest of all plants that spring up from seeds that are sown. In less than a year's time the tiny grain of mustard springs up rapidly to become the sizeable mustard plant. There is an amazing difference in size between the sown mustard seed and the six to twelve foot high offspring plant that springs from it.
When our Lord told the parable of the Mustard Seed to illustrate the **"Reign of the Heavens"** (St. Matt. 13:31), *i.e.,* the final understanding of the Truth of His Words, He phrased the parable in such a way as to emphasize the end stage of the growth of the mustard seed: "**when it may be increased** *(auxano)* **it is greater than the vegetables and becomes a tree**" (St. Matt. 13:32 Literal Trans.).
St. Matthew was careful to retain this emphasis because the reign of understanding is reserved for the end (St. Mark 4:22; St. Luke 8:17; 12:12; 17:30; Jer. 23:20; 30:24; Isaiah 30:20; 52:15; 54:11-13; Dan. 11:33-35; 12:3; Zeph. 3:9; Prov. 1:23; 19:20; 2 Macc. 2:7-8; Sirach 16:21-22 (LV); 31:22 Hebrew Text; 33:6; 39:16-17,21,34; Enoch 1:2; 37:2; 38:3; 51:3; 100:6; 104:10-12; 2 Bar. 51:7-9; 4 Ezra 7:31,35,77; Romans 2:16; 11:25; I Cor. 2:7; 4:5; Coloss. 2:2-3; 2 Thess. 2:6-10; I Tim. 2:6; Heb. 6:5; I Peter 1:10-12; 2 Peter 1:19; Dead Sea Scrolls; I Qp Hab. 7:1-5; I Qh 9:23-24; I Qm 16:11; Midrash Rabbah on Eccle. 2:1 *etc.*).
It is when the time is ripe and all things have increased that we shall see the plant sprung up from the mustard seed become a glorious "tree." We shall see it *transformed* into a "tree" *(dendron)* and know that a "tree" *(dendron)* is no "vegetable" *(lachanon)* nor is a "shrub" *(thamnos, batos)* a "tree" *(dendron).* The evangelists knew the Greek word for "shrub" or "bush." *i.e.,* *batos,* for they used it (St. Mark 12:26, St. Luke 6:47; 20:37; Acts 7:30-35) but they were careful to use the word "tree" *(dendron)* in the parable of the mustard seed (St. Matt. 13:32; St. Luke 13:19) by what right does *The New American Bible* change the word tree into "shrub" and *The Living Bible* "great tree" (St. Luke 13:19) into "bush"?

*"**FOLLOW**": "He that comes to wisdom shall rest *(kataskenoo)* securely" (Sirach 4:15 Sept. Codex Vaticanus Text). He shall rest just as securely as "*the birds of heaven (that) come and shelter (kataskenoo) in*" (St. Matt. 13:32) the Wisdom of the Lord.

*"**REST**": In the parable of the Mustard Seed all three evangelists use the Greek word *kataskenoo* which literally means "to tent down" *(kata*=down; *skene*=tent). *Kataskenoo* is variously rendered "dwell," "lodge," "rest," "shelter" and "nest" in the English versions of the Gospels. However, *kataskenoo* strictly means "to rest" or "to take shelter" temporarily and not to "lodge," "dwell" or "nest" permanently. For we rest temporarily in hope until our hope is fulfilled. Thus in the Septuagint of Psalm 16:9 (Acts 2:26) David says: "my flesh shall rest *(kataskenoo)* in hope" *(elpis).* David rests in the promises of our Lord and in His Wisdom, for in the book of Proverbs (1:33 Sept.) Wisdom herself says: "he that hearkens to me shall rest *(kataskenoo)* in hope" *(elpis).* To rest in "hope" *(elpis)* upon the marvellous Wisdom of the Lord is to rest in "safety" *(elpis)* and "confidence" *(elpis).* His Wisdom is there in the tiniest of things small as a grain of mustard. So let us keep the least of His things and "let us hold fast the confession of our hope *(elpis)*. . .for He who promised is faithful" (Heb. 10:23) and He shall bring to light in the end—His wonderful knowledge (Isaiah 11:9).

*"*TSEL*" means "shadow" or "shade" in Hebrew. Thus when the Alexandrian Jewish scribes rendered the Hebrew Text of Ecclesiastes 7:12 into the Greek of the Septuagint they used the Greek word for "shade" or "shadow": *skia.* When the blazing "sun of justice" (Mal. 4:2) comes forth to scorch away all wickedness from this earth "healing" shall only be found under the shadow of "His wings" (Mal. 4:2). Then indeed "Wisdom is a shade *(tsel; skia)* that. . .revives the life of him who has it" (Eccle. 7:12) provided he has also had the "water of good understanding *(tebunah)* to drink" (Sirach 15:3 Hebrew Text).

Is 45:15 Jn 8:59 Jn 12:36	"Truly Thou art a God who hidest Thyself, O God of Israel the Saviour."
Pr 25:2 Jb 17:4	"It is the glory of God to hide a thing"* And keep the "heart *(leb)* from understanding" it Until the time comes for His Truth to be revealed.
Jn 16:13-14 Is 52:13-15	God hides His great Wisdom in the lowly and least* of things Because in the Day He shall be glorified, the height of His exaltation is measured from the base.
Si 1:23 Sept. Si 1:23 Sept.	"He will hide His Words for a season" as a tiny mustard seed sown in *"His field"* (St. Matt. 13:24, 31). "And the lips of many shall declare His understanding" when they see His *vegetable** grown higher than the rest of them.
Mt 13:32	They shall be utterly astonished and acclaim His Wisdom When they see the high vegetable transformed into a tree. *"So that the birds of heaven come and shelter in its branches"*
Ws 5:6 L.V. Ml 4:1-2	Because the wise birds know that the rising "sun of Understanding" becomes the blazing orb of Justice at noon.
	"He who has ears to hear let him hear" And let him tremble because the Day is at hand.
Jb 12:7	"Ask now the beasts and they shall teach thee; ask the birds of *heaven* and they shall tell thee," To flock to Him and seek His shelter while there is yet some time.
Jb 35:11	For it is the Lord "who teaches us more than the beasts of the earth and makes us *wiser* than the birds of *heaven.*"
Si 14:22,26-27	"Blessed is the man that shall come to an end in Wisdom he shall set his children under her shelter and shall rest under her branches. By her he shall be covered from the heat and he shall lodge in her glory."
Qo 7:11	So follow* the birds! and rest* under her protection. "For Wisdom is an advantage to those who see the sun" of Understanding rise up in that Day.
Qo 7:12 Qo 7:12	"Wisdom is a shadow" *(tsel)** and a shelter from the burning judgment that comes at noon. "The advantage of the Knowledge of Wisdom is that Wisdom revives *(chayah)* the life of him who has it"... Who has the life of Truth within him on that Day of Days.

185

*"**BROUGHT FORTH**": Mysteries remain hidden until they are brought forth and when that happens they are no longer "mysteries" but "revelations." In the parable of the Mustard Seed as found in St. Matthew, the "Mysteries of the Kingdom of Heaven" (St. Matt. 13:11) are as it were hidden inside the tiny grain of mustard sown in his field, waiting for the time when all that has been sown in the ground shall come to light.

God hides His greatest Mysteries in the smallest things so as to give the largest reward to those who have held fast the least of His things (St. Matt. 5:19-20). In His time it was relatively easy for the "ground" to hold fast the respectable seeds of Mosaic teaching but it required faith and perseverance to hold on to the apparently insignificant teachings of our Lord. In the reign of understanding it is the revelation of these little things that shall tower as a "tree" over all that was sown in His field so that all may see the glorious wisdom and understanding which was hidden within that humble seed. Then all the people shall flock to Him, as "the birds of heaven" in the parable did, to the "Tree" that was once a little seed.

*"**FIELD**": When our Lord told the parable of the Good Seed and the Darnel (St. Matt. 13:24-30) He spoke about "a man who sowed good seed" of "wheat" "in his field" (vv. 24,25) and He continued speaking to the "crowds" (vv. 2-3,34) telling "them" "another parable": the parable of the Mustard Seed (vv.31-32) which was also sown "in his field" (St. Matt. 13:24,31). Thus the phrase, "in his field," continued to evoke the imagery of a field where grain was sown. Because of the restrictions imposed on farmers by the Oral Law, the ears of His listeners must have pricked up when our Lord commenced the parable of the Mustard Seed saying: "The **Kingdom of Heaven is like to a grain** (*kokkos*=singular: one grain) **of mustard which a man sowed in his field**." Hearing about this singular grain must have made the crowd smile for the following reasons: the Oral Law decreed that a field where wheat or barley had been sown could be bordered by sowing the edges of it with condiment seeds similar to mustard, *viz.*, cummin, fennel, caraway and dill (all these are used in the Middle East to flavor bread) but a field of grain could *not* be bordered by sowing *mustard*: "they may not flank a field of grain with mustard" (Kilaim 2:8 Mishnah). The explanation given for this restriction is that mustard seeds grow up to become exceptionally large plants which tend to hide a field of grain and make it appear like a field of mustard instead. However, the Oral Law frequently provided "loopholes" even for the mustard seeds, it ruled that if a field of grain had a small unsown patch within or to the side of it of not more than "two of a quarter of one *kab's* space he may sow it with mustard seed; but if three of a quarter of one *kab's* space he may not sow them with mustard seed since it might appear like a field of mustard" (Kilaim 2:9). Thus to avoid giving scandal in that "field" our Lord wisely limited the sowing of mustard in His parable to one solitary grain! The poor mustard seeds were indeed discriminated against by the Oral Law for another ruling decreed that "lettuce and wild lettuce, chicory and wild chicory, the leek and wild leek, the coriander and wild coriander. . .are not accounted Diverse Kinds" (Kilaim 1:2) which means to say that "chicory and wild chicory" or "the leek and wild leek" could be sown together and share the same garden bed but not mustard and wild mustard for "although mustard and wild mustard are like to each other they are accounted Diverse Kinds" (Kilaim 1:5) and as such they could not be sown together or occupy the same plot. This was particularly ironic because another loophole in the Oral Law allowed ordinary (Jewish) "Mustard and *Egyptian* mustard" to be sown together, for they "are not accounted Diverse Kinds" (Kilaim 1:2) but ordinary "Mustard and wild mustard" were to remain forever estranged. How sad—because the word for "wild mustard" in Hebrew is "mustard of the field" and if the field was in Israel it meant that ordinary Jewish mustard and Israelite mustard were forbidden to be in the same garden bed.

As the old Rabbi said: "It takes wisdom to sweeten the mustard" (Midrash Rabbah on Song of Songs 1:8).

*"**COUNSEL**": The common Hebrew word for "tree": *ets,* is closely related to the Hebrew word for "counsel": *etsah.* In the parable of the Mustard Seed (St. Matt.) the "birds of heaven" come to the "tree" of His revealed wisdom, knowledge, and understanding of the Truth. "The birds of heaven come and shelter in its branches" because these wise birds know that all the ingredients of good counsel (*etsah*) are found in that Tree (*ets*) of the Lord.

Thus Jeremiah (6:6) uniquely and wisely said against false Jerusalem: "hew down (her) *counsel*" (*etsah*) instead of saying "hew down (her) trees" (*ets*) for in the enigmatic (Numbers 12:6-8) words of prophecy, a counsellor is a tree and vice versa as Ezra the wise scribe knew when he said that "the trees of the field took counsel" (4 Ezra 4:13).

It depends on the "tree" (*ets*) whether the "counsel" (*etsah*) received is good or bad for "an instruction of vanities is the tree itself" (Jer. 10:8 Literal Translation) of the foolish who flock to it. Jeremiah, to whom "the Lord hath given. . . .Knowledge" (Jer. 11:18) that forewarned him of the evil intent of his enemies, in turn quoted them as saying of him: "Let us destroy the tree (*ets*) and the fruit (*lechem*=bread) thereof" (Jer. 11:19) or in other words "let us get rid of Jeremiah and his good counsel." For evil people prefer to "ask counsel at their trees (*ets*) or stocks (*ets*) and their staff declares (falsely) unto them. . .to cause them to err for they have gone a-whoring from under their God" (Hosea 4:12). Only the Tree of the Lord gives good and true counsel. Consequently, in later Hebrew *etsah* became a word for "trees" as well as "counsel" (*See* Erubim 67b B. Talmud; Erubim VIII 25b; Sabb. III 6a; Sukk. I 52c, Jer. Talmud).

Great Mysteries are concealed in the least of things
To remain hidden until they are brought* forth.

The Lord hid His great Understanding in the little mustard grain
that He sowed in His field* of Truth,
The field where the good seed of His Word was sown.

In the time of the Harvest,
When we shall have brought forth the fruit of His Word,
We shall become aware of the large fully grown plant by the side
of His field,

The plant that sprung up from the mustard seed.

We shall then be able to discern it because the fruit brought forth
from His Word is the fruit of Understanding.

Ps 147:5

Ps 145:3

It shall take all our understanding to make us truly realize how
much more He understood.
And we shall discover that everything we possess is nothing
compared to what belongs to Him.

Then shall our eyes suddenly see
His large plant become an incomparable Tree.

Ezk 17:23;
31:6,12
Dn 4:12,21-22

And the birds of heaven shall come and shelter in its branches
For protection and advice.

Pr 16:16 Sept.

Because "the brood of Wisdom" and "the brood of
Understanding" know that the place for good "counsel"* (etsah)
is the "Tree" (etsah) of the Lord.

Pr 3:18

And before the end all the nations of the world shall come to it
To His Tree of Life and Wisdom and True Knowledge.

Have some fruit of True knowledge from an understanding
branch

*Jb 12:11
Si 36:19

But examine* it very closely before you partake of it.

Then bite into it
and learn—

That the beauty on the outside of His fruit is Wisdom
And the goodness inside of it: Truth.

Eat and live!!

*"**HIDDEN**": The sower, when he sows, covers up the seed, for which reason today he is called by the Arabs a *kafir* (Lit., "he who covers up").

*"**WORD**": The hidden Wisdom and Understanding of our Lord is placed as a grain of mustard in the same field where the "good seed" (St. Matt. 13:24) of His Word has been sown. We are the ground in His field and if we hold fast to all His seeds however small and trivial they may seem to be, we shall bring forth the fruit of understanding the wisdom of His Word. In the end it is those who have held fast the least of His things—to the last jot and tittle—who shall bring forth the greatest of fruits (St. Matt. 5:19).
Among the Jews no word of a Scriptural text was considered superfluous for even the slightest and apparently most trivial element of a text was believed to contain profound truths (*See* Bereshith Rabbah 68 *et seq.*). The figurative language behind the parable of the Mustard Seed is very apt because in Rabbinic circles the skillful fine argumentation of a Scriptural text by disciples was known as *pilpul hatalmaddim, i.e.,* "seasoned" discussion. The word *pilpul* in Rabbinic terminology means the scholarly penetration that arrives at a sound conclusion through minute and exhaustive investigation. *"Ba'al pilpul"* was the term given to a "master of ingenious disputation and deduction" (B. Talmud: Baba Bathra 145b, Tosefta VII.5; Shabbath 31a; Baba Metzia 85b; Aboth VI.5; Baraita B.B. 145b; Terumah 16a; Ketuboth 103b; Jer. Talmud: Terumoth *IV.* 42d; Horayoth *III.*48c). The word *pilpul* itself means "pepper corn," sharp and penetrating as mustard is to the palate or the term *"pilpul"* to the "discernment" *(taam)* "good judgment" *(taam; Ps. 119:66)* and "taste" *(taam)* of the "understanding" *(taam).* "For as the mouth tasteth (and discerns) so does an understanding heart" (Sir. 36:19).
So let us hold fast His "mustard seed" and we shall explain the grain. "If you have faith as a grain of mustard" "and do not doubt" (St. Matt. 17:20; St. Mark 12:23) in His Words, you will someday overturn all stumbling blocks and become a greater expounder than the *"pilpulist"* who was called an "uprooter of mountains" but yet was limited in his understanding (Berakoth 64a; Horayoth 14a. *See also* Sanhedrin 24a; Tamid 32a; Yebamoth I 3a; Exodus Rabbah XV. 4).

*"**INCREASED**": St. Matthew 13:32 is written in the Greek Aorist tense and it literally reads: "but when it may be increased" *(auxano).* The statement is both indefinite and conditional for it is written: "but when." The Greek word *auxano,* commonly rendered "grown," actually means "increased" *(auxano)* as in I Cor. 3:7: "God gives the increase" *(auxano).* For the Word of God does not "grow up" *(anabaino)* like we do, "the Word of God increases" *(auxano)*—Acts 6:7, and if we hold it fast we shall "increase *(auxano)* in every way unto Him who is the Head, into Christ" (Eph. 4:15).

*"**WE**": In the time of the harvest, the fruit brought forth from the "good seed" is the full ear of wheat. Allegorically it may be called the "fruit of understanding" because it is composed of perfectly ordered rows of children seeds and to be able to do that takes understanding. The "fruit of understanding" may be also called the "fruit of the light" (Eph. 5:9 Lit. Trans.) for it sprung forth from the "light" that was "sown for the righteous" (Ps. 97:11).
The good ground that brings forth this "fruit" gradually becomes aware of the extent of the wisdom and understanding of our Lord that was hidden as it were like an insignificant grain of mustard in the same field where His word was sown. As the fruit of light matures, awareness of the hidden Wisdom and Understanding of our Lord increases in the heart of the ground which now acknowledges that His heavenly plant surpasses all earthly growth. Then, when the fruit has become fully perfected with all His Words well arrayed within the ground shall exalt His hidden greatness and make manifest His glorious Truth. "Who, as I, can proclaim *(qara)*[1] and declare it and set it in order *(arak)*"? saith the Lord (Isaiah 44:7). For His "Wisdom orders all things well" and "God orders all things rightly" (Wisdom 8:1; 12:15 Latin Vulgate). And "who shall order His Words with judgment"? (Ps. 111 (112):5 Latin Vulgate) "Who shall magnify Him as He is?" (Sirach 43:31) "What man can set in order a song of praise to tell of His wondrous works?" (Midrash Rabbah on Ps. 40:5). For "man knows not the order *(erek)*[2] of Understanding" (Job 28:13), until he shall have brought forth the fruit of His Word. Hold fast to the seed!

[1] *Qara* is also the Hebrew verb for "to read" (*See* Exod. 24:7; Deut. 17:19; 31:11; Josh. 8:34,35; 2 Kings 5:7; 19:14; 23:2; Neh. 8:8, 18; 9:3; Isaiah 29:11; 34:16; Jer. 36:6,8,10,13,14,15,21,23; Hab. 2:2. etc.). As a noun *aara* is the term for a "Biblical scholar" (*See* Kidd. 49a; Ber. 30b; Pesikta Shubah p. 165b; Yalkut to Hos. 533; Ab. Zar. 40a B. Talmud) and a *"qara* text" is the Rabbinic term for the authoritative or definitive scriptural text. (*See* Ber. 2a; 27a; 29b; 30b; Sanh. 45b; 71a; Ket. 56a; Yeb. 40a, B. Talmud. *See also* 2 Baruch 27:14-15; 28:1). Thus Rabbi Eliezer (c.1st Cent. A.D.) read Isaiah 44:7; "who, as I can read *(qara)* and declare it and set it in order," commenting that Holy Scripture is purposely not arranged in proper order and only God knows the true order of its arrangement, adding that the dead would resurrect if man was able to arrange the sections of Holy Scripture in their proper order (*See* Midrash Rabbah on Psalm 3:1 sect. 2; 2 Cor. 3:14-16; Rom. 11:7, 8, 10, *15*).

[2] *Erek.* Job 28:13 is usually rendered "man knows not the price *(erek)* thereof." However, the most ancient commentaries and texts rightly rendered it in the sense of "setting in order" or the "ordering" of it. The ancient scribal marginal notation of Exodus 40:4 defines *erek* as "the order thereof." *Erek* is spelled the same way as *arak* ("to set in order") in Hebrew. Thus Exodus 40:7, 23 reads: "Thou shalt bring in the table and set in order *(arak)* the things that are to be set in order *(erek)* upon it. . .and he set the bread in order" *(erek)* or literally "he set in order, the order *(erek)* of the bread."

Mt 13:31
Mt 13:31
The Mysteries of the *"Kingdom of Heaven"* remain hidden* as a tiny *"grain of mustard"* by the side of His Word.*
There to remain until the fruit of the good seed is brought forth by the ground in His field.

The good seed is brought forth as wheat: in the time of the Harvest,
When all things that are sown have increased and come to light.

Mt 13:32
Mt 13:32
In the same season *"when it may be increased"** as well
We shall become aware that His plant *"is greater than the vegetables and becomes a Tree"*

Because then, in the time of the Harvest
We* shall have exalted it in His own Words.

189

CHAPTER 8

THE PARABLE OF THE MUSTARD SEED

According to St. Mark 4:30-32

[30] And He said, "To what shall we liken the Kingdom of God? And to what parable shall we compare it?

[31] As a grain of mustard which when it may be sown in the ground is smaller than all the seeds that are in the ground.

[32] But when it is sown it comes up and becomes greater than all the vegetables and makes great branches so that the birds of heaven are able to shelter under its shade."

Literal Translation.

*"**GROWN**" or better still, "increased": "when it may be increased" (St. Matt. 13:32) depends on *us:* the "ground" in His field.

*"**SOWN**": "When it may be sown" (St. Mark 4:31) depends on *Him:* the Sower. Yet no man knows the time for it is the Father in heaven who gives the "rain" (St. Matt. 5:45), *i.e.,* the "early rain" that prepares the soil and brings the Sower to *sow* and the "latter rain" that brings the Lord of the Harvest to *gather* the fruits it matured.

*"**HARVEST**": All things mature and become fulfilled in the time of the harvest. His glorious Wisdom and Understanding become unveiled in the time of the harvest because by then we shall have brought forth His Words in the proper order needed to praise Him worthily. In the end it is through Understanding that we shall unearth His Wisdom and exalt it as a tree to be seen by all because it is left for us to glorify Him (St. John 7:3-4,6; 16:14; 17:9-10). In the prophetic Psalm 56:10 (Sept.) which is titled: "do not destroy" save "for the end," the Psalmist sings: "For Thy Mercy has been magnified even to the heavens and Thy Truth *(aletheia)* to the clouds" just like a tree! Remember that the "Light" that was sown (Ps. 97:11) springs up from the earth as "Truth" revealed (Ps. 85:11) that it may be "magnified" and exalted by our praise (Ps 56:10). Thus Wisdom says: "I was exalted *(hupsoo)* like a cedar in Lebanon and (exalted) as a cypress tree upon the mountains of Hermon. I was *exalted* like a palm tree in En-gaddi. . .as a plane tree by the water was I *exalted*" (Sirach 24:13-14 Sept.) because Wisdom knows that she is exalted by the same *ground* that exalts trees and brings forth Truth to magnify it. The good ground that understands the Word lifts up His Wisdom and Truth to exalt it like a tree *"so that* the birds of heaven *come* and shelter in its branches" (St. Matt. 13:32) to receive the fruits of His counsel and sing the praises of His Truth. "Wisdom *nested* with faithful men" (Sirach 1:15 Sept.) as a seed in the good ground of their hearts, and Wisdom became a tree to shelter and shade them in turn. "Blessed is the man. . .who sets his *nest* in her (Wisdom's) foliage and *lodges* among her *branches* seeking refuge from the heat in her shade" (Sirach 14:20,26,27 Hebrew Text Ms. A, Geniza fragment), for "by her (Wisdom) he shall be covered from the heat, and shall lodge in her glory" (Sirach 14:27 Sept.). "Among men of Truth hath Wisdom been established—forever" (Sirach 1:15 emended Syriac Text.) because men of Truth are true and they possess the Truth that is needed to establish Wisdom. Remember that "Truth lodges with them that practice her": men of Truth (Sirach 27:9 Sept. (v. 10) L.V.; St. John 3:21).

*"**NEED**": "For the Lord is *truthful* in all His *Words* and *kind* in all His *works*" (Ps. 145:13, 17 Latin Vulgate and Syriac Text).

The Mysteries of the Kingdom of Heaven remain secret until **grown.***
The Mystery of the Kingdom of God remains secret until **sown,***

The Kingdom of **Heaven** is made manifest in our understanding which becomes fully perfected in the time of the Harvest* when all things have then matured.

The Kingdom of God is made manifest soon after it is sown Because it becomes evident in the goodness, mercy and love springing forth from those who hold His seed fast.

Mk 4:31
Aorist tense

The Mystery of the Kingdom of God is like a tiny grain of mustard hidden in the hand of the Sower And there it remains until *"it may be sown."*

He does not sow it until we are ready to receive it And it does not grow unless we give it all our self.

Si 33:10
Mk 4:31
Mk 4:28

For we are *"the ground"* in His field And *"of itself the ground bears fruit,"* Provided the seed is sown and the ground accepts it.

Lk 17:20

When the infinite power and glory of God becomes infinitesimally small, It is in order that it may be sown in us and enter our hearts unnoticed.

He decreases so that He may increase in us.

But for Him to increase in us requires maximum effort on our part And we must give Him all that we are or He will not flourish in the ground of our hearts.

Mk 4:31
L.T.

Among *"all the seeds of those on the ground"* His seed is sown as the smallest, So that it may exercise our faith to hold on to it, And reward our endurance if we succeed.

Mt 5:17-20

For indeed those who hold fast to the least of His things Shall bring forth the greatest.

Jn 1:14

And what is more they shall grow up to become someone like Him "Full of grace and Truth."

Mk 4:32

And full of *"great branches"* made to give *"shelter"* and *"shade"* To those in need.*

193

*"WAY": The parable of the Mustard Seed is a "parable of *understanding*" (Sirach 6:35 Greek and Hebrew Texts). This type of parable calls for close attention and earnest consideration on our part or else the hidden truths in it: "the subtleties of parables. . .the secrets of parables" (Sirach 39:2 L.V.: Prov. 1:3; Wisdom 8:8 Sept.) shall escape our notice. It takes great effort for "the finding out of parables is a wearisome labour of mind" (Sirach 13:26 Sept.) and much more so the finding out of the parables of understanding. Therefore "be eager to hear every saying of God and do not let the parables of understanding escape you" (Sirach 6:35 Latin Vulgate and Greek Texts).

"Many parables such as this (toioutos) *He spoke to them"* (St. Mark 4:33 Literal Translation). St. Mark said this, following the narration of the parable of the Mustard Seed because our Lord told the same parables over again with slight variations designed to convey a separate truth in each instance. Thus in the gospel according to St. Mark, just before telling the parable of the Mustard Seed to set forth the mystery of the Kingdom of God, our Lord said: *"To what parable* (parabole) *shall we set it alongside* (paraballo)?" (St. Mark 4:31). We shall set it alongside the same parable of the Mustard Seed as told by Him to set forth the mysteries of the Kingdom of *Heaven* (as recorded in St. Matt. 13:31-32) and wait for someone who understands to be able to discern the difference between these "parables of understanding."

The lord told the parable of the Mustard Seed in three distinct ways to set forth three separate events:
(1) The sowing of Understanding (The Kingdom of Heaven) in His *"field"* and how it is to be made manifest in the end (The form of this parable found in the gospel according to St. Matthew).
(2) The sowing of the Kingdom of God in the *"ground"* and how it is made manifest in us (The form of this parable found in the Gospel according to St. Mark).
(3) The casting of the Kingdom of God: Himself, in His own *"garden"* and the effect of His Presence in our midst (The form of this parable found in the gospel according to St. Luke).

In St. Matthew,
Our Lord began the parable by stating an accomplishment: *"the Kingdom of Heaven is like a grain of mustard which a man took and sowed in his field."* In this instance the **sowing** is definite and it was done **"in his field"** but the **increase** is **indefinite** and **conditional:** *"but when it may be increased."* When the time comes that it may be increased, an extraordinary thing happens, the grain of mustard which is seen to have developed into something *"greater than the vegetables"* suddenly *"becomes a tree."* It becomes a tree for a reason: *"so that the birds of heaven come and shelter in its branches."* (Note parallel increase in size in Daniel 2:35).

In St. Mark.
The **sowing** is **indefinite** and **conditional:** but *"when it may be sown,"* and the tiny seed is sown upon the **"ground."** But *"when it may be sown,"* the **growth** is **definite** for *"it grows* (anabaino=to ascend in growth) *and becomes greater than all the vegetables."* In the narrative pattern of the parable of the Mustard Seed as retained in St. Mark there is no mention of a tree and all our attention is drawn to the *"great branches"* that the larger plant **"makes"[2]** *(poieo)* **"so that** *the birds of heaven are able to shelter under its shade."* For in this instance of telling the parable our Lord asked for collaboration on our part: *"to what shall we liken the Kingdom of God and to what parable shall we compare it?"* and, having invited our participation he graciously gives the limelight to the *"branches":* the **"great[3]** *branches".*

In St. Luke.
The form of the parable preserved by St. Luke is the one He told without qualifications. Both the **casting** of the grain *and* the **increase** are **unconditional:** *"The Kingdom of God is like a grain of mustard which a man took and cast into his own* garden *and it increased and became a great tree and the birds of heaven sheltered in its branches."* In this instance He also asked a rhetorical question but He did not solicit collaboration from His listeners: *"to what is the Kingdom of God like and to what shall I liken it?"* for on this occasion He was illustrating, by parable, the incarnate Kingdom of God: Himself. God is incomparable, there is no setting alongside in this form of the parable and there are no vegetables mentioned and no intermediate stage, the *"grain" "increased"* to *"a great Tree"* and when it did so *"the birds of heaven came and sheltered in its branches."* Notice also in St. Luke that He did not "sow" the grain "in his field" or "upon the ground" but **"cast"** it *"into* his own garden."

[1] "parable" *(parabole).* In all the rest of the forty-nine times it is used in the New Testament the word *parabole* means "parable," *i.e.*, a narrative from which a moral or spiritual truth is drawn, not a "comparison."

[2] "makes" *(poieo).* The Greek word *poieo* is an active verb meaning "to make," "to do," "to create" and "to work." It implies *active effort* in making the "branches" for a specific purpose, *viz.*, to provide shelter for the "birds of heaven." The usual word for "putting forth" branches or leaves is *ekphuo* (See St. Matt. 24:32; St. Mark 13:28). *Ekphuo* is derived from *ek*="out" and *phuo*="to bring forth," "to produce." In contradistinction to *poieo* it does not imply active effort.

[3] "great branches". Since in this form of telling the parable (as preserved in St. Mark), our Lord asked for our participation, He generously directs attention to the "branches" and makes no mention of a "Tree." He honors the "branches" as Wisdom herself honored her branches saying of them: "My branches are the branches of honor and grace" (Sirach 24:16). The word "branches" in this form of the parable is particularly appropriate in describing the role of a disciple (St. John 15:5) or "son" because in Holy Scripture a "son" (ben) or "daughter" (bath) is figuratively speaking a "branch" of the parent tree:
"The branch (ben) Thou madest strong for Thyself" (Ps. 80:15).
"Whose branches (bath pl.) run over the wall" (Gen. 49:22).
It is through the "branches" that the Tree shelters the unfortunate and it is through the "branches" that it gives fruit to the hungry. The abundance and sweetness of the fruits in the branches bear witness in turn to the excellence of the Tree (St. John 15:8).

194

Our Lord asked for our collaboration when He told the parable of the mustard seed in such a way* as to set forth the mystery of the Kingdom of God.

Mk 4:30

Thus in St. Mark He said: *"To what shall we liken the Kingdom of God and to what parable shall we compare it?"*

He asks for our cooperation because the Kingdom of God is sown for us
And it is up to us to make it grow and flourish in the ground of our hearts.

But the Lord does not sow His dominion in us
Unless we are ready to receive it and accept His rule.

Mk 4:31
Aorist Tense

And so He said: *"when it may be sown"* and made the time indefinite
Because the sowing depends on the Sower who knows the state of the ground.

Mk 4:31

But when it may be sown and is accepted by the ground, the growth is definite.
For *"when it may be sown it grows up and becomes greater than the vegetables"*

Day by day,

Mk 4:32
Mk 4:32

The Kingdom of God is made manifest in its growth
And in the loving Mercy of its *"great branches"* that are *made*
"so that the birds of heaven are able to shelter under its shade."

There to rejoice in the ground that held fast to the least of His seeds and thereby brought forth something greater than the vegetables:

The vegetables sprung forth from those who held fast other seeds instead of His.

195

CHAPTER 9

THE PARABLE OF THE MUSTARD SEED

According to St. Luke 13:17-19

[17] And when He had said these things all His adversaries were put to shame and all the people rejoiced over all the glorious things that were being done by Him.
[18] He said therefore, "To what is the Kingdom of God like? and to what shall I liken it?
[19] It is like to a grain of mustard which a man took and cast into his own garden: and it increased and became a great tree and the birds of heaven sheltered in its branches."

Literal Translation.

*"SONS OF THE TREE": "To fear the Lord is the root of Wisdom and Wisdom's branches are length of days" (Sirach 1:20). "In length of days: Understanding" (Job 12:12) and so Wisdom's branches understand and bear fruit of praise for Him: "The branches of trees exalt my Words" (Ps. 151:3 Psalm Scroll Cave 11, Dead Sea Scrolls). There shall be fruit in the branches if they remain attached to the Lord and let His life giving graces course through them. Otherwise they shall wither and "when the *branches* are withered they shall be broken off and the women shall come and set them on fire because it is a people of no *understanding*" (Isaiah 27:11), a people without fruit in their branches. Hold fast the Seed of His Word and you shall become "Trees of Righteousness the planting of the Lord that He might be glorified" (Isaiah 61:3) by the fruits of your branches (St. John 15:8; Heb. 12:11; St. James 3:18; Ps. 1:1,3).

*"NO COMPARISON": God can *liken* Himself to a Tree, *e.g.*, "I am like a...Tree" (Hosea 14:8) but He never compares Himself to anything because a comparison is the setting alongside of one thing to another. Comparisons presuppose similarity and who is like unto God that we may place him alongside the Lord? We can "compare ourselves with ourselves" (2 Cor. 10:12 L.V.) and we can try "comparing spiritual things with spiritual" (I Cor. 2:13) but who can compare God to anyone? (Ps. 89:6).
St. Luke (13:17-19) preserves the form of the parable of the Mustard Seed as told by our Lord in response to the exultation of the people over *"all the glorious things that were being done by Him. He said* **therefore,"** the same parable of the Mustard Seed in such a way as to acknowledge their praise and also to praise *"His own garden"* before the crowd that was gathered on this occasion, *"in one of the synagogues"* (St. Luke 13:10, 14), *not* "by the sea side" (St. Matt. 13:1, 31; St. Mark 4:1,3).
In this instance our Lord praised Himself just as it was said that "Wisdom shall praise herself" as a "Tree" (Sirach 24:1, 12-17) for our Lord is "the Wisdom of God" (St. Luke 11:49; I Cor. 1:24,30; Col. 2:3). Thus there are no other "seeds" or "vegetables" in this form of the parable retained by St. Luke and there are no prerequisites and no intermediate stage between the "grain" and the "great Tree" sprung forth from it. Remember that something "like a grain of mustard" is not a grain of mustard because a grain of mustard never increases to become "a great Tree." To be like, is not to be the same. When He also said: "I am like an evergreen fir tree, from Me is your fruit found" (Hosea 14:8), He does not intend to make us consider eating fir cones. He said: "like an evergreen fir tree" because most of the fruits of the Holy Land which the Israelites knew and partook of came from deciduous trees whose leaves faded and shriveled away every Fall but God is not like a fruit tree "whose leaf fadeth" (Isaiah 1:30). When He likens Himself to a tree He is like a very special "great Tree" whose leaves are forever green and whose fruit is out of this world. He was indeed in our midst as a great Tree sprung up from something as small as a grain of mustard is to us.

*"GOD": In Holy Scripture (Isaiah 1:29; 61:3; Ezek. 31:4) one of the Hebrew words for "tree" in the *plural* form is *elim* ("trees"). *Elim* is never used in the singular because it would then have to be rendered *El*, the formal Hebrew word for "God." Another Hebrew word *elah* means "oak tree" or "turpentine tree" (Gen. 35:4; Judges 6:11, 19; I Kings 13:14; Isaiah 6:13, etc.) but it is also the Hebrew-Aramaic word for "God," especially as regards the worship due to Him (Ezra 6:18; 7:15,19; Dan. 3:17, etc.). Again, another Hebrew word for "oak" is *allah* (Josh 24:26) which is of course the Arabic word for "God." Thus it was not inappropriate for Him to liken Himself to a tree.
There is great Wisdom hidden in the parable of the Mustard Seed for man begins life as a little "bundle" *(tseror)* smaller than a "grain" *(tseror)* of mustard. The little "bundle" grows to become big as a large "vegetable" *(yarak)*. A "vegetable" *(yarak)* may look, "bright" *(barak. See* Midrash Rabbah on Song of Songs 6:11) but if that "vegetable" opens its mouth before the time all it will be able to do is to "expectorate" *(yarak)* and "spit" *(yarak)*. Therefore it must be patient and continue to hold fast the Word until it shall increase to the size of a "large plant" *(siach)* or "bush" *(siach)*. Then it will be able to "talk" *(siach)*, "speak" *(siach)*, "commune" *(siach)* and "declare" *(siach)* the wonders of the Lord and "meditate" *(siach)* on them. Someday, when the time comes, that "bush" *(siach)* may become a little "tree" *(etsah)* full of good "advice" *(etsah)* or better still, it may choose to be part of the great Tree as one of its very own understanding branches.
It is written: "They shall return and dwell beneath His shade" (Hosea 14:7).

*"GARDEN": The expression "garden" signifies "woman" (Pirke Rabbi Eliezer, chapter 21). The "garden enclosed and barred" is used as a simile for the "chaste virgin bride" (Midrash Rabbah on Canticles 4:12). Early rabbinic Meshalim (Parabolic teaching) commented that a garden was the most precious gift a king could give to his dearest child (Deut. Rabbah 5:7; Yalkut I Sect. 907). In Holy Scripture, the Hebrew word *ganzak* (I Chr. 28:11) and *genazim* (Esther 3:9; 4:7) mean "treasuries." Both these words are derived from *gan, gannah* and *gennah* the Hebrew-Aramaic words for "garden." All of these in turn are closely related to the verb *ganan* which means "to defend." For gardens were "defended" *(ganan)* by being made into "enclosures" *(gan, gannah)* to "shield" *(magan)* them from the cupidity of outsiders. Great care was taken to keep a garden clear of weeds, the surveillance and assiduous tillage that a garden frequently required provided material for the rabbinic parables found in the Midrash and Talmud (See Exodus Rabbah 2.2; Leviticus Rabbah 4:5; Numbers Rabbah 15.25; Sanhedrin 91a; Yebamoth 216, etc.). A garden was kept enclosed and barred to protect it from thieves. In turn "thieves" *(ganab, ganabim)* got their name from their habit of "stealing" *(ganab)* things from a "garden" *(gan, gannah)*. The act itself of stealing things from a garden constituted the definition of "robbery": "that which is guarded within a garden it is forbidden to take—the taking would be robbery; but that which is not guarded in a garden may be taken, and the taking is not robbery" (Pesikta Rabbati Pisk. 21:19). Water is scarce in the Holy Land and a garden is a valuable piece of property for it betokens an independent water supply from a fountain, well or spring. In the rich imagery of Holy Scripture the terms "garden" and "well watered" are synonymous (See Canticles 4:15; Isaiah 51:3; 58:11; Jer. 31:8; Sirach 24:42 etc.). "A garden causes what is sown in it to spring up" (Isaiah 61:11) because it is well watered and kept free from noxious weeds. (cont'd.)

198

Ho 14:8 En 32:6	The sons* of the Tree are the understanding branches But the "Tree of Wisdom" is the Lord Himself.
Mt 12:28 Lk 11:20 Lk 13:18	He *is* the Kingdom of God. And when He asked: *"To what shall I liken the Kingdom of God": Himself,* He made no* comparisons.
	There are no other "seeds" or "vegetables" in the parable of the mustard seed as preserved by St. Luke.
Is 46:5	Because the Lord said: "To whom will you liken Me as an equal? And to what shall you compare Me as though we were alike?"
Is 44:7 Is 46:9	"Who is like Me?" "For I am God, and there is no other; I am God and there is none like Me."
	Only God can liken Himself to something But He never compares Himself to anything He has made.
Is 40:18	Do not try to compare Him with others. For "to whom will you liken God? and to what likeness shall you compare Him?"
Ps 35:10 Jr 10:6	"O Lord, who is like unto Thee?" "There is none like unto Thee, O Lord."
Lk 13:19	Even as a Seed the Lord is incomparable And only God* can increase to be: **"a great** *Tree"*
Lk 13:19 Sg 4:12	When He sowed Himself: He *"cast" (ballo)* Himself *"into His own garden"* Because His own garden* is "a garden enclosed."
Lk 13:19	In that holy ground His seed *"increased (auxano) and became (ginomai) a great Tree"*
Lk 13:19 Lk 13:19 Lk 13:17	And *"it came to pass" (ginomai)* that *"the birds of heaven did shelter in its branches"*, There to rejoice *"over all the glorious things that were being done by Him."*
	And shall be done again.
Is 61:11	"For as the earth brings forth its shoots And as a *garden* causes what is sown in it to spring up So the Lord will cause righteousness and praise to spring forth before all the nations"
	When the time is ripe.

199

(cont'd.)

In the parable of the Mustard Seed as retained in St. Luke our Lord did not say "sow" *(speiro)* as He did in the two other instances He narrated this parable (St. Matt. 13:31; St. Mark 4:31,32) but said "cast" *(ballo)* instead and thus kept "His own garden" inviolate. The concept of the inviolability of the Lord's own garden is found in the rabbinic parables of Rabbi Eliezer ben Hyrcanus (1st Century A.D.), he used to say: "Peer not into the garden of the Holy One, blessed be He; if thou hast looked in, do not enter. . .for if thou didst peer and enter. . .in the end thou wilt be cut off from the world" (Tanna di ben Eliahu, Ch. 7). For "the Lord's own garden" was the place where He kept His most secret thoughts and to "peer into His garden" meant to "look into the Divine secrets" (Tosefta Hagigah II. 234; Bacher Ag. Tan. I. 340). Philo Judaeus (c.20 B.C.-40 A.D.) often used the garden of Paradise as an image for theosophical inquiry (Philo Q. and A. Gen. Sect. 51 *re.* Gen. 1.6 foll. *See also* 2 Cor. 12:3-4). It is only fitting that St. Luke who told us about the Incarnation of the Word of God should also preserve for us the form of this parable wherein the Lord praises His mother and Himself. In St. Luke we find that the grain of mustard increased to become a great Tree for both the Seed and the garden are wonderfully unique and incomparable.

"Grace is like a garden of blessings" (Sirach 40:17; St. Luke 1:28; 2:52).

"The fear of the Lord is a Paradise of blessing" (Sirach 40:27).

200

The Parable of the Mustard Seed
And its Hidden Differences

According to St. Matthew 13:31-32

³¹ Another parable He set before them saying, "The *Kingdom of Heaven* is like to a grain of mustard which a man took and *sowed* in *his field.*
³² It is the least indeed of all the seeds but *when it may be increased* it is greater than the vegetables and *becomes* a *tree* so that the birds of heaven come and shelter in its branches."

Literal Translation.

According to St. Mark 4:30-32

³⁰ And He said, "To what shall *we* liken the *Kingdom of God?* And to what parable shall *we* compare it?
³¹ As a grain of mustard which *when it may be sown in the ground* is smaller than all the seeds that are in the *ground.*
³² But when it is sown *it comes up* and becomes greater than all the vegetables and *makes great branches* so that the birds of heaven are able to shelter under its shade."

Literal Translation.

According to St. Luke 13:17-19

¹⁷ And when He had said these things all His adversaries were put to shame and all the people rejoiced over all the glorious things that were being done by Him.
¹⁸ He said *therefore*, "To what is the *Kingdom of God* like? and to what shall *I* liken it?
¹⁹ It is like to a grain of mustard which a man took and *cast* into *his own garden;* and *it increased* and *became* a *great tree* and the birds of heaven sheltered in its branches."

Literal Translation.

The Hidden Treasure — The Pearl — The Net — The Scribe

Go to work early in the field of the Lord
And remain there tilling and delving.

Be attentive and regardful in your task
For it is in the field of His Word that He has hidden Wisdom.

Rejoice! when you discover the greatness of His treasure
Because manifest Wisdom reveals that you now understand.

But be prudent and take means to acquire by learning
What you desire to draw forth from the ground of His field.

Buy! for with the silver of your understanding you can get
Wisdom's gold
And with the gold of Wisdom go about obtaining fine jewels of
discernment to set aright.

There will come a time when in your searching you shall find that
single most precious Pearl
Which cannot be possessed unless you sell all that you hold.

Then love shall give you courage to leave learning aside
And merit by His friendship to keep true Knowledge.

They who know the Lord watch over His things and strive for the
sake of His glory.
They take counsel to establish by judgment the honor of His
Truth.

For only when His justice is done shall Peace reign over the world
And Bounty distribute His goods to the hungry.

*"**THE FIELD**": The original Greek Text preserves the generic definitive form: "in (*en*) the (*to*) field" *(agro)*, for the treasure is hidden in the same field where the Sower sowed the Word.

CHAPTER 10

THE PARABLE OF THE HIDDEN TREASURE

St. Matthew 13:44

"The Kingdom of heaven is like unto a treasure hidden in the* field; which a man found and hid; and from the joy thereof went and sold what things he had and bought that field."

Literal Translation.

*"**DIG**": "Dig after the words of the Torah ("Teaching" or "Law") as for secret treasures" (Midrash Rabbah on Canticles I.1).

Ws 8:5	"What is richer than Wisdom?"
Jb 28:16	For Wisdom "cannot be valued in the gold of Ophir, in precious onyx or sapphire,"
Ws 7:9	And "in the sight of Wisdom all gold is as a little sand."
Pr 8:11	"Wisdom is better than jewels,"
Pr 3:15 Sept.	"She is more valuable than precious stones."
Jb 28:18	"The price of Wisdom is above pearls."
Ws 7:13	O! "the riches of Wisdom!"
Si 41:12 M.T.	The "thousands of treasures of Wisdom!"
Ws 7:14 L.V.	"Wisdom is an infinite treasure to all mankind."
Bar 3:14	"Learn where Wisdom is"
T.L. 13:7	Because "Wisdom is great wealth of honour and a goodly treasure to all that find her."
Bar 3:15 Sept. & L.V.	"Who has found the place of Wisdom and who has come into her treasures?"
Jb 28:18 L.V.	"Wisdom is drawn out of secret places."
Pr 2:4 L.V.	Therefore "seek her as for silver and. . .dig* for her as for a treasure."
Ba 3:23	"Search after the Wisdom that is in the ground. . ."
Si 32:18 Sy	"A wise man will not leave Wisdom when it is hidden."
Si 39:1 L.V.	A "wise man will seek out Wisdom"—in the same field where His Word was sown.
Si 11:4	In there he will search for "hidden truths because the works of the Most High are wonderful, secret and hidden"
Pr 25:2	For "it is the glory of God to conceal a thing" *(dabar).*
Pr 25:2	And our business "is to search out a matter" *(dabar).* The matter of His precious "Word" *(dabar).*
Jb 28:20,21	"Wisdom. . .is hid from the eyes of all living and concealed from the birds of the heavens"
Ws 8:6	Because His Words of Wisdom are hidden in the heart of the ground where "understanding works."
Si 39:17 M.T.	"The utterance of God's mouth is His treasure."
Ps 119:162	"I rejoice in Thy Words as one that finds rich spoil."

*"**JOY THEREOF**": The Greek text literally reads: "from (*apo*) the (*tes*) joy (*charas*) thereof" (*autou*). It may seem awkward at first sight to have it read thus but not if we remember that hidden "Wisdom" that is found "shall be turned for you into joy"—the joy of discovering her by your understanding (Sirach 6:28 L.V.).

*"**LEARNING**": "He that has learned many things shall show forth understanding" (Sirach 34:9 Latin Vulgate). He shall show forth understanding when he brings all the things he has learned to light.

*"**PROV. 3:13**": "Happy is the man who finds Wisdom and the man who brings forth (*puq*) Understanding." The Hebrew word *puq* means to "bring forth", "draw out," and "to cause to go out."

*"**NO UNDERSTANDING**": "The wicked. . .have neither knowledge nor understanding" (Ps. 82:4,5). "The ungodly man does not understand knowledge" (Prov. 29:7 Sept.). "But knowledge is easy to a man of understanding" (Prov. 14:6).

*"**BE GOOD**": Because sin "does not allow understanding to work in men" (Test. of Simeon 4:8 Greek B Text, Armenian and Slavonic I Texts).

*"**HAPPINESS**": "Happy are thy men, happy are these thy servants, which stand continually before thee and hear thy wisdom" (I Kings 10:8).

208

Si 40:18,19 "Better than. . .he that findeth a treasure. . .is he that findeth Wisdom."
Ws 6:13 L.V. "Wisdom. . .is found by them that seek her."
Mt 13:44 By them that seek her secret treasure in *"the field"* of the Lord.

Si 6:27 Sept. "Search and seek and Wisdom shall be made known to you."
Si 6:28 Sept. And when "at last you shall find the place of rest of Wisdom"—
Si 6:28 L.V. "Wisdom shall be turned for you into joy."

Mt 13:44 Then you shall be like the man in the parable who *"from the joy* thereof went and sold what things he had and bought that field"* where he found the hidden treasure.

But not before he hid and covered up the treasure again,
Ba 3:32 Sept. & L.V. For he was a prudent man who "found Wisdom out with his understanding."

Ws 8:6 Sept. He found the treasure because "understanding works" it digs and delves and labors mightily to bring to light the glory of His Word.

Pr 12:23
2Ba 54:13 Having come upon the treasures of His Wisdom: "the prudent man conceals his knowledge" of "the treasures of Wisdom beneath"—
Pr 29:11 For he knows that "a wise man defereth and keepeth it till afterwards."

Until he can through acquired learning* establish the Truth of His Word.
Pr 18:15 M.T. "The understanding of the prudent man buys knowledge" for that purpose.

Pr 3:13* For it is one thing to find out the Lord's hidden Wisdom
But another thing to bring it forth from His field.

Si 1:8 Sy & Aram
Pr 4:57
Pr 16:16 L.T. "One there is who has dominion over all the treasures of Wisdom."
"Buy Wisdom" from Him.
"How much better to buy Wisdom than gold."

But no one can buy Wisdom without first acquiring understanding.
Pr 17:16 Sept. For "a man without understanding will not be able to purchase Wisdom."

T.L. 13:7
Frag. Aram.
Jb 28:28 If the wicked "shall not find the treasures of Wisdom nor shall they discover her hidden things,"
It is because evil men have no* understanding.

Jb 28:28 Understanding is given only to those who are good.

So be* good and keep digging
And someday you shall be happy and wise.

Pr 3:13 L.T. "O! the happiness* of a man who *finds* Wisdom!"

209

CHAPTER 11

THE PARABLE OF THE PEARL OF GREAT PRICE

St. Matthew 13:45-46

45 "Again, the Kingdom of heaven is like to a man, a merchant, seeking beautiful pearls, 46 who on finding one pearl of great price, went away and sold all that he had and bought it."

*"**TAUGHT**": God teaches man true knowledge of Himself that we may love Him and He placed in the soul of man a deep hunger for true knowledge: "Since Thou hast fashioned man thou hast created him with a love of Knowledge" (Books of Adam and Eve 27:3, 1st Century A.D.). "Lord. . .Thou knowest all things" (Esther 13:11,12 L.V.; St. John 21:17). "Knowledge has Thou of all things" (Esther 13:26 L.V.).

*"**FRIEND**": The Lord confides and gives Knowledge to His friends (St. John 15:15; St. Mark 4:10,34; 13:4) and His friends are those who do His commands (St. John 15:14). "The friendship of the Lord is for those who reverence Him and He *makes known* to them His Covenant" (Ps. 25:14). "trust in the Lord with all thine heart; and lean not unto thine own understanding" (Prov. 3:5), but "subject your understanding (to God) and your ears will be instructed with words of Knowledge" (Prov. 12:1). "Covet My Words and love them and you shall have instruction" (Wisdom 6:12 L.V.; 6:11 Sept.). We treasure the words of a friend, and because the friend knows that we love and keep them, he reveals his innermost thoughts to us. "Let a man get himself a friend. . .to whom he will entrust all his secrets" (Pirke Aboth 1:6 Jer. Talmud). The Hebrew word for a "confidant" or "close friend" is *yada* which also means "to know."
Be taught by God for "instruction is to them that use it. . .as a precious stone which every way it is turned, it is admired" (Prov. 17:8 Sept.). "There is nothing so much worth as a well instructed soul" (Sir. 26:14) who has learned from the Lord. "How precious are Thy friends *(rea)* unto me, O God" (Ps. 139:17 Hebrew Text. *See* Midrash R. on Ps. 116:15) for they know Thy "thoughts" *(rea* as in Ps. 139:2). "There is nothing so precious as a faithful friend. . .a faithful friend is an elixir of life" (Sirach 6:15,16 RSV), he is a priceless jewel.
"The Lord teaches the humble" (Ps. 25:9). Be good and humble for "then shalt thou understand the fear of the Lord and shalt find the Knowledge of God" (Prov. 2:5)—through His friendship. Thus to Abraham the "friend" of God (2 Chr. 20:7) were directed these words from the Lord: "What you cannot understand I will make known to thee for thou art pleasing in My sight and I will tell thee what is kept in My heart" (Apocalypse of Abraham). "Abraham was a friend (of God) because he kept the Commandments of God" (Zadokite Fragment 4:2 see also v.3 and Isaiah 41:8; Jubilees 19:9; 30:21; St. James 2:23).
Daath is the common Hebrew word for "Knowledge," it is derived from the Ugaritic word: *daat* which means "friend." Other Hebrew words for "Knowledge" are *manda* (as in Dan. 2:21; 5:12) and *madda* (as in 2 Chr. 1:10,11, 12) both of these words are derived from the Akkadian word for "friend": *madu.* The friends of God receive His Knowledge that they may rejoice in His Truth and praise Him with all their understanding.
"He has given Wisdom to them that love Him" (Sir. 1:10). "For to make known the glory of the Lord is Wisdom given and for recounting His many deeds is Wisdom revealed to man so as to make known to simple folk His might and to explain to the senseless His greatness" (Cave 11, Dead Sea Scroll Psalm 154:5-8). "Grant me Understanding, O Lord, in Thy law and teach me Thine ordinances that many may hear of Thy deeds and peoples may honor Thy glory" (Ps. 155:9, Psalm Scroll found in Cave 11). "Hath not the Lord made the saints to declare all His wonderful works, which the Lord Almighty hath firmly settled to be established for His glory?" (Sirach 42:27 Latin Vulgate and Psalm 73:28; 118:17,28; Ps. 145:10-12; Sirach 42:22 Syriac, 50:28-29 Sept.; Isaiah 52:13; I John 2:20; I Tim. 2:4; I Cor. 2:11-16 and Psalm 9:1-2).

*"**KNOWLEDGE**": By diligent and persevering effort we find Wisdom through our understanding. Having found Wisdom we learn that the greatest Wisdom is to reverence the Lord, keep His Commandments and do good because thereby we gain His friendship. The friends of the Lord are taught by Him and receive from Him the gift of true Knowledge. With the Knowledge of God, His friends then undertake to glorify Him and do justice for the sake of His Truth.
Therefore "seek Wisdom and improve Understanding by Knowledge" (Prov. 9:6 Sept.), but remember that only the friends of God are "the initiate in the Knowledge of God and the chooser of His works" (Wisdom 8:4) for we are given Knowledge to judge, *i.e.,* to choose the good and reject what is evil and to praise Him. He "Himself gave me an unerring knowledge of the things that are." (Wisdom 7:17) for true Knowledge comes only from God. "In the fullness of His *Knowledge* God *distinguished.* . .and *differentiated"* (Sir. 33:8) and in the fullness of time He shall teach His friends to do the same (Ps. 149:9).

Better than the man who finds Wisdom is the one who
understands and keeps it in righteousness
For he shall be taught* by God.

Si 42:19 L.V.   "The Lord knows all Knowledge."
Ps 94:10,11   "He who teaches man Knowledge" is "the Lord."

But we must first be righteous if we are to be taught by Him
2 P 1:5   For the Knowledge of God is a personal thing: a holy thing
that the Lord gives only to those who are good

2 M 6:30   Because only the good can truly understand His "holy
Knowledge."

Qo 8:17   "A wise man" may fear the Lord
Pr 28:2   But "a man of understanding" has put that fear into practice
Jn 15:14   and proved himself a friend* of God.

Dn 2:21   The Lord "gives Knowledge to those who have understanding"
Ps 111:10   "A good understanding have all those who *do* His Commands"
Ws 2:12,13   Thus "the righteous. . .have the Knowledge of God."

Qo 2:26   "To the man who is good in His sight the Lord gives Wisdom,
Knowledge and joy,"
Pr 2:6   The joy that comes from understanding the Truth of His Word.

Is 28:9   "To whom shall He teach Knowledge
And whom shall He make to understand?"
Ps 96:3   That he may thereby "declare His glory among the nations and
His wonders among all peoples?"

Si 38:6 L.V.   For "the Most High gives Knowledge to men that He may be
Ps 73:28   honored in His wonders,"
Si 42:22 Sy   And praised in His Truth.
Ps 71:22
Ps 25:12   "Who is the man who fears the Lord?
him will the Lord instruct. . ."

Pr 15:33   "The fear of the Lord is the instruction of Wisdom."
Pr 1:7   "The fear of the Lord is the beginning of Knowledge" as well.

Pr 21:11   The Knowledge* we receive when we understand His Wisdom.

Si 21:13 L.V.   "The perfection of the fear of the Lord is Wisdom and
Understanding"
For we need these two witnesses to tell the good from the bad.

Is 5:16   "The Lord of hosts shall be exalted in judgement."
His Truth shall be made manifest when we expose the lie.

*"MOST VALUABLE": The pearl was considered "most precious" among all jewels (*See* Pliny's *Hist. Natur.* Vol. IX, 35,54, n. 106; Vol. XXXVII 4, 15s,n. 55,62). Even up to the 11th Century Al-Tifaschi, an Arabian Lithologist, classified the pearl as the most valuable of all precious stones (*cf* J. Ruska in *Naturwiss. Wochenschrift* N.F. IV).

*"HIDDEN KNOWLEDGE": "It is the custom of those skilled in the Law and who know its secrets, to utter their pearls to their disciples under a very hidden sense" (Zohar, Synopsis, Tit-1; Maimonides, Mor, Nebh. Par. I cap. 71). In reproof, one Rabbi said to another: "after I removed (Lit. "uncovered") the potsherd you found the Pearl," *i.e.,* if it were not for my elucidation on the matter you would not have found the Truth (Pearl) you now claim to have brought forth (Jer. T. Maaseroth V end; 52a B.T.; Kethubim IX. 33b B. Talmud).

In the time of our Lord the pearl was regarded as a very costly and rare jewel.

The Talmud mentions "a pearl that is worth thousands of Zuzim" and "a pearl that has no price" (Baba Bathra 146a; Yer. Ber. 9.12d). A Rabbinic parable related that the most valuable* treasure of a king was his "choicest pearl" (Neflaoth Israel).

The pearl was also regarded as a life-giving substance and in the case of severe illness in the wealthy, a pearl was crushed and put in a vessel containing medicinal liquid or wine and given to them to drink (Baba Bathra 146a vid., JMEOS XV, p.43 ff., M.A. Canney). The proverbial beauty of a pearl made it a symbol of heavenly perfection, "the garment of light" was made from a pearl (Midrash Rabba Genesis 20:12), the gates of the heavenly Jerusalem were of pearls (Rev. 21:21). Manna was white as a pearl (Yoma 75a).

"Wherever it may be, a pearl remains a pearl" (Megillah 15a).

The Greek word for "pearl" *(margarites)* as used in the gospel is derived from the Sanskrit *mangara* which means both "pearl" and "pureness."

Allegorically the seventy wise elders were compared to a string of pearls around the neck of Moses (Midrash Rabba on Song of Songs 1:10). Moses and Aaron were compared to a pair of fine pearls side by side (Midrash Rabba on Song of Songs 4:5,1).

The Soul was considered to be "a priceless pearl" (Yer. Kilaim 9:32c and Yer. Abodah Zarah 2:41a). Prayer was also referred to as a pearl (Berakoth 32b).

In Rabbinic circles hidden* knowledge or understanding of a Scriptural text was a Rabbi's "precious pearl" too precious to be revealed or openly discussed (Baba Bathra 123b; Yebamoth 72b, 92b, 94a; Pirke Aboth di Rabbi Nathan 33a; Semahoth 47b; Midrash Rabba on Numbers 14:4).

In the Oral Laws of *Ona'ah* (Mishnah) against overpricing goods, the pearl was one of the few things not subject to the Laws of *Ona'ah* for the reason that the buyer of a pearl looks for a second one to match it (Baba Bathra 78a; Baba Metzia 4:8; *ibid.*, Gemara 58b). Thus a merchant who went about seeking fine pearls invariably sought to match them in perfect pairs. He sought the beautiful complement.

In the parable of the Hidden Treasure the man who found the treasure discovered it in someone else's field. The merchant in the parable of the Pearl of Great Price was also a stranger in the eyes of the Jews because ancient Israel had no merchant class. Private citizens did their transactions in the village squares where the market was held. The peasants sold in the market the produce of their fields, the herdsmen their animals and the craftsmen their wares on a direct basis from producer to consumer without any intervention by a middleman (2 K. 7:1).

Real commerce was in the hands of the foreign Canaanite-Phoenician trade merchants. They were the universal agents (Isaiah 23:28; Ezek. 27:1-3; Neh. 13:16). In the Bible the very word "Canaanite" means "merchant" (Job 41:6; Prov. 31:24; Zech 14:21), often in a derogatory sense (Isaiah 23:8; Hosea 12:7; Zeph. 1:11). In the general repentance and reign of righteousness that would come in the "Day of the Lord" (Zech 14:1) the great sign of purification was that "in that Day there shall be no more merchants *(Canaanites)* in the House of the Lord" (Zech 14:21).

*"PAIR": The merchant in the parable seeks only beautiful things choosing the finest among precious pearls. He deals only in beautiful and good things. "All the works of the Lord are good" (agathos)—Sirach 39:33. But "look upon the works of the Most High they are two and two, and one against another" (Sirach 33:15 Latin Vulgate). For in this world "all things are double, one against another and He has made nothing imperfect, one thing establishes the good of another" (Sirach 42:24-25) just as one true word establishes another bearing witness to the Truth. "Oh! that God would speak and open His lips to you, and that He would declare to you the secrets of Wisdom! that they are double (kephel) to the understanding" (tushiyah)—Job 11:6. "Tushiyah" is the skillful understanding required to bring about an undertaking to complete success. It implies ability to contrive the venture with the aid of Wisdom, Understanding, Knowledge and Counsel. The ones who possess "tushiyah" are the "wise in heart." i.e., those who are both wise and understanding. Needless to say only the righteous have Wisdom in themselves (Ps. 37:30; Prov. 10:31; Sir. 27:12; 43:37 L.V.). Thus "the Lord lays up tushiyah for the righteous" (Prov. 2:7) for we know that all Wisdom, Understanding, Knowledge and Counsel belong to the Lord (Sir. 1:1; Prov. 8:14; Jer. 32:19; Dan. 2:21) and tushiyah as well for "with Him is strength and tushiyah" (Job 12:16) indeed "the Lord of Hosts is wonderful in counsel and excellent in tushiyah" (Isaiah 28:29 see also Jer. 32:19).
But as for the wicked "He breaks the devices of the crafty so that their hands cannot execute tushiyah" (Job 5:12). The Lord prevents them from succeeding in their schemes. The word tushiyah implies "a saving work leading to deliverance and help to others."
"The Lord lays up skillful understanding for the righteous" (Prov. 2:7) because it is through tushiyah that they will be able to seize and grasp the Truth of His word.
"The lot of Truth" (Sirach 17:20 Latin Vulgate) belongs to the righteous and the wages of the righteous is Truth (Isaiah 61:8) for they understand, and it is they who "shall fully make known tushiyah" (Job 26:3 Literal Trans.), when everyone shall see the abundant fruits of their understanding. In the end "the man of tushiyah shall see Thy Name" (Micah 6:9) for that righteous man shall grasp and behold Truth. The Lord said "I am the Truth" (St. John 14:6). "Truth is the name of God"—Sanhedrin 1.18a (Jerusalem Talmud).

*"WISE": when he "sold all that he had" he stopped being a "merchant." He no longer "erred" because he no longer "traveled" from one place to another. Both in Hebrew and Greek the word "to err" is the same word for "to travel." "Be still and know"—Ps. 46:10 (Vide Sirach 51:13 Sept. and Sir. 51:13 Hebrew Text, Dead Sea Scrolls Cave 11).

Si 26:29 Sy	The wise man looked upon the merchant with disapproval: "With great difficulty shall the merchant keep himself from wrongdoing"
Si 27:1 Sept.	"Many have sinned for the sake of gain."
Si 27:2 Sept.	"Sin will thrust itself between buyer and seller as a nail sticks fast between the joinings of stones."
Kidd 82a P.A. 2:6 Er 55b	And the Rabbis warned: "He who has much business does not become wise." "The study of the Torah is not found among merchants." How shall they understand His Word who have set their hearts to ponder upon other things?
Mt 19:23	"Hardly shall a rich man enter the Kingdom of heaven." Indeed with difficulty shall he understand the Wisdom of God.
P.A. 4:14 Si 38:24 M.T.	Therefore "have little business and be busied in the Torah" For "he that has little business can become wise."
	Hold fast to the Word that you may learn to love it And be taught to understand it by the Lord your God.
Ps 119:99-100 Ps 111:10 Jn 3:21	For in the keeping and doing of His Word We shall be given to see the light of His Truth.
	The poor man seeks treasure to become rich. The rich man seeks to buy things precious and rare.
	A learner seeks Wisdom to be wise. A wise man seeks the pair* that establishes His Wisdom.
Ps 27:1	He searches until he finds the one Truth beyond compare, Giving strength and life to his own soul.
Rm 1:28 AV Ph 3:8	This is the Truth possessed by those who believe in the Lord And who are willing to sell all things to keep Him by their side.
Pr 3:18	Far greater than the joy of finding Wisdom Is the happiness of holding Wisdom fast in the fear of the Lord.
Si 25:10-11 Sept.	"How great is he who finds Wisdom! But he is not above him that fears the Lord, The fear of the Lord surpasses all things, He that holds it fast to whom shall he be likened?"
Mt 13:45,46	He shall be likened *"to a man, a merchant seeking beautiful pearls, who on finding one pearl of great price, went away sold all that he had and bought it"* To *keep it* and become truly wise.*

*"EQUATE": In the Book of Proverbs (2:1-2,9) the wise father tells his sons: "My son, if you receive my words and treasure my commandments with you, making your ear attentive to Wisdom and incline your heart to understanding. . .then you will understand righteousness and justice and right things" *(mesharim*="equal things"). If we also do the same as regards His Words and His Commandments we shall be able to "make an agreement" *(mesharim* as in Daniel 11:6) between "things that are equal" *(mesharim* as in Ps. 17:2 A.V.) proving them to be "things that are right" *(mesharim* as in Isaiah 45:19). "By stringing together parable to parable King Solomon drew out the secrets of the Torah" (Midrash Rabbah to Song of Songs I.1, Sect. 8).

*"DISCOVER": "Just as it is said that a field labourer digging a plot in order to plant some tree, by unlooked for good fortune, happened upon a treasure. . ." (Philo. *Quod, Deus Imm.* XX. 91) so do we sometimes light upon the treasures of His Wisdom when we work in His field.

*"LIGHT": "A Text (of Holy Scripture) which is not fully explained in its own place is illuminated by another text" (The 32 Middoth by Rabbi Eliezer ben R. Jose, c. 2nd C. A.D.). "An understanding man is he who can deduce one thing from another" (Midrash in Libnath Hasappir).

*"MATCH THE PEARLS": "I string together like pearls, the words of the Torah with those of the prophets and those of the prophets with those of the Hagiographers; and therefore the words of the Torah rejoice as on the day when they were *revealed* in the flames of Sinai'" (Rabbi Ben Asai, *c.* 110 A.D. and Midrash Rabbah on Leviticus 16 and Song of Songs 1:10). Exposition of the words of the Torah was done by "linking together the words of the Torah in the proper way," *i.e.,* with skill (Midrash Rabbah on Song of Songs 1:10.2) as when one matches like a wise merchant: the pearls of His Wisdom. In the Old Testament the doubling of a thing establishes it (Genesis 41:32. *See also* Test. of Napthali 7:4 Hebrew Text and Akkadian lament in the Rawlinson Text from excavated cuneiform tablets at Nippur fragment III. 3-8). If "a dream in the morning appeared twice with the same meaning" it was certain to happen (Sippar Text. No. 55, also Ber. 55b B.T.; Ibn Ezra and R. Malbim *re.* Gen. 41:32). Also before matched pearls can be strung they must be bored through. In Rabbinic circles "a borer of pearls" was one able to enter into the depths of a Scriptural Text (Midrash Rabbah on Song of Songs 1:10).

*"KEEP IT": The wise merchant having found Truth concentrates all his efforts in keeping it. "I have refrained my feet from every evil way, that I may keep Thy Word" (Ps. 119:101). For "through Thy precepts I get understanding therefore I hate every base way" (Ps. 119:104). Those who keep the Word of God are taught by Him. Therefore "take fast hold of instruction and do not let her go; keep her for she is thy life" (Prov. 4:13). "My son, attend to My Words and incline your ears to My sayings. Do not let them depart from your eyes; but keep them in the midst of your heart. For they are life to him who finds them and health to all his flesh" (Prov. 4:20-22). The Word of God is life to them who find and *keep* it. We hold on to Life. Let us get on with the business of "holding fast the Word of Life" (Philippians 2:16; I John 1:1). The pearl was esteemed not only as the most precious of jewels but also as a life-giving substance. This parable provided an excellent analogy to Proverbs 3:1-2, 18,22; 4:10, 13,22; 6:23; 8:35; 9:10-11; 10:17; 11:19, 30; 12:28; 13:14; 14:27; 16:22; 19:23 (Sept.); 21:21; 22:4; Psalm 34:12-14; Prov. 30:14-16, 19-20. "The fear of the Lord is life to man" (Prov. 19:23 Sept.). "In the fear of the Lord there is no want and with it there is no need to seek support" (Sirach 40:26c Masada Scroll). "If you desire Wisdom keep the Commandments and the Lord will give her freely unto you" (Sirach 1:26), you will no longer have to search and exchange for her like the wise and understanding merchant but will possess her in the knowledge given to you through your friendship with the Lord: "He who is understanding in business finds good; but most happy is he that trusts in God" (Prov. 16:20 Sept.) and gives up all business to be with Him "for the Lord *gives* Wisdom and from His mouth comes Knowledge and Understanding" (Prov. 2:6) for His friends. Thus "the love of God is honorable Wisdom" (Sirach 1:14 L.V.). Indeed the Lord "has given Wisdom to them that love Him" (Sir. 1:10 L.V.).

*"THE LORD": The early church Fathers interpreted the Pearl as representing Christ our Lord and the Knowledge derived from His teaching. *See* the following sources:
Clement of Alexandria. *Paed.* (Migne P.8.540 c)
Ephrem Syr. (Migne 2.269b and 2.274c opera omnia-Asemani)
Ephrem Antiochenus. *frag.* (Migne 86.2109 a)
Isidorus Pelusiota (Migne 78.1273a) and (Migne 78.301b)
Hesychius Hier. *Serm.*5 (Migne 93.1416a)
Germanus I Constantinop. *Contempl.* (Migne 98.385a)
Chrysostom *Hom. 1.3 in St. John* (8.4d.)
Methodius *De Creatis* (Migne 18.332a)
Theodoretus Cyr. *Comment. Dan.* (Migne 81.496)
Also Acts of John 109 and Chrysippus Hier. *Enc. in B.M.V.* (Patrol. Orient. I p.337.5)
The hidden treasure in the field of the Lord is "the treasure that fails not for it is the Wisdom of God." "Whosoever desires to become a merchant let him buy for himself the field and the treasure that is in it." "Let us sell all our possessions and buy for ourselves the Pearl that we may be rich." "Jesus our Lord is God, the Son of God. . .and the Pearl" (Aphrahat, c.337 A.D., *Demonstrations* Section 10 Paragraph B; 6 Paragraph 1; 17 Paragraph 1. Nicene and Post-Nicene Fathers Series 2 Vol. 13, Eerdmans). "Christ the Power of God; and the Wisdom of God"; "Christ in whom are hid all the treasures of Wisdom and Knowledge" (I Cor. 1:24; Col. 2:2,3). "The good pearls are the Law and the Prophets; the one of the great price is the Knowledge of the Saviour" (Hugh of St. Victor, c. 1140 A.D., in his *Annot. in St. Matthew*). "Cleave unto Him for He is thy life and the length of thy days" (Deut. 2:20).

218

A wise man is like the merchant in the parable in that he seeks to equate* the pearls of His Wisdom and array them before us so that we may understand the Truth of His Word. The task of searching and gathering requires ability in discerning the genuineness of His precious things and skill in rightly pairing them.

Midr. R
Sg 1.1,9

Pr 25:2

A humble student determined to "seek after the words of the Torah as for hidden treasure" may in the process suddenly discover* the concealed Wisdom of God and then through acquired learning and understanding bring it forth from His field. Having done so he becomes rich in Wisdom and like the merchant he begins to search with skill and perception for even more precious things. He has become a connoisseur.

Just as by striking two flints together we can produce light* so by equating two things in Holy Scripture we may obtain the true answer. If the wise man seeks to match* the pearls of His Wisdom it is in order to fashion the ornament that makes manifest the beauty of His Truth, and establishes it.
He continues searching until he discovers that far more gratifying than finding and pairing Wisdom is to hold Wisdom fast and keep* it in Truth.

Pr 23:23

Jb 27:6

"Buy the Truth and sell it not." We keep it and "sell it not" when through filial reverence for the Lord we come to possess the Truth in righteousness.
Whosoever keeps the Truth holds on to the Lord and thereby possesses in Him all Wisdom, Understanding and Knowledge.

Si 25:16 L.V.

"The fear of God is the beginning of love for Him" and love for God is holding Him fast so that He abides in us and we in Him.

Jn 14:21,23
Jn 15:4,7

1 Co 13:6

To abide with the Lord is to be instructed by Him. Whosoever is taught by God understands all things and "rejoices. . .in the Truth."
He no longer searches for he has found in the Lord* the fulfillment of all desire.

Si 2:15
Jn 14:15,21,23
1 Jn 5:2-3

We keep what we love.

Mt 13:46

But who can love more than one thing at a time?
And so—"finding **one** pearl of great price he went away and sold all that he had and bought it"

Mt 13:46
Eph 3:19

Because he fell in love with that "**one** Pearl" he now held.

1 P 1:22

"Love one another intensely."

CHAPTER 12

THE PARABLE OF THE NET

St. Matthew 13:47-50

[47] "Again, the Kingdom of heaven is like a net cast into the sea and gathering of every kind: [48] which when it was filled they drew to the shore and sitting chose the good into vessels but the corrupt they cast out.

[49] Thus shall it be at the completion of the age; the angels will come forth and will separate the wicked from the midst of the just [50] and will cast them into the furnace of fire: there shall be weeping and gnashing of teeth."

*"**REVEALED**": "He reveals the deep and secret things" (Daniel 2:22). "He reveals the profoundest secrets" (Sirach 42:19 Hebrew Text). For if "you cannot plumb the depths of the heart of man nor perceive the things that a man is thinking; how then can you search out God who made all these things and know His mind or comprehend his purpose?" (Judith 8:14).

The secret things of God are not found out, unless they are revealed to His own in His good time. "Just as one can neither seek out nor know what is in the deep of the sea, even so, no one upon earth is able to see My son until the time of His day" (4 Ezra 13:52).

*"**THEREIN**": It is in "the deep" (Sirach 43:23 Hebrew Text) that His deep things are kept reserved for the Day of His exaltation. "The dumb and lifeless water (of the sea) produced living things that all people might declare Thy wondrous works" (2 Esdras 6:48).

Qo 7:24	"That which is far off and exceeding deep who can find it out?"
Jb 38:16	"Have you walked in search of the deep"
Si 42:18 L.V.	As "He has searched out the deep" and "walked in the bottom of
Si 24:5 Sept.	the deep?"
Jb 12:7 Sy	"Can you understand the deep things of God?"
Rm 11:33	
Is 40:28	For "there is no searching of His understanding."
1 Co 2:6-16	The secret things of God are not found; they are revealed.*
Pr 20:5	"The words of a man's mouth are as deep waters"
	But far more profound are the Words of God.
Si 24:39 L.V.	"For His thoughts are more vast than the sea
Is 55:8-9	And His counsels more deep than the great ocean."
Pr 20:5	"Counsel in the heart of man is like deep water."
Is 29:15 Sept.	"But woe unto them that are deep of heart to hide their counsel
	from the Lord"
Pr 20:5	Because "a man of understanding will draw it out" and bring to
Is 45:1-6	light what was hidden in the darkness.
Mi 4:12	The wicked "know not the thoughts of the Lord, neither do they
2 Tm 3:2,7	understand His counsel"
Si 43:37 L.V.	Because only "to the righteous He has given Wisdom" and
Dn 2:22 L.V.	"reveals deep and hidden things" to them alone.
Jb 12:22	For them "He uncovers deep things out of darkness."
Ps 63 (64):6,7	He makes known that "a man shall approach the deep heart, and
L.V. & Sept.	God shall be exalted."
Is 52:13-15	When the deep and hidden thoughts of His heart shall be then
	revealed!
Ps 92:5	"O Lord. . .Thy thoughts are very deep"
Ps 36:6	And "Thy judgments are a great deep."
Ps 107:24	"See the works of the Lord and His wonders in the deep"
Si 43:25 M.T.	"For therein* are marvels, the most wondrous of His works."
Ps 139:17	Behold "how precious are Thy thoughts unto us, O God,
	And how vast the sum of them."

*"WISDOM": "Joseph, the mighty one of God, caught me as a fish with his wisdom and by his spirit (Understanding) brought me into subjection for life" (Joseph and Asenath VII.22 Syriac Text).

*"DARK SAYINGS"="riddles" (chidah): "the words of the wise and their riddles" (Prov. 1:6) by which they test the wisdom and understanding of others.

*"COUNSELS": All His Commandments or Laws are given to us as good counsels which we are free to submit or reject (Deut. 30:10,15,19). For those who have chosen to be bound by His Laws He wills life but by the same token those who have chosen not to be bound by them or have forsaken them have thereby chosen death for themselves. Nevertheless, whether we accept to be bound to His Laws or not, His will prevails over all things as a great net spread over all the living. Those who submit to His counsels place themselves willingly under the bonds of His directive precepts which are meant to guide us towards the good and restrain us from evil. When the Jewish Alexandrian scribes translated the Hebrew Text of Sirach 6:25 into the Greek of the Septuagint they rendered "grieve not under the bonds of wisdom" into "chafe not under the counsels of Wisdom" for it meant the same thing to them. Thus in the early writings, known as the Corpus Hermetica we read: "when the period was completed the counsels by which all things were held together was loosened (as a rope) by God's design" (Corp. Herm. 1:18, Edited by W. Scott, Clarendon Press, Oxford, 1936). The Lord Himself in Ezekiel refers to the covenant as "the bond of the covenant" (Ezekiel 20:37 Hebrew Text). In the Midrash Debarim Rabba 10:1, God's will is compared to a golden chain for those who obey (honor) and iron fetters (dishonor) to those who do not.
The counsel of God is an effectual operation, a "steering" as it were. Thus in the Book of Sirach it is written that "He guides the world in the span of His hand (enclosing and steering it as in a dragnet) and all things are obedient unto His will; for He is King of all things and by His power separating among them the holy things from the profane" (Sirach 18:3 Greek Cursive MSS. 70, 106, 248). Just as the wise fishermen shall do when it is time to bring His net ashore. For then "they" that handle (taphas) the Law" (Jer. 2:8) shall "surprise" (taphas) and "take" (taphas) captive every presumption of the scoffers. They shall be able to do so because through their fidelity to the Law they shall have acquired tachbuloth, the effective "wise counsels" needed to wage a successful war against an enemy. For tachbuloth is "counsel and strength" (Job 12:13; Isaiah 11:2; 36:5) the "counsel and strength for the war" (2 K. 18:20) we must wage against His enemies. It is through tachbuloth that the adversary is encompassed and entrapped. "Every purpose is established by counsel (etsah) and with good counsel (tachbuloth) is war waged" (Prov. 20:18). "Where there is no tachbuloth (wise counsels) the people fall" (Prov. 11:14). Therefore be faithful and "by wise counsels (tachbuloth) thou shalt make thy war" (Prov. 24:6) against the evil one and expose his rotten lies.
Let us be good that we may truly understand and "acquire tachbuloth" (Prov. 1:5) and be guided by Him (Job 23:14; Isaiah 44:26) so as to be able to champion His cause with good judgment (Prov. 12:5). "With whom shall you find the fight for the Law (Torah)? with him in whose hands are wise counsels" (tachbuloth) or "bundles of laws" (Leviticus Rabbah sect. 21 Munich MS.).
The word tachbuloth is derived from the Hebrew word for "rope" and the verb "to steer." Thus the Rabbis said that "tachbuloth" is "the art of steering" (Pesikta Rabbati 47 sect. 4) which is after all what "wise counsel" is, for it is through "good counsel" (tachbuloth) that a man is able to steer a right course of action either to govern or wage war for the sake of justice. In later Hebrew a "capable lawyer" was called a tachmoni and even the ancient Egyptians knew that it is through the wise counsel that comes from superior knowledge that one is able to enmesh and bring a culprit to justice. In an invocation to Thoth, the Egyptian god of wisdom, who was the Scribe of the gods, the court scribes made this prayer: "O Moon (Thoth) establish his cause against him and so steer that we may drag the wicked man across"—to judgment (Instruction of Amen-em-Opet fol. L. 15 Papyrus 10474 British Museum).
So "strive for the Truth (aletheia) unto death, and the Lord God shall fight for thee" (Sirach 4:28 Sept.) and the "world" (kosmos) too where His Word was sown (Wisdom 5:20). Hold fast the cords of the Law and the Lord shall give you strength to "bring forth judgment for the sake of Truth" (Isaiah 42:3) and then you shall bring to light all the deep and hidden counsels enclosed by the Net of the Lord: your Understanding.

224

The net of Wisdom* is Understanding
And by it are gathered the hidden things both good and bad.

Si 47:14-15 M.T. and Sy	O! Solomon "how wise thou wast in thy youth, thou didst gather parables like the sea through thine understanding and didst fill it with dark* sayings."

To be gathered and brought to light by those who understand.

Pr 4:7 Hab 1:16 Si 6:28,29 M.T. & Sy	Therefore "with all thy getting get understanding" For through it your portion shall be made fat And "in the end you shall rejoice in Wisdom and her *net* shall become the foundation of your strength."

The strength possessed by those who understand the Truth of His Word.

Si 6:25 Sept. Si 6:25 M.T. Si 6:24 Sept.	Now, "chafe not under the counsels* of Wisdom." "Grieve not under her bonds." "Bring your feet under her fetters and your neck into her chain."

Ws 6:18 Si 6:29 Sy Jn 15:14 Ps 105:18-21 Gn 41:42	Let the "Laws of Wisdom" hold you fast. For "her bonds shall become your robe of glory and her chain an ornament of gold," When you shall have earned through them the friendship of the Lord.

The friends of God possess the Knowledge of God and with it zeal for Him,
The zeal that seeks to vindicate His Truth.

Is 59:14 Dn 8:12	Because "Truth is fallen in the street"; Truth is "thrown to the ground" When there is no one to uphold it.

Si 32:16 M.T. Is 42:3	"They who fear the Lord discern His judgment" And know that "He shall bring forth judgment for the sake of Truth."

Because the glory of God is Truth revealed in all its brightness.

Si 4:21 L.V. Is 28:26 Targ. Zc 8:16	Before He judges the Lord makes manifest all that is concealed. He opens up "the treasures of Knowledge and the understanding of justice" to His friends "for instruction in judgment." Because it is they who shall "execute the judgment of Truth" and by their understanding gather all the facts before Him.

Mt 13:43	"He who has ears to hear let him hear!" and be good.

Si 4:15 M.T. Si 3:32 L.V. Si 45:26 Sept.	For "he that listens to Wisdom shall judge for the sake of Truth" And "a wise heart that has understanding will abstain from sins and have success in the works of justice."

*"**NET**": The Greek word for "net" used in St. Matthew 13:47 is *sagene* which means a large "seine" net or "dragnet." The word *sagene* is derived from *satto* meaning "heavily laden" as a *sagene* was sometimes half a mile long and would indeed be heavily laden during optimal conditions. This large net was leaded below so that it swept the bottom of the sea when dragged. On the surface it was supported by corks. The *sagene* was carried out to sea by boats so as to encompass a large marine area and when it was full, the distant ends of the net were brought together and the heavy contents were slowly dragged in to be emptied upon the shore by the fishermen.

From the noun *sagena* the Greeks derived the verb *sageneuo* which means "to completely surround and entrap" all the inhabitants of a land (Herodotus ch.3.149; ch. 6.31). The Hebrew word that would correspond to *sagene* is *mikmereth*. It is interesting to note that the Hebrew word for "net" and also "utter destruction and annihilation" is the same word *cherem* from a root meaning "to enclose." Another word for "net" is *metsodah* derived from a root signifying "to lie in wait" (*See* Syriac Text of this parable).

In the rich word imagery of Holy Scripture the wicked are said to lie in wait for the just, ready to spring their evil "net" on the unsuspecting (Ps. 9:15; 10:9; 35:7 *etc.*).

The Chaldeans were described as plundering and overwhelming the inhabitants of Israel as it were by netting them (Habacuc 1:6,9,15-17). The just man prayed to be delivered from the "net" and "snare" of his foes (Ps. 25:14; 31:4) and he hoped that "the wicked" would "fall into their own nets" (Ps. 141:10; 9:15; 35:8).

The swift judgment of God was expressed in the simile of His spreading a net (Job 19:6; Ezekiel 12:13; 17:20; 32:3 etc.). The wiles of a temptress were a net of enticement (Prov. 29:5). Thus the word *gedilim* means both "lies" and "twisted thread" such as that used to weave a net. Even today the Arabic word *saraja* means "to braid hair" and also "to tell a lie."

Allegorically "he who arranges Mishnahs (teaching) in order" is compared to a "net weaver" (Erubim 72, B. Talmud) and in an ancient Akkadian Text a god called Nabu was described as being the "acquirer of learning," the word "acquirer" being derived from *asis* and *asasu* which mean in Akkadian "to catch in a net" or "to snare" (*Zeitschrift fur Assyrologie* 4.252).

In Rabbinic terminology to "spread" one's "net" over an opponent was to have been able to overcome him in an argument through superior knowledge (Midrash Rabba on Genesis VII sect. 4).

From the word *paras:* "to spread," comes the word *parash:* "to declare distinctly" (Ezra 4:18). In the wonderful Wisdom of our Lord we learn that before good men of understanding can handle their net to gather the facts, they must know how "to interpret" *(pesher)* a thing and understand that the word *pesher* is derived from the root *sher* which means "to travel around" or "to encircle" an area completely as fishermen do when they spread their *sagene* into the sea. To be able to guide the net they must possess "skillful understanding" *(sekel)* as Jacob did when he "guided his hand with) *sekel"* (Genesis 48:14). Furthermore, since the *sagene* is a great net they must know how to steer it aright, and to do that takes "good counsel" *(tachbuloth)* so as to see that "it is turned round about by *tachbuloth"* (Job 37:12) competently, to catch all kinds of things so as to "draw out" *(mashah)* the secrets of the "parable" *(mashal)* of the net.

The wise and understanding fishermen keep watch and so they know when the net is *"filled"* and the time has come for them to draw it ashore that they may discern *"every kind"* of thing that is enclosed within it.

They work together then to apply the power of understanding vigorously because that net is very deep indeed and so great that only God was able to *"cast"* it.

When they have finally brought the net ashore they have "to uncover" *(gallah)* the folds in order to be able "to reveal" *(galah)* the contents of the haul and with "understanding" *(bin)* "distinguish" *(bin)* the good from the bad. Then with the knowledge of God they shall "judge" *(din)* and execute the justice that exposes and *"casts out"* all lies and "successfully vindicates" *(tushiyah*=ability to exalt well) His Truth.

For Truth becomes known through the judgment that upholds it and the justice that brings "salvation" *(teshuah)* to the just.

In that Day everyone shall understand for "He shall utterly remove. . .the face-covering cast over all people and the woven veil that is spread over all the nations" (Isaiah 25:7) like a great net *(See* Eph. 4:18; 2nd Cor. 3:14-18; Rom. 11:7-8, 25; St. Matt. 13:11).

*"**SUBMITTED**": The Net holding fast those who do the will of God shall empower them to "bring every thought into captivity to the obedience of Christ" (2 Cor. 10:5). When "the sea is no more" (Rev. 21) it is His Net that shall deliver us and enable us to bring to light all that is deeply hidden, "for our knowledge He has folded up the sea" (Job 11:6 Tur-Sinai Transl. *See also* Isaiah 11:9; Habacuc 2:14). Submit to His will in faith and the day shall come when you shall understand the reason for His actions and merit then to gather in abundance His "full knowledge of the Truth" (2 Tim. 2:25) but beware of "the snare of the devil" (*ibid*.v.26) that imprisons the undiscerning who do his evil desires. Pray "that they who have been taken captive by the devil may recover themselves out of his snare, so as to serve the will of God" (2 Tim. 2:26). Exchange nets that "having been set free from sin you have become the slaves of justice" (Rom. 6:8). For it is His servants who shall wield the great Net of His Understanding to the glory of His Truth.

*"**LAW**": The binding Law is referred to as "the Law of life and good understanding" (Sirach 45:5, Hebrew Text) because those who hold fast "the Law of life" (Sirach 17:11) and do it "shall live" (St. Luke 10:28. *See also* Lev. 18:5; Deut. 30:15; 32:46-47; Neh. 9:29; Ezek. 20:11; St. Matt. 19:17; Rom. 10:5; Gal. 3:12).

They shall *also* understand for it is written that "a good understanding have those that do His Commandments" (Ps. 111:10; 19:11; 119:100; Sir. 4:17, 18; St. John 3:21; I John 3:24; Eph. 1:17-18; Neh. 9:20).

"Keep therefore and do them for that *is* your wisdom and your understanding" (Deut. 4:6).

Thus: "the book of the Commandments of God and the Law that endures forever, all they that hold it fast are ordained to live but such as forsake it shall die" (Baruch 4:1,2).

*"**UNDERSTANDING**": It takes "Understanding" *(binah)* to "make" *(banah)* something beautiful out of a little thing (Gen. 2:22), just as it takes "understanding" *(bin)* to "weave" *(binyatah)* a net.

"In the sea towns they call plaiting (nets) *binyata"* (Pirke R. Nathan 4:2).

Mt 13:47	*"Again, the Kingdom of heaven is like a net* cast into the sea."*
Ps 103:19	"The Lord has established His throne in the heavens and His Kingdom [in the heavens] rules over all."
Ps 135:6	"Whatever the Lord wills He does in the heavens and on earth, in the sea and the depths of the sea."
Ps 33:11	"The counsel of the Lord stands forever and the designs of His heart unto all generations."
Eph 1:11	Everything is ordained by Him and His will prevails over all things.
P.A. 3:20	His sovereignty and justice encompass all His works as a "net spread over all the living."
Hab 1:4	To some it may appear that the net is slacked and His judgment long in coming,
2 P 3:9	But remember that "The Lord is not slack concerning His promises in the way some men consider to be slackness; but He is patient towards us, not willing that anyone should perish but that all should come to repentance" and be saved.
	Repent!
	Repent!
2 Tm 2:25	Understand and turn to Him before He draws the cords of "His
Dn 9:13 AV	net"
Jb 19:6	
	to execute His justice.
Qo 9:12	Woe to the wicked who shall be "snared in an evil time"
Qo 9:12	for when "the net. . .falls suddenly upon them" they shall not
Ps 9:16	escape.
Pr 29:6 Sept.	But let the just rejoice for although "a great snare is spread for a sinner it shall be joy and gladness for the righteous"
	Because with the very same cords of the Law they submitted* to, Wisdom shall weave for them their net of understanding.
Si 32:15 M.T.	Truly "he that seeks out the Law* shall be filled thereby but the dissembler shall be snared by it."
Pr 19:8	And "he that keeps understanding shall find good things," he shall draw them out, gather them, and bring them to light,
	With the net of his understanding.*

*"**DEVISED**": The wicked "devises wicked devices to destroy the poor with lying words" (Isaiah 32:7).

*"**SEA**": To the Semitic mind the sea represented all that was inscrutable, immense, deep and unfathomable: "O! sage. . .where is the man of your standing? Where is the scholar who can oppose you? For your understanding is a river whose spring never fails, an immense sea which knows no decrease"—Babylonian Tablet No. 34505, Lines 223-24 (British Museum).
In the ancient Canaanite and Babylonian cosmogony the sea was the dwelling place of Wisdom. *Apsu:* "the deep" was also called "the house of Wisdom." From "the deep" came forth the word and wisdom of Ea, the creative deity, and "lord of wisdom." This conception of the "deep" being the "house of wisdom" is reflected in sacred scripture: "your heart is lifted up and you have said I am God and I sit in the seat of God in the heart of the seas" (Ezekiel 28:2). The seat of Wisdom is Understanding: "an understanding man is a throne of Wisdom" (Prov. 12:23 Sept.). Wisdom is given to praise God (Sir. 4:31, 33) and to judge and execute the justice that establishes His Truth. Thus it is written that: "the rule of an understanding man is well ordered" (Sir. 10:1 Sept.) and "a king shall reign and *understand* and shall execute judgment." (Jer. 23:5 Sept.).
We understand in the heart: "God made. . .the heart for understanding" (Test. of Naphtali 2:8); "a heart He gave them to understand" (Sir. 17:6; Enoch 14:3; Palest. Targum on Deut. 29:2-4). "The heart of the understanding one will comprehend a parable" (Sir. 3:29 Greek Text) such as the one about the Net and realize that "the heart of man is deep beyond all things. . ." (Jer. 17:9 Sept.) even deeper than the deepest ocean "for you cannot find the depths of the heart of man" (Judith 8:14).
Understand now that the counsels and deliberations of the Lord are profound and unfathomable: "Thy judgments are a great deep" (Ps. 36:6) and "by His eloquent understanding He makes an arsenal out of the deep" (Sir. 43:23 Greek and Hebrew Levi Text), for when the time comes for judgment He will array his deep Words as a weapon against those who have scoffed at them (St. John 12:48).
In the meantime He "has shut up the deep and sealed it" (Prayer of Manasses vv. 3-4) and "He has covered up the foundations of the sea for by them [the depths] He does judge peoples" (Job 36:30,31). Did He not say to wicked Tyre: "I shall bring up the deep upon thee"? (Ezekiel 26:19) to crash it down upon the proud with all the hidden power of His Understanding. "The sea speaks, yea, even the strength of the sea saying. . ." (Isaiah 23:4 Sept.): "your justice would have been as the waves of the sea" (Isaiah 48:18 Latin Vulgate) had you listened to His Words and kept them in your heart.
The dark impenetrable depths of the sea provided an apt simile of the covert sought by God's enemies (Dan. 7:2-3; Amos 9:3, *etc.*) who are "deep of heart to hide their counsel from the Lord" (Isaiah 29:15 Sept.) not remembering that "He searcheth out the deep and the heart and all *their* secrets for the Most High possesses Knowledge" (Sir. 42:18, Masada Scroll) and "His word penetrates the mighty deep" (Sirach 43:23, Masada Scroll) there to "examine their crafty devices: for the Lord knows all that can be known" (Sir. 42:18 Greek Text and Latin Vulgate), for "the works of all flesh are before Him and there is nothing hid from His eyes" (Sir. 39:24 Latin Vulgate). Never forget that "by His Knowledge the depths are broken up" (Prov. 3:20) and by His Understanding He "binds the flood and brings forth what is hid to light" (Job 28:11) and reveals at the bottom all the deep things hidden in the darkness. "The works of Truth and the works of deceit are done in the hearts of men and each one of them the Lord knows and there is no time at which the works of men can be hid" (Test. of Judah 20:3,4; Prov. 6:16, 18) from Him, though the heart of man be deeper than the sea.
"I said, I will be wise; but it was far from me. That which is far off and exceedingly deep, who can find it out?" (Eccle. 7:24). For "Wisdom's Understanding is more full than the sea, and her counsel greater than the deep" (Sir. 24:29 Codex Vaticanus, Cursives 248,254 and Syriac Text).

*"**WITH THEM**": "Every work that is corruptible shall fail in the end: and the worker thereof shall go with it. And every excellent work shall be justified and the worker thereof shall be honored therein" (Sirach 14:20-21 Latin Vulgate).
"All the works of the Lord are good and. . .in time they shall all be well approved" (Sir. 39:33,34 Greek Text), by those who have good understanding.

Rm 11:34 Si 18:4 Ps 107:24	"Who has known the Understanding of the Lord?" "Who can search out His mighty works?"
Si 11:4 L.V. 1 Co 2:10 Ps 92:5	For "His works are wonderful, secret and hidden" And "the deep things of God" are most profound.
Rm 11:33	"O! the depths of the riches of the Wisdom and Knowledge of God, how unsearchable are His judgments and how inscrutable His ways."
En 63:3	O Lord "all Thy Mysteries are deep and numberless." Who can bring them to light unless he understands?
Is 29:15 Rev. 2:24 Ps 116:3	And who shall discern the deep things of evil unless he receives true Knowledge from God? That he may thereby fathom "the depths of Satan" wherein are devised* "the snares of hell."
Jr 17:19 Sept. Ps 64:6 Mt 13:47	Because like a sea*: "The heart of man is deep beyond all things, it *is* the man"— And in the heart of man are made *"all kinds"* of things both good and bad Depending on who rules inside of him.
Dn 2:9 Jn 8:44	For in the heart of the wicked are "prepared lying and corrupt words" by the "father of lies" And in the heart of the righteous the net that shall trap them.
Si 27:30 L.V. Ps 119:163,104	The day is coming when "wicked counsel shall be rolled back upon the author of it," By those who "abhor lying" and "hate every false way."
Si 32:16 Sy	For "they who fear the Lord understand His judgment and draw forth great Wisdom with skill from their hearts."
Pr 22:21	So that they may with Wisdom and Understanding make known "the certainty of His Words of Truth" And with Power cast out the lies that sought to confound it.
Mt 13:48 Si 27:32 L.V. Pr 5:22	When the times are "fulfilled" *(pleroo)* and the net is *"filled" (pleroo).* "They shall perish in a snare that are delighted with the fall of the just" And "his own iniquities shall capture the wicked."
Eph 4:29 1 Co 15:33 Mt 13:48	Then shall their "corrupt *(sapros)* words" be flung away with* them, as all "rotten" *(sapros)* things shall be.

*"**HIS JUDGMENT**": "The judgment of God is according to Truth" (Rom. 2:2 Literal Translation). Ask Light from the Lord for "proving what is acceptable to the Lord" (Ephesians 5:10), and what is acceptable to the Lord is nothing but the Truth. "The spiritual man judges all things" (I Cor. 2:15) according to the Truth, for he knows that "the works of His hands are Truth" (Pirke Aboth 3:23; Psalm 19:9).
"He will judge the world with righteousness and the peoples with His Truth" (Ps. 96:13).
"He will judge me in the righteousness of His Truth" (Community Rule 11:14 Dead Sea Scrolls).

*"**CORRUPT** (sapros)": The Greek word sapros in St. Matt. 13:48 means "rotten" or "corrupt" such as the "rotten" (sapros) trees and fruits in St. Matt. 7:17,18; St. Luke 6:43. These are the only instances the word sapros is used in the gospels. In the epistles it is found only in Ephesians: "let no corrupt (sapros) word proceed out of your mouth but (only) that which is good for edifying as fits the occassion, that it may impart grace to those who hear" (Eph. 4:29). The disciples of our Lord knew that what proceeds from the mouth springs forth from the heart, "for out of the heart the mouth speaks" (St. Matt. 12:34). "A good (agathos) man out of the good (agathos) treasure of his heart brings forth good (agathos) things" (St. Matt. 12:35). Nothing "corrupt" (sapros) or "rotten" (sapros) comes forth from the heart of a good man. "The good (kalos) Word of God" (Heb. 6:5) is "a living Word and active" (Heb. 4:12) for it is a "Word of Life" (Philip. 2:16) full of the Life of Truth and also full of Wisdom for it comes from God. The book of Sirach tells us that Wisdom is fragrant giving "forth the aroma of spices. . .like choice myrrh. . .a pleasant odor like galbanum, onychia and stacte and like the fragrance of frankincense" (Sirach 24:15). The Word of God is holy and nothing holy is corrupt (Ps. 16:10; Acts 13:35). Thus those who are good are as a fragrant sacrifice unto Him: "Hearken unto Me, ye holy children. . .give ye a sweet odor as frankincense. . .send forth fragrance" (Sirach 39:13, 14) and to the wicked our Lord exhorts: "Put away each one of you, your evil practices. . .and. . .I will accept you as a sweet smelling fragrance" (Ezek. 30:39, 41). The same imagery is found in Judith 16:16; 2 Cor. 2:15; Eph. 5:2. The gifts that good people give to God are also as a fragrant sacrifice to him (Philip. 4:18) but not so the "dead things. . .the (lawless) works of men's hands" (Wisdom 13:10). The presumptuous man "makes a dead thing with lawless hands" (idem.v. 17) and "for life beseeches the dead thing" (idem.v. 18). They who trust in lifeless things become just as dead as their own works (Deut. 4:25-28; Ps. 115:4-8; 135:15-18, etc.), for there is no life in their lies. To the Jews "lies" (sheqer) are an "abomination" (sheqets) just as unlawful and abominable as unclean fish (Lev. 11:10-13) or rotten flesh (Lev. 7:18). They hated and abominated all wilful perversity because "the Lord hates all abomination of error and they that fear Him shall not love it" (Sirach 15:13 Latin Vulgate) but abominate it as a "rotten" (sapros) thing. The errors of those who attempt to pervert His Word become corrupt things devoid of the "fragrance of His Knowledge" (2 Cor. 2:14). What was thought to be "sweet" shall "stink" in the end (Isaiah 3:24).
Behold "the sea. . .therein are marvels the most wondrous of His works. . .through Him the end of these things is fragrant" (euodia)—(Sirach 43:26 Greek Text Codex Alexandrinus) but not the end of the evil hidden counsels of those who deny His Words, the end of them is "putrid" (sapros), their "every work rotteth and consumeth away and the worker thereof shall go the same" (Sirach 14:19 Greek Text). "For the wisdom of the flesh is death, but the Wisdom of the Spirit: life and peace" (Romans 8:6).

*"**PRODUCE**": "Dead things (rephaim) are brought forth (chil) from under the waters and the inhabitants thereof" (Job 26:5), the dead things produced in the dark depths of the heart of the wicked who have no understanding (Prov. 21:16).

*"**SIR. 4:11**": "Wisdom breathes life into her children" (Latin Vulgate) and enlightens all who give heed to her" (Syriac Text). "It is the spirit that gives life. . .the words that I have spoken to you are spirit and life" (St. John 6:63). "Whosoever findeth Wisdom findeth life" (Prov. 8:35).

*"**CASTING IT**": "If an understanding man hears a wise word he will commend it and add unto it but when one of no understanding hears it, it displeases him and he mocks at it and casts it behind his back" (Sirach 21:15 Greek and Syriac Text). In the end his own foolish rotten words will be cast out for the Life of Truth is not in them. "He will reject every work grounded on unrighteousness. Woe to you sinners"—(Enoch 97:6,7). Never forget that those who cast His words and His "Law behind their backs" (Neh. 9:26) cast Him aside (I Kings 14:9; Ezek. 23:35) and shall be punished (Exod. 34:6-7; Numbers 14:18; Deut. 5:9-10).

*"**ALTER**": "The things which are written may not be altered" (Test. of Isaac, Cod. Copt. Vat. 61 f. 164a). "For the Word of the living God is not as the words of men: for the Lord, the Ruler of all worlds is the Unchangeable" (Palestinian Targum on Numbers 23 and 27. See also Eccle. 3:14; Sirach 18:6; 42:21, etc.).

The fulness of Wisdom is Understanding.
The fulness of Understanding is the Knowledge of God.
The fulness of Knowledge is Judgment for the sake of Truth.

Ws 8:4 L.V.	"Wisdom teaches the Knowledge of God and is the chooser of His works" Because Wisdom possesses Knowledge to teach and to choose.
Lv 10:10 L.V.	For we are given "Knowledge to discern between holy and unholy, between clean and unclean and to teach."
Dt 30:19 Mt 13:48	Choose His things then, for they are life to your soul And *"cast out"* the things of the evil one for they are death and corruption to those who hold them fast.
Jr 15:19	"If you will separate the precious from the vile you will be as My mouth," says the Lord.
Pr 2:6	And you shall know how to judge and to choose because "out of His mouth comes Knowledge and Understanding,"

The understanding and knowledge we need to execute His* judgment.

Jn 8:16-18	But no one executes His justice without first taking counsel before the Lord.
Mt 13:48	And so —*"when the net was filled they drew to the shore and sitting (they) chose the good (kalos) into vessels but the corrupt* (sapros) they cast out."*
Jb 9:32 Jb 34:4	They worked *together* for "we. . .come together in judgment." Therefore "let us choose to us judgment, and let us know among ourselves what is good," So that we may separate it and treasure it in vessels but cast out what is rotten and corrupt.

And what is corrupt and rotten is that which comes from

2 Tm 3:8 Tt 1:15	"men of corrupt minds" who "resist the Truth" and whose "mind and conscience are defiled."

1 Tm 6:5 Eph 4:9 Sir 4:11*	It is "men of corrupt understanding" who produce* rotten *(sapros)* words" *(logos)* for there is no life in them nor Wisdom.
2 Co 2:17 2 Co 4:2 Dn 2:9 Pr 1:29 Sept.	Furthermore they "debase the Word of God" by "handling the Word of God deceitfully" casting it* behind their backs to substitute instead their own "lying and corrupt words." "Because they hate Wisdom and do not choose the Word of the Lord."
Ws 18:4 Dt 4:2 Mk 7:13	They do their works of deceit in the darkness far from "the incorrupt light of the Law" which decreed that no man shall alter* His Words for it thereby makes void His Wisdom.

231

*"GOOD" *(kalos):* "For we are not able to understand that which is good *(agathos)* as Thou art our Creator" (2 Baruch 14:15), for "no one is good *(agathos)* but God alone" (St. Luke 19:20).

*"RISE":"My Word will require it of him. . .My Word shall take vengeance on him" (Targum Onkelos and Palestinian on Deut. 19).

*"SOME TRANSLATIONS": *Jerusalem Bible* (English and French editions); *La Sainte Bible* (Maredsous Edit.); *Sagrada Biblia* (Nacar-Colunga); *Sagrada Biblia* (Bover-Cantera), etc.

*"VESSELS" *(aggos-aggeion):* During the time of our Lord it was customary for fishermen to put their netted fish into vessels containing water or brine. Strabo (c.63 B.C.-25 A.D.), a contemporary Greek geographer, related (Book XVI .2) that large quantities of fish preserved in casks were exported from Tarichea, a fishing center located on the south shore of Lake Galilee *(See also* Josephus Bell. Jud. Book II, 21.8). Even as late as 1924 an eyewitness (F. Dunkel in *Biblica 24,* p. 383) wrote that the fishermen of Lake Galilee deposited their catch in water-filled clay tanks so as to keep the fishes alive and fresh.
In addition to the obvious advantages of conserving fish in *vessels,* the Oral Law supplied fishermen with certain legal inducements for doing so. The Mishnah stipulated that: "all things enclosed in vessels containing water are free from restrictions" (Hullin 67a), *i.e.,* they are legally "clean." So that even if forbidden fish (Lev. 11:9-12) were to be accidentally included with the rest, they too became acceptable by virtue of being also enclosed within that particular vessel. The Rabbis also ruled that after fish were caught they became susceptible to uncleanness if they died but not if they were transferred into water-filled vessels to preserve them alive *(Uktzin* 2.8). Obviously "rotten" *(sapros)* things have no hope of living for who would choose to "keep" *(shamar-tereo)* and "preserve" *((shamar-tereo)* them in vessels? In His time fish-skins were prized and made into vessels for "vessels made of fish skins are not susceptible to any uncleanness" (Kelim 24:11).
The vessels used by the fishermen had to be "vessels that have been finished in purity" (Hagigah 20b) and free from leaky cracks. It was not legally feasible to use "baskets" because on the other hand the Oral Law decreed that all "basket fish" or exposed fish were to be presumed "unclean" (Machshirin 6:3). Never forget that the baker lost his head because he had upon it "three baskets full of holes" *(chori)*—Genesis 40:16 Literal Translation.
As the good old Rabbi said: "when a vessel has a hole, it is a heap of rubbish, for it is no longer regarded as a vessel" (Sepher Mordecai Maharam, Rabbi Meir in the Massoreth Ha Massoreth of Elias Levith), for it has become like a leaky "basket" that does not hold water because it is full of holes.
"They who have rejected the Word of the Lord, what Wisdom is in them?" (Jer. 8:9). "From him who has not, even what he thinks that he has will be taken away" (St. Luke 8:18). "Ye that trust vainly in falsehood shall fall" (Isaiah 28:17 Sept.). All that have been ashamed of Him and of His words shall be ashamed, (St. Mark 8:38; St. Luke 9:26) for "whoever rejects Wisdom and instruction. . .their hope is vain, their labors are unprofitable and their works are useless" (Wisdom 3:11).
St. Matthew knew the words for "basket" *(viz. kophinos* and *spuris)* for he used them (St. Matt. 14:20; 15:37; 16:9,10) but he *retained* the word "vessels" in the parable of the Net because our Lord said "vessels" and not "baskets." Let the modern scribes be careful and more faithful in rendering His Words, and less presumptuous in their conjectures. Let them remember that His thoughts and His ways are far above our own (Isaiah 55:8-9).

*"STORED": A young but learned man was referred to as "a *new* vessel full of *old* wine," *i.e.,* full of Wisdom and *stored* knowledge (Aboth 4:20). The Hebrew word for "old wine" means literally "stored wine."

*"THEREIN": "I have treasured the words of His mouth more than my necessary food" (Job 23:12). "A *good* vessel encloses a word in its heart but a broken one lets it out" (The words of Ahikar, Aramaic Text, Ch. VII fol. 105). "The Torah (Law) is like water which is. . .kept in earthen vessels" (Midrash Chazitha on Cant. 1:2).

232

Qo 2:14 Mt 13:49	God judges what is good *(agathos)* and evil *(poneros)* and in the end He shall send forth His angels to *"separate the wicked from the midst of the just."*
Heb 5:14	We judge what is good* *(kalos)* and bad *(sapros-kakos)* and we shall discern what is true and false when we become holy.
2 Tm 1:8 Col 1:5 Ps 117:2	"Do not be ashamed of the testimony of our Lord" because "the Word of the Truth of the gospel" proceeded from the mouth of the Lord and "the Truth of the Lord remains forever."
Jn 12:48 Jb 16:9 Sept.	Be patient and hold fast, for the time shall come when His Word shall rise* to judge those who have cast It aside.
Mt 13:48 Jr 8:8 RSV Jr 28:15	In the translations of the parable of the Net there are some* who have supplanted His Word *"vessels"** (aggeion) for their word "baskets" thus making the "people trust in a lie" and rendering His Wisdom folly in the eyes of His countrymen.
2 Co 4:7 2 Tm 2:19-21	Because to the Jews "man" is a "vessel" and precious things or even fish must not be put into "baskets" if they are long to remain good and clean. To them the substitute word "basket" is a "dud" that construes to make His parable pointless.
4 Ezr 4:11	You who have cast His Word aside: "how then shall your vessel be able to understand the way of the Most High?"
Ps 51:6 Stob. Herm. Exc. 26.4	If you "desire Truth in the inward parts" do not forget that to the ancients "Nature is the maker of the mortal frames and the fashioner of the vessels into which souls are put,"
Si 17:7 Rm 8:23 Si 21:14 Sept.	And into which Wisdom and Knowledge are stored* as well. Is it not written that "the heart of a fool is like a broken vessel and he will hold no Knowledge?"
	Perhaps because he has become like a leaky "basket."
	Hold fast! Be holy and you shall be whole.
P.A. 4:20	"Regard not the vessel but that which is therein" And that which should be therein* are His holy Words.
L.B. 21:8 P.A. 2:8	Listen now "while the good vessel of the body is still with you," And understand that a good disciple is "like a vessel lined with lime which loses not one drop" of His wonderful Wisdom.

233

*"*KALOS*": "Incline thine ear to the words of wise men, hear also my word, and apply thine understanding that thou mayest know that they (the words) are good" *(kalos)*—Proverbs 22:17 Sept. "Hear me, ye wise, and ye understanding ones, hearken unto that which is good" *(kalos)*—Septuagint Alternate Text. Bear witness to Him for He "spoke...well" *(kalos)*—St. John 19:23. In His time true teachers were called *didaskalos (See* St. Matt. 10:24,25; St. Mark 10:17; St. Luke 6:40; Eph. 4:11; 1 Tim. 2:7, etc.). The word *didaskalos* is derived from *didasko*="to teach" and *kalos*="good," *i.e.,* a "teacher of good *(kalos)* things." This is further emphasized in Titus 2:3 wherein the women are exhorted to be among themselves: *kalodidaskalos,* literally "good teachers of good things." Thus the word for "doctrine" in the Gospels and Epistles is *didaskalia, i.e.,* "good teaching." Good teachers taught "good *(kalos)* things." In the Parable of the Net it is these "good *(kalos)* things" which are deposited into the *"vessels"* of the righteous, through the "sound wisdom" *(tushiyah)* of those who understand, for it is the Truth within the good things of His Word that shall "deliver" *(teshuah)* them. So "hold fast...that good *(kalos)* thing which was deposited unto you to keep by the Holy Spirit" (2 Tim. 2:14). Be also good and kind for "acceptable is the man that shows mercy and lends: he shall order his words with judgment" (Ps. 111 (112):5 Sept. and Latin Vulgate). If we are good *(agathos)* and have kept our trust in Him we shall see that "He has made everything beautiful *(kalos)* in His time" (Eccle. 3:11 Sept.) and we shall also realize then, that even in this life, the wicked had been "disabled from recognizing the things that were good" *(kalos)*—Wisdom 10:8.

*"*CORRUPT*": "Take care that there proceed no corrupt word out of thy mouth" (Testament of Isaac. folio 14). "I desire to reason with God; first showing that ye are forgers of lies, ye are followers of corrupt doctrines" (Job 13:3-4 as quoted by St. Gregory in his commentary on Job). "As the sea keeps the living but casts off from itself the dead things" (St. Gregory on Job Book V.3), so let us cast off all corrupt doctrines from the depths of our hearts.

*"*PROVING*": "Now therefore, children, hearken unto me and I will open your eyes to see and understand the works of God and to choose what He approves and reject what He hates" (Zadokite Fragment 3:1).

234

1 Th 5:21 1 Tm 2:3;5:4 Heb 6:5	"Prove all things and hold fast that which is good" *(kalos*)* And that which is "good *(kalos)* and acceptable" is the "good *(kalos)* Word of God."
2 Tm 1:13,14 Lk 8:15	"Hold fast the form of sound words. . .that good *(kalos)* thing which was deposited unto you to keep" in the "good *(kalos)* and honest" *(agathos)* vessel of your heart.
1 Tm 1:10	"If there be any other thing that is contrary to sound teaching," Throw it out!
2 Tm 4:4	For the time is here "when people will not endure sound doctrine but having itching ears they will accumulate for themselves teachers to suit their own likings and will turn away from listening to the Truth and wander into fables."
1 Tm 6:20 1 Tm 6:5	"Guard what has been entrusted to you, avoid the godless chatter and contradictions of what is falsely called Knowledge." Have nothing to do with the "perverse disputings of men of corrupt minds deprived of the Truth."
2 Tm 3:8 2 Co 2:17	For these "men of utterly corrupted minds. . .resist the Truth." And vainly try to "adulterate the Word of God."
Eph 4:29	"Let no corrupt* *(sapros)* word *(logos)* spew out of your mouth," For what is "rotten" *(sapros)* is malodorous and shall be flung away.
Tt 2:3 Tt 1:9 Tt 1:9 Jr 23:36	But instead, be "teachers of good things" *(kalodidaskalos),* "holding fast the faithful Word." So that you "may be able by sound doctrine to exhort and also to confute those who contradict it," Those who "have perverted the Words of the living God."
Is 5:24 1 Tm 1:15;4:9	Despise not "the Word of the Holy One of Israel" Because His Word "is a faithful Word and worthy of all acceptation."
Rev 22:6 2 Co 2:14	Treasure the Words of the Lord for His "Words are faithful and true" and they are full of "the fragrance of His Knowledge."
2 Co 4:7	"We have this treasure in earthen vessels" that the glory may be His.
Rev. 22:7 Tt 2:7 Eph 5:10	"Blessed is he that keeps the Words" of God For he shall go about "teaching uncorruptedly" *(adiaphthoria)* And "proving* what is acceptable to the Lord."

CHAPTER 13

THE PARABLE OF THE SCRIBE

St. Matthew 13:51-52

[51] "Do ye understand all these things?" They say to Him: "Yes." [52] So He said to them: "Therefore every scribe instructed as regards the Kingdom of heaven is like to a man, a householder, who brings forth out of his treasure things new and old."

Literal Translation.

*"ORDER": God arranges all His things in beautiful order (St. Matt. 6:29; St. Luke 12:27), for "all His ways are according to His ordering" (Sirach 33:14 L.V.), and "He set in order His works forever" (Sirach 16:27). As the Book of Wisdom (11:21 L.V.) says: "by measure, number and weight Thou didst order all things" (*See also* Wisdom 12:15; 15:1 L.V.; Job 28:25; Isaiah 40:12, 26; 28:25, 26; 4 Esdras 4:5, 36-37; Testament of Naphtali 2;3; I Enoch 41:5; 43:2; Philo *Somn.* 2:29 and *Mut.* Sect. 40, etc.). If Qoheleth "was wise. . .and set in order many parables" (Eccle. 12:9) how much more the Author of all Wisdom Himself as we shall see for "He has set to order the mighty works of His Wisdom" (Sirach 42:21).

This wonderful order is evident in the way He put forth His parables. In the instances (St. Matt. 13:2-9, 24-34; St. Mark 4:1-9, 21-33) He fed the crowds by setting before them as food for thought the following parables: the Sower, the Secretly Growing Seed, the Good Seed and Darnel, the Grain of Mustard and the Leaven. In these are found all the ingredients and means to make true bread, *viz.*, the "good seed" of "wheat," the "ears of grain," the "meal," the "mustard" relish, the "leaven," the "fire" and the "furnace."

We see again His marvelous foresight and order in the sequence in which He put forth these parables to the crowd. He commences with the "going forth" *(outside)* of the Sower to sow His good seed (St. Matt. 13:3; St. Mark 4:3; St. Luke 8:5) then proceeds to: (a) the various types of soil, (b) the gradual process of growth, (c) the watchfulness of the lone worker, (d) the inattentiveness of those who slept, (e) the subsequent disparity of seed, (f) the fruition and the harvesting.

The parables of the Sower, the Secretly Growing Seed, the Good Seed and Darnel are followed by the parable of the Mustard Seed. For in His time it was customary to sow the grain first and then border a small portion of the field with seeds of condiment vegetables such as mustard, used in making bread relish.

This group of parables conclude with the parable of the Leaven: the transformation of the wheat meal by the hidden yeast, a work done *inside* a house.

He then dismissed the crowd and told His disciples in private four special parables which are linked to one another, *viz.*, The Hidden Treasure, the Pearl, the Net and the Scribe. Through these parables which He told to them alone, they were to learn the art of breaking the Bread of God with understanding, revealing to the faithful thereby, the goodness of His Truth within. For Wisdom, understanding, knowledge and good judgment are needed (Acts 6:3,6,8,10) to serve His true Bread and to divide it properly. His disciples were to "teach all nations" (St. Matt. 28:19-20) but they had first to be instructed in "the way of Understanding" (Prov. 9:6). Besides being disciples they also had to be faithful servants (St. Matt. 10:24-25; 24:45-46; St. Luke 12:42-44) "showing all good fidelity that they might set to order (*kosmeo*) the teaching of God our Saviour" (Titus 2:10). All teaching is progressive. The special parables of our Lord deal with the three basic steps of learning, *viz.*, diligence (the Hidden Treasure), discerning inquiry (the Pearl) and good judgment (the Net) leading to the stage where the student becomes an instructor now able to distribute knowledge from his own store (the Scribe). Thus the first three special parables are joined to each other by the word "again" (St. Matt. 13:45, 47) and only after His disciples answered in the affirmative to His question: "Have you understood all these things?" (St. Matt. 13:51), did our Lord introduce the fourth special parable saying: "*Therefore (lit.,* "because of this") *every scribe instructed as regards the Kingdom of Heaven is like to a man, a householder who brings forth out of his treasure things new and old*" (*idem*.v. 52). For they who are instructed by the Lord (St. Mark 4:34), in the order of His Wisdom, receive true Knowledge from Him and it is "by Knowledge that the storerooms are filled with all precious and pleasant riches" (Prov. 24:4), to be dispersed by the lips of the wise (Prov. 15:7). "Wise men store up Knowledge" (Prov. 10:14) for this purpose. But the disciple must listen closely and love to learn for "whosoever loves instruction loves Knowledge" (Prov. 12:1) and loves Wisdom as well for Wisdom said that she shall: "divide substance to them that love Me and fill their treasuries with good things. If I declare to you the *things* of today *(new)*, I will remember also to recount the *things* of old" (Prov. 8:21 Sept. *See also* St. John 4:14; 14:26; Isaiah 42:9 Sept.).

The special parables of light are enacted in three distinct areas: the land (The Hidden Treasure), the coast (the Pearl) and the sea (the Net); encompassing the course of the sun across the heavens from east to west—sunrise to sunset. In the geography of the Holy Land, the sea (Mediterranean) is situated directly west of the land area. Thus the word *yam* in Hebrew means both "sea" and "west."

The group of the special parables commence appropriately in the land, *i.e.*, the area "in front of" *(quedem)* or "before" *(quedem)* the sea. Fittingly the word *(quedem)* is also the most common Hebrew word for "east." The parable of the Hidden Treasure "precedes" *(quedem)* the rest for he began His life in our midst in the east symbolically. The gospels begin by telling us about "His star in the east" *(anatole*="east" in Greek) which was seen by "wise men from the east" *(anatole)* for "through the tender mercy of our God. . .the East *(anatole)* from on high has visited us to give light" (St. Matt. 2:2, 9, 10; St. Luke 1:78, 79). "Whose name is the East" *(anatole)*—Zech. 6:12 Septuagint.

Let us then go "east" *(mizrach* is another word for "east" in Hebrew) where His things are "sown" *(mizrach)* and there "inquire" *(b'qr)* in the "early morning" *(b'qr)* whether we but may "hire out" *(sakar)* to "work for wages" *(sakar)* in His field at "daybreak" *(shachar)*. But let us get up "early" *(shachar)* because "morning" *(or)* is the time for "light" *(or)*. The "dawn" *(shachar)*of understanding is here, go about then "diligently seeking" *(shachar)* and "searching" *(shachar)* for the hidden treasures of Wisdom in the field of the Lord. For Wisdom said that "those who seek me early *(shachar)* shall find me" (Prov. 8:17) and "he that diligently seeks *(shachar)* good procures acceptance" (Prov. 11:27) and gets the job (St. Matt. 24:42, 44-47; St. Luke 12:40, 42-44).

Understanding works, it "plows" *(charash)* the ground of His teaching and delves into it, and when it finds the treasures of His Wisdom it "conceals" *(charash)* them and "holds its peace" *(charash)* until it can successfully bring them to light. The treasures of Wisdom endow the finder with discernment and desire for finer things (Ps. 111:7,8,2). The laborer becomes a merchant connoisseur in search of precious things: beautiful pearls which he shall "skillfully devise" *(charash)* and "fasten" *(hokmah)* with "Wisdom" *(hokmah)* pair by pair to fashion a glorious ornament. The merchant is no longer bound to the soil as the laborer was but is now "free" *(chophshi)* to go about "seeking" *(chaphas)* "loose" *(chophesh)* pearls.

Since he knows that these precious things are traded for by the "shores" *(choph)* of the sea, he "travels" *(arach)* along that route comparing *(arak)* and matching *(arak)* the "several" *(chophshith)* pearls into perfect pairs. Until one day while in the "coast" *(gelilah)* there was "uncovered" *(gelah)* and "revealed" *(gelah)* to him a solitary most precious pearl worth all the rest, and that is the wonderful Truth that there is nothing more valuable than the friendship of God. To hold (cont'd)

238

Mt 13:52	A *"scribe instructed as regards the Kingdom of heaven,"* understands the Wisdom of God, And knows that the Lord does all things in perfect order.*
	The parables of the Sower, the Good Seed and Darnel, the Grain of Mustard and the Leaven He spoke to the crowds. Those of the Hidden Treasure, the Pearl, the Net and the Scribe, He told His disciples in private.
	To the multitudes He gave Bread and to His chosen ones: right judgment. For they were chosen to bear witness to the glory of His Truth and to proclaim it.
	He gave us His Words to sow and to reap.
Hab 2:3	But between the sowing and harvesting there is a long tarrying, So that in watching and waiting we may yearn for Him.
Mt 13:33 Si 15:3	The leaven of His teaching is hidden in the mass until the dough becomes transformed and rises, Then ready to be made "Bread of Understanding" for His famished ones.
Rm 13:11 1 Co 15:34	Arise! Arise! Be roused from your sleep.
1 Co 4:5	For the Lord comes "to bring to light the things now hidden by the darkness and make manifest the secret counsels of the hearts."
1 Co 4:5 Ps 47:7 A.V.	"Then everyman shall have praise of God" And "sing. . .praises with understanding."
2 M 2:8 Jr 30:24; 23:20	For "then shall the Lord disclose these things" And thus "in the latter days you shall understand" them.
2 P 1:19 1 P 4:13	In the meantime, though the night lingers, hold fast to His Words and have faith in Him, "That when His glory shall be revealed you may also be glad with exceeding joy,"
Ws 3:9 1 Co 4:1 Si 20:19 L.V. Lk 12:42	Because then, "they that trust in Him shall understand Truth" and as "stewards of the Mysteries of God" they shall "distribute with right understanding": the good things of the Lord.

and keep His love is worth the sacrifice of giving up all that we possess, for what makes a man truly rich is knowing the Lord who is all Wisdom and Knowledge. The friends of the Lord know and love Him and "possess *(echo)* God in full knowledge" (Romans 1:28) as long as they "have" *(echo)* and "hold fast" *(echo)* His friendship like a precious pearl (St. John 15:14). He whom the Lord loves is "initiated into the Knowledge of God and is a chooser of His works" (Wisdom 8:4) and by His Knowledge he discerns "between holy and unholy, between clean and unclean" (Lev. 10:10 L.V.) and between good and evil (Gen. 2:9) so that he may "take out the precious from the vile" (Jer. 15:9)—His Truth from all falsehood. The wise merchant who acquired the Pearl of great price "saw and considered it well—looked upon it and received instruction" (Prov. 24:32). "When a wise man is instructed he receives knowledge" (Prov. 21:11) and with knowledge comes zeal for the Lord (Romans 10:2). They who are given true Knowledge by God are "zealous for that which is good" (I Peter 3:13). "All the works of the Lord are good and...in due season...in time they shall all be well approved" (Sir. 39:33,34; Eccle. 3:11). "The works of His hands are Truth and judgment" (Ps. 111:7). When the time comes for Him to "bring forth judgment for the sake of Truth" (Isaiah 42:3), His friends shall "draw in *(mashak*=to draw in, to drag in) the Law" (Sir. 32:17 Heb. Text) like a dragnet "to execute the judgment of Truth" (Zech. 8:16). Then, just as an execution of judgment is followed by the allocation of goods, the parable of the Net (St. Matt. 13:47-50) is succeeded by the parable of the Scribe—Householder (St. Matt. 13:51-52). And thus what was kept hidden as a "Treasure" *(thesauros)* in the beginning (St. Matt. 13:44) is brought forth from the "Treasury" *(thesauros)* in the end (St. Matt. 13:52).

*"**SCRIBE**": In His time as well as the four centuries preceding it, "the burden of the Word of the Lord" was entrusted to the Scribes, *i.e.,* the *Sopherim.* The Hebrew word *sopher* (scribe) is derived from the Assyrian words *shaparu=*"to send" and *shataru=* "to write." Thus an Assyrian "overseer" was called a *shatar* and a written "document;" a *shetara.* Later on the Jewish Rabbis elucidated that the "scribes" were called *sopherim* because they "counted" or "numbered" *(saphar)* all the letters of the Torah (Kidd. 30a B.T.).

It was the scribes who brought the oral collections that comprise the Pentateuch, Prophets, Psalms and Wisdom lore into written form. The Holy Bible as we have it today is mainly the work of the scribes. They took great pains to render faithfully into writing the inspired Word of God for they believed then as today in its sacred character (*See* Babylonian Talmud sections Sanhedrin 10:1; 74b; 99a; Gittin 60a; B. Bathra 15a; Jebamoth 79a; Megillah 3:3; Aboth 3:8; Midrash Rabbah on Song of Songs 5:11; Exod. 6:2; 10:1; Vayikrah 19 para. 2; Mekhilta on Exod. 15:7, etc.). They dealt with the holy and so the scribes lived accordingly and were held in high esteem by the Jews then as today (*See* Midrash Rabbah on Song of Songs I.2; Numbers VIII. 4; XIV. 4, etc.). They were the "men of understanding" enrolled chiefly from among the Hassidim (righteous ones) and are the just men referred to in the prophecies of Daniel 11:33, 35; 12:3. Their prototype *par excellence* was Ezra the faithful scribe (Ezra 7:6, 11-12; Neh. 8:1,4,9,13; 12:26,36). But from the time of Ezra, the priest-scribe, non-priestly Israelites gradually began to assume the functions of the priest-scribes, forming by themselves an independent class of scripture scholars. In Hellenic times and the Roman occupation when the Jewish priesthood fell into disrepute for neglecting the Law and collaborating with their pagan overlords, it was no longer the priests but the popular scribes, who were the zealous guardians of the Law. From that time to the Time of our Lord they were the real teachers of the people over whose spiritual life they held complete sway. In the New Testament they were referred to as the *grammateis* ("learned in writings"), *nomikos* ("learned in Law") and *nomodidaskaloi* ("teachers of the Law"). The people addressed them as "Lord" *(kurie),* "teacher" *(didaskale),* "master" *(epistata),* "master-guider" *(kathegetes),* "Father" *(pater, abba)* and "my great one" *(rabbi, rabboni).* These learned scribes became accepted as the final arbiters of any discussion particularly as regards points of Law or judgment: "Have I a book or a scribe *(grammateus)* by me that I may stand and put man to silence?" (Job 37:20 Sept.). Their erudition was so proverbial that eventually the words "scribe" *(sopher)* and "wise man" *(hakam)* became synonymous. Thus in the Talmud contemporary scribes are referred to as the "wise men" *(ha-khamim)* and there was great respect for their knowledge (*See* B. T. Orlah 3:9; Jebamoth 2:4; 9:3; Sotah 9:15; Sanhedrin 11:3; Kelim 13:7; Parah 11:4-6; Tohoroth 4:7, 11 etc.).

Yet "wise" as the "scribes" had come to be known they had one thing in common: they all started out as simple disciples at the feet of a master-scribe and were subjected to the "discipline" *(musar)* of his "instruction" *(musar)* for to be "taught." *(yasar)* then was to be "chastised" *(yasar)* and "goaded" *(malamad)* until one "learned" *(lamad)*. Thus later on the Rabbis modestly explained that their title "Rabbi" *(lit.,* "my great one") meant simply "master" in opposition to "slave," no doubt recalling the slave-like status they had during their discipleship (Aboth 1:3; Eduyoth 1:13). For the disciple-scribes had to undergo a long period of instruction before they could qualify as full-fledged scribes. They had to pore long over the many scrolls and dig deep into the field of His Word before they would be able to come upon the treasures of His Wisdom. They had much to learn before they would be able to bring forth from their own treasury things new and old, to give to the rest. Their day of learning commenced at dawn for they remembered that he who gets up early in the morning to study shall teach by night (Exod. Rabbah s.47, edit. Wilna).

The Jewish scribes took good care of the burden of the Word that was entrusted to them and they handled the Word with great reverence for they were taught that: "He who touches a Word of God touches the pupil of His eye" (Yalkut on Prov. 27:3). As disciples they were enjoined by their masters that "he who forgets a tenet of his instruction in the Law, to him Scripture imputes the wilful forfeiture of his life" (Aboth 3:8), and so they were careful and showed great fidelity copying the words of a text from one scroll to another and in quoting Holy Scripture during their discussions. They knew that the honor of the Lord was bound up in His word (See "*Die agada der Palastinsichen Amoraer*" by W. Bacher, vol. I p. 126; Yalkut of Rabbi Machir bar Abba Mari on Zechariah, ed. A.W. Greenup, London 1909 p. 32; Yalkut on Proverbs, edit. L. Grunhut, Frankfort 1902 p. 66a; Mekhilta de R. Ismael on Exodus 15:7; Yalkut Shimeoni on Exod. 15:7; Siphre on Numbers 10:35, etc.). They were zealous in their task, remembering the accusation of our Lord through the prophet Hosea against the priests who were derelict in teaching and transmitting the Law: "They have changed My glory into shame" (Hosea 4:7 strict literal translation of the Hebrew Text). When out of extreme reverence the Scribes sometimes emended a text, they were careful to note the emendation and acknowledge the original text. The disciple scribes were admonished by their master: "My son, be careful because thy work is the work of the heavens, if thou omittest one single letter or addest a single letter thou dost as a consequence destroy the whole world" (Rabbi Ismael 120 A.D. in Sotah 20a B.T.). Yet they were also encouraged to persevere in their diligence for "he who makes himself a slave in this world on account of the Words of the Torah will be free in the world to come" (Baba Metzia 85b. B.T.). They exulted in their prestige: "The Words of the *Sopherim* are more beloved than the Words of the Torah" (Berakoth 1:7 Jer. Talmud); "the words of the scholars are better than the wine of the Law" (Midrash Rabbah on Song of Songs 1:2; *See also* Jer. Talmud: Ber. 8a; 13; B. Metzia 33a; Chagigah 10a). When He laid the burden of the care of His Words upon their shoulders, not only were they entrusted with the glory and honor of His Word but they themselves were to bask in its uncovered radiance. Thus the wise Ben Sirach said: "Wisdom's yoke was to me for glory" (Sirach 51:17 Hebrew and Syriac text) because "Wisdom exalts to glory those who hold her fast" (Sirach 1:19 Sept.). Wisdom and the Torah are one and the same thing (Sirach 24:23) to the Jews, thus "the yoke of the Torah" (Pirke Aboth 3:8) and "Wisdom's yoke" are synonymous.

So "bring. . .your neck into Wisdom's yoke; put your shoulder under her and be not grieved with her bonds. . .for in the end. . .she shall be turned for you into gladness and. . .you shall put her on as a robe of honor and set her upon you as a crown of joy" (Sirach 6:24,25,28,31).

Be a good and loyal child of Wisdom, defend her from those who scoff at her Words. Remember that "Wisdom is justified by her children" (St. Matt. 11:19; St. Luke 7:35).

"Magnify Wisdom and she shall exalt you, embrace her and she shall honor you" (Proverbs 4:8). "Upon the person of the scribe He shall lay His honor" (Sirach 10:5) for it is left to the scribe to bring forth the glory of His Word.

Si 10:5	"Upon the person of the scribe* He shall lay His honor."
Ml 1:1	The honor that is bound up within "the *burden* of the Word."
Jn 8:31-32;15:3; 17:19 1 P 1:22	And then the Lord shall wait until that burden placed upon him shall have fully perfected the disciple scribe.
Lk 6:40	For "the disciple is not above his Teacher but everyone when he is perfected shall be as his Teacher."
Si 39:8 Sept. 51:26 M.T. Zc 12:1	Then able to bring forth to His honor— the Truth found within "the burden of the Word of the Lord."
Mt 10:24-25	"The disciple is not above his Master, nor the servant above his Lord, It is enough for the disciple that he be as his Master and the servant as his Lord."
Mt 13:52	That the servant may become a *"householder"* And the disciple, a master *"scribe."*
Jb 22:21 L.V.	When the time comes for the glory of the Lord to be revealed, They who have kept His Word shall bring forth Truth to Him as Fruit from a hidden Seed.
Col 2:23	So that all may see, hear, partake and fully understand it And acknowledge that the Lord is God.
Mt 13:52 Si 1:17 Sept.	In the end *"every scribe instructed"* by the Lord *"is like a man, a householder who brings forth out of his treasure things new and old."*
Lk 6:45 Mt 12:35 Ws 8:9 Pr 8:21 Sept.	He is like "a good man" who "out of the good treasure of his heart brings forth that which is good." And that which is good are the true things found within "the burden of the Word": the "good things" He promised we shall have.
Jr 23:33 Sg 7:13	For within "the burden of the Lord" are "all manner of choice fruits new and old. . .kept for you"— To bring forth and distribute for Him.
Jn 6:63	So hurry up and open the treasury of your heart and bring forth the good things of His burden: true Words full of "Spirit and Life."
Am 8:11-13	For there is "a famine in the land" and the poor are weak and hungry.
Mt 21:41 Ps 1:3	Make haste! because He comes for His "fruits in their season" To divide and apportion them soon,
Si 24:25-27	In this vintage time of Understanding.

The Parables of

St. Matt. 13:44-52

The Hidden Treasure

44 "The Kingdom of heaven is like unto a treasure hidden in the field; which a man found and hid; and from the joy thereof went and sold what things he had and bought that field."

Literal Translation.

The Pearl of Great Price

45 "*Again*, the Kingdom of heaven is like to a man, a merchant, seeking beautiful pearls, 46 who on finding one pearl of great price, went away and sold all that he had and bought it."

The Net

47 "*Again*, the Kingdom of heaven is like a net cast into the sea and gathering of every kind: 48 which when it was filled they drew to the shore and sitting chose the good into vessels but the corrupt they cast out.

49 Thus shall it be at the completion of the age; the angels will come forth and will separate the wicked from the midst of the just 50 and will cast them into the furnace of fire: there shall be weeping and gnashing of teeth."

The Scribe

51 "*Do ye understand all these things?*" They say to Him: "Yes". 52 So He said to them: "Therefore every scribe instructed as regards the Kingdom of heaven is like to a man, a householder, who brings forth out of his treasure things new and old."

Literal Translation.

245

We are the dough.
Humility rests in knowing we are dust:
Flour which the waters of Baptism through the Holy Spirit forms into dough.

Meekness is letting ourselves be handled by Him,
By His hands that knead and press the mass to be shaped into the Mould he desires:
Christ Jesus—His Son.

It does not matter if He places us into the oven next
Because by the Leaven of His Word we know that He is making Bread out of us.

When the Loaf is done He takes it out awhile
For it has risen and is almost bursting with the generosity that seeks to give itself.

He then takes it in His hands breaks it and gives it to the rest to eat,
This Bread which is us
That through us others may partake of His Goodness.

This is the daily Bread that He gives to the world.
Yesterday, today and tomorrow
God works.

He is always making Bread.

CHAPTER 14

THE PARABLE OF THE LEAVEN

According to St. Matthew 13:33.

[33] Another parable He spoke to them: "The Kingdom of heaven is like leaven which a woman took and hid in three measures of meal, until the whole was leavened."

THE PARABLE OF THE LEAVEN

According to St. Luke 13:20-21

[20] And again He said: "To what shall I liken the Kingdom of God? [21] It is like leaven which a woman took and hid in three measures of meal until the whole was leavened."

Mt 13:19
Lk 8:11

Si 15:3

The parables portraying the increase of "the Word of the Kingdom" begin with the parable of the Sower who sows "the Seed" which "is the Word of God" and they end with the parable of the Leaven, *i.e.*, the making of the Bread of the Word: "the *bread of understanding*" it.

See p. 101

Pr 9:5

Pr 9:5
Si 15:3

We know the many instances in which the Word of God is likened to "seed" or "wheat." In turn, the content of the Word or the understanding of its Teaching is likened to "bread" given to us. Thus Wisdom says to him who is without understanding: "Come eat of my *bread.*" Wisdom says that to him who is "a man who fears the Lord. . .and who holds to the Law. . .she will feed him with the *bread of understanding.*"

Targ. Is 32:6

For he who fears the Lord and keeps His Commandments is a righteous man and "the righteous. . .desire *instruction* even as one that hungers desires *bread.*"
If we hunger and desire in all innocence to imbibe the Word of God as "milk," we shall grow up to be strong enough in all good judgment to partake the more solid food of understanding His Word (1 Peter 2:2; I Cor. 3:2-3; Heb. 5:12-14).

T.L. 18:6
En 49:3

Pr 12:11

En 82:3

Ask of the Father the Holy "Spirit of Understanding" and you shall find and enjoy the good things of His Word (St. Matt. 7:9-11; St. Luke 11:11-13). But first let us take good care of the ground of our hearts and go about keeping it clear of all weeds because "he that tills his own ground shall be satisfied with *bread* but they that pursue vanities are void of *understanding*" and let us also pay close attention to His Words for they that "listen with the ear that they may learn. . .Wisdom. . .shall eat thereof better than good food."

Thus the Rabbis traditionally considered the Torah as "meal" and "bread" (*See* Genesis Rabbah XLIII. 6; Exod. R. XLVII. 5,7; Eccle. R. XII. 4,7; Cant. R. VIII. 2; Lam. R. Introd. sect. 23; Aboth R. Nathan, Ch. 18; Sifre Deut. sect. 45 on Deut. 11.18, 22; Mechilta to Exod. XVI. 31; Yalkut to Cant. 1.1, sect. 980; Midrash on Ps. 119 sect. 24; Bacher's Palest. Amoraer I. 490; II. 396; Kiddushin 30b; B. Bathra 16a; Gittin 67a; Shoher Tob 41.7; Tanh. Ekeb. sect. 2; Pesachim 84a; Yoma 46a; Yebamoth 49b; B.T.; Jer. Shekalim V. init. p. 48c; Sotah IX. 14, etc.).

But before the "wheat" of the Word can be made into "bread," the grain must be ground into meal and passed through a sieve. And before the flour can be moulded into loaves, water must be poured upon it to convert it into dough. The leaven of His Teaching hidden within it is then kneaded along with the mass, there to remain hidden until it has pervaded throughout and enlightened the whole.

In the time of our Lord and even today in many parts of the Middle East, leavened bread is prepared by "hiding" or inserting into a fresh mass of dough an unbaked fully fermented batch of dough retained the previous day for this purpose. The retained lump of fermented dough is called *chamets* in Hebrew and since this was the common "leaven" found in a household, *chamets* is the usual word for "leaven" in Holy Scripture. *Chamets* ("leaven" or, *lit.*, "soured" dough) contains within it the active yeast principle, the "leaven" *per se* which is called *seor.* Unmixed "leaven" *(seor)* was usually made anew once a year during the time of vintage by kneading millet or fine bran with grape juice (Pliny, *Hist. Nat.* 18.26). However, hardly anyone kept "leaven" in this liquid form for it was far more convenient to retain leaven in "sour dough" *(chamets)* from day to day. Leavened bread was made with *chamets* leaven.
The usual Hebrew word for common "bread" is *lehem* and since ordinary bread then as today is made with leaven, the word *lehem*

as a rule means "leavened bread." To eat leavened bread is also to eat "leaven" consequently the very word "leaven" *(chamets)* by itself is applied to "leavened bread":

Exod. 12:15. . . . ."Whosoever eats *leavened* bread" *(chamets)*
Exod. 13:37. . . . ."There shall be no "*leavened* bread" *(chamets)*
Exod. 23:18. . . . ."My sacrifice with "*leavened* bread" *(chamets)*
Deut. 16:3. . . . ."Thou shalt eat no *leavened* bread" *(chamets)*

Thus when our Lord said "beware of the leaven of the Pharisees" (St. Luke 12:1) He meant beware of their false "bread." "*True* bread" (St. John 6:32) comes from God.

In Hebrew, the freshly kneaded "dough" while still in the kneading trough and before it rises is called *arisah* a word which also means "cradle," "nursery," or the "cradle stage" of early childhood. Risen dough is called *batsek* (*lit.*, "swollen" or "grown" dough).

Gn R. XIV.1

When the dough had become fully fermented by the batch of "leaven" *(chamets)* inserted into it, two portions were nipped off and separated "from the very center" of the leavened mass. One was the small fresh batch of *chamets* which was retained to be used as "leaven" the following day, and the other was the portion called *challah, viz.*, the "first fruits" of the dough, *i.e.*, the Lord's portion. For the Israelites were enjoined by the Law that "when Nb 15:19,20 ye eat of the bread of the land ye shall separate a portion as a gift to the Lord. . .ye shall separate *challah* from the first of your dough as a gift." Moreover this was to be done by them Nb 15:21 "throughout your generations." Thus even today when Jewish women make bread they separate *challah* from the dough. However, since the destruction of the Temple, the *challah* portion is no longer given to the priests to be consumed by them (Numbers 18:8,12,24,26; Deut. 18:4) but is instead burned in a specially made fire. This is done as an abiding gesture that still acknowledges *challah* to be the Lord's "hallowed portion" *(terumah)* separate from "common" *(chullin)* dough. The *challah* was separated from the center of the dough just after the batch of *chamets* was removed from it (Yoreh Deah 324). Thus there is no difference in composition between *chamets* and *challah;* yet the former is "profane" and the latter "sacred." Allegorically, yesterday's "rejected" *chamets* that was set aside, is able to transform the dough that receives it in its midst today. In the process the *chamets* becomes the *challah* of the new mass just as the rejected stone becomes the chief corner stone through the Lord's doing (St. Matt. 21:42; St. Mark 12:10; St. Luke 20:17).

Mt 13:33
Lk 13:20-21

Mt 13:1

The parable of the Leaven is found both in St. Matthew and St. Luke. The Gospel according to St. Matthew retains the form of the parable as told by our Lord to the multitude "by the seaside," on the occasions He told them the parables of the Sower, the Good Seed and Darnel, and the Mustard Seed.

Lk 13:10

St. Luke preserves the parable of the Leaven in the manner it was spoken by our Lord on a **different** occasion when "He was teaching in one of the synagogues on the Sabbath." While there, He spoke to the people the parable of the Mustard Seed and the parable of the Leaven in response to their acclamation. Thus on that particular occasion just as He did when He spoke the parable of the Mustard Seed to them, He prefaced the parable of the Lk 13:20 Leaven also: "He said **again** *(palin)* to what shall I liken the Kingdom of God?"

St. Matthew preserves for us the parable of the Leaven as told by our Lord to illustrate the development of "the Reign of the heavens," *i.e.*, the advent of the Understanding of the wonderful Wisdom and Knowledge of God hidden in our Lord's teaching.

Lk 12:1

Lk 17:20

Pes. 2:2

All teaching contains its own leaven: its active principle that either enlightens or corrupts the mass depending on the type of leaven it is. Elsewhere in St. Matthew (16:6,11-12) our Lord described the false "teaching of the Pharisees and the Sadducees" as a "leaven" capable of affecting the heart of the people imperceptibly but just as thoroughly as leaven affects dough. Thus He resolutely warned His disciples: *"First of all* beware of the leaven of the Pharisees" because the counsel we "take in" has a profound effect on us. By the same token, just as there is good and bad advice, there is also good and evil leaven. The leaven of His teaching has within it the active good principle that comes and does its hidden work "without observation" in the hearts of those who have accepted His Teaching. Slowly but surely in them the leaven of His Word enlightens and prepares them to undergo the trials (Acts 14:22) that shall prove and transform them for Him.

Leaven, through its fermentative action, makes the dough porous, it aerates and lightens it. As the dough becomes wholly leavened it becomes distinguishable from unleavened dough by its smooth, shiny and golden appearance. Furthermore, leavened dough resounds when tapped. Thus the Rabbis referred to hard unleavened dough as "deaf *(cheresh)* dough" or "dumb dough" *(cheresh* also means "deaf and dumb," *see* Terumoth 1:2 B.T.). Conversely leavened dough may be said to be a dough that "hears."

CHAPTER 15

THE PARABLE OF THE LEAVEN

According to St. Matthew 13:33.

³³ Another Parable He spoke to them: "The Kingdom of heaven is like leaven which a woman took and hid in three measures of meal, until the whole was leavened."

*"LEAVEN WITHIN": Good doctrine bears within itself its own "light" that gives understanding to those who occupy themselves with it and follow its counsels (Prov. 6:23; Pss. 19:8; 97:11; 119:105, 130). This "light" (or) may be aptly likened to "leaven" (seor) hidden within the mass, for just as the action of leaven in due time makes dough shiny, lighter and easier to mould so does perseverance in study render a "hard" subject light and easy to grasp.
In the Oral Law (Mishnah) the rabbis commented on the fact that there is intrinsic leaven in all dough, flour and cereal grains (Pesachim 2:7,8; 3:1,2-5). Therefore, in the preparation of unleavened bread for the Passover, great care was taken to make sure that the particular grain to be used was dry and intact. The unleavened dough itself was never left standing more than eighteen minutes (distance time) as otherwise it was presumed to have become si'ur ("leavened by itself") and thereby unsuitable to be made into matzah ("unleavened bread"). Thus even today because of all the precautions taken to insure its proper preparation, unleavened Passover bread is called shamira ("watched") matzoth.
There is a quality of austerity in unleavened bread, it is the bread of nomads and of warriors on the march for it is bread that can be prepared in haste as it was on the Passover night of the Lord (Exod. 12:12). Thus in Holy Scripture unleavened bread is called "the bread of affliction" or "sorrow" (Deut. 16:3) made as it were under duress. The Jews consider the Law a sacred obligation and they refer to it as the "yoke of the Law" (Pirke Aboth 3:7-8; 6:6; Sirach 6:25; 51:26; Pss. of Sol. 7:8; 17:32; Acts 15:10; Gal. 5:1). Acknowledging the austerity of its discipline (Wisdom 6:17-18) yet nevertheless aware of the salutary effects derived from compliance to the Law of God, the rabbis sagely noted that the Hebrew word for "unleavened bread" and "Commandments" have identical consonants (Mekhilta Piska Bo 10a). And perhaps because we have to strive when we attempt to conform ourselves to His Commandments, the Hebrew word for "to contend with" or "to strive against" and the word for "unleavened bread" is the same word: matzah.
On the other hand because of its assuasive or softening action on the dough, leaven was said to have a pacifying effect: "Great is Peace for Peace is to the world as leaven is to dough" (Perek Hashalom 1:1 in Derek Erez Zuta B.T., Wilna Edit. See also Bacher's Agada der Palest. A moraer I, 136). Consequently judges who mercifully mitigated their verdicts in passing judgment were praised in these terms: "Blessed be the judge who leavens his judgment" (David Kimchi as noted in Lightfoot's Horae Hebr. II, 334.).
We now see the wisdom of ordaining unleavened bread to be always the bread of the solemn Passover season and leavened bread to be the bread of the joyful Feast of Weeks (Exod. 34:22; Lev. 23:15-17). When a wandering people are finally able to settle in their own land they change the staple of their diet from unleavened to the tastier leavened bread for they have more time and leisure then to prepare it in peace. If unleavened bread is the bread of the dispersed, leavened bread is the bread of the gathered. And if unleavened bread is the bread of the Sower, leavened bread is the bread of the Harvestman come home to enjoy the fruits of the seed. If we keep and partake the unleavened bread of His word we shall some day eat the leavened bread of understanding it.

Thus to "knead" the dough of the Torah, i.e., to be occupied in the study of the Law or Teaching of the Lord is to become aware of the mysterious action of His hidden "leaven" upon the mass of Teaching. In due time a diligent student notices that the "dough" of the Law (Torah) becomes less dense and more pliant to his probing if he has faithfully observed its precepts. Acquiring learning then becomes easier for him and study itself a source of great joy for he shall understand at last what he long struggled to comprehend.
The wise men of old knew that the keeping and doing of the Lord's will as found in the Law brought to the doer its own reward, viz., understanding the Truths contained therein (Ps. 111:10). Thus the Psalmist sang:
"Oh, how I love Thy teaching (Torah)! it is my meditation all the day
Thy commandment makes me wiser than my enemies for it is ever with me" (Ps. 119:97-98). The Psalmist knew that His Commandments make those who keep them wise because they are full of light within:
"The Commandment is a lamp and the Teaching (torah) a light" (Prov. 6:23). Thus the faithful young scribe exulted:
"I have more understanding than all my teachers for Thy Testimonies are my meditation. I understand more than the elders because I keep Thy Precepts" (Ps. 119:99-100). He understood for he knew that: "Through Thy Precepts I get Understanding" (Ps. 119:104a).
To understand is to turn to the Lord (Isaiah 6:10) and "hate every false way" (Ps. 119:104b) and run the way of His Commandments (Ps. 119:32) and thereby gain once more His friendship (St. John 15:14). The wise rabbis knew this. For in one of the oldest Tractates of the Talmud a rabbi commented on Jeremiah 16:11: "They have deserted Me," says the Lord, "and have not kept My Law," interpreting this to mean in the Words of the Lord: "Would that they had deserted Me but yet kept My Law (Torah) for the leaven which is in it would have brought them back to Me" (Pesikta de Rab Kahana Piska XV, 120b-121a., S. Buber, edit.). In other words, they who come to a true understanding (which the Lord has hidden as a "leaven" within the mass of His Teaching) will in awe, discover in the Teaching (Torah) the infinite Wisdom and Knowledge of God. In their astonishment they shall then turn, repent and acknowledge Him. For to recognize the greatness of a work is to want to know the author and sing forth his praise. "Give me understanding and I shall keep Thy Law; yes I shall observe it with my whole heart" (Ps. 119:34).
"Make me to understand the way of Thy Precepts and I shall tell of Thy wondrous works" (Ps. 119:27).

258

Si 11:4 L.V.	"His works are glorious secret and hidden"
Pr 25:2	For "it is the glory of God to hide a thing"
	That we may bring it to light and give glory to Him.
	God hides the understanding of His marvelous Wisdom as a "leaven" within the mass of His Teaching.
Kal. R. 54a	And "whosoever occupies himself with the Teaching (Torah)...
B.T.	to him are revealed the secret meanings of the Teaching," by the leaven* within.
Pr 29:18	Therefore "happy is he who keeps the Teaching" (Torah),
Si 21:11 Sept.	For "he that keeps the Teaching of the Lord gets the understanding thereof."
Si 32:15 Sept.	And thus "he that seeks out the Teaching shall be filled thereby" with the bread of understanding it.
Ps 119:18	"Open Thou mine eyes, that I may behold the hidden things of Thy Law"
Is 6:10	For when we understand we shall turn to Thee, O Lord.
Ps 119:34	"Give me Understanding and I shall keep Thy Law; yes I shall observe it with my whole heart."
Ps 119:32	"I will run the Way of Thy Commandments when Thou shalt enlarge my understanding."
Ps 119:4	Therefore, "Thou hast commanded us to keep Thy Precepts diligently,"
Ps 119:104	For "through Thy Precepts we get understanding."
Ps 111:10	Indeed, "a good understanding have all those that do" Thy
Ps 119:100,98	Commands.
Si 1:26 Sept.	"If you desire Wisdom, keep the Commandments and the Lord will give her unto you."
Dt 4:5,6	"Behold, I have taught you statutes and judgments...keep therefore and do them for this is your Wisdom and Understanding in the sight of the nations."
Si 6:37 M.T.	"Meditate in the fear of the Most High and think upon His Commandments continually; Then He will instruct your heart, and He will make you wise in that which you desire."
	Hunger with all desire to understand His Word, And He will feed you with the Bread of Understanding.
Jn 14:6, 14; 15:16; 16:23-24	But ask Him for it in the Name of the Lord,
Col 2:3	"In whom are hid all the treasures of Wisdom and Knowledge."

259

*"**FEAST OF WEEKS**" known as *Shovuos* and also called Pentecost, is the feast that commemorates the anniversary of the giving of the Law on Mt. Sinai.

*"**SHEAF OF BARLEY**": Our Lord taught throughout the countryside (St. Matt. 4:23,25; St. Mark 1:39) and several times by the Sea of Galilee. On one occasion when "He began **again** *(palin)* to teach by the sea side" (St. Mark 4:1), He told the multitude the parable of the Secretly Growing Seed. This parable is preserved for us by the Gospel according to St. Mark (4:26-29). On that occasion our Lord also told the crowd the particular versions of the parables of the Sower and the Mustard Seed retained by St. Mark. However, on that day He did not tell the multitude the parable of the Leaven; for it was on that occasion that He told them the parable of the Secretly Growing Seed, and the seed in that parable is a grain of barley. We may safely deduce that, because the man's whole attention in that parable is directed to the progressive growth of the seed from hidden kernel to the full ear of grain in the *sheaf*. And in the barley harvest it is the chosen sheaf that is the "first fruits" of the Lord. No one is allowed to eat leavened bread during *barley* harvest time because barley is invariably harvested in the Passover season: the season of Unleavened Bread. It would have therefore been inappropriate to include the parable of the Leaven in that day's set of parables.

Although the parable of the Mustard Seed was elsewhere (St. Matt. 13:31-33; St. Luke 13:18-21) paired with that of the Leaven, it was nevertheless told alongside the parable of the Secretly Growing Seed in the Gospel according to St. Mark for it was customary to eat leavened *and* unleavened bread with mustard relish (Pesachim 2:8, Mishnah).

There were no restrictions in the time of the *wheat* harvest, everyone then was allowed to eat leavened bread. Thus on another occasion also "by the sea side" (St. Matt. 13:1) when our Lord told the multitude another "harvest" parable, *viz.,* the parable of the Good Seed and Darnel, He also included at that time the parable of the Leaven, because the "Good Seed" in that parable were grains of "wheat" (St. Matt. 13:24,25,29,30). And it is from the new grains of wheat that the *leavened* loaves "first fruits of the wheat harvest" (Exod. 34:22) were made. We know there is no difference in composition between *chamets* ("leaven") and *challah* ("firstfruits of the dough"). The baked leavened loaves in turn were also called *challah* (pl.) by the Rabbis (Menachoth 3:6). Thus the *chamets* of today may become tomorrow's holy *challah*, (first fruits of the dough) and *challah* become the most holy bread: "the first fruits to the Lord" (Lev. 23:17).

There were two grain harvests in the Holy Land: the barley harvest which occurred around the solemn Passover season, and the wheat harvest which took place fifty days later during the joyful celebration of the Feast* of Weeks (Pentecost). In each one of these harvests, first fruits were offered to the Lord. The first fruit offering of the *barley* harvest was the Omer, a specially chosen sheaf* of barley from the best portion of the growth. The first fruit offering of the *wheat* harvest was not a sheaf of grain but the two leavened loaves of bread made from fine flour of the new wheat crop "two wave loaves. . .of fine flour. . .baked with leaven; they are the first fruits unto the Lord."

Lv 23:17

Lv 23:10

Lv 23:20

Fifty days were reckoned from the presentation of the "**sheaf** *(omer)* of the first fruits" of the *barley* harvest to the presentation of the leavened "**bread** of the first fruits" of the *wheat* harvest. Accordingly, the days before the Feast of Weeks were always reckoned as the first, second, third, etc., since the presentation of the "omer" sheaf. These "omer days" were kept in close count, for the Feast of Weeks (Pentecost) was eagerly anticipated "just as one who is expecting the most faithful of his friends is wont to count the days and hours to his arrival" (Maimonides in *Moreh Nebukim*). This was so because the Jews considered the giving of the Torah in Mt. Sinai to be the object of the Passover deliverance and Exodus from Egypt. Thus the Feast of Weeks is also designated by them as *Chag ha Azereth* ("Feast of the Conclusion") and the "Season of the giving of our Law." They were festive and grateful to the Lord on this occasion because even today devout Jews "delight in the Law of the Lord" (Pss. 1:2; 112:1; 119:16,24,47,70,77,92,143,162,174; Sir. 4:18; 15:6 L.V.; 51:20 L.V.; Wisd. 8:18; Rom. 7:22, etc.), they "delight in understanding" it (Prov. 18:2; Neh. 8:12; Pss. 19:8; 119:14, 72,97,103-104, 111, 127-128, 130; Prov. 2:10; 3:13; 24:13-14; 29:18; Sir. 21:11 Sept. and Apoc. of Baruch 15:5; Jer. 15:16; St. Luke 24:32, etc.).

Let us too "rejoice in the Truth" (1 Cor. 13:6; Philip. 1:18;2 John v.4; 3 John v.3) for "we have the understanding of Christ" (1 Cor. 2:16; 1:24,30; Col. 2:2-3; 3:16; St. John 14:6). And let us also be good and hold fast to the Truth that we may bring forth the fruit of acknowledging it. For we are born unto "the acknowledging of the Truth" (2 Tim. 2:25; Titus 1:1; Philemon v.6; Col. 2:2-3) but this witnessing is "according to godliness" (Titus 1:1). Only the good who have brought forth "the fruits of righteousness" (Philip 1:11; Heb. 12:11; St. James 3:18), shall receive from within these "fruits" the seeds of His praise as their reward (1 Cor. 4:5; Sir. 15:9-10; 39:33-34; Eccle. 3:11).

If there is an interim of waiting between the reaping of the barley sheaf *(omer)* and the baking of the wheaten leavened loaves, it is so that we may keep and be nourished in this interval by "the unleavened bread of sincerity and Truth" (1 Cor. 5:8). Hold fast! for the Day will surely come when He shall give us the leavened bread of understanding.

CHAPTER 16

THE PARABLE OF THE LEAVEN

According to St. Luke 13:20-21

[20] And again He said: "To what shall I liken the Kingdom of God?
[21] It is like leaven which a woman took and hid in three measures of meal until the whole was leavened."

*"**BETHLEHEM**": It is well known that Bethlehem was the birthplace of King David, the progenitor of the Judah line of kings. What is less well known is that Benjamin, the eponymous ancestor of Saul the Benjaminite, first king of Israel, was also born in the immediate vicinity of Bethlehem (Gen. 35:16,19; 48:7; Josh. 15:60 Sept.). Thus from Bethlehem stemmed the two great royal families of Israel: Benjamin and Judah.

In the wisdom of God it was fitting that these two ruling houses should derive their origin from the little town of the "House" *(Beth)* of "Bread" *(lehem)*, for kings are chosen to feed and guide the people (2 Sam. 5:2), providing sustenance and security for them (Micah 5:2, 4). Therefore as the "signs" (I Sam. 10:7) of Divine predilection and clues to the role he was to act as King, Saul was told by Samuel that he would find two men resting "by Rachel's sepulchre (in the outskirts of Bethlehem) in (the shade) of the landmark *(gebul*="marker" or "landmark," usually a large stone pillar. *See* Gen. 35:20) of Benjamin at sun protection" *(zelzah*="sun shade," *i.e.,* "noon"). This was the sign that King Saul of the tribe of Benjamin was to be a shelter to his people like a "House" *(Beth)*. Samuel also told Saul that he was to receive "two loaves of bread" *(See* I Sam. 10:2-4) as he went further along his journey. This of course, was the "sign" that the King was to provide "Bread" *(Lehem)* for his people.

It was important to have situated the "two men by Rachel's sepulchre in the landmark of Benjamin at sun shade" (I Sam. 10:2) because there at that particular spot in the land of Canaan, the tribe of Benjamin received from God the right to have the first King of Israel chosen from among their ranks. For all the rest of Jacob's children were born outside the land of Canaan. Benjamin alone was born in the promised land. Moreover, only Benjamin was the son of "Israel" (Gen. 32:22-28; 35:9-10, 14-22), all the rest were children of "Jacob."

We are meant to ponder over the "signs" in Holy Scripture, for the wisdom of God is hidden in His "signs" and "to ponder upon Wisdom is perfect understanding" (Wisdom 6:15; Ps. 49:3; Sirach 15:20-21; 16:23; Prov. 24:32). Pondering and setting in order is the work of our understanding (Prov. 16:1; Eccle. 12:9; Pirke Aboth 5:22; St. Luke 2:19,51).

The King of Kings who came to us from the line of David (St. Matt. 1:1-16; St. Luke 1:32; 2:4) "was born in Bethlehem" (St. Matt. 2:1). For He was born not only to be "Emmanuel" ("God with us") but also God within us as our Food: the Bread of our souls. Yet in His wonderful humility and as a great lesson for us, He chose to be born not in a "house" in the town called the "House of Bread" but in a stable (or storehouse) where barley and wheat are kept and there He was placed in a grain bin or "manger." Because all bread making commences where the grain is kept.

Another lesson he gave to us is that all saviours who free the oppressed from their bonds are they themselves helpless babes at birth, even more so when they have been "swaddled" or bound up in bands (Wisdom 7:45), and so it is written:

"Unto you is born this day in the city of David a Saviour, who is Christ the Lord and this will be a sign for you: you will find a babe wrapped in swaddling clothes and laid in a manger" (St. Luke 2:12).

God does all things exceedingly well. Thus He who is our nourishment was born in Bethlehem and chose to live in Nazareth. Because "Nazareth" is the "place of watching" (in Hebrew-Aramaic). A good King shepherds his people and like a good shepherd he watches over and provides for them (Micah 5:1,3).

264

St. Luke retains the parable of the Leaven as spoken by our Lord on a different occasion and for a more personal reason. He was at the time "teaching in one of the synagogues on the Sabbath" and had just healed a woman suffering from severe curvature of the spine when He was rebuked by the "ruler of the synagogue" for healing on the Sabbath. Our Lord's wonderful answer to that charge elicited the admiration of the crowd and "all the people rejoiced at the glorious things that were done by Him." It was then and *"therefore"* that He spoke the parables of the Mustard Seed and the Leaven in response to the acclamation of the crowd, but in this instance directing the parables to Himself. Thus he prefaced each of these parables there with the same phrase: *"To what shall I liken the Kingdom of God?"* He likened the perfect Reign of God's will in Himself to the tiny mustard seed that increased to become "a great Tree" providing the shelter of good counsel and "rest" to those in need. He also likened the Reign of God in Himself to leaven transforming the mass and readying it to be made True Bread for our souls.

Lk 13:10

Lk 13:14

Lk 13:17

Lk 13:v.18

Lk 13:18,20

Lk 13:19
Mt 11:28

Both the mustard grain and the leaven are inconspicuous and hidden in their beginnings but they become manifest in the end, one as "a great tree" giving shelter and shade and the other in the large amount of dough ready to be made bread. These two parables are paired, for Wisdom gives shelter and shade (Sir. 14:26-27; 24:13-15; Prov. 3:18; 1:33 Sept; Enoch 32:6) and also provides for us the bread of understanding (Prov. 9:5; Sir. 14:3; 4 Ezra 8:4; Midrash R. on Ps. 119 sect. 24). Is this not the reason why the King of Kings was born in Bethlehem?* A good shepherd "tends," he not only provides food for his lambs but guides them into shelter as well.

In the Gospel according to St. Luke our Lord likens the Kingdom of God to *"leaven which a woman took and hid in three measures of meal" (aleuron)*. The words "meal" and "dough" are used interchangeably in the Hebrew and Greek Texts of Holy Scripture for example:

1 S 28:24
M.T.& Sept.
2 S 13:8 idem.

"The woman. . .took meal *(qemach-aleuron)* and kneaded it."

"Tamar. . .took dough *(batsek-stais)* and kneaded it."

St. Matthew and St. Luke used the word *aleuron* instead of the more common word *stais* because the Greek word *aleuron* strictly means "wheat meal" as distinguished from *alphiton:* "barley meal." Both evangelists knew that once a year at the Feast of Weeks two leavened loaves of bread made out of *wheaten* meal

Lv 23:20
Men. 7:1 B.T.

were offered up to the Lord as "bread of the first fruits," and it is these holy leavened loaves, made out of the grain of the new wheat crop, which are significant in the Parable of the Leaven.

265

*"TOWARDS WICKEDNESS": Presumptuous thoughts were also said to act as a bad "leaven" in the "dough" of man puffing him up with false pride (Horeb Edoth II.204, Hirsch edit.). Conversely, the wise taught that from the very beginning God implanted "the fear of the Lord" in the heart of man (Sirach 1:14) and the "inclination" or "inward counseling" (*yetzer*) towards good (Sirach 33:13). Consequently, Man has a *Yetzer ha tob* ("of good") in him to combat the "evil inclination" *(yetzer ha ra)* he incurred (Enoch 98:4) since the Fall (Sirach 15:11-20; 33:14). There is a constant battle in the heart of man between his opposite inclinations (Romans 7:15-25) but man's free will decides his fate (Pirke Aboth 3:24). "The wages of sin is death" and corruption, and the reward of good is incorruption and "eternal life through Jesus Christ our Lord" (Romans 6:23; 5:12; Ezek. 18:4,20; I Cor. 15:48-50).

Let us hold on to him and the good leaven of His Teaching. "He that keepeth the Law becomes master of his inclinations" (Sirach 21:11). So "rouse up your good inclination and you will not sin" (Midrash Rabbah Ruth VIII.1). "Let a man stir up *(ragaz*="to agitate," "to foment" as leaven does) his good inclination (*Yetzer ha tob*) against his bad" (Berakoth 5a B.T.). "Depart from sin and it will turn aside from thee" (Sirach 7:2 Greek and Heb. Text; Gen. 4:7). "Resist the devil and he will flee from you" (St. James 4:7).

*"KEEP WISDOM": for it says in the Book of Wisdom (6:18-20) that "the love of Wisdom is the keeping of her Laws, and the giving heed to her Laws is assurance of incorruption *(aphtharsia)*, and incorruption brings one near to God; so the desire for Wisdom leads to a kingdom": The "Kingdom" of God's Reign in our hearts.

Mt 13:33	In the parable of the Leaven as retained by St. Matthew, the "meal" is the Teaching and the "leaven"—the knowledge of the Understanding of our Lord.
Lk 13:20-21	In the parable of the Leaven as preserved by St. Luke, the "dough" is our humanity and the "leaven"—the Lord.

We know that the rabbis often likened the Torah to "wheat," "flour" and "meal." In addition, they likened Man to "dough" (Gen. Rabbah XIV.1; XVII.8; Tan. Ber. I, 28; III, 53; Tan. Noah I and Mezora 9; Shabbath 31b B.T.; 2.5b. Jer.T.; Tosephta Kiddushin V.2; Berakoth 17a B.T.; Yalkut to Proverbs 962; *see also* Philo in *De Sacr. Abel et Cain* 33).

Gn 2:6-7 Jb 10:9;33:6 Si 17:1	For Adam was kneaded and formed from the dust of the moistened ground by the hands of the Lord, just as dough is kneaded and formed into loaves *(idem.)*.

And because the Jews considered Man to be the crowning point of creation, the best and holiest part of it, they referred to Adam as *challah*, *i.e.*, the sacred portion of the earth-mass which the Lord had formed (Gen. R. XIV.1; *see* Gen. 2.7-8,19; Pss. 90:2; 95:5; Isaiah 45:18). As *challah*, Man is the portion of creation God keeps for Himself, the "first fruits" that He claims as His very own.

But although he was created to be the *challah* ("first fruits of the *dough*") of creation, Adam forfeited this honor the moment he disobeyed the Lord and accepted within himself the "evil suggestion," *i.e.*, the *yetzer* ("counsel") *ha-ra* ("of evil") of the Tempter. Having considered Adam "the first fruits of the dough," the rabbis aptly described the wicked counsel of the Devil as an evil "leaven" at work in the "dough" of Man predisposing him towards* wickedness (R. Abahu commentary on Gen. 6:6; Gen. Rabbah XXXIV. 10; Berakoth 17a B.T.; 7d Jer. T.; Sifre Deut. sect. 45 re Deut. 11:18). Needless to say the "evil leaven" is death to the "dough."

Kidd 30b B.T.	However, in His great mercy the Lord "created the Torah for healing." For within the Torah is the good leaven of His life-giving counsel (Deut. 30:14-19; St. John 6:63,68; 12:49-50; 14:6, 23-24; 1 John 1:1). Remember that "the Spirit of Truth" is within the Truth and does His work of sanctifying us—through the Truth (St. John 14:17; 15:26; 16:13-14; 17:17, 19). "The Word
Heb 4:12	of God is living and active." It is by holding fast "the implanted Word" (St. James 1:21) that we shall be able to "purge *(ekkathairo)* out the old leaven" and "be a new dough" (1 Cor. 5:7) because we are made "clean *(katharos)* through the Word" (St. John 15:3).
Dt 4:40;6:1-2 Pr 7:2; 9:16 Pss 19:8; 119:9,11	Therefore keep His Commandments and ponder over His Words. "If you study the Torah you will not fall into the power of the *yetzer ha-ra* or evil leaven" (Kiddushin 30b. B.T.). Because the Teaching of God is full of the Wisdom of His good counsel. Then shall you know that "Wisdom...is...incorruptible" and like good leaven "she is more active than all active things, pervading and penetrating all things by reason of her pureness *(katharotes)*...hence nothing polluted creeps into her" (Wisdom 7:22,24,25) or into those who keep* Wisdom in the "dough" of their good hearts. Hold fast then the "Word of Life": "the very Word of God at work in you who keep the faith" for the "Word...heals all things" (Philip. 2:16; 1 Thess. 2:13; Wisdom 16:12).

*"**WISE WOMAN**": The ancient Syriac Text and the Curetonian Syriac MS. (British Museum) retain the qualification "wise" before "woman" in the parable of the Leaven.

*"**THREE MEASURES**": The word *saton* used in the Gospels is derived from the Aramaic word for the Hebrew dry measure called *seah*. Three *seahs*=1 *epha*, approximately 48-60 lbs. of flour, more than enough to make a loaf of leavened bread the size of a man or two loaves each the size of a grown boy or girl. So large an amount was three *seahs*, or "measures" that the rabbis commented thus: "a man can lift a *seah* himself; he can carry two *seahs* if his companion lifts it on his back; he can carry three with the help of his companion" (Midrash Rabbah on Numbers XVI. 14, see also Mid Rabbah on Ruth V.8 and Rabbi Johanan's oblique commentary that Ruth must have been a strong woman to be able to lift that amount by herself). There is a lot of "dough" in Man. Thus the "two leavened loaves" offered up to the Lord in behalf of all the people of God were made from 3 *seahs* or "measures" of meal (Mishnah Menahoth 6:6, *see also* 7:1). And although the flour for these two loaves was sifted and reduced from three *seahs* to three fifths of a *seah*, nevertheless "each loaf was seven handbreadths long, four handbreadths wide and four fingerbreadths thick" (Maimonides *Book of Temple Service* Sect. Daily offerings, Paragraph 10).

The rabbis blamed Eve for introducing the evil leaven that corrupted Adam, the pure "dough" of the Lord (Gen. Rabbah XVII. 8; *see also* Sir. 25:24; Book of Adam and Eve XVI-XIX; 2 Cor. 11:3; 1 Tim. 2:14). They also said that consequently as a punishment Woman was given the task of making bread and lighting the lamps *(idem.*, Gen. Rabbah).

The early fathers of the Church also commented that the old leaven of wickedness came with the sin of Eve and the new leaven by the sinlessness of Mary: the new Eve. Thus through the blessed Virgin the old leaven of iniquity was replaced by the transforming leaven of good.

Man provides the grain and oil; Woman the bread and light. There are many references in Holy Scripture to the making of bread by women. Hence appropriately in the parable of the Leaven it was "a woman" who "*took (lambano*="to take" or "to receive") *and hid in three measures of meal,*" the *"Leaven"* of the Lord.

Lk 13:31

Lk 15:8   Again, in the parable of the Lost Coin it is a woman who lit the lamp.

Moreover, the wisdom of God is often clothed in the imagery of a woman. Wisdom is a mother in Sirach 15:2; Wisd. 7:12; a bride and mistress in Prov. 9:1-6; Sir. 15:2; Wisdom 7:28; 8:16-21; a sister in Prov. 7:4; a little girl in Prov. 8:30 and a nurse in Sirach

Q 11 D.S.S. Fg.   51:16. It is only fitting that "she" should be the one then who prepares the "bread of understanding" (Sirach 15:3) for us.

The "woman" in the parable "hid" (*enkrupto*="to hide in") the "leaven" for women are wonderful in hiding things (Gen. 31:34-35; Exod. 2:2; Heb. 11:3; Josh 2:6; 6:17; 2 Sam. 17:19; 2 Kings 6:29; 11:2-3; 2 Chr. 22:11-12, etc.). They also hide themselves (St. Luke 1:24) until it is time to bring forth what was hidden.

Mk 4:22
Lk 8:17;   If things are hidden it is so that they may become manifest in the
12:2   end. "For there is nothing hid except to be made manifest; nor is anything secret except to come to light."

Lk 13:21   Being a "wise* woman," the woman in the parable hid the leaven "*in three* measures (saton) *of meal,*" because "*three measures*" is the amount of flour needed to make a loaf of leavened bread the size of a man, or two loaves each the size of a child.

And there in the "dough" of Man, the Leaven of His Word remains hidden until the whole mass is transformed into holy "leaven" itself.

Rm 11:6   For if the first fruit of the dough *(challah)* is holy so shall the whole lump also be,
Provided it has accepted and worked along with His Leaven within.

*"**MYSTERY**": "All that has happened in the world, the beginning is obscure (*aphanei*="not apparent", "hidden") but the end manifest" (4 Ezra 9:5,6; I Cor. 13:12).
God reigns in the hearts of those who obey Him and to them He gives "the Holy Spirit," "the Spirit of Understanding" (Acts 5:32; Pss. of Solomon 17:42; Enoch 49:3; Test. of Levi 18:7; Prov. 15:4 Sept.; 1:24; Job 20:3; 32:8; Neh. 9:20; Thanksgiving Hymn 12:11-12). The Lord gives "the Spirit of Wisdom and of revelation in the knowledge of Him so that the eyes of your understanding being enlightened you may know" (Eph. 1:17,18) and having been "transformed by the renewing of your understanding. . .you may be able to know the will of God as to what is good and pleasing to Him and perfect" (Romans 12:2). It is for this reason that He gives the Spirit of Understanding to those who believe in Him for "who shall know how to please the Lord except by Wisdom and the Holy Spirit?" (Wisdom 9:17).

Remember that "God is at work in you both to will and to work for His good pleasure" (Eph. 2:10). Let us obey Him so that we "may be filled with the Knowledge of His will in all Wisdom and spiritual Understanding. . .walking worthy of the Lord, fully pleasing to Him, bearing fruit in every good work and increasing in the knowledge of God" (Col. 1:9-10). For as we "increase in the knowledge of Him," "the fruits of. . .Understanding" (Sir.37:23) will abound in us. It is this "fruit" that the Father seeks in us (St. John 15:1-5,8,16) because a wise father is glorified in the understanding of his children. What else does a father want but "a son, a man of understanding"? (Sirach 47:12). Who else is the Son of Man but He who is the Son of God and *understands all things*? Walk in His Light (St. John 12:34-35; 8:12) and repent, for the Day of swift judgment is not far behind "the Day when the Son of Man is revealed" (St. Luke 17:30).

The Mystery of the Kingdom of God is the great mystery of the work of God in the hearts of those who believe in His Son, the Lord Jesus Christ (Gal. 2:16; 3:26). It is a work intended to have us "conformed to the image of His Son" (Rom. 8:29), through the action of the Holy Spirit in us. The Kingdom of God is the Mystery of the restoration of our understanding and knowledge of God. We lost this holy knowledge through the disobedience of our first parents (Rom. 5:19). We regain it through "the obedience of Christ" (2 Cor. 10:5; 5:18-19) who set us an example of "obedience unto righteousness" (Romans 6:16; St. John 17:17,19), when "He humbled Himself and became obedient unto death" (Philip. 2.8) for our sanctification (Heb. 5:8-9). For this reason "God sent forth His Son. . .to redeem us. . .that we might receive the adoption of sons," "having destined us in love to be His sons through Jesus Christ according to the purpose of His will, to the praise of the glory of His grace" (Gal. 4:4,5; Eph. 1:5,6). It is therefore through Him, in Him, and by Him that we are remade and renewed to become "in Christ Jesus. . .a new creation" (Gal. 6:15 AV). "Consequently, if anyone is in Christ, he is a new creation; the old has passed away, behold, the new has come" (2 Cor. 5:17) and he shall again see all things clearly, having been "transformed by the renewal of 'his' understanding" (Rom. 12:2). As His "children" we shall merit then "to share in the inheritance of the saints in light" (Col. 1:12). For the reward of those who keep and obey "the Word of the Truth of the Gospel" is "fruit" from it (Col. 1:5,6): "the fruit of light" (*phos*) for "proving what is acceptable to the Lord" (Eph. 5:9,10). Thus "Light" and "Understanding" are the lot of the just, the benefit bestowed on them for bringing forth "fruits of righteousness. . .unto the glory and praise of God" (Philippians 1:11). The wise men of old knew that the reward of the righteous is "the lot of Truth" (Sirach 17:20 L.V.; Isaiah 38:18-19; Test. of Levi 18:8; Test. of Judah 24:4a BS Text; Thanksgiving Hymns 4:25-26; 10:28-29; 11:26-31; 14:15; Zadokite Document 13:12; 4 Qp Isaiah d 13:12, D.S.S.; Targum of the Amidah. *See also* St. James 3:2) and light and understanding in it (Wisdom 3:9; 6:22; Prov. 3:35; Sirach 4:11 Heb. Text; Enoch 6:27; 48:6; 61:4-5; 108:12; War Scroll 11:9-10, 15-16; 13:6-9; 17:6-7; Community Rule 11:5-8; Thanksgiving Hymns 3:21-22. *See also* Col. 1:12-13, 26; St. Luke 24:45). These are given to enable us to praise and exalt the Lord well (Pss. 119:7; 149:1,5-6; Prov. 21:28; Eccle. 3:11; Sirach 14:21 L.V.; 15:9-10; 17:7-8 L.V.; 39:33 Sept. 42:17 Sept.; 42:22 Syriac and 51:22 Hebrew Text. *See also* 1 Cor. 4:5) and champion His cause (Isaiah 54:17; Prov. 16:1; Wisdom 9:17-19 L.V.; Sirach 51:29 Sept.; 51:37 L.V. *See also* St. Luke 21:15).

"The Mystery of the Kingdom of God," "the Mystery which was kept secret. . .but now is made manifest" (St. Mark 4:11; Rom. 16:25) and which "He has made known to us in all wisdom and understanding" is "the Mystery of His will according to His good pleasure which He set forth in Christ as a plan for the fulness of time, to unite all things in Him, things in heaven and things on earth. . .for the praise of His glory" (Eph. 1:9-10,12). "This Mystery is Christ in (*en*) you the Hope of Glory" (Coloss. 1:27) and the salvation of those who believe in Him and obey His Commands. For the Lord Jesus Christ is the Incarnate Word of God which we accept in our hearts as a seed, a Leaven which works in us through the Holy Spirit to transform us into "being born again, not of corruptible seed but by the incorruptible Seed of the Word of God which lives and abides forever" (I Peter 1:23). "Of His own will He brought us forth by the Word of Truth that we should be a kind of first fruits of His creatures" (St. James 1:18) becoming "partakers of the divine nature having escaped from the corruption that is in the world" (2 Peter 1:4) and in the "dough" of man (Eph. 2:3; Rom. 5:12,19,21; Ps. 51:7; Job 14:4).
"The Mystery of godliness" "is the power that works in us" enabling us to "put on the new nature which is renewed in full knowledge after the image of its Creator" (I Tim. 3:16; Eph. 3:20; Col. 3:10)—provided we keep "obeying the Truth through the Spirit" (I Peter 1:22). If we persevere to the very end in keeping the seed of His Commands we shall become in ourselves a Tree of Knowledge able to tell good from evil and able to give the hungry "bread" from the fruits of our understanding.
Obey Him and keep His Seed so that it may be said of the "ground" (*adamah*) from which Adam was made: That it brought forth "Trees" (*elim*) of knowledge and "judges" (*elohim*). And made in its heart "Bread" (*lehem*) of "God" (*elohim*) for Him.

Col 1:26-29;2:3	The Kingdom of God is a Mystery* that remains hidden until it has accomplished its work. Then, it is revealed in those who have followed His counsels and obeyed His commands.
Mk 4:11 Gal. 3:26 Jn 1:12,13 1 Jn 5:1	"The Mystery of the Kingdom of God" is the revelation that the Lord dwells in those who have faith in Him and keep His Word in their hearts.
1 Jn 2:5	For "whosoever keeps His Word, truly in him is the love of God perfected," The love that seeks to form His Son in us.
Col. 4:3 Eph. 3:16 2 Co 4:16 Lk 8:11,5 Gal 4:19 1 Jn 5:1,18 Col 1:27	"The Mystery of Christ" is the Mystery of the "inner man" increasing in the hearts of those who have kept His Word. "For the Word of God" is "His Seed": the Seed that forms Him in us through the Holy Spirit, so that we may be begotten of Him. Treasure "this Mystery. . .which is Christ in *(en)* you. . ."
1 Co 15:45	The Word of God is a holy leaven that transforms the dough which receives it within. And when the dough is wholly leavened, behold, it becomes leaven itself ready to quicken others for Him, Because there is *life* in leaven.
Mt 5:13,14	If we are "the light of the world" and "the salt of the earth," we are also in Him, the Leaven that shall transform the mass; Provided we have become ourselves wholly leavened by Him.
Si 2:5-8 Ws 3:5-9 1 P 1:7;4:12-13	Then, if we must suffer, let us take heart knowing that when the dough has become fully leavened it is placed in the fire to make it Bread.
2 Co 7:4;1:4-7; 4:14-18 Ph 3:10-12 Heb 2:9-10	Let us therefore "be exceedingly joyful in all our continuous tribulation," because the end of our suffering is to rise with Him.
Jm 1:4	Be patient now and persevere for when the trial is over we shall truly understand
Heb 12:10-11 Si 4:19-21 L.V. Rm 5:3-5 Col 4:3-4	And know that it is in the furnace of His Love that we are cleansed and made into Bread of Understanding. This is the Bread of God to the praise of His glory And for the feeding of His lambs.
Jewish Prayer Ps 104:14; Jb 24:5 L.T.	Blessed art Thou, O Lord God, King of the Universe, who bringeth forth Bread from the heart of the ground.

271

2 S 7:28   "O Lord God, You are God
and Your Words are Truth."

Ps 118:27 M.T.   "God is the Lord who has given us Light."

ACKNOWLEDGMENTS

The author wishes to express his gratitude to the Missionary Oblates of Mary Immaculate, St. Peter's Province; the Librarians of Trinity College, Dublin; St. Paul's University, Ottawa; the Jewish Theological Seminary of America, Princeton, and Andover Harvard Theological Libraries. Many thanks to J.A., who patiently typed the manuscript, and to H.E., for her faith and kind encouragement throughout the years.

¡ Que Dios se los pague como El bien sabe!

BIBLIOGRAPHY

Hebrew Bible

Kahle, P., **Prolegomena to Kittel's Biblia Hebraica.** Leipzig: 1937.
Kittel, R., **Biblia Hebraica,** 2d and 3d editions. Leipzig: 1912,
1937.

Greek Bible (Septuagint)

Rahlf, A., **Septuaginta,** 2 volumes. Stuttgart: 1935.
Swete, H.B., **The Old Testament in Greek,** 3 volumes. Cambridge:
1922.

The Book of Wisdom

Deane, W.J., **The Book of Wisdom.** Oxford: 1881.
Gregg, J.A.F., **The Wisdom of Solomon.** Cambridge: 1909.
Grimm, C.L.W., **Das Buch der Weisheit.** Leipzig: 1860.
Reider, J., **The Book of Wisdom.** Philadelphia: Dropsie College,
1957.

Sirach (Ecclesiasticus)

Fritzsche, O., **Libri Apocryphi Veteris Testamenti Graece.**
Leipzig: 1871.
Hart, J.H.A., **Ecclesiasticus, The Greek Text of Codex 248.**
Cambridge: 1909.
de Lagarde, Paul, **Libri Veteris Testamenti Apocryphi Syriace,**
(Syriac Text). Leipzig: 1871.
Levi, Israel, **The Hebrew Text of the Book of Ecclesiasticus.**
Leiden: 1969.
Oesterley, W.O.E., **Ecclesiasticus.** Cambridge: 1912.

Apocrypha and Pseudoepigrapha

Bernard, J.H., editor, **Odes of Solomon.** Cambridge: 1912.
Box, G.H., and J.L. Landsman, trans., **Apocalypse of Abraham.**
London: SPCK, 1918.
————, **II Esdras (IV Ezra),** (Syriac). Longon: SPCK, 1917.
————, **Testament of Abraham.** London: SPCK, 1927.
Bogaert, Pierre, trans., **Apocalypse of Baruch** (2 Baruch, 3
Baruch) Syriac and Greek. Paris: Éditions Cerf, 1969.
Brock, S.P., and E.J. Brill, trans., **Testament of Job** (Greek).
Leiden: 1967.
Brooks, E.W., trans., **Joseph and Asenath** (Greek). London:
SPCK, 1918.
Charles, R.H., Adam and Charles Black, trans., **Apocalypse of
Baruch** (2 Baruch, 3 Baruch) Syriac and Greek. Oxford: 1896.
————, and W.O.E. Oesterley, trans., **Idem.** London: SPCK,
1929.
————, **The Apocrypha and Pseudoepigrapha of the Old
Testament,** 2 volumes. Oxford: 1913.
————, Adam and Charles Black, trans., **Ascension of Isaiah**
(Ethiopic and New Greek and Latin Translations of Slavonic
Versions). Oxford: 1900.
————, ————, trans., **Assumption of Moses** (Latin), Oxford:
1897.
————, **The Book of Enoch** or I Enoch, (Ethiopic), 2d Ed.
Oxford: 1912.
————, and Adam and Charles Black, trans., **Book of Jubilees**
(Ethiopic). Oxford: 1902.
————, **Testaments of the Twelve Patriarchs** (Greek and
Armenian-Slavonic variants). Oxford: 1908.
Conybeare, F.C., **Testament of Solomon** (Greek). *Jewish Quarterly Review,* Oct. 1898.
Ferrar, Wm. John, trans., **Assumption of Moses** (Latin). London:
SPCK, 1918.

Fleck, F.F., Testament of Solomon (Greek). German trans. 1837.
Gaselee, S., trans. and ed., Testament of Isaac and Jacob (Coptic).
London: SPCK, 1927.
Gray, G.B., trans., Psalms of Solomon (Syriac). Oxford: Charles,
1913.
Harris, J. Rendel, Psalms of Solomon (Syriac). Cambridge: 1909.
James, M.R., trans., Testament of Abraham (Greek). Cambridge:
1892.
Kautzch, E., Die Apocryphen und Pseudoepigraphen des Alten
Testaments. 1900.
Malan, Rev. S.C., trans., The Book of Adam and Eve (Ethiopic).
Edinburgh: William and Norgate, 1882.
Morfill, W.R., trans., The Book of the Secrets of Enoch
(Slavonic). Oxford: 1896.
Odeberg, Hugo, trans., 3 Enoch or The Hebrew Book of Enoch.
Cambridge: 1928.
Oesterley, W.O.E., trans., II Esdras (IV Ezra)—Latin and Syriac.
London: Methuen, 1933.
Mai, Angelo, trans., Testament of Job (Greek). Rome: 1833.
Philonenko, M., trans., Joseph and Asenath (Greek). Leiden:
Studio Post Biblica XIII, 1968.
Schodde, G.H., Book of Jubilees. Oberlin, Ohio: 1888.
Stone, M.E., trans., Testament of Levi (Armenian). Jerusalem: St.
James Press, 1969.

Targums of the Old Testament (Aramaic).
Etheridge, J.W., The Targums. (English trans. The Pentateuch) 2
vols. London: 1865.
Sperber, A., ed., The Bible in Aramaic, 4 vols. London: 1959.
Stenning, J.F., The Targum of Isaiah. Oxford: 1949.

Dead Sea Scrolls
Dupont-Sommer, A., ed., The Essene Writings from Qumran.
Ohio: Meridian Books, 1962.
Gaster, T.H., The Dead Sea Scriptures. New York: Anchor Books,
1964.
Vermes, G., The Dead Sea Scrolls in English. London: Penguin
Books, 1965.
Brownlee, W.H., ed., Manual of Discipline (Community Rule-IQS)
Yale: BASOR, 1951.
Leaney, A.R.C., The Rule of Qumran and Its Meaning
(Community Rule). Philadelphia: Westminster Press, 1966.
Wernberg-Moller, P., The Manual of Discipline (Community
Rule). Leiden: 1957.
Van Der Ploege, J., Le Rouleau de la Guerre (War Rule IQM).
Leiden: 1959.
Yadin, Y., ed., The Scroll of the War of the Sons of Light Against
the Sons of Darkness (War Rule IQM). Jerusalem: Bialik Institute,
1956.
Holm-Neilson, Svend, Hodayot, Psalms from Qumran
(Thanksgiving Hymns, Hymn Scroll IQH). Aarhus, Denmark:
1960.
Mansoor, Menahem, The Thanksgiving Hymns. Grand Rapids,
Mich: Eerdmans Publishers, 1961.

The Zadokite Documents—CD
Rabin, Chaim, ed., The Zadokite Documents. Oxford: 1954.
Schechter, S., Fragments of a Zadokite Work. Cambridge: 1910.

Patrology
Asemani, J.S., Bibliotheca Orientalis, 4 vols. Rome: 1728.
Fabricius-Harle, Bibliotheca Graeca, 14 vols. Hamburg: 1808.
Frankenberg, W., Evagrius Ponticus. Berlin: 1912.
Graffin, R., Patrologia Syriaca, 2 vols. Paris: 1894.
————, Patrologia Orientalis, idem. Paris: 1903.
Migne, J. P., Demonstrations Evangeliques, 20 vols. Paris: 1853.
————, Patrologi Graeciae, 2d series, 166 vols. Paris: 1866.

————, **Patrologie Latinae**, 217 vols. Paris: 1855.
————, **Scriptura Sacrae Cursus**, 28 vols. Paris: 1845.
General Works: **Ante-Nicene, Nicene and Post-Nicene Fathers**. 38 vols. Grand Rapids, Mich.: Eerdmans, 1955-67.

Ancient Near Eastern Texts
Egyptian
    1. Maxims of Ptah-Hotep
       Caminos, R.A., **Literary Fragments in the Hieratic Script**. Oxford: 1956.
       Zaba, Z., **Les Maximes de Ptah-Hotep**. Prague: 1956.
    2. Instructions of Merikare
       Volten, A., trans., in **Analecta Aegyptica IV**. Copenhagen: 1945.
    3. Teachings of Amen-em-Opet
       Budge, E.A.W., **The Teaching of Amen-em-Apt, Son of Kanaht**. London: 1923.
       Marzal, A., **Le Enseñanza de Amenenope**. Madrid: 1965.
    4. Instructions of Ankhsheshanqy
       Glanville, S.R.K., trans., **The Instructions of Onchsheshonqy**. London: British Museum, Cat. Dem. Papyri, Vol. II.
Sumero-Akkadian and Ugaritic Literature
       Gordon, C.H., **Ugaritic Manual**. Rome: 1955.
       de Langhe, R., **The Cuneiform Texts of Ras Shamra-Ugarit** (French). Paris: 1945.
       Shaeffer, C.F.A., **The Cuneiform Texts of Ras Shamra-Ugarit** (English). 1930.
       Van Dijk, J.J.A., **La Sagesse Sumero-Accadienne**. Leiden: E.J. Brill, 1953.
Babylonian
       Langdon, S., "Babylonian Wisdom," **Babyloniaca VII**, 1923, pp. 129-229.
General Works
       Driver, G.H., **Canaanite Myths and Legends**. 1956.
       Gordon, C.H., **Ugaritic Literature**. 1949.
       Pritchard, J.B., **Ancient Near Eastern Texts Relating to the Old Testament**. Princeton: 1955.
Rabbinic Works
Midrashim (Rabbah)
       Braude, W.G., ed. and trans., **Midrash on Psalms**, 2 vols. New Haven: Yale University Press, 1959.
       Buber, S., ed., **Midrash Lekah Tob**, 2 vols. Wilna: Romm, 1884.
       ————, ed., **Midrash Shemuel**. Wilna: 1925.
       ————, ed., **Midrash Tanhuma**, 3 vols. Wilna: 1885.
       ————, ed., **Midrash Tehillim**. Wilna: 1891.
       Eisenstein, J.D., ed., **Ozar Midrashim**. New York: Reznick and Menschel, 1928.
       Freedman, H., and M. Simon, eds. and trans., **Midrash (Rabbah)**, 10 vols. Soncino Press, 1961.
       Hallevy, E.E., ed., **Midrash Rabbah**, 8 vols. Tel Aviv: 1965.
       Jellinek, Adolf, ed., **Beth-ha Midrash**, 6 vols. Jerusalem: Bamberger and Wahrman, 1938.
       Lauterbach, Jacob zur, ed. and trans., **Mekilta de R. Ishmael**, 3 vols. Philadelphia: Jewish Publishing Society, 1935.
Mishnah
       Danby, Herbert, ed. and trans., **The Mishnah**. London and New York: Oxford University Press, 1933.
Pesikta Rabbati
       Braude, W.G., ed. and trans., **Pesikta Rabbati**, 2 vols. New Haven: Yale University Press, 1968.
       Buber, S., ed., **Pesikta de Rab Kahana**. Siebert, Lyck, 1868.
Pirke
       Friedlander, G., ed. and trans., **Pirke de Rabbi Eliezer**. New York: Hermon Press, 1965.
       Goldin, Judah, ed. and trans., **The Fathers (Pirke Aboth According to Rabbi Nathan)**. New Haven: Yale University Press, 1965.

Talmud
Babylonian

Talmud Babli (Hebrew). Wilno: Romm, 1927.
Talmud Babli (English) Epstein, I., ed., The Talmud Babli with Minor Tractates, 35 vols. Soncino Press, 1935-52.

Jerusalem

Behrend, B.Z., ed., Talmud Yerushalmi (Hebrew). Posen: Manash, Krotoschin, 1866.
Schwab, M., ed., Le Talmud de Jérusalem (French), 11 vols. 1878.

Yalkut

Simeon, R., of Frankfurt, ed., Yalkut Shimeoni. Warsaw, 1876.
————, Idem. Wilno: 1898.

General Works

Die Agada der Babylonischen. Frankfurt: 1913.
Die Agada der Tannaiten, 2 vols. Strassburg: 1890.
Bacher, W., ed., Die Agada der Palastinischen Amoraer, 3 vols. Strassburg: 1899.
Jastrow, M., ed. and comp., A Dictionary of the Targumin, the Talmud Babli and Yerushalmi, and the Midrashic Literature, 2 vols. New York: Pardes Publishing Co., 1950.
Singer, I., ed., The Jewish Encyclopedia. New York: Funk and Wagnalls, 1906.
Strack, H.L., ed., Dikduke Sopherim. Leiden: 1912.
————, and P. Billerbeck, Kommentatar zum Neuen Testament aus Talmud und Midrasch. 3 vols. Munich: 1928.

Concordances

Cruden, Alexander, Cruden's Complete Concordance of the Old and New Testaments and the Apocrypha. London: Frederick Warner and Co.
Hatch, E. and H. Redpath, Concordance to the Septuagint, 2 vols. Oxford: 1897.
Strong, James, Strong's Exhaustive Concordance of the Bible. Nashville: Abingdon Press.
Thompson, Rev. Newton, and Raymond Stock, Complete Concordance to the Bible. St. Louis: Herder, 1964.
Young, Robert, Analytical Concordance to the Bible. New York: Funk and Wagnalls.

Miscellaneous

Colson, F.W., and H.G. Whitaker, Philo Judaeus (English translation). London: 1929.
Drummond, J., ed., Philo Judaeus, 2 vols. London: 1888.
Guillamont, Puech, Quispel, Till and Al Masih, eds., The Gospel According to Thomas (Nag Hammadi Papyri). New York: Harper & Bros., 1959.
Scott, W., ed., Corpus Hermeticum, 4 vols. Oxford: 1936.
Thackeray, H. St. John, and R. Marcus, eds., Josephus, 8 vols. London: Loeb Classical Library.

NOTE:

This is only a partial listing of texts consulted.

Let the many islands be glad

Ps. 97:1